KF
4549
.U5
1956x

THE SUPREME COURT
Speaks

THE SUPREME COURT
Speaks

By JERRE S. WILLIAMS

AUSTIN : 1957

UNIVERSITY OF TEXAS PRESS

KF
4549
.U5
1956x

Library of Congress Catalog Card No. 55–8473
© 1956 by the University of Texas Press
Second printing

Printed in Austin, Texas, by the Printing Division
of the University of Texas

To
Mary Pearl

Foreword

THIS BOOK WAS WRITTEN in an attempt to let the United States Supreme Court tell its history in its own words. Much has been written about the Court, but it occurred to me some time ago that the opinions of the justices, those significant documents that *reproduce* rather than *describe* its history, have not been made readily available to the layman who would wish to know them. Yet these opinions constitute a plentiful reservoir of some of the greatest and most meaningful American political and social literature.

Cases to be included were chosen with three considerations in mind. First, I wished to select those which are of moment both historically and currently, those giving proof of the constant role the Supreme Court has played in vitalization of the Constitution; second, those cases engendering opinions that have merit as truly great literature; and finally those that reveal in interesting fashion the broad sweep of the legal problems which confront our Court, a scope that may not be readily realized by the casual observer. Some cases, of course, embody in themselves all three criteria of selection. No attempt has been made to offer a representative opinion of each justice, mainly because such a scheme could not have accomplished the fulfillment of the other criteria, but the reader will find examples from the pens of those considered to be the "great" justices in the Court's history. Some of the opinions have been presented in full; where excerpting has been done, it was usually in the interest of eliminating technical legal matters and the side issues that accompany almost every case. The text of the Constitution is given in Appendix I, so that reference may be made if desired; in Appendix II a chronological table of all Supreme Court justices will be found.

The powerful role which the Supreme Court has played in our national life would seem scarcely to need emphasis, yet it is easy for us to forget how much we are all actually indebted to the Court's decisions for the further securing of our liberties under the Constitution. Chief Justice Hughes said, "The Constitution is what the judges say it is." And James M. Beck in his book *The Constitution of the United States* (1922) likened the Supreme Court to a continuing constitutional convention, revising and applying the Constitution to keep it alive and vibrant. If these observations be apt, and surely they are, then it is well for the reader of the Court's opinions to be continually reminded of the human side of the Court. The Supreme Court is an institution. But it is a human institution composed of nine honored men who bear the awesome responsibility of keeping American life and American liberties secure. The "handing down" of a Supreme Court decision is a potent historical event, widely publicized and widely commented upon. The justices are at once concerned in an intimate and personal way with every living being in the United States and at the same time are engaged in an exercise of statecraft in broadest measure.

A brief description of the routine operation of the Court as the vehicle of this process of human decision may aid the reader at the outset. The membership of the Court has varied in number from six to ten justices, but since 1869 the number has been established at nine. The judges are political appointees, yet for over one hundred and fifty years they have shown a magnificent disdain for political ties to those who appointed them. They have manifested independence and courage worthy of their role.

In earlier days, the Court commonly met only for one or two months of the year because cases were so few. Today the Court convenes for a new term on the first Monday of every October, and usually adjourns the first or second Monday in June in completion of its term. Typically, during this October to June period, the Court meets for one or two weeks to hear oral argument in the cases before it, and then recesses for two or three weeks to write its opinions. The most exciting time to the observer is a Court meeting on the first Monday after a recess. It is on those days that the bulk of the decisions are delivered, decisions often destined to have the widest repercussions throughout the world. The ut-

FOREWORD

most secrecy is preserved before the decisions are publicly announced. This is the reason that the printing of the opinions has not been done by the Government Printing Office, but has traditionally been retained in the absolute control of the Court itself.

The Supreme Court has original jurisdiction in those few cases involving ambassadors of foreign nations and in cases in which a state is a party. All other cases reach the Court by way of review of decisions of the highest courts of the states or of lower federal courts. In only a few vital situations is the Supreme Court compelled by law to hear and decide these appealed cases. The great bulk of cases come under a procedure which lawyers know as "petitions for certiorari," which simply means that the person appealing is asking the court to hear his case. The Court may in its discretion agree to hear it or decline to do so. Most of the cases brought are considered briefly and only in sufficient detail to provide a basis for declining to hear and decide them—to "deny the petition for certiorari." This restricted right of appeal is grounded in the fact that if the Court were compelled to hear every case that litigants wanted it to hear the work load could not be handled by a dozen such courts, let alone one. In exercising this most delicate power to decide which cases to hear, the Court uses rather detailed criteria. The short answer, however, is that the Court will hear only those cases which capture its attention as significant. In the actual mechanical process, if three or more justices vote to hear a case then the Court will hear it.

If the Court consents to hear a case, or if it is one of those cases where the Court is compelled to take jurisdiction, the attorneys for each side file written briefs and are afforded the opportunity to argue the case orally before the justices. In the early days of the Court, argument on a given case often extended for several days. Now, except for special dispensation, argument is limited to one hour for each side. This argument is popularly supposed to consist of ringing oratorical efforts by opposing counsel locked in formal debate, and in earlier times this was not an inaccurate picture. More and more in recent years, however, the argument has taken the form of a mere skeletal statement by the lawyer, with the crux of it consisting of answers to piercing verbal questions directed to the lawyer by the justices. This process undoubtedly places a greater burden upon the lawyer than does the fixed address to the Court. But it enables rapid progress to the very heart of a case, and argument precisely upon those matters which most concern the justices. While argument before the Court is, therefore, spontaneous and fresh, it is by no means extemporaneous. Rather, the modern way simply means that the advocate before the Court must be so thoroughly in command of his case that he can answer any question or any line of attack.

After the oral argument, the case is considered in one of the regular Saturday conferences of the justices. These conferences are highly secret, as might be supposed. They are the Supreme Court at the supreme moment of deliberation and decision making. But enough information has filtered out of the conferences from time to time so that we know in general what takes place. The Chief Justice presides, and he briefly states the facts and issues of the case to be decided. There follows a lively and informal discussion among the justices until all significant aspects have been exposed to the searching light of nine powerful legal minds. After thorough consideration, the vote is taken. The junior justice votes first, and there is voting up the ascending scale of seniority until the Chief Justice casts the final vote. If the Chief Justice is part of the majority, he designates the justice who will write the opinion for the Court. If he is not on the majority, then the senior justice on the majority assigns the opinion. The dissenting justices, if there are any, work out more informally who will write the dissenting opinion or opinions. Any justice, whether in majority or dissent, is free to write his own opinion concurring or dissenting.

After the decision has been agreed upon and the opinions assigned, the justices write the initial drafts of the opinions. In rough or proof form they are circulated for comment and amendment among those justices who have indicated they will concur. Then redone, they are recirculated for final agreement. On the Monday that the decision is rendered, summaries of the various opinions are delivered orally by the justices in open court, and the full opinions are filed with the clerk of the Court. This is "decision day," the culmination of that mysterious yet ordinary human process which builds granite monuments to liberty out of the mental travail of human beings.

In acknowledging aid received in the preparation of this manuscript I must stress the skill and devotion of one who as a lawyer combines legal ability of the highest order with feminine intuition, as always of unassessable quantity and quality. This is my wife, Mary Pearl Williams. Every word of this manuscript was exposed to her critical abilities and intuition. Whatever its over-all merit, it is much the better as the result of her contribution. My brother, Dr. Daniel Day Williams, had much to do with the original conception of this volume. Discussions with him revealed that theologians, among others, felt a strong need for ready access to the work of the Supreme Court. In addition, he read the manuscript and made significant suggestions. Finally, I must express an infinite obligation to the memory of my father, Wayne C. Williams, lawyer, educator, public servant, and author, who more than any other person taught me the majesty and priceless worth of the American Constitution and of this nation which has been built under the aegis of our great charter of human freedom and human dignity.

Contents

Foreword . . . . *page* vii

PART ONE—John Marshall: Architect of
 the Federal System
1. "This is of the very essence of judicial duty" . . . 3
    Marbury v. Madison 6
2. "It is the case, then, and not the court, that gives
    the jurisdiction" 11
    Martin v. Hunter's Lessee 14
3. "A thing may be necessary, very necessary, absolutely
    or indispensably necessary" 29
    McCulloch v. The State of Maryland . . . 32
4. "Commerce, undoubtedly, is traffic, but it is something
    more; it is intercourse" 51
    Gibbons v. Ogden 54

PART TWO—The Civil War and Its Aftermath
1. "Neither Dred Scott himself, nor any of his family,
    were made free" 65
    Dred Scott v. Sandford 68
2. "The highest honor of sovereignty is untarnished faith" . 80
    Ableman v. Booth 81

3. "It is no loose, unorganized insurrection" . . . 89
   Prize Cases 90
4. "A law for rulers and people, equally in war
   and in peace" 97
   Ex parte Milligan 99
5. "The Constitution deals with substance,
   not shadows" 105
   Cummings v. Missouri 107
6. "Government would be paralyzed in the paralysis
   of the people" 114
   Legal Tender Cases 116
7. "The natural and proper timidity and delicacy
   which belongs to the female sex" 124
   Bradwell v. Illinois 124
8. "An indestructible Union, composed of
   indestructible States" 127
   Texas v. White 129
9. "The one pervading purpose" 131
   Slaughterhouse Cases 133
10. "No man in this country is so high that he is
    above the law" 139
    United States v. Lee 140
11. "The foundation of a republic is the virtue of
    its citizens" 144
    Trist v. Child 145
12. "The gradual process of judicial inclusion
    and exclusion" 150
    Davidson v. New Orleans 151
13. "It is the State action that is prohibited" . . . 154
    Civil Rights Cases 156
14. "Their graves shall not remain unknown
    or unhonored" 166
    United States v. Gettysburg Railway . . . 167

PART THREE—The Supreme Court Enters the Twentieth Century

1. "Neagle fired two shots from his revolver" . . . 173
   In re Neagle 174
2. "The settled law of income taxation" . . . 185
   Pollock v. Farmers' Loan and Trust Company . . 187

3. "With better grace and greater cogency" . . . 191
    Holden v. Hardy 192
4. "The 14th Amendment does not enact Mr.
    Herbert Spencer's Social Statics" 199
    Lochner v. New York 200

PART FOUR—The Era of Holmes

1. "The ultimate good desired is better reached by
    free trade in ideas" 205
    Abrams v. United States 211
2. "Every idea is an incitement" 213
    Gitlow v. New York 214
3. "Those who won our independence by revolution
    were not cowards" 216
    Whitney v. California 219
4. "The greatest dangers to liberty lurk in insidious
    encroachment by men of zeal" 224
    Olmstead v. United States 225
5. "Not a universal, inexorable command" 230
    Burnet v. Coronado Oil & Gas Co. . . . 231
    Smith v. Allwright 234
6. "A strong public desire is not enough" . . . 236
    Pennsylvania Coal Company v. Mahon . . 238
7. "I do not believe in such apologies" 241
    Tyson & Brother v. Banton 242
8. "Because they believe more than some of us do in the
    teachings of the Sermon on the Mount" . . . 244
    United States v. Schwimmer 244
9. "And that is enough" 247
    Herbert v. Shanley Co. 248
10. "The stockyards are but a throat through which
    the current flows" 249
    Stafford v. Wallace 251
11. "The strike became a lawful instrument in a lawful
    economic struggle" 255
    American Steel Foundries v. Tri-City Central
        Trades Council 256

PART FIVE—Chief Justice Hughes and the Court of the "Nine Old Men"

1. "A growth from the seeds which the fathers planted" . . 265
   Home Building & Loan Association v. Blaisdell . . 268
2. "For adequate reason" 274
   Nebbia v. New York 276
3. "Frank recognition that language may mean what it says" 283
   United States v. Butler 286
4. "We are asked to shut our eyes to the plainest facts of our national life" 292
   Carter v. Carter Coal Company 295
   National Labor Relations Board v. Jones & Laughlin Steel Corp. 296
5. "The haunting fear when journey's end is near" . . 304
   Helvering v. Davis 305
6. "We are to keep the balance true" 309
   Palko v. Connecticut 311
   Snyder v. Commonwealth of Massachusetts . . 316

PART SIX—The Modern Supreme Court

1. "The compulsion is to bear false witness to his religion" . 321
   Minersville District v. Gobitis 323
2. "Compulsory unification of opinion achieves only the unanimity of the graveyard" 329
   West Virginia Board of Education v. Barnette . . 332
3. "Have done with this business of judicially examining other people's faiths" 349
   United States v. Ballard 350
4. "And I should think I would then have thought" . . 353
   McGrath v. Kristensen 354
5. "This is not just a little case over bus fares" . . 357
   Everson v. Board of Education of Ewing Tp. . . 360
6. "We are a religious people" 373
   Zorach v. Clauson 375
7. "We cannot bind the government to wait until the catalyst is added" 383
   Dennis v. United States 386
8. "The imminence of great disorder" 395
   Feiner v. New York 396

9. " 'Another such victory and I am undone' " . . . 401
    Beauharnais v. Illinois 402
10. "Such wheat overhangs the market" 407
    Wickard v. Filburn 409
11. "Separate educational facilities are inherently
    unequal" 416
    Brown v. Board of Education of Topeka . . . 418
Epilogue 425
Appendix I—The Constitution of the United States . . 429
Appendix II—The Justices of the United States
    Supreme Court 449
Index 455

PART ONE

John Marshall: Architect of the Federal System

ONE

Chapter 1

"This is of the very essence of judicial duty"

IN THE YEAR 1800 there was a revolution in the United States. It was a peaceful revolution, accomplished by the ballot in the democratic tradition. But it was surely a revolution in the sense that it effected an abrupt alteration in the direction of government.

During the presidential term of John Adams, 1797–1801, the rival political parties, the Federalists and the Democratic-Republicans, took definitive form. Their tenets were modified versions of the earlier Jefferson-Hamilton opposing alignments, particularly in regard to distrust of centralized government and confidence in the people's capacity to govern (Jefferson) and advocacy of strong national government by an "elite" and distrust of the people's capacity (Hamilton). Increasingly throughout these four years, the Federalists, with President Adams as leader, found themselves in public disfavor. The dramatic power of Vice-President Jefferson, leader of the Democratic-Republicans, and his confrere James Madison was a vital political force against the unpopular, but politically equally vital, aristocratic and almost monarchial bent of the Federalists.

As the public disfavor toward them grew, the Federalists fought back with all the power of a party in control. The culmination was the passage of the infamous Alien and Sedition Acts of 1798, which were designed to make unlawful any criticism of the government tending to bring it "into contempt or disrepute." While the constitutionality of these laws was never tested, there can be no doubt that they were an invalid infringement of freedom of speech. Indeed, many years later the Supreme Court said as much in a case that did not directly involve their validity. Jefferson himself, though the Vice-President, was the author of the Kentucky Resolutions protesting the unconstitutionality of the laws. Madison wrote similar resolutions passed by the legislature of Virginia.

The bitter debate over the Alien and Sedition Acts and the Virginia and Kentucky resolutions was merged with the presidential campaign of 1800. The popular tide flowed to the party of Thomas Jefferson, and he was elected. But the Federalists were not to be denied their final moments of power. Between the election on December 3, 1800, and the inauguration of Jefferson on March 4, 1801, the Federalists undertook to fill all open offices with good party men. One such appointment by outgoing President Adams was that of John Marshall, his Secretary of State and a loyal Federalist, to be the third Chief Justice of the United States Supreme Court. Another appointment, seemingly obscure, was destined also for an important historical role—the commission of William Marbury on March 2, 1801, as justice of the peace for the District of Columbia.

In December of 1801, Marbury, together with three other Federalist appointees, applied to the United States Supreme Court for an order compelling James Madison, Jefferson's Secretary of State, to deliver their commissions as justices of the peace. It was revealed that the appointments had been signed and sealed by the outgoing Secretary of State, but in the press of winding up affairs the commissions had not been delivered. Jefferson, upon his inauguration, had directed Madison to withhold delivery of these appointments. The neglectful Secretary of State who had not delivered the commissions before Jefferson's inauguration was, of course, John Marshall. And now Marshall sat as Chief Justice of the Court to which Marbury's application was made.

John Marshall and Thomas Jefferson were related, Marshall's grandmother and Jefferson's mother being first cousins. But the two men had never been close, and politically they were poles apart. In fact, much of the history of the next twenty-five years was to be the story of a running battle between Jefferson and his followers, as the party in power, and John Marshall, often assailed but almost invulnerable in his position as Chief Justice of the United States. The first manifestations of this running battle were the open threats of Jefferson's party that Marshall would be impeached if he held against them in Marbury's case.

That Marbury should bring his lawsuit directly in the United States Supreme Court was unusual, even though the defendant was the Secretary of State. The circumstance of his doing so set the stage for Marshall's master stroke. The jurisdiction of the Supreme Court is defined in the Constitution: the Court is entitled to take original jurisdiction in a narrowly defined class of cases, and in all other cases has only the power of review over lower court decisions. Marbury's case was clearly one which was not entitled to be heard by the Supreme Court as a matter of original jurisdiction. Normally in such a situation any court will simply decline to hear the case and leave the litigant free to bring his suit again in the proper court. But also in the picture was the Judiciary Act of 1789, which had set up the details of procedure in the federal courts. This statute was written by Senator Oliver Ellsworth, of Connecticut, a distinguished constitutional lawyer in his own right who became Chief Justice in 1796, Marshall's immediate predecessor.

There was nothing controversial about the Judiciary Act. But Marshall saw language in it which could be interpreted to authorize the Supreme Court to hear cases such as Marbury's, an interpretation of course that would put the statute in violation of the Constitution. The statute's wording was vague and ambiguous, and if such a question were presented today we would confidently expect the Court to interpret the statutory words to avoid conflict with the Constitution. But not John Marshall. Here was to be the master stroke.

Marshall held that the Court could not hear Marbury's case because of the constitutional restrictions. So far the decision was favorable to Jefferson. But Marshall also held that the Judiciary Act attempted to give the Supreme Court power to hear a case such as this. Thus, the statute was unconstitutional. Marshall had established the power of the Court to declare acts of Congress unconstitutional.

Today, after one hundred and fifty years of the exercise of the Supreme Court's power to declare statutes unconstitutional, it is difficult for us to realize what a sweeping assertion of power Marshall's decision was in 1803. True, there was strong sentiment that the Court should have this authority. But the framers of the Constitution had ducked the issue. And more significantly, Jefferson and his party were completely and bitterly opposed to the lodging of such power in any court. Indeed, Jefferson's well-developed political philosophy viewed courts as dangerous undemocratic institutions which had to be tolerated to settle private controversy but should be allowed no further power. Jefferson saw the dangers in Marshall's decision, dangers from his point of view. But

Marshall had effectively blocked active attack: the decision appealed to the widespread feeling that the courts should have this power of judicial review of the legislation—and further, Jefferson and his party had ostensibly won the case. While a sophisticated political philosopher such as Jefferson could perceive what Marshall had done, how could he arouse less perceptive followers? Criticizing the decision could hardly be effective. For he had won the case!

Thus was the all-important principle established: the Supreme Court has the power to declare acts of Congress unconstitutional. True, there have been other attacks upon the principle at later times, yet the power remains. If Marshall had chosen to proclaim the doctrine again, on some other occasion and in less skillful fashion, impeachment might have resulted and the doctrine might have died. But never again in the entire period of Marshall's tenure on the Supreme Court did he declare an act of Congress unconstitutional.

Marshall was Chief Justice for thirty-five years. The tremendous impact of his judicial service upon our system of government will be evaluated later. But he began his term with the most significant and fateful decision of all, the case upon which all our constitutional law is based—*Marbury v. Madison*.

MARBURY v. MADISON

Supreme Court of the United States, 1803, 1 Cranch 137

MARSHALL, C. J.:

The question,* whether an act, repugnant to the constitution, can become the law of the land, is a question deeply interesting to the United States; but happily, not of an intricacy proportioned to its interest. It

---

* In this quotation of the opinion, and in all other such quotations to follow, a typographical convention has been used for the reader's convenience: to denote, as here, a quotation from which preliminary remarks have been deleted, the first line runs full to the left margin; to denote one which begins with the Justice's opening remarks, deep paragraph indentation has been made.

seems only necessary to recognize certain principles, supposed to have been long and well established, to decide it.

That the people have an original right to establish, for their future government, such principles, as, in their opinion, shall most conduce to their own happiness is the basis on which the whole American fabric has been erected. The exercise of this original right is a very great exertion; nor can it, nor ought it, to be frequently repeated. The principles, therefore, so established, are deemed fundamental. And as the authority from which they proceed is supreme, and can seldom act, they are designed to be permanent.

This original and supreme will organizes the government, and assigns to different departments their respective powers. It may either stop here, or establish certain limits not to be transcended by those departments.

The government of the United States is of the latter description. The powers of the legislature are defined and limited; and that those limits may not be mistaken, or forgotten, the constitution is written. To what purpose are powers limited, and to what purpose is that limitation committed to writing, if these limits may, at any time, be passed by those intended to be restrained? The distinction between a government with limited and unlimited powers is abolished, if those limits do not confine the persons on whom they are imposed, and if acts prohibited and acts allowed, are of equal obligation. It is a proposition too plain to be contested, that the constitution controls any legislative act repugnant to it; or, that the legislature may alter the constitution by an ordinary act.

Between these alternatives there is no middle ground. The constitution is either a superior paramount law, unchangeable by ordinary means, or it is on a level with ordinary legislative acts, and, like other acts, is alterable when the legislature shall please to alter it.

If the former part of the alternative be true, then a legislative act contrary to the constitution is not law; if the latter part be true, then written constitutions are absurd attempts, on the part of the people, to limit a power in its own nature illimitable.

Certainly all those who have framed written constitutions contemplate them as forming the fundamental and paramount law of the nation, and, consequently, the theory of every such government must be, that an act of the legislature, repugnant to the constitution, is void.

This theory is essentially attached to a written constitution, and, is consequently, to be considered, by this court, as one of the fundamental principles of our society. It is not therefore to be lost sight of in the future consideration of this subject.

If an act of the legislature, repugnant to the constitution, is void, does it, notwithstanding its invalidity, bind the courts, and oblige them to give it effect? Or, in other words, though it be not law, does it constitute a rule as operative as if it was a law? This would be to overthrow in fact what was established in theory; and would seem, at first view, an absurdity too gross to be insisted on. It shall, however, receive a more attentive consideration.

It is emphatically the province and duty of the judicial department to say what the law is. Those who apply the rule to particular cases, must of necessity expound and interpret the rule. If two laws conflict with each other, the courts must decide on the operation of each.

So, if a law be in opposition to the constitution; if both the law and the constitution apply to a particular case, so that the court must either decide that case comfortably to the law, disregarding the constitution; or conformably to the constitution, disregarding the law; the court must determine which of these conflicting rules governs the case. This is of the very essence of judicial duty.

If, then, the courts are to regard the constitution, and the constitution is superior to any ordinary act of the legislature, the constitution, and not such ordinary act, must govern the case to which they both apply.

Those, then, who controvert the principle that the constitution is to be considered, in court, as a paramount law, are reduced to the necessity of maintaining that courts must close their eyes on the constitution, and see only the law.

This doctrine would subvert the very foundation of all written constitutions. It would declare that an act which, according to the principles and theory of our government, is entirely void, is yet, in practice, completely obligatory. It would declare that if the legislature shall do what is expressly forbidden, such act, notwithstanding the express prohibition, is in reality effectual. It would be giving to the legislature a practical and real omnipotence, with the same breath which professes to restrict their powers within narrow limits. It is prescribing limits, and declaring that those limits may be passed at pleasure.

That it thus reduces to nothing what we have deemed the greatest improvement on political institutions, a written constitution, would of itself be sufficient, in America, where written constitutions have been viewed with so much reverence, for rejecting the construction. But the peculiar expressions of the constitution of the United States furnish additional arguments in favour of its rejection.

The judicial power of the United States is extended to all cases arising under the constitution.

Could it be the intention of those who gave this power, to say that in using it the constitution should not be looked into? That a case arising under the constitution should be decided without examining the instrument under which it arises?

This is too extravagant to be maintained.

In some cases, then, the constitution must be looked into by the judges. And if they can open it at all, what part of it are they forbidden to read or to obey?

There are many other parts of the constitution which serve to illustrate this subject.

It is declared that "no tax or duty shall be laid on articles exported from any state." Suppose a duty on the export of cotton, of tobacco, or of flour; and a suit instituted to recover it. Ought judgment to be rendered in such a case? Ought the judges to close their eyes on the constitution, and only see the law?

The constitution declares "that no bill of attainder or ex post facto law shall be passed."

If, however, such a bill should be passed, and a person should be prosecuted under it; must the court condemn to death those victims whom the constitution endeavors to preserve?

"No person," says the constitution, "shall be convicted of treason unless on the testimony of two witnesses to the same overt act, or on confession in open court."

Here the language of the constitution is addressed especially to the courts. It prescribes, directly for them, a rule of evidence not to be departed from. If the legislature should change that rule, and declare one witness, or a confession out of court, sufficient for conviction, must the constitutional principle yield to the legislative act?

From these, and many other selections which might be made, it is apparent, that the framers of the constitution contemplated that instrument as a rule for the government of courts, as well as of the legislature.

Why otherwise does it direct the judges to take an oath to support it? This oath certainly applies in an especial manner, to their conduct in their official character. How immoral to impose it on them, if they were to be used as the instruments, and the knowing instruments, for violating what they swear to support!

The oath of office, too, imposed by the legislature, is completely demonstrative of the legislative opinion on this subject. It is in these words: "I do solemnly swear that I will administer justice without respect to persons, and do equal right to the poor and to the rich; and that I will faithfully and impartially discharge all the duties incumbent on me as ———, according to the best of my abilities and understanding, agreeably to the constitution and laws of the United States."

Why does a judge swear to discharge his duties agreeably to the constitution of the United States, if that constitution forms no rule for his government? If it is closed upon him, and cannot be inspected by him?

If such be the real state of things, this is worse than solemn mockery. To prescribe, or to take this oath, becomes equally a crime.

It is also not entirely unworthy of observation, that in declaring what shall be the supreme law of the land, the constitution itself is first mentioned; and not the laws of the United States generally, but those only which shall be made in pursuance of the constitution, have that rank.

Thus, the particular phraseology of the constitution of the United States confirms and strengthens the principle, supposed to be essential to all written constitutions, that a law repugnant to the constitution is void; and that courts, as well as other departments, are bound by that instrument.*

---

* At the end of each majority opinion of the United States Supreme Court there are a few words which in technical language actually direct the disposal of the case. Throughout the book these concluding words are omitted without indication by ellipses. Where ellipses do appear at the end of the printed opinion they indicate that a concluding portion of the body of the opinion is omitted.

Chapter 2

*"It is the case, then, and not the
court, that gives the jurisdiction"*

IMPEACHMENT was threatened against John Marshall shortly after his decision in *Marbury v. Madison*. Because the case itself ill-afforded grounds for open attack upon him, as we have already seen, the route was to be more indirect. After the successful impeachment and conviction of two federal lower court judges, the House of Representatives in 1804 impeached Associate Justice Chase of the United States Supreme Court. Jefferson and his party had hereby launched the plan, and it was an openly avowed plan, to impeach all the justices of the Supreme Court, including Marshall. Thus would the Court be reconstituted with Democratic-Republicans in sympathy with the national administration. Chase, irascible and domineering, was the obvious first choice. But from many high political sources came statements that there was to be a clean sweep.

The trial of the impeachment in the Senate was a dramatic public spectacle. Marshall himself testified, though rather ineffectively. But the Jeffersonians' plan misfired. Chase was acquitted, largely through the brilliant efforts of his head defense counsel, the noted lawyer Luther Martin. Marshall and his court were secure, at least for the time being.

The relations between Marshall and the Jeffersonians were not destined to improve, however. Only two years thereafter, Jefferson and Marshall were again brought to swords' points by one of the most bizarre episodes in American history—the alleged treason of Aaron Burr. Burr had been Jefferson's Vice-President, and he was a brilliant young man of exciting promise. No one has ever known for certain what he had in mind when he conferred with General James Wilkinson, commander of United States forces in the Mississippi Valley and governor of Upper Louisiana. Whether Burr's outfitted military expedition was to invade Mexico or set up a new nation in what was then westernmost United States is buried in the mists of the past. But Jefferson and his party were convinced that the treasonable alternative was correct. Burr and his conspirators were indicted. Marshall was destined to play the decisive role in opposition.

The Constitution requires that there can be no conviction for treason without confession in open court unless there are two witnesses to the same overt treasonable act. Twice did Marshall apply this constitutional mandate strictly to thwart the prosecution of Burr and his henchmen, first in the Supreme Court decision releasing two of Burr's associates on the ground that no treason had been shown, and again when he himself presided over the United States Circuit Court at the trial of Aaron Burr for treason. His appearance as a trial judge was in the normal course of events because of the earlier practice of the Supreme Court justices of traveling "in circuit" and hearing cases in lower federal courts. It was Marshall's detailed and strict interpretation of the constitutional requirements in treason trials that led to Burr's acquittal.

Again there were threats to impeach Marshall. But at some time in his career Marshall must have become somewhat inured to them— they came so often. And other cases followed, all with the strong nationalist bent and all evoking bitter criticism from the party in power.

A year after Jefferson's retirement from the Presidency he wrote James Madison, "It will be difficult to find a character of firmness enough to preserve his independence on the same bench with Marshall." The prophetic wisdom of these words came to the test in 1811 when, with the appointment of Justices Gabriel Duval and Joseph Story by President Madison, the Supreme Court for the first time contained a majority of Democratic-Republicans. Story's appointment was the significant one. A young man of surpassing intellectual stature, he was the acknowledged master of the common law in the United States. While a follower of Jefferson and Madison, he not infrequently revealed his intellectual independence in those days when "party regularity" had not attained the fetishistic level of today.

By all standards of preparation for the high post of Justice of the United States Supreme Court, Story was pre-eminently qualified. The Jeffersonians could hope that with a man who was Marshall's equal in intellectual stature sympathetic to their cause, the days of Supreme Court "obstructionism" would be dead. Again was John Marshall underestimated by his foes.

Marshall was a man with a mission. His powerful intellect was enforced by deep moral conviction and propelled by a most vigorous and winsome personality. He was noted for the delightfulness of his informal conversation and the keenness of his wit. Somewhat indolent, he countered his lack of scholarship by the sheer impact of the reasoning and logic of his magnificent mind. Instead of the anticipated clash of the great intellects of Marshall and Story, there was an incredible blending. Story was captivated and then captured.

Thus it fell to Story in his first constitutional decision almost to surpass Marshall in his nationalistic leanings, if that were possible. The hopes of the Jeffersonians were blasted. A case came to the Court involving rival grants of land in Virginia. One grant stemmed from the state and one from the British government before the Revolution. Marshall disqualified himself from hearing the case because of a family relation on the side of the ultimate winner. The Supreme Court, in an opinion by Justice Story, held against the grant of the state of Virginia. Normally this would have ended the litigation, as the state supreme court would be expected to issue court process to carry out the decision. But the Supreme Court of Virginia openly defied the decision and refused to issue the proper legal process upholding it! Remember, this was Virginia, the home of the Jeffersonians and the seat of the opposition to Marshall and the Court.

Back the case went to Washington. Story again delivered the opinion of the Court—an opinion which surely reached the ultimate in the doctrine of federal supremacy over the states. Story held that the Virginia court *must* follow the mandate of the Supreme Court, and indirectly hinted that if this were not done the Supreme Court would issue legal process against the Virginia justices personally, compelling their acquiescence upon threat of contempt. The possible spectacle of a judge of the highest court of a state being called to account before the United States Supreme Court under pain of possible fine or jail sentence is certainly the acme of federal supremacy over the states. The spectacle never took place. The Supreme Court of Virginia acquiesced.

Story's opinion, one of his longest, was one of his ablest. It is magnificently reasoned, as might be expected from a meticulous scholar, but its very thoroughness makes it a somewhat difficult opinion to read and understand. Less than half of it is printed here.

Also presented is the concurring opinion of Justice William Johnson. Johnson was the first Democratic-Republican appointee to the Court, named by Jefferson in 1804. He was a young man of only indifferent qualifications as far as experience was concerned. After service in the legislature of South Carolina, he became a trial judge in that state and was serving in that capacity when Jefferson appointed him to the Court at the age of thirty-three. Johnson served on the Court for thirty years. A man of quiet scholarship, he wrote exceedingly well. His personal feelings are beautifully expressed in this concurring opinion, which is a masterpiece of conciliation. But with all its conciliatory skill and its disapproval of Story's threat of compulsory process against the state judges, there remains the undercore of unshakable belief that the Supreme Court must not be defied, that it must endure as truly the supreme court of the land—small solace indeed for the Virginia Jeffersonians from their first Court appointee.

MARTIN v. HUNTER'S LESSEE

Supreme Court of the United States, 1816, 1 Wheaton 304

STORY, J.:

This is a writ of error from the Court of Appeals of Virginia, founded upon the refusal of that court to obey the mandate of this court, requiring the judgment rendered in this very cause, at February term, 1813, to be carried into due execution. The following is the judgment of the Court of Appeals rendered on the mandate: "The court is unanimously of opinion that the appellate power of the Supreme Court of the United States does not extend to this court, under a sound construction of the constitution of the United States; that so much of the 25th section of the act of Congress to establish the judicial courts of the United States, as extends the appellate jurisdiction of the Supreme Court to this court, is not in pursuance of the constitution of the United States; that the writ of error, in this cause, was improvidently allowed under the authority of that act; that the proceedings thereon in the Supreme Court were, *coram non judice,* in relation to this court, and that obedience to its mandate be declined by the court."

The questions involved in this judgment are of great importance and delicacy. Perhaps it is not too much to affirm that, upon their right decision, rest some of the most solid principles which have hitherto been supposed to sustain and protect the constitution itself. The great respectability, too, of the court whose decisions we are called upon to review, and the entire deference which we entertain for the learning and ability of that court, add much to the difficulty of the task which has so unwelcomely fallen upon us. It is, however, a source of consolation that we have had the assistance of most able and learned arguments to aid our inquiries; and that the opinion which is now to be pronounced has been weighed with every solicitude to come to a correct result, and matured after solemn deliberation.

Before proceeding to the principal questions, it may not be unfit to dispose of some preliminary considerations which have grown out of the arguments at the bar.

The constitution of the United States was ordained and established, not by the states in their sovereign capacities, but emphatically, as the preamble of the constitution declares, by "the people of the United States." There can be no doubt that it was competent to the people to invest the general government with all the powers which they might deem proper and necessary; to extend or restrain these powers according to their own good pleasure, and to give them a paramount and supreme authority. As little doubt can there be that the people had a right to prohibit to the states the exercise of any powers which were, in their judgment, incompatible with the objects of the general compact; to make the powers of the state governments, in given cases, subordinate to those of the nation, or to reserve to themselves those sovereign authorities which they might not choose to delegate to either. The constitution was not, therefore, necessarily carved out of existing state sovereignties, nor a surrender of powers already existing in state institutions, for the powers of the states depend upon their own constitutions; and the people of every state had the right to modify and restrain them, according to their own views of policy or principle. On the other hand, it is perfectly clear that the sovereign powers vested in the state governments, by their respective constitutions, remained unaltered and unimpaired, except so far as they were granted to the government of the United States.

These deductions do not rest upon general reasoning, plain and obvious as they seem to be. They have been positively recognized by one of the articles in amendment of the constitution, which declares, that "The powers not delegated to the United States by the constitution, nor prohibited by it to the states, are reserved to the states respectively, or to the people."

The government, then, of the United States, can claim no powers which are not granted to it by the constitution, and the powers actually granted, must be such as are expressly given, or given by necessary implication. On the other hand, this instrument, like every other grant, is to have a reasonable construction, according to the import of its terms; and where a power is expressly given in general terms, it is not to be restrained to particular cases, unless that construction grow out of the context expressly, or by necessary implication. The words are to be taken in their natural and obvious sense, and not in a sense unreasonably restricted or enlarged.

The constitution unavoidably deals in general language. It did not suit the purposes of the people, in framing this great charter of our liberties, to provide for minute specifications of its powers, or to declare the means by which those powers should be carried into execution. It was foreseen that this would be a perilous and difficult, if not an impracticable, task. The instrument was not intended to provide merely for the exigencies of a few years, but was to endure through a long lapse of ages, the events of which were locked up in the inscrutable purposes of Providence. It could not be foreseen what new changes and modifications of power might be indispensable to effectuate the general objects of the charter; and restrictions and specifications which, at the present, might seem salutary, might, in the end, prove the overthrow of the system itself. Hence its powers are expressed in general terms, leaving to the legislature, from time to time, to adopt its own means to effectuate legitimate objects, and to mold and model the exercise of its powers, as its own wisdom and the public interests should require.

MARTIN V. HUNTER'S LESSEE

With these principles in view—principles in respect to which no difference of opinion ought to be indulged—let us now proceed to the interpretation of the constitution, so far as regards the great points in controversy.

The third article of the constitution is that which must principally attract our attention. The first section declares, "the judicial power of the United States shall be vested in one Supreme Court, and in such other inferior courts as the Congress may, from time to time, ordain and establish." The second section declares, that "the judicial power shall extend to all cases in law or equity, arising under this constitution, the laws of the United States, and the treaties made, or which shall be made, under their authority; to all cases affecting ambassadors, other public ministers and consuls; to all cases of admiralty and maritime jurisdiction; to controversies to which the United States shall be a party; to controversies between two or more states; between a state and citizens of another state; between citizens of different states; between citizens of the same state, claiming lands under the grants of different states; and between a state or the citizens thereof, and foreign states, citizens, or subjects." It then proceeds to declare, that "in all cases affecting ambassadors, other public ministers and consuls, and those in which a state shall be a party, the Supreme Court shall have original jurisdiction. In all the other cases before mentioned the Supreme Court shall have appellate jurisdiction, both as to law and fact, with such exceptions, and under such regulations, as the Congress shall make."

Such is the language of the article creating and defining the judicial power of the United States. It is the voice of the whole American people solemnly declared, in establishing one great department of that government which was, in many respects, national, and in all, supreme. It is a part of the very same instrument which was to act not merely upon individuals, but upon states; and to deprive them altogether of the exercise of some powers of sovereignty, and to restrain and regulate them in the exercise of others.

Let this article be carefully weighed and considered. The language of the article throughout is manifestly designed to be mandatory upon the legislature. Its obligatory force is so imperative that Congress could not, without a violation of its duty, have refused to carry it into operation. The judicial power of the United States shall be vested (not may be vested) in one supreme court, and in such inferior courts as Congress may, from time to time, ordain and establish. Could Congress have lawfully refused to create a supreme court, or to vest in it the constitutional jurisdiction? "The judges, both of the supreme and inferior courts, shall hold their offices during good behavior, and shall, at stated times, receive, for their services, a compensation which shall not be diminished during their continuance in office." Could Congress create or limit any other tenure of the judicial office? Could they refuse to pay, at stated times, the stipulated salary, or diminish it during the continuance in office? But one answer can be given to these questions: it must be in the negative. The object of the constitution was to establish three great departments of government; the legislative, the executive and the judicial departments. The first was to pass laws, the second to approve and execute them, and the third to expound and enforce them. Without the latter it would be impossible to carry into effect some of the express provisions of the constitution. How, otherwise, could crimes against the United States be tried and punished? How could causes between two states be heard and determined? The judicial power must, therefore, be vested in some court, by Congress; and to suppose that it was not an obligation binding on them, but might, at their pleasure, be omitted or declined, is to suppose that, under the sanction of the constitution they might defeat the constitution itself; a construction which would lead to such a result cannot be sound. . . .

If, then, it is the duty of Congress to vest the judicial power of the United States, it is a duty to vest the whole judicial power. The language, if imperative as to one part, is imperative as to all. If it were otherwise, this anomaly would exist, that Congress might successively refuse to vest the jurisdiction in any one class of cases enumerated in the constitution, and thereby defeat the jurisdiction as to all; for the constitution has not singled out any class on which Congress are bound to act in preference to others. . . .

It being, then, established that the language of this clause is imperative; the next question is as to the cases to which it shall apply. The answer is found in the constitution itself. The judicial power shall extend to all the cases enumerated in the constitution. As the mode is not limited, it may extend to all such cases, in any form in which judicial power may be exercised. It may, therefore, extend to them in the shape of original or appellate jurisdiction, or both; for there is nothing in the nature of the cases which binds to the exercise of the one in preference to the other.

In what cases, (if any) is this judicial power exclusive, or exclusive at the election of Congress? It will be observed that there are two classes of cases enumerated in the constitution, between which a distinction seems to be drawn. The first class includes cases arising under the constitution, laws, and treaties of the United States; cases affecting ambassadors, other public ministers and consuls, and cases of admiralty and maritime jurisdiction. In this class the expression is, "and that the judicial power shall extend to all cases"; but in the subsequent part of the clause which embraces all the other cases of national cognizance, and forms the second class, the word "all" is dropped seemingly *ex industria*. Here the judicial authority is to extend to controversies (not to all controversies) to which the United States shall be a party, &c. From this difference of phraseology, perhaps, a difference of constitutional intention may, with propriety, be inferred. It is hardly to be presumed that the variation in the language could have been accidental. It must have been the result of some determinate reason; and it is not very difficult to find a reason sufficient to support the apparent change of intention. In respect to the first class, it may well have been the intention of the framers of the constitution imperatively to extend the judicial power either in an original or appellate form to all cases; and in the latter class to leave it to Congress to qualify the jurisdiction, original or appellate, in such manner as public policy might dictate....

This leads us to the consideration of the great question as to the nature and extent of the appellate jurisdiction of the United States. We have already seen that appellate jurisdiction is given by the constitution to the Supreme Court in all cases where it has not original jurisdiction; subject, however, to such exceptions and regulations as Congress may prescribe. It is, therefore, capable of embracing every case enumerated in the constitution, which is not exclusively to be decided by way of original jurisdiction. But the exercise of appellate jurisdiction is far from being limited by the terms of the constitution to the Supreme Court. There can be no doubt that Congress may create a succession of inferior tribunals, in each of which it may vest appellate as well as original jurisdiction. The judicial power is delegated by the constitution in the most general terms, and may, therefore, be exercised by Congress under every variety of form, of appellate or original jurisdiction. And as there is nothing in the constitution which restrains or limits this power, it must, therefore, in all other cases, subsist in the utmost latitude of which in its own nature, it is susceptible.

As then, by the terms of the constitution, the appellate jurisdiction is not limited as to the Supreme Court, and as to this court it may be exercised in all other cases than those of which it has original cognizance, what is there to restrain its exercise over state tribunals in the enumerated cases? The appellate power is not limited by the terms of the third article to any particular courts. The words are, "the judicial power (which includes appellate power) shall extend to all cases," &c.; and "in all other cases before mentioned the Supreme Court shall have appellate jurisdiction." It is the case, then, and not the court, that gives the jurisdiction. If the judicial power extends to the case, it will be in vain to search in the letter of the constitution for any qualification as to the tribunal where it depends. It is incumbent, then, upon those who assert such a qualification to show its existence by necessary implication. If the text be clear and distinct, no restriction upon its plain and obvious import ought to be admitted, unless the inference be irresistible.

If the constitution meant to limit the appellate jurisdiction to cases pending in the courts of the United States, it would necessarily follow that the jurisdiction of these courts would, in all the cases enumerated in the constitution, be exclusive of state tribunals. How otherwise could the jurisdiction extend to all cases arising under the constitution, laws and treaties of the United States, or to all cases of admiralty and maritime jurisdiction? If some of these cases might be entertained by state tribunals, and no appellate jurisdiction as to them should exist, then the appellate power would not extend to all, but to some, cases. If state tribunals might exercise concurrent jurisdiction over all or some of the other classes of cases in the constitution without control, then the appellate jurisdiction of the United States might, as to such cases, have no real existence, contrary to the manifest intent of the constitution. Under such circumstances, to give effect to the judicial power, it must be construed to be exclusive; and this not only when the *casus foederis* should arise directly, but when it should arise, incidentally, in cases pending in state courts. This construction would abridge the jurisdiction of such courts far more than has been ever contemplated in any act of Congress.

On the other hand, if, as has been contended, a discretion be vested in Congress to establish, or not to establish, inferior courts at their own pleasure, and Congress should not establish such courts, the appellate jurisdiction of the Supreme Court would have nothing to act upon, unless it could act upon cases pending in the state courts. Under such circumstances it must be held that the appellate power would extend to state courts; for the constitution is peremptory that it shall extend to certain enumerated cases, which cases could exist in no other courts. Any other construction, upon this supposition, would involve this strange contradiction, that a discretionary power vested in Congress, and which they might rightfully omit to exercise, would defeat the absolute injunctions of the constitution in relation to the whole appellate power.

But it is plain that the framers of the constitution did contemplate that cases within the judicial cognizance of the United States not only might but would arise in the state courts, in the exercise of their ordinary jurisdiction. With this view the sixth article declares, that "this constitution, and the laws of the United States which shall be made in pursuance thereof, and all treaties made, or which shall be made, under the authority of the United States, shall be the supreme law of the land, and the judges in every state shall be bound thereby, anything in the constitution or laws of any state to the contrary notwithstanding." It is obvious that this obligation is imperative upon the state judges in their official, and not merely in their private, capacities. From the very nature of their judicial duties they would be called upon to pronounce the law applicable to the case in judgment. They were not to decide merely according to the laws or constitution of the state, but according to the constitution, laws and treaties of the United States—"the supreme law of the land.". . .

It must, therefore, be conceded that the constitution not only contemplated, but meant to provide for cases within the scope of the judicial power of the United States, which might yet depend before state tribunals. It was foreseen that in the exercise of their ordinary jurisdiction, state courts would incidentally take cognizance of cases arising under the constitution, the laws and treaties of the United States. Yet to all these cases the judicial power, by the very terms of the constitution, is to extend. It cannot extend by original jurisdiction if that was already rightfully and exclusively attached in the state courts, which (as has been already shown) may occur; it must, therefore, extend by appellate jurisdiction, or not at all. It would seem to follow that the appellate power of the United States must, in such cases, extend to state tribunals; and if in such cases, there is no reason why it should not equally attach upon all others within the purview of the constitution.

It has been argued that such an appellate jurisdiction over state courts is inconsistent with the genius of our governments, and the spirit of the constitution. That the latter was never designed to act upon state sovereignties, but only upon the people, and that if the power exists, it will materially impair the sovereignty of the states, and the independence of their courts. We cannot yield to the force of this reasoning; it assumes principles which we cannot admit, and draws conclusions to which we do not yield our assent.

It is a mistake that the constitution was not designed to operate upon States, in their corporate capacities. It is crowded with provisions which restrain or annul the sovereignty of the states in some of the highest branches of their prerogatives. The tenth section of the first article contains a long list of disabilities and prohibitions imposed upon the states. Surely, when such essential portions of state sovereignty are taken away, or prohibited to be exercised, it cannot be correctly asserted that the constitution does not act upon the states. The language of the constitution is also imperative upon the states as to the performance of many duties. It is imperative upon the state legislatures to make laws prescribing the time, places, and manner of holding elections for senators and representatives, and for electors of President and Vice-President. And in these, as well as some other cases, Congress have a right to revise, amend, or supersede the laws which may be passed by state legislatures. When, therefore, the states are stripped of some of the highest attributes of sovereignty, and the same are given to the United States; when the legislatures of the states are, in some respects, under the control of Congress, and in every case are, under the constitution, bound by the paramount authority of the United States; it is certainly difficult to support the argument that the appellate power over the decisions of state courts is contrary to the genius of our institutions. The courts of the United States can, without question, revise the proceedings of the executive and legislative authorities of the states, and if they are found to be contrary to the constitution, may declare them to be of no legal validity. Surely the exercise of the same right over judicial tribunals is not a higher or more dangerous act of sovereign power.

Nor can such a right be deemed to impair the independence of state judges. It is assuming the very gound in controversy to assert that they possess an absolute independence of the United States. In respect to the powers granted to the United States, they are not independent; they are expressly bound to obedience by the letter of the constitution; and if they should unintentionally transcend their authority, or misconstrue the constitution, there is no more reason for giving their judgments an absolute and irresistible force than for giving it to the acts of the other co-ordinate departments of state sovereignty.

The argument urged from the possibility of the abuse of the revising power is equally unsatisfactory. It is always a doubtful course to argue against the use or existence of a power, from the possibility of its abuse. It is still more difficult, by such an argument, to ingraft upon a general power a restriction which is not to be found in the terms in which it is given. From the very nature of things, the absolute right of decision, in the last resort, must rest somewhere—wherever it may be vested it is susceptible of abuse. In all questions of jurisdiction the inferior, or appellate court, must pronounce the final judgment; and common sense, as well as legal reasoning, has conferred it upon the latter. . . .

It is further argued that no great public mischief can result from a construction which shall limit the appellate power of the United States to cases in their own courts; first, because state judges are bound by an oath to support the constitution of the United States, and must be presumed to be men of learning and integrity; and secondly, because Congress must have an unquestionable right to remove all cases within the scope of the judicial power from the state courts to the courts of the United States, at any time before final judgment, though not after final judgment. As to the first reason—admitting that the judges of the state courts are, and always will be, of as much learning, integrity, and wisdom, as those of the courts of the United States (which we very cheerfully admit), it does not aid the argument. It is manifest that the constitution has proceeded upon a theory of its own, and given or withheld powers according to the judgment of the American people, by whom it was adopted. We can only construe its powers, and cannot inquire into the policy or principles which induced the grant of them. The constitution has presumed (whether rightly or wrongly we do not inquire) that state attachments, state prejudices, state jealousies, and state interests, might sometimes obstruct, or control, or be supposed to obstruct or control, the regular administration of justice. Hence, in controversies between states; between citizens of different states; between citizens claiming grants under different states; between a state and its citizens, or foreigners, and between citizens and foreigners, it enables the parties, under the authority of Congress, to have the controversies heard, tried, and determined before the national tribunals. No other reason than that which has been stated can be assigned, why some, at least, of those cases should not have been left to the cognizance of the state courts. In respect to the other enumerated cases—the cases arising under the constitution, laws, and treaties of the United States, cases affecting ambassadors and other public ministers, and cases of admiralty and maritime jurisdiction—reasons of a higher and more extensive nature, touching the safety, peace, and sovereignty of the nation, might well justify a grant of exclusive jurisdiction.

This is not all. A motive of another kind, perfectly compatible with the most sincere respect for state tribunals, might induce the grant of appellate power over their decisions. That motive is the importance, and even necessity of uniformity of decisions throughout the whole United States, upon all subjects within the purview of the constitution. Judges of equal learning and integrity, in different states, might differently interpret a statute, or a treaty of the United States, or even the constitution itself. If there were no revising authority to control these jarring and discordant judgments, and harmonize them into uniformity, the laws, the treaties, and the constitution of the United States would be different in different states, and might, perhaps, never have precisely the same construction, obligation, or efficacy, in any two states. The public mischiefs that would attend such a state of things would be truly deplorable; and it cannot be believed that they could have escaped the enlightened convention which formed the constitution. What indeed, might then have been only prophecy, has now become fact; and the appellate jurisdiction must continue to be the only adequate remedy for such evils. . . .

On the whole, the court are of opinion that the appellate power of the

United States does extend to cases pending in the state courts; and that the 25th section of the judiciary act, which authorizes the exercise of this jurisdiction in the specified cases, by a writ of error, is supported by the letter and spirit of the constitution. We find no clause in that instrument which limits this power; and we dare not interpose a limitation where the people have not been disposed to create one.

Strong as this conclusion stands upon the general language of the constitution, it may still derive support from other sources. It is an historical fact that this exposition of the constitution, extending its appellate power to state courts, was, previous to its adoption, uniformly and publicly avowed by its friends, and admitted by its enemies, as the basis of their respective reasonings, both in and out of the state conventions. It is an historical fact that at the time when the judiciary act was submitted to the deliberations of the first Congress, composed, as it was, not only of men of great learning and ability, but of men who had acted a principal part in framing, supporting, or opposing that constitution, the same exposition was explicitly declared and admitted by the friends and by the opponents of that system. It is an historical fact that the Supreme Court of the United States have, from time to time, sustained this appellate jurisdiction in a great variety of cases, brought from the tribunals of many of the most important states in the Union, and that no state tribunal has ever breathed a judicial doubt on the subject, or declined to obey the mandate of the Supreme Court, until the present occasion. This weight of contemporaneous exposition by all parties, this acquiescence of enlightened state courts, and these judicial decisions of the Supreme Court through so long a period, do, as we think, place the doctrine upon a foundation of authority which cannot be shaken, without delivering over the subject to perpetual and irremediable doubts. . . .

We have not thought it incumbent on us to give any opinion upon the question, whether this court have authority to issue a writ of *mandamus* to the Court of Appeals to enforce the former judgments, as we do not think it necessarily involved in the decision of this cause.

It is the opinion of the whole court that the judgment of the Court of Appeals of Virginia, rendered on the mandate in this cause, be reversed, and the judgment of the District Court, held at Winchester, be, and the same is hereby affirmed.

JOHNSON, J., *concurring*:

It will be observed in this case, that the court disavows all intention to decide on the right to issue compulsory process to the state courts; thus leaving us, in my opinion, where the constitution and laws place us—supreme over persons and cases as far as our judicial powers extend, but not asserting any compulsory control over the state tribunals.

In this view I acquiesce in their opinion, but not altogether in the reasoning, or opinion, of my brother who delivered it. Few minds are accustomed to the same habits of thinking, and our conclusions are most satisfactory to ourselves when arrived at in our own way.

I have another reason for expressing my opinion on this occasion. I view this question as one of the most momentous importance; as one which may effect, in its consequences, the permanence of the American Union. It presents an instance of collision between the judicial powers of the Union, and one of the greatest states in the Union, on a point the most delicate and difficult to be adjusted. On the one hand, the general government must cease to exist whenever it loses the power of protecting itself in the exercise of its constitutional powers. Force, which acts upon the physical powers of man, or judicial process, which addresses itself to his moral principles or his fears, are the only means to which governments can resort in the exercise of their authority. The former is happily unknown to the genius of our constitution, except as far as it shall be sanctioned by the latter; but let the latter be obstructed in its progress by an opposition which it cannot overcome or put by, and the resort must be to the former, or government is no more.

On the other hand, so firmly am I persuaded that the American people can no longer enjoy the blessings of a free government, whenever the state sovereignties shall be prostrated at the feet of the general government, nor the proud consciousness of equality and security, any longer than the independence of judicial power shall be maintained consecrated and intangible, that I could borrow the language of a celebrated orator [Patrick Henry], and exclaim: "I rejoice that Virginia has resisted."

Yet here I must claim the privilege of expressing my regret that the opposition of the high and truly respected tribunal of that state had not been marked with a little more moderation. The only point necessary to be decided in the case then before them was, "whether they were bound to obey the mandate emanating from this court." But in the judgment entered on their minutes, they have affirmed that the case was, in this court, *coram non judice,* or, in other words, that this court had not jurisdiction over it.

This is assuming a truly alarming latitude of judicial power. Where is it to end? It is an acknowledged principle of, I believe, every court in the world, that not only the decisions, but everything done under the judicial process of courts, not having jurisdiction, are, *ipso facto,* void. Are, then, the judgments of this court to be reviewed in every court of the Union? And is every recovery of money, every change of property, that has taken place under our process, to be considered as null, void, and tortious?

We pretend not to more infallibility than other courts composed of the same frail materials which compose this. It would be the height of affectation to close our minds upon the recollection that we have been extracted from the same seminaries in which originated the learned men who preside over the state tribunals. But there is one claim which we can with confidence assert in our own name upon those tribunals—the profound, uniform, and unaffected respect which this court has always exhibited for state decisions, give us strong pretentions to judicial comity. And another claim I may assert, in the name of the American people; in this court, every state in the Union is represented; we are constituted by the voice of the Union, and when decisions take place, which nothing but a spirit to give ground and harmonize can reconcile, ours is the superior claim upon the comity of the state tribunals. It is the nature of the human mind to press a favorite hypothesis too far, but magnanimity will always be ready to sacrifice the pride of opinion to public welfare.

In the case before us, the collision has been, on our part, wholly unsolicited. The exercise of this appellate jurisdiction over the state decisions has long been acquiesced in, and when the writ of error, in this case, was allowed by the president of the Court of Appeals of Virginia, we were sanctioned in supposing that we were to meet with the same acquiescence there. Had that court refused to grant the writ in the first instance, or had the question of jurisdiction, or on the mode of exercising jurisdiction, been made here originally, we should have been put on our guard, and might have so modeled the process of the court as to strip it of the offensive form of a mandate. . . .

I should feel the more hesitation in adopting the opinions which I express in this case were I not firmly convinced that they are practical, and may be acted upon without compromitting the harmony of the Union, or bringing humility upon the state tribunals. God forbid that the judicial power in these states should ever, for a moment, even in its humblest departments, feel a doubt of its own independence. Whilst adjudicating on a subject which the laws of the country assign finally to the revising power of another tribunal, it can feel no such doubt. An anxiety to do justice is ever relieved by the knowledge that what we do is not final between the parties. And no sense of dependence can be felt from the knowledge that the parties, not the court, may be summoned before another tribunal. With this view, by means of laws, avoiding judgments obtained in the state courts in cases over which Congress has constitutionally assumed jurisdiction, and inflicting penalties on parties who shall contumaciously persist in infringing the constitutional rights of others—under a liberal extension of the writ of injunction and the *habeas corpus ad subjiciendum,* I flatter myself that the full extent of the constitutional revising power may be secured to the United States, and the benefits of it to the individual, without ever resorting to compulsory or restrictive process upon the state tribunals; a right which, I repeat again, Congress has not asserted; nor has this court asserted, nor does there appear any necessity for asserting.

Chapter 3

*"A thing may be necessary, very necessary,
absolutely or indispensably necessary"*

THAT THE GREATEST court opinion in American jurisprudence is John Marshall's 1819 opinion in *McCulloch v. Maryland,* most, if not all, students of American law agree. Greatest does not mean best written. In his later years, Marshall tended more and more to construct complex sentences difficult to follow, and there are difficult sentences here; but the inexorable logic shines through as does the vision that the Constitution and our form of government must endure. Here in one masterful picture Marshall paints the whole panorama of the federal system as it must be to live and endure. The Chief Justice was now at the peak of his powers and had his Court solidly behind him. In case after case, he had been building the constitutional structure with consistent plan and imperishable materials. The political winds blew, and always against him. But Marshall withstood and built on and on.

The Bank of the United States, Alexander Hamilton's fiscal brain child, was a most powerful financial institution, engaged in banking at all levels. Such a strong federal institution was too much for the Jeffersonians. The states must gain the fiscal power through their own banks. And so it came to pass—the Bank of the United States was allowed to die in 1811. The states chartered the banks the people needed.

Chaos was the immediate result. There were no developed state banking controls, and financial brigands took over the banking business. The banks issued mountains of notes, their values fluctuating wildly from day to day. Banks opened and closed overnight. Financial panic began to develop. Madison determined that there would have to be a rebirth of the United States Bank to avert financial collapse. The Second United States Bank was chartered in 1816.

Conditions, however, went from bad to worse. If the new bank had been as skillfully and conservatively managed as its predecessor, it would probably have alleviated the situation; but it fell into the pattern of the state banks. There was wild speculation. Notes of other banks were honored on the basis of favoritism. Local branches of the United States Bank fell into default themselves. Popular dissatisfaction with financial affairs now turned on the institution which was supposed to have saved the day.

The states began to search for means to drive the Second United States Bank out of existence. By 1819 no less than nine states had laws designed to make it impossible for the bank to maintain branches or transact business within their borders. One such state was Maryland. Upon all bank notes issued by a bank not chartered by the state, Maryland levied a 2 per cent tax (1 per cent on the larger bills). This scheme automatically drove all United States Bank notes out of circulation in the state, since no one would accept, for example, a ten-dollar note which was worth only nine dollars and eighty cents when a note worth its ten-dollar face value issued by a state bank was the alternative.

The Baltimore branch of the United States Bank refused to pay the state tax. Suit was brought against the cashier, James W. McCulloch, to recover penalties for nonpayment. The argument of the case in the United States Supreme Court took place in the charged atmosphere of financial panic and during debate in the Congress over a resolution to abolish the United States Bank. The case was argued for nine days, with the greatest constitutional lawyers of that time, and perhaps of all time, in full array. Arguing for the federal government were Daniel Webster, William Pinkney, and William Wirt. Answering for Maryland were Luther Martin, Joseph Hopkinson, and Walter Jones. Pinkney spoke for three days, and it is generally conceded that his argument was one of the all-time pinnacles of legal advocacy. Marshall's opinion, delivered only three days after the nine-day argument was concluded, follows the pattern of Pinkney's speech very closely.

Marshall's opinion is divided into two basic parts. He first addresses himself to the difficult question whether the federal government has the authority to create a United States Bank. His powerful development of constitutional theory on this question speaks for itself. But one should particularly note the skillful and fascinating way in which he establishes that the critical word, "necessary," in the "necessary and proper" clause of the Constitution, actually means no more than "appropriate." Further, particular attention should be paid to the statement on page 44, beginning with the words, "Let the end be legitimate," for here we find Marshall's summary of the breadth of federal power. And broad it is. Marshall went far beyond the requirements of the case itself to dispel forever the notion that federal power must be minutely construed so as to create a domain of narrow and unchangeable boundaries.

Then, in the second portion of the opinion, Marshall set out to build the ramparts which will protect this broad federal power from outside encroachment, particularly by the states. In assessing the threat of Maryland's tax, Marshall uttered his famous statement, "The power to tax involves the power to destroy," which was, in fact, almost an exact paraphrase of a statement which Webster had made in argument.

When Marshall was done he left no lingering doubt—the Supreme Court would not allow the national power to be reduced to the impotency of the national powers under the Articles of Confederation. Made just as clear was the determination to insist that the states recognize the national government for what it was, truly the government of a nation.

The volcano of "states' rights" erupted. Never had an opinion of Marshall's been so bitterly attacked. Newspapers began with a broadside on the Chief Justice so vituperative that it could have been designed only to drum him off the Court. Then, more formal steps were taken. The Virginia legislature passed a resolution condemning the decision and insisting on a constitutional amendment that would create a "super supreme court" over Marshall's Court to decide questions involving the distribution of powers between state and federal governments. Ohio followed with a bitter resolution threatening to pass laws forbidding any Ohio judge to recognize the existence of the United States Bank in any way and forbidding Ohio jailors to accept any prisoner committed to custody on suit by the United States Bank. The resolution called for other states to act also. And they did. Pennsylvania proposed a constitutional amendment forbidding the federal government to establish a bank with powers which extended beyond the District of Columbia. Indiana, Illinois, and Tennessee also passed condemnatory resolutions.

Once again destiny took a hand and Marshall was saved. The fateful dispute over slavery entered the picture late in 1819 when the applications of Missouri and Maine for statehood were before Congress. State legislatures, rushing to get on record with respect to this issue of transcendent importance which culminated with the Missouri Compromise in 1820, gradually began to pass over Marshall's decision, and Marshall again was secure.

While Marshall's decision was to endure to become for all time the leading exposition of the breadth of federal power, the United States Bank did not endure. It lived only until Andrew Jackson's second term as President. Jackson always strongly opposed the bank. In a violent political controversy after his re-election, he simply withdrew the nation's funds from the bank, and its charter was allowed to expire. Coincidentally, the principal adviser to Jackson in this affair was his Attorney General, Roger Brooke Taney, the man he appointed Chief Justice after Marshall's death in 1835.

Thus did Marshall establish and secure the principle that our federal government must be truly national, with the power to endure for ages to come. It is difficult to see how, without Marshall, our nation could have survived *as* a nation these many generations. Jefferson, in spite of all his greatness, had such sweeping ideas on states' rights and a weak central government with a weak judiciary that he might have sowed the seeds of national collapse. But Marshall effectively barred the way. In *McCulloch v. Maryland,* Marshall gave us a living and vital Constitution, one which could be molded to the needs of the future, could indeed meet the challenge of an Atomic Age surely far beyond the foresight even of a man so gifted.

McCULLOCH v. THE STATE OF MARYLAND
Supreme Court of the United States, 1819, 4 Wheaton 316

MARSHALL, C. J.:

In the case now to be determined, the defendant, a sovereign state, denies the obligation of a law enacted by the legislature of the

Union, and the plaintiff, on his part, contests the validity of an act which has been passed by the legislature of that state. The Constitution of our country, in its most interesting and vital parts, is to be considered: the conflicting powers of the government of the Union and of its members, as marked in that constitution, are to be discussed; and an opinion given, which may essentially influence the great operations of the government. No tribunal can approach such a question without a deep sense of its importance, and of the awful responsibility involved in its decision. But it must be decided peacefully, or remain a source of hostile legislation, perhaps of hostility of a still more serious nature; and if it is to be so decided, by this tribunal alone can the decision be made. On the Supreme Court of the United States has the constitution of our country devolved this important duty.

The first question made in the cause is, has Congress power to incorporate a bank?

It has been truly said that this can scarcely be considered as an open question, entirely unprejudiced by the former proceedings of the nation respecting it. The principle now contested was introduced at a very early period of our history, has been recognized by many successive legislatures, and has been acted upon by the judicial department, in cases of peculiar delicacy, as a law of undoubted obligation.

It will not be denied that a bold and daring usurpation might be resisted, after an acquiescence still longer and more complete than this. But it is conceived that a doubtful question, one on which human reason may pause, and the human judgment be suspended, in the decision of which the great principles of liberty are not concerned, but the respective powers of those who are equally the representatives of the people, are to be adjusted; if not put at rest by the practice of the government, ought to receive a considerable impression from that practice. An exposition of the constitution, deliberately established by legislative acts, on the faith of which an immense property has been advanced, ought not to be lightly disregarded.

The power now contested was exercised by the first Congress elected under the present constitution. The bill for incorporating the bank of the United States did not steal upon an unsuspecting legislature, and pass unobserved. Its principle was completely understood, and was opposed with equal zeal and ability. After being resisted, first in the fair and open field of debate, and afterwards in the executive cabinet, with as much persevering talent as any measure has ever experienced, and being supported by arguments which convinced minds as pure and as intelligent as this country can boast, it became a law. The original act was permitted to expire; but a short experience of the embarrassments to which the refusal to revive it exposed the government, convinced those who were most prejudiced against the measure of its necessity and induced the passage of the present law. It would require no ordinary share of intrepidity to assert that a measure adopted under these circumstances was a bold and plain usurpation, to which the constitution gave no countenance.

These observations belong to the cause; but they are not made under the impression that, were the question entirely new, the law would be found irreconcilable with the constitution.

In discussing this question, the counsel for the state of Maryland have deemed it of some importance, in the construction of the constitution, to consider that instrument not as emanating from the people, but as the act of sovereign and independent states. The powers of the general government, it has been said, are delegated by the states, who alone are truly sovereign; and must be exercised in subordination to the states, who alone possess supreme dominion.

It would be difficult to sustain this proposition. The convention which framed the constitution was indeed elected by the state legislatures. But the instrument, when it came from their hands, was a mere proposal, without obligation, or pretensions to it. It was reported to the then existing Congress of the United States with a request that it might "be submitted to a convention of delegates, chosen in each state by the people thereof, under the recommendation of its legislature, for their assent and ratification." This mode of proceeding was adopted; and by the convention, by Congress, and by the state legislatures, the instrument was submitted to the people. They acted upon it in the only manner in which they can act safely, effectively, and wisely, on such a subject, by assembling in convention. It is true, they assembled in their several states—and where else should they have assembled? No political dreamer was ever wild enough to think of breaking down the lines which separate the states, and of compounding the American people into one common mass. Of consequence, when they act, they act in their states.

But the measures they adopt do not, on that account, cease to be the measures of the people themselves, or become the measures of the state governments.

From these conventions the constitution derives its whole authority. The government proceeds directly from the people; is "ordained and established" in the name of the people; and is declared to be ordained, "in order to form a more perfect union, establish justice, insure domestic tranquillity, and secure the blessings of liberty to themselves and to their posterity." The assent of the states, in their sovereign capacity, is implied in calling a convention, and thus submitting that instrument to the people. But the people were at perfect liberty to accept or reject it; and their act was final. It required not the affirmance, and could not be negatived, by the state governments. The constitution, when thus adopted, was of complete obligation, and bound the state sovereignties.

It has been said that the people had already surrendered all their powers to the state sovereignties, and had nothing more to give. But, surely, the question whether they may resume and modify the powers granted to government does not remain to be settled in this country. Much more might the legitimacy of the general government be doubted, had it been created by the states. The powers delegated to the state sovereignties were to be exercised by themselves, not by a distinct and independent sovereignty, created by themselves. To the formation of a league, such as was the confederation, the state sovereignties were certainly competent. But when, "in order to form a more perfect union," it was deemed necessary to change this alliance into an effective government, possessing great and sovereign powers, and acting directly on the people, the necessity of referring it to the people, and of deriving its powers directly from them, was felt and acknowledged by all.

The government of the Union, then (whatever may be the influence of this fact on the case), is, emphatically, and truly, a government of the people. In form and in substance it emanates from them. Its powers are granted by them, and are to be exercised directly on them, and for their benefit.

This government is acknowledged by all to be one of enumerated powers. The principle, that it can exercise only the powers granted to it, would seem too apparent to have required to be enforced by all those arguments which its enlightened friends, while it was depending before the people, found it necessary to urge. That principle is now universally admitted. But the question respecting the extent of the powers actually granted, is perpetually arising, and will probably continue to arise, as long as our system shall exist. . . .

If any one proposition could command the universal assent of mankind, we might expect it would be this—that the government of the Union, though limited in its powers, is supreme within its sphere of action. This would seem to result necessarily from its nature. It is the government of all; its powers are delegated by all; it represents all, and acts for all. Though any one state may be willing to control its operations, no state is willing to allow others to control them. The nation, on those subjects on which it can act, must necessarily bind its component parts. But this question is not left to mere reason; the people have, in express terms, decided it by saying, "this constitution, and the laws of the United States, which shall be made in pursuance thereof," "shall be the supreme law of the land," and by requiring that the members of the state legislatures, and the officers of the executive and judicial departments of the states shall take the oath of fidelity to it.

The government of the United States, then, though limited in its powers, is supreme; and its laws, when made in pursuance of the constitution, form the supreme law of the land, "anything in the constitution or laws of any state to the contrary notwithstanding."

Among the enumerated powers, we do not find that of establishing a bank or creating a corporation. But there is no phrase in the instrument which, like the articles of confederation, excludes incidental or implied powers; and which requires that everything granted shall be expressly and minutely described. Even the 10th amendment, which was framed for the purpose of quieting the excessive jealousies which had been excited, omits the word "expressly," and declares only that the powers "not delegated to the United States, nor prohibited to the states, are reserved to the states or to the people"; thus leaving the question, whether the particular power which may become the subject of contest has been delegated to the one government, or prohibited to the other, to depend on a fair construction of the whole instrument. The men who drew and adopted this amendment had experienced the embarrassments resulting from the insertion of this word in the articles of confederation, and probably omitted it to avoid those embarrassments. A constitution, to contain an accurate detail of all the subdivisions of which its great powers will admit, and of all the means by which they may be carried into execution, would partake of a prolixity of a legal code, and could scarcely be embraced by the human mind. It would probably never be understood by the public. Its nature, therefore, requires, that only its great outlines should be marked, its important objects designated, and the minor ingredients which compose those objects be deduced from the nature of the objects themselves. That this idea was entertained by the framers of the American constitution, is not only to be inferred from the nature of the instrument, but from the language. Why else were some of the limitations, found in the ninth section of the 1st article, introduced? It is also, in some degree, warranted by their having omitted to use any restrictive term which might prevent its receiving a fair and just interpretation. In considering this question, then, we must never forget that it is a constitution we are expounding.

Although, among the enumerated powers of government, we do not find the word "bank" or "incorporation," we find the great powers to lay and collect taxes; to borrow money; to regulate commerce; to declare and conduct a war; and to raise and support armies and navies. The sword and the purse, all the external relations, and no inconsiderable portion of the industry of the nation, are entrusted to its government. It can never be pretended that these vast powers draw after them others of inferior importance, merely because they are inferior. Such an idea can never be advanced. But it may with great reason be contended, that a government, entrusted with such ample powers, on the due execution of which the happiness and prosperity of the nation so vitally depends, must also be entrusted with ample means for their execution. The power being given, it is the interest of the nation to facilitate its execution. It can never be their interest, and cannot be presumed to have been their intention, to clog and embarrass its execution by withholding the most appropriate means. Throughout this vast republic, from the St. Croix to the Gulf of Mexico, from the Atlantic to the Pacific, revenue is to be collected and expended, armies are to be marched and supported. The exigencies of the nation may require that the treasure raised in the north should be transported to the south, that raised in the east conveyed to the west, or that this order should be reversed. Is that construction of the constitution to be preferred which would render these operations difficult, hazardous, and expensive? Can we adopt that construction (unless the words imperiously require it) which would impute to the framers of that instrument, when granting these powers for the public good, the intention of impeding their exercise by withholding a choice of means? ...

The government which has a right to do an act, and has imposed on it the duty of performing that act, must, according to the dictates of reason, be allowed to select the means; and those who contend that it may not select any appropriate means, that one particular mode of effecting the object is excepted, take upon themselves the burden of establishing that exception. ...

But the constitution of the United States has not left the right of Congress to employ the necessary means for the execution of the powers conferred on the government to general reasoning. To its enumeration of powers is added that of making "all laws which shall be necessary and proper, for carrying into execution the foregoing powers, and all other powers vested by this constitution, in the government of the United States, or in any department thereof."

The counsel for the State of Maryland have urged various arguments, to prove that this clause, though in terms a grant of power, is not so in effect; but is really restrictive of the general right, which might otherwise be implied, of selecting means for executing the enumerated powers.

In support of this proposition, they have found it necessary to contend, that this clause was inserted for the purpose of conferring on Congress the power of making laws. That, without it, doubts might be entertained whether Congress could exercise its powers in the form of legislation.

But could this be the object for which it was inserted? A government is created by the people, having legislative, executive, and judicial powers. Its legislative powers are vested in a Congress, which is to consist of a senate and house of representatives. Each house may determine the rule of its proceedings; and it is declared that every bill which shall have passed both houses, shall, before it becomes a law, be presented to the President of the United States. The 7th section describes the course of proceedings, by which a bill shall become a law; and then, the 8th section enumerates the powers of Congress. Could it be necessary to say that a legislature should exercise legislative powers in the shape of legislation? After allowing each house to prescribe its own course of proceeding, after describing the manner in which a bill should become a law, would it have entered into the mind of a single member of the convention that an express power to make laws was necessary to enable the legislature to make them? That a legislature, endowed with legislative powers, can legislate, is a proposition too self-evident to have been questioned.

But the argument on which most reliance is placed, is drawn from the peculiar language of the clause. Congress is not empowered by it to make all laws, which may have relation to the powers conferred on the government, but such only as may be "necessary and proper" for carrying them into execution. The word "necessary" is considered as controlling the whole sentence, and as limiting the right to pass laws for the execution of the granted powers, to such as are indispensable, and without which the power would be nugatory. That it excludes the choice of means, and leaves to Congress, in each case, that only which is most direct and simple.

Is it true that this is the sense in which the word "necessary" is always used? Does it always import an absolute physical necessity, so strong that one thing, to which another may be termed necessary, cannot exist without that other? We think it does not. If reference be had to its use, in the common affairs of the world, or in approved authors, we find that it frequently imports no more than that one thing is convenient, or useful, or essential to another. To employ the means necessary to an end, is generally understood as employing any means calculated to produce the end, and not as being confined to those single means, without which the end would be entirely unattainable. Such is the character of human language, that no word conveys to the mind, in all situations, one single definite idea; and nothing is more common than to use words in figurative sense. Almost all compositions contain words, which, taken in their rigorous sense, would convey a meaning different from that which is obviously intended. It is essential to just construction, that many words which import something excessive should be understood in a more mitigated sense—in that sense which common usage justifies. The word "necessary" is of this description. It has not a fixed character peculiar to itself. It admits of all degrees of comparison; and is often connected with other words, which increase or diminish the impression the mind receives of the urgency it imports. A thing may be necessary, very necessary, absolutely or indispensably necessary. To no mind would the same idea be conveyed by these several phrases. This comment on the word is well illustrated by the passage cited at the bar, from the 10th section of the 1st article of the constitution. It is, we think, impossible to compare the sentence which prohibits a state from laying "imposts or duties on imports or exports, except what may be absolutely necessary for executing its inspection laws," with that which authorizes Congress "to make all laws which shall be necessary and proper for carrying into execution" the powers of the general government, without feeling a conviction that the convention understood itself to change materially the meaning of the word "necessary," by prefixing the word "absolutely." This word then, like others, is used in various senses; and in its construction, the subject, the context, the intention of the person using them, are all to be taken into view.

Let this be done in the case under consideration. The subject is the execution of those great powers on which the welfare of a nation essentially depends. It must have been the intention of those who gave these powers to insure, as far as human prudence could insure, their beneficial execution. This could not be done by confiding the choice of means to such narrow limits as not to leave it in the power of Congress to adopt any which might be appropriate, and which were conducive to the end. This provision is made in a constitution intended to endure for ages to come, and, consequently, to be adapted to the various crises of human affairs. To have prescribed the means by which government should, in all future time, execute its powers, would have been to change, entirely, the character of the instrument, and give it the properties of a legal code. It would have been an unwise attempt to provide, by immutable rules, for exigencies which, if foreseen at all, must have been seen dimly, and which can be best provided for as they occur. To have declared that the best means shall not be used, but those alone without which the power given would be nugatory, would have been to deprive the legislature of the capacity to avail itself of experience, to exercise its reason, and to accommodate its legislation to circumstances. If we apply this principle of construction to any of the powers of the government, we shall find it so pernicious in its operation that we shall be compelled to discard it. The powers vested in Congress may certainly be carried into execution, without prescribing an oath of office. The power to exact this security for the faithful performance of duty, is not given, nor is it indispensably necessary. The different departments may be established; taxes may be imposed and collected; armies and navies may be raised and maintained; and money may be borrowed, without requiring an oath of office. It might be argued, with as much plausibility as other incidental powers have been assailed, that the convention was not unmindful of this subject. The oath which might be exacted—that of fidelity to the constitution—is prescribed, and no other can be required. Yet, he would be charged with insanity who should contend that the legislature might not superadd, to the oath directed by the constitution, such other oath of office as its wisdom might suggest.

So, with respect to the whole penal code of the United States: whence arises the power to punish in cases not prescribed by the constitution? All admit that the government may, legitimately, punish any violation of its laws; and yet, this is not among the enumerated powers of Congress. The right to enforce the observance of law, by punishing its infraction, might be denied with the more plausibility because it is expressly given in some cases. Congress is empowered "to provide for the punishment of counterfeiting the securities and current coin of the United States," and "to define and punish piracies and felonies committed on the high seas, and offenses against the law of nations." The several powers of Congress may exist, in a very imperfect state, to be sure, but they may exist and be carried into execution, although no punishment should be inflicted in cases where the right to punish is not expressly given.

Take, for example, the power "to establish post-offices and post-roads." This power is executed by the single act of making the establishment. But, from this has been inferred the power and duty of carrying the mail along the post-road, from one post-office to another. And, from this implied power, has again been inferred the right to punish those who steal letters from the post-office, or rob the mail. It may be said, with some plausibility, that the right to carry the mail, and to punish those who rob it, is not indispensably necessary to the establishment of a post-office and post-road. This right is indeed essential to the beneficial exercise of the power, but not indispensably necessary to its existence. So, of the punishment of the crimes of stealing or falsifying a record or process of a court of the United States, or of perjury in such court. To punish these offenses is certainly conducive to the due administration of justice. But courts may exist, and may decide the causes brought before them, though such crimes escape punishment.

The baneful influence of this narrow construction on all the operations of the government, and the absolute impracticability of maintaining it without rendering the government incompetent to its great objects, might be illustrated by numerous examples drawn from the constitution, and from our laws. The good sense of the public has pronounced, without hesitation, that the power of punishment appertains to sovereignty, and may be exercised whenever the sovereign has a right to act, as incidental to his constitutional powers. It is a means for carrying into execution all sovereign powers, and may be used, although not indispensably necessary. It is a right incidental to the power, and conducive to its beneficial exercise.

If this limited construction of the word "necessary" must be abandoned in order to punish, whence is derived the rule which would reinstate it, when the government would carry its powers into execution by means not vindictive in their nature? If the word "necessary" means "needful," "requisite," "essential," "conducive to," in order to let in the power of punishment for the infraction of law; why is it not equally comprehensive when required to authorize the use of means which facilitate the execution of the powers of government without the infliction of punishment?

In ascertaining the sense in which the word "necessary" is used in this clause of the constitution, we may derive some aid from that with which it is associated. Congress shall have power "to make all laws which shall be necessary and proper to carry into execution" the powers of the government. If the word "necessary" was used in that strict and rigorous sense for which the counsel for the state of Maryland contend, it would be an extraordinary departure from the usual course of the human mind, as exhibited in composition, to add a word, the only possible effect of which is to qualify that strict and rigorous meaning; to present to the mind the idea of some choice of means of legislation not strained and compressed within the narrow limits for which gentlemen contend.

But the argument which most conclusively demonstrates the error of the construction contended for by the counsel for the state of Maryland, is founded on the intention of the convention, as manifested in the whole clause. To waste time and argument in proving that without it Congress might carry its powers into execution, would be not much less idle than to hold a lighted taper to the sun. As little can it be required to prove, that in the absence of this clause, Congress would have some choice of means. That it might employ those which, in its judgment, would most advantageously effect the object to be accomplished. That any means adapted to the end, any means which tended directly to the execution of the constitutional powers of the government, were in themselves constitutional. This clause, as construed by the state of Maryland, would abridge, and almost annihilate this useful and necessary right of the legislature to select its means. That this could not be intended, is, we should think, had it not been already controverted, too apparent for controversy. We think so for the following reasons:

1st. The clause is placed among the powers of Congress, not among the limitations on those powers.

2d. Its terms purport to enlarge, not to diminish the powers vested in the government. It purports to be an additional power, not a restriction on those already granted. No reason has been, or can be assigned for thus concealing an intention to narrow the discretion of the national legislature under words which purport to enlarge it. The framers of the constitution wished its adoption, and well knew that it would be endangered by its strength, not by its weakness. Had they been capable of using language which would convey to the eye one idea, and, after deep reflection, impress on the mind another, they would rather have disguised the grant of power than its limitation. If, then, their intention had been, by this clause, to restrain the free use of means which might otherwise have been implied, that intention would have been inserted in another place, and would have been expressed in terms resembling these. "In carrying into execution the foregoing powers, and all others," &c., "no laws shall be passed but such as are necessary and proper." Had the intention been to make this clause restrictive, it would unquestionably have been so in form as well as in effect.

The result of the most careful and attentive consideration bestowed upon this clause is, that if it does not enlarge, it cannot be construed to restrain the powers of Congress, or to impair the right of the legislature to exercise its best judgment in the selection of measures to carry into execution the constitutional powers of the government. If no other motive for its insertion can be suggested, a sufficient one is found in the desire to remove all doubts respecting the right to legislate on that vast mass of incidental powers which must be involved in the constitution, if that instrument be not a splendid bauble.

We admit, as all must admit, that the powers of the government are limited, and that its limits are not to be transcended. But we think the sound construction of the constitution must allow to the national legislature that discretion, with respect to the means by which the powers it confers are to be carried into execution, which will enable that body to perform the high duties assigned to it, in the manner most beneficial to the people. Let the end be legitimate, let it be within the scope of the constitution, and all means which are appropriate, which are plainly adapted to that end, which are not prohibited, but consist with the letter and spirit of the constitution, are constitutional.

That a corporation must be considered as a means not less usual, not of higher dignity, not more requiring a particular specification than other means, has been sufficiently proved. If we look to the origin of corporations, to the manner in which they have been framed in that government from which we have derived most of our legal principles and ideas, or to the uses to which they have been applied, we find no reason to suppose that a constitution, omitting, and wisely omitting, to enumerate all the means for carrying into execution the great powers vested in government, ought to have specified this. Had it been intended to grant this power as one which should be distinct and independent, to be exercised in any case whatever, it would have found a place among the enumerated powers of the government. But being considered merely as a means, to be employed only for the purpose of carrying into execution the given powers, there could be no motive for particularly mentioning it. . . .

If a corporation may be employed indiscriminately with other means to carry into execution the power of the government, no particular reason can be assigned for excluding the use of a bank, if required for its fiscal operations. To use one, must be within the discrimination of Congress, if it be an appropriate mode of executing the powers of government. That it is a convenient, a useful and essential instrument in the prosecution of its fiscal operations, is not now a subject of controversy. All those who have been concerned in the administration of our finances, have concurred in representing its importance and necessity; and so strongly have they been felt, that statesmen of the first class, whose previous opinions against it had been confirmed by every circumstance which can fix the human judgment, have yielded those opinions to the exigencies of the nation. Under the confederation, Congress, justifying the measure by its necessity, transcended perhaps its powers to obtain the advantage of a bank; and our own legislation attests the universal conviction of the utility of this measure. The time has passed away when it can be necessary to enter into any discussion in order to prove the importance of this instrument, as a means to effect the legitimate objects of the government.

But, were its necessity less apparent, none can deny its being an appropriate measure; and if it is, the degree of its necessity, as has been very justly observed, is to be discussed in another place. Should Congress, in the execution of its powers, adopt measures which are prohibited by the constitution; or should Congress, under the pretext of executing its powers, pass laws for the accomplishment of objects not entrusted to the government, it would become the painful duty of this tribunal, should a case requiring such a decision come before it, to say that such an act was not the law of the land. But where the law is not prohibited, and is really calculated to effect any of the objects entrusted to the government, to undertake here to inquire into the degree of its necessity, would be to pass the line which circumscribes the judicial department, and to tread on legislative ground. This court disclaims all pretentions to such a power. . . .

After the most deliberate consideration, it is the unanimous and decided opinion of this court that the act to incorporate the bank of the United States is a law made in pursuance of the constitution, and is a part of the supreme law of the land. . . .

It being the opinion of the court that the act incorporating the bank is constitutional, and that the power of establishing a branch in the state of Maryland might be properly exercised by the bank itself, we proceed to inquire:

2. Whether the state of Maryland may, without violating the constitution, tax that branch?

That the power of taxation is one of vital importance; that it is retained by the states; that it is not abridged by the grant of a similar power to the government of the Union; that it is to be concurrently exercised by the two governments; are truths which have never been denied. But, such is the paramount character of the constitution that its capacity to withdraw any subject from the action of even this power, is admitted. The states are expressly forbidden to lay any duties on imports or exports, except what may be absolutely necessary for executing their inspection laws. If the obligation of this prohibition must be conceded—if it may restrain a state from the exercise of its taxing power on imports and exports—the same paramount character would seem to restrain, as it certainly may restrain, a state from such other exercise of this power, as is in its nature incompatible with, and repugnant to, the constitutional laws of the Union. A law, absolutely repugnant to another, as entirely repeals that other as if express terms of repeal were used.

On this ground the counsel for the bank place its claim to be exempted from the power of a state to tax its operations. There is no express provision for the case, but the claim has been sustained on a principle which so entirely pervades the constitution, is so intermixed with the materials which compose it, so interwoven with its web, so blended with its texture, as to be incapable of being separated from it without rending it into shreds.

This great principle is, that the constitution and the laws made in pursuance thereof are supreme; that they control the constitution and laws of the respective states, and cannot be controlled by them. From this, which may be almost termed an axiom, other propositions are deduced as corollaries, on the truth or error of which, and on their application to this case, the cause has been supposed to depend. These are, 1st. That a power to create implies a power to preserve. 2d. That a power to destroy, if wielded by a different hand, is hostile to, and incompatible with these powers to create and to preserve. 3d. That where this repugnancy exists, that authority which is supreme must control, not yield to that over which it is supreme.

These propositions, as abstract truths, would, perhaps, never be controverted. Their application to this case, however, has been denied; and, both in maintaining the affirmative and the negative, a splendor of eloquence, and strength of argument seldom, if ever, surpassed, have been displayed. . . .

It is admitted that the power of taxing the people and their property is essential to the very existence of the government, and may be legitimately exercised on the objects to which it is applicable, to the utmost extent to which the government may choose to carry it. The only security against the abuse of this power is found in the structure of the government itself. In imposing a tax the legislature acts upon its constituents. This is in general a sufficient security against erroneous and oppressive taxation.

The people of a state, therefore, give to their government a right of taxing themselves and their property, and as the exigencies of government cannot be limited, they prescribe no limits to the exercise of this right, resting confidently on the interest of the legislator, and on the influence of the constituents over their representative, to guard them against its abuse. But the means employed by the government of the Union have no such security, nor is the right of a state to tax them sustained by the same theory. Those means are not given by the people of a particular state, not given by the constituents of the legislature, which claim the right to tax them, but by the people of all the states. They are given by all, for the benefit of all—and upon theory, should be subjected to that government only which belongs to all.

It may be objected to this definition, that the power of taxation is not confined to the people and property of a state. It may be exercised upon every object brought within its jurisdiction.

This is true. But to what source do we trace this right? It is obvious that it is an incident of sovereignty, and is co-extensive with that to which it is an incident. All subjects over which the sovereign power of a state extends, are objects of taxation; but those over which it does not extend, are, upon the soundest principles, exempt from taxation. This proposition may almost be pronounced self-evident.

The sovereignty of a state extends to everything which exists by its own authority, or is introduced by its permission; but does it extend to those means which are employed by Congress to carry into execution—powers conferred on that body by the people of the United States? We think it demonstrable that it does not. Those powers are not given by the people of a single state. They are given by the people of the United States, to a government whose laws, made in pursuance of the constitution, are declared to be supreme. Consequently, the people of a single state cannot confer a sovereignty which will extend over them.

If we measure the power of taxation residing in a state, by the extent of sovereignty which the people of a single state possess, and can confer on its government, we have an intelligible standard, applicable to every case to which the power may be applied. We have a principle which leaves the power of taxing the people and property of a state unimpaired; which leaves to a state the command of all its resources, and which places beyond its reach, all those powers which are conferred by the people of the United States on the government of the Union, and all those means which are given for the purpose of carrying those powers into execution. We have a principle which is safe for the states, and safe for the Union. We are relieved, as we ought to be, from clashing sovereignty; from interfering powers; from a repugnancy between a right in one government to pull down what there is an acknowledged right in another to build up; from the incompatibility of a right in one government to destroy what there is a right in another to preserve. We are not driven to the perplexing inquiry, so unfit for the judicial department, what degree of taxation is the legitimate use, and what degree may amount to the abuse of the power. The attempt to use it on the means employed by the government of the Union, in pursuance of the constitution, is itself an abuse, because it is the usurpation of a power which the people of a single state cannot give.

We find, then, on just theory, a total failure of this original right to tax the means employed by the government of the Union, for the execution of its powers. The right never existed, and the question whether it has been surrendered, cannot arise.

But, waiving this theory for the present, let us resume the inquiry, whether this power can be exercised by the respective states, consistently with a fair construction of the constitution.

That the power to tax involves the power to destroy; that the power to destroy may defeat and render useless the power to create; that there is a plain repugnance, in conferring on one government a power to control the constitutional measures of another, which other, with respect to those very measures, is declared to be supreme over that which exerts the control, are propositions not to be denied. But all inconsistencies are to be reconciled by the magic of the word CONFIDENCE. Taxation, it is said, does not necessarily and unavoidably destroy. To carry it to the excess of destruction would be an abuse, to presume which, would banish that confidence which is essential to all government.

But is this a case of confidence? Would the people of any one state trust those of another with a power to control the most insignificant operations of their state government? We know they would not. Why, then, should we suppose that the people of any one state should be willing to trust those of another with a power to control the operations of a government to which they have confided the most important and most valuable interests? In the legislature of the Union alone, are all represented. The legislature of the Union alone, therefore, can be trusted by the people with the power of controlling measures which concern all, in the confidence that it will not be abused. This, then, is not a case of confidence, and we must consider it as it really is.

If we apply the principle for which the state of Maryland contends, to the constitution generally, we shall find it capable of changing totally the character of that instrument. We shall find it capable of arresting all the measures of the government, and of prostrating it at the foot of the states. The American people have declared their constitution, and the laws made in pursuance thereof, to be supreme; but this principle would transfer the supremacy, in fact, to the states.

If the states may tax one instrument, employed by the government in the execution of its powers, they may tax any and every other instrument. They may tax the mail; they may tax the mint; they may tax patent-rights; they may tax the papers of the custom-house; they may tax judicial process; they may tax all the means employed by the government, to an excess which would defeat all the ends of government. This was not intended by the American people. They did not design to make their government dependent on the states.

Gentlemen say they do not claim the right to extend state taxation to these objects. They limit their pretensions to property. But on what principle is this distinction made? Those who make it have furnished no reason for it, and the principle for which they contend denies it. They contend that the power of taxation has no other limit than is found in the 10th section of the 1st article of the constitution; that, with respect to everything else, the power of the states is supreme, and admits of no control. If this be true, the distinction between property and other subjects to which the power of taxation is applicable, is merely arbitrary, and can never be sustained. This is not all. If the controlling power of the states be established; if their supremacy as to taxation be acknowledged; what is to restrain their exercising this control in any shape they may please to give it? Their sovereignty is not confined to taxation. That is not the only mode in which it might be displayed. The question is, in truth, a question of supremacy; and if the right of the states to tax the means employed by the general government be conceded, the declaration that the constitution, and the laws made in pursuance thereof, shall be the supreme law of the land, is empty and unmeaning declamation. . . .

The court has bestowed on this subject its most deliberate consideration. The result is a conviction that the states have no power, by taxation or otherwise, to retard, impede, burden, or in any manner control the operations of the constitutional laws enacted by Congress to carry into execution the powers vested in the general government. This is, we think, the unavoidable consequence of that supremacy which the constitution has declared.

We are unanimously of opinion that the law passed by the legislature of Maryland, imposing a tax on the Bank of the United States, is unconstitutional and void.

This opinion does not deprive the states of any resources which they originally possessed. It does not extend to a tax paid by the real property of the bank, in common with the other real property within the state, nor to a tax imposed on the interest which the citizens of Maryland may hold in this institution, in common with other property of the same description throughout the state. But this is a tax on the operations of the bank, and is, consequently, a tax on the operation of an instrument employed by the government of the Union to carry its powers into execution. Such a tax must be unconstitutional.

Chapter 4

*"Commerce, undoubtedly, is traffic, but
it is something more; it is intercourse"*

MARSHALL'S pre-eminent part in the task of defining a workable federal system was not yet done. There remained a consideration of the constitutional power by which the federal government was enabled to control the internal matters of the nation, those matters calling for uniform regulation. This, of course, was the federal power over interstate commerce. Again, Marshall was to define the power with a perception which makes the words as pragmatic and precise in this day as when they were written.

The legislature of the state of New York had awarded to Robert Fulton, Robert Livingston, and their associates a thirty-year monopoly in the operation of steamboats on the waters of the state. No steam-propelled vessels could be operated in New York without a license from Fulton and Livingston under the terms of the monopoly.

When steam-powered ferries under Fulton and Livingston license began to operate across the Hudson river to New Jersey, New Jersey interests began to compete by means of unlicensed ferry service into New York. As the vessels entered the New York harbors, however, the state insisted that the requisite license be obtained. Natural dissatisfaction of the New Jerseyites led to a New Jersey statute authorizing any citizen who had had his steam vessel seized by New York to seize any New York vessel in New Jersey waters. Buccaneers on the Hudson! Connecticut also passed a statute forbidding any New York steam vessels the privilege of entering Connecticut waters.

Dissatisfaction with the New York monopoly was felt by many New Yorkers themselves, who considered that the monopoly was a vicious stifling of competition. In fact, in the political tenor of the times generally, monopoly was viewed with great public disfavor. Such was the background of the case of *Gibbons v. Ogden.*

Aaron Ogden operated a ferry across the Hudson from New York to New Jersey, holding a license from the monopoly. Thomas Gibbons began to compete with him operating under a federal coastwide trade license. Ogden sued Gibbons in the New York State courts to obtain an injunction prohibiting him from operating in New York waters. Chancellor Kent, undoubtedly the greatest judge of that time outside the Supreme Court and considered by many the peer of the Supreme Court justices, granted the injunction. Kent could find nothing invalid in the New York monopoly and no conflict with the federal law regulating coastwise trade.

As thus posed, the case came to Marshall and the Supreme Court. Arguing for Gibbons—against the New York monopoly—was Daniel Webster. And this was his finest argument. Yet Marshall did not accept it in full. Marshall's opinion, probably his greatest after *McCulloch v. Maryland,* follows the same two-point outline of his opinion in that case. First, Marshall addresses himself to the question whether the federal power over interstate commerce extends within the boundaries of a state. His development of the constitutional meaning on this point is again an epic of broad national power. Particularly to be noted is his summary on page 57, beginning with the words, "The genius and character of the whole government seem to be...." The summary constitutes a definition of the federal power over commerce in which the cases of the present day can be precisely and accurately fitted. Characteristically, Marshall went far beyond the case before him to explore thoroughly the deceptively simple words giving the national government the power over interstate commerce. When he was done the words were vital; a commanding and essential federal power was established for all time.

He then turned to the question of state encroachment on the federal power thus established. But he refrained in this case from implying a constitutional prohibition (which he had implied in his opinion in *McCulloch v. Maryland*), though Webster had so argued. Marshall came to the very threshold of doing so, but then he turned away and decided the case merely upon a conflict between the federal coastwise statute and the state monopoly, thus avoiding a constitutional inhibition directed against state regulation of interstate commerce when there was no statutory conflict with federal control. It remained for Justice Johnson, in a concurring opinion which surpassed Marshall in nationalism, to insist that the Constitution should be found to imply a prohibition against state control of interstate commerce—that the power of regulation was exclusively in the federal government. This is the same Justice Johnson who was the first Democratic-Republican appointee to the Supreme Court and the author of the conciliatory opinion in *Martin v. Hunter's Lessee*. Marshall's evangelism in his mission caused his converts to outdo him!

Marshall's prophetic insight is never more clearly revealed than in this opinion. Subsequent events have inescapably revealed that Johnson's concept was wrong and Marshall's was right. Later cases showed the necessity for the retention by the states of some power over interstate commerce when the exercise of that power did not come into conflict with federal control. Yet, in his early recognition of this necessity, Marshall did not detract from the broadly established federal power. His decision made it quite clear that when state regulation had any tendency to conflict with federal control, the federal control was supreme.

For the first and only time in his stewardship as Chief Justice, Marshall found a major constitutional opinion the object of praise rather than fervent condemnation, but for the almost irrelevant reason that he had struck down an unpopular monopoly. Nevertheless, praise it was. In the next Congress, a resolution was introduced by a small clique to "pack" the Court with three additional members, but the debate over the resolution turned into a succession of eulogies of Marshall and the Court. This must have been as a great symphony to the tired ears of a man then seventy-one years old.

Marshall's work in building the constitutional foundation was largely done, although he continued to write important decisions for ten more years. Once one of his opinions was flatly repudiated by President Jackson's open defiance—but this was a puny effort against an impregnable fortress. When Marshall died in 1835, at the age of eighty, even his enemies had reluctantly sensed the measure of the man. He was the Great Chief Justice.

GIBBONS v. OGDEN
Supreme Court of the United States, 1824, 9 Wheaton 1

MARSHALL, C. J.:

As preliminary to the very able discussions of the constitution, which we have heard from the bar, and as having some influence on its construction, reference has been made to the political situation of these states, anterior to its formation. It has been said that they were sovereign, were completely independent, and were connected with each other only by a league. This is true. But when these allied sovereigns converted their league into a government, when they converted their Congress of Ambassadors, deputed to deliberate on their common concerns, and to recommend measures of general utility, into a legislature, empowered to enact laws on the most interesting subjects, the whole character in which the states appear, underwent a change, the extent of which must be determined by a fair consideration of the instrument by which that change was effected.

This instrument contains an enumeration of powers expressly granted by the people to their government. It has been said that these powers ought to be construed strictly. But why ought they to be so construed? Is there one sentence in the constitution which gives countenance to this rule? In the last of the enumerated powers, that which grants, expressly, the means of carrying all others into execution, Congress is authorized "to make all laws which shall be necessary and proper" for the purpose. But this limitation on the means which may be used, is not extended to the powers which are conferred; nor is there one sentence in the constitution which has been pointed out by the gentlemen of the bar, or which we have been able to discern, that prescribes this rule. We do not, therefore, think ourselves justified in adopting it. What do gentlemen mean by a strict construction? If they contend only against that enlarged construction which would extend words beyond their natural and obvious import, we might question the application of the term, but should not controvert the principle. If they contend for that narrow construction which, in support of some theory not to be found in the constitution, would deny to the government those powers which the words of the grant, as usually understood, import, and which are consistent with the general views and objects of the instrument; for that narrow construction, which would cripple the government and render it unequal to the objects for which it is declared to be instituted, and to which the powers given, as fairly understood, render it competent; then we cannot perceive the propriety of this strict construction, nor adopt it as the rule by which the constitution is to be expounded. As men, whose intentions require no concealment, generally employ the words which most directly and aptly express the ideas they intend to convey, the enlightened patriots who framed our constitution, and the people who adopted it, must be understood to have employed words in their natural sense, and to have intended what they have said. If, from the imperfection of human language, there should be serious doubt respecting the extent of any given power, it is a well-settled rule that the objects for which it was given, especially when those objects are expressed in the instrument itself, should have great influence in the construction. We know of no reason for excluding this rule from the present case. The grant does not convey power which might be beneficial to the grantor, if retained by himself, or which can enure solely to the benefit of the grantee, but is an investment of power for the general advantage, in the hands of agents selected for that purpose; which power can never be exercised by the people themselves, but must be placed in the hands of agents, or lie dormant. We know of no rule for construing the extent of such powers, other than is given by the language of the instrument which confers them, taken in connection with the purposes for which they were conferred.

The words are: "Congress shall have power to regulate commerce with foreign nations, and among the several states, and with the Indian tribes."

The subject to be regulated is commerce; and our constitution being, as was aptly said at the bar, one of enumeration, and not of definition, to ascertain the extent of the power it becomes necessary to settle the meaning of the word. The counsel for the appellee would limit it to traffic, to buying and selling, or the interchange of commodities, and do not admit that it comprehends navigation. This would restrict a general term, applicable to many objects, to one of its significations. Commerce, undoubtedly, is traffic, but it is something more; it is intercourse. It describes the commercial intercourse between nations, and parts of nations, in all its branches, and is regulated by prescribing rules for carrying on that intercourse. The mind can scarcely conceive a system for regulating commerce between nations, which shall exclude all laws concerning navigation, which shall be silent on the admission of the vessels of the one nation into the ports of the other, and be confined to prescribing rules for the conduct of individuals, in the actual employment of buying and selling or of barter.

If commerce does not include navigation, the government of the Union has no direct power over that subject, and can make no law prescribing what shall constitute American vessels, or requiring that they shall be navigated by American seamen. Yet this power has been exercised from the commencement of the government, has been exercised with the consent of all, and has been understood by all to be a commercial regulation. All America understands, and has uniformly understood, the word "commerce" to comprehend navigation. It was so understood, and must have been so understood, when the constitution was framed. The power over commerce, including navigation, was one of the primary objects for which the people of America adopted their government, and must have been contemplated in forming it. The convention must have used the word in that sense; because all have understood it in that sense, and the attempt to restrict it comes too late. . . .

The word used in the constitution comprehends, and has been always understood to comprehend, navigation within its meaning; and a power to regulate navigation is as expressly granted as if that term had been added to the word "commerce."

To what commerce does this power extend? The constitution informs us, to commerce "with foreign nations, and among the several states, and with the Indian tribes."

It has, we believe, been universally admitted that these words comprehend every species of commercial intercourse between the United States and foreign nations. No sort of trade can be carried on between this country and any other, to which this power does not extend. It has been truly said, that commerce, as the word is used in the constitution, is a unit, every part of which is indicated by the term.

If this be the admitted meaning of the word, in its application to foreign nations, it must carry the same meaning throughout the sentence, and remain a unit, unless there be some plain intelligible cause which alters it.

The subject to which the power is next applied, is to commerce "among the several states." The word "among" means intermingled with. A thing which is among others, is intermingled with them. Commerce among the states cannot stop at the external boundary line of each state, but may be introduced into the interior.

It is not intended to say that these words comprehend that commerce which is completely internal, which is carried on between man and man in a state, or between different parts of the same state, and which does not extend to or affect other states. Such a power would be inconvenient, and is certainly unnecessary.

Comprehensive as the word "among" is, it may very properly be restricted to that commerce which concerns more states than one. The phrase is not one which would probably have been selected to indicate the completely interior traffic of a state, because it is not an apt phrase for that purpose; and the enumeration of the particular classes of commerce to which the power was to be extended, would not have been made had the intention been to extend the power to every description. The enumeration presupposes something not enumerated; and that something, if we regard the language or the subject of the sentence, must be the exclusively internal commerce of a state. The genius and character of the whole government seem to be, that its action is to be applied to all the external concerns of the nation, and to those internal concerns which affect the states generally; but not to those which are completely within a particular state, which do not affect other states, and with which it is not necessary to interfere, for the purpose of executing some of the general powers of the government. The completely internal commerce of a state, then, may be considered as reserved for the state itself.

But, in regulating commerce with foreign nations, the power of Congress does not stop at the jurisdictional lines of the several states. It would be a very useless power if it could not pass those lines. The commerce of the United States with foreign nations, is that of the whole United States. Every district has a right to participate in it. The deep streams which penetrate our country in every direction, pass through the interior of almost every state in the Union, and furnish the means of exercising this right. If Congress has the power to regulate it, that power must be exercised whenever the subject exists. If it exists within the states, if a foreign voyage may commence or terminate at a port within a state, then the power of Congress may be exercised within a state.

This principle is, if possible, still more clear, when applied to commerce "among the several states." They either join each other, in which case they are separated by a mathematical line, or they are remote from each other, in which case other states lie between them. What is commerce "among" them; and how is it to be conducted? Can a trading expedition between two adjoining states commence and terminate outside of each? And if the trading intercourse be between two states remote from each other, must it not commence in one, terminate in the other, and probably pass through a third? Commerce among the states, must, of necessity, be commerce with the states. In the regulation of trade with the Indian tribes, the action of the law, especially when the constitution was made, was chiefly within a state. The power of Congress, then, whatever it may be, must be exercised within the territorial jurisdiction of the several states. The sense of the nation, on this subject, is unequivocally manifested by the provisions made in the laws for transporting goods, by land, between Baltimore and Providence, between New York and Philadelphia, and between Philadelphia and Baltimore.

We are now arrived at the inquiry, What is this power?

It is the power to regulate; that is, to prescribe the rule by which commerce is to be governed. This power, like all others vested in Congress, is complete in itself, may be exercised to its utmost extent, and acknowledges no limitations, other than are prescribed in the constitution. These are expressed in plain terms, and do not affect the questions which arise in this case, or which have been discussed at the bar. If, as has always been understood, the sovereignty of Congress, though limited to specified objects, is plenary as to those objects, the power over commerce with foreign nations, and among the several States, is vested in Congress as absolutely as it would be in a single government, having in its constitution the same restrictions on the exercise of the power as are found in the constitution of the United States. The wisdom and the discretion of Congress, their identity with the people, and the influence which their constituents possess at elections, are, in this, as in many other instances, as that, for example, of declaring war, the sole restraints on which they have relied, to secure them from its abuse. They are the restraints on which the people must often rely solely, in all representative governments.

The power of Congress, then, comprehends navigation within the limits of every State in the Union; so far as that navigation may be in any manner, connected with "commerce with foreign nations, or among the several states, or with the Indian tribes." It may, of consequence, pass the jurisdictional line of New York, and act upon the very waters to which the prohibition now under consideration applies. . . .

In our complex system, presenting the rare and difficult scheme of one general government, whose action extends over the whole, but which possesses only certain enumerated powers, and of numerous state governments, which retain the exercise of all powers not delegated to the Union, contests respecting power must arise. Were it even otherwise, the measures taken by the respective governments to execute their acknowledged powers, would often be of the same description, and might, sometimes, interfere. This, however, does not prove that the one is exercising, or has a right to exercise, the powers of the other. . . .

It has been contended by the counsel for the appellant, that, as the word "to regulate" implies in its nature, full power over the thing to be regulated, it excludes, necessarily, the action of all others that would perform the same operation on the same thing. That regulation is designed for the entire result, applying to those parts which remain as they were, as well as to those which are altered. It produces a uniform whole, which is as much disturbed and deranged by changing what the regulating power designs to leave untouched, as that on which it has operated.

There is great force in this argument, and the court is not satisfied that it has been refuted.

Since, however, in exercising the power of regulating their own purely internal affairs, whether of trading or police, the states may sometimes enact laws, the validity of which depends on their interfering with, and being contrary to, an act of Congress passed in pursuance of the constitution, the court will enter upon the inquiry, whether the laws of New York, as expounded by the highest tribunal of that State, have, in their application to this case, come into collision with an act of Congress, and deprived a citizen of a right to which that act entitles him. Should this collision exist, it will be immaterial whether those laws were passed in virtue of a concurrent power "to regulate commerce with foreign nations and among the several states," or in virtue of a power to regulate their domestic trade and police. In one case and the other, the acts of New York must yield to the law of Congress; and the decision sustaining the privilege they confer, against a right given by a law of the Union, must be erroneous.

This opinion has been frequently expressed in this court, and is founded as well on the nature of the government as on the words of the constitution. In argument, however, it has been contended that if a law, passed by a state in the exercise of its acknowledged sovereignty, comes into conflict with a law passed by Congress in pursuance of the constitution, they affect the subject, and each other, like equal opposing powers.

But the framers of our constitution foresaw this state of things, and provided for it, by declaring the supremacy not only of itself, but of the laws made in pursuance of it. The nullity of any act, inconsistent with the constitution, is produced by the declaration that the constitution is the supreme law. The appropriate application of that part of the clause which confers the same supremacy on laws and treaties, is to such acts of the state legislatures as do not transcend their powers, but, though enacted in the execution of acknowledged state powers, interfere with, or are contrary to the laws of Congress, made in pursuance of the constitution, or some treaty made under the authority of the United States. In every such case, the act of Congress, or the treaty, is supreme; and the law of the state, though enacted in the exercise of powers not controverted, must yield to it.

In pursuing this inquiry at the bar, it has been said that the constitution does not confer the right of intercourse between state and state. That right derives its source from those laws whose authority is acknowledged by civilized man throughout the world. This is true. The constitution found it an existing right, and gave to Congress the power to regulate it. In the exercise of this power, Congress has passed "an act enrolling or licensing ships or vessels to be employed in the coasting trade and fisheries, and for regulating the same." The counsel for the respondent contend that this act does not give the right to sail from port to port, but confines itself to regulating a pre-existing right, so far only as to confer certain privileges on enrolled and licensed vessels in its exercise.

It will at once occur, that, when a legislature attaches certain privileges and exemptions to the exercise of a right over which its control is absolute, the law must imply a power to exercise the right. The privileges are gone, if the right itself be annihilated. It would be contrary to all reason, and to the course of human affairs, to say that a state is unable to strip a vessel of the particular privileges attendant on the exercise of a right, and yet may annul the right itself; that the state of New York cannot prevent an enrolled and licensed vessel, proceeding from Elizabethtown, in New Jersey, to New York, from enjoying, in her course, and on her entrance into port, all the privileges conferred by the act of Congress; but can shut her up in her own port, and prohibit altogether her entering the waters and ports of another state. To the court it seems very clear, that the whole act on the subject of the coasting trade, according to those principles which govern the construction of statutes, implies, unequivocally, an authority to licensed vessels to carry on the coasting trade. . . .

Powerful and ingenious minds, taking, as postulates, that the powers expressly granted to the government of the Union are to be contracted, by construction, into the narrowest possible compass, and that the original powers of the States are retained, if any possible construction will retain them, may, by a course of well digested, but refined and metaphysical reasoning, founded on these premises, explain away the constitution of our country, and leave it a magnificent structure indeed, to look at, but totally unfit for use. They may so entangle and perplex the understanding, as to obscure principles which were before thought quite plain, and induce doubts where, if the mind were to pursue its own course, none would be perceived. In such a case it is peculiarly necessary to recur to safe and fundamental principles, to sustain those principles, and when sustained, to make them the tests of the arguments to be examined.

PART TWO

The Civil War and Its Aftermath

TWO

Chapter 1

*"Neither Dred Scott himself, nor any
of his family, were made free"*

THE TRAGEDY of human bondage grew into the tragedy of war between brothers. Surely a nation could not be more sorely tried. The cataclysm of the Civil War was at hand. Although somewhat withdrawn from the immediacy of political affairs, the Supreme Court could not be expected to avoid participation in so violent an upheaval, but the justices could have felt little foreboding of the role the court was to play in precipitating the conflict.

In the years following the death of John Marshall, the complexion of the Supreme Court gradually changed. The Democratic party of Jackson and his followers had its roots in the South, just as had its parent, the Democratic-Republicans. Thus, most of the men appointed to the Court from the time of Jackson were southerners. The most important of these appointments was that, in 1836, of Roger Brooke Taney, of Maryland, to succeed John Marshall as Chief Justice.

Taney came to the court in his fifty-ninth year. He was without judicial experience but had gained pre-eminence as a constitutional lawyer and cabinet member. Always bitterly opposed to the United States Bank, as Jackson's Attorney General he had counseled the President in the controversial withdrawal of funds. When the Secretary of the Treasury refused to follow Jackson's orders to withdraw the government's deposits from the bank, Taney accepted a recess appointment as Secretary and did Jackson's bidding. This action was a bitter blow to Senators Webster and Clay, who led the majority of the Senate in favoring the bank. The Senate passed a resolution of censure of Taney and refused to confirm his appointment as Secretary of the Treasury.

Shortly thereafter, in 1835, Jackson appointed Taney to the Supreme Court to take the place of Justice Duval. The Senate refused to confirm. Less than a year later, however, when Taney was named to succeed John Marshall, the Senate majority having changed, the appointment was approved.

Taney was at least close to being a worthy successor of Marshall. True, his views were more parochial than Marshall's: the Constitution was to be interpreted strictly by Taney's Court. But the changes were to be merely in the superstructure; Marshall's foundation remained secure. This is the nature of the work of courts. Marshall's decisions were already so deeply engrained in the structure of government that the new cases grew out of innovations; they were not attempts to do away with the old.

Always feeble physically, Taney was nevertheless gifted with a clear and precise mind. He particularly exhibited the talent to write simply, forcefully, and persuasively. But there is one blot upon his career as Chief Justice, a stain so livid that much of his truly valuable contribution is obscured. The blot is the case of *Dred Scott v. Sandford*.

In 1857 the nation was on the brink of conflict. The morbid cancer of slavery seemingly could not be cured. Compromise after compromise had been tried, but each had proved to be only a temporary palliative. One such attempt was the Missouri Compromise of 1820. Its validity was destined to be challenged by the defense in the case brought by Dred Scott, a Negro, to have himself and his family declared free of the bonds of slavery. His claim was that he had been taken by his owner to "free territory," as defined by the Missouri Compromise, and thus had his servitude been ended.

The case came to decision in an atmosphere of unquenchable controversy over the slavery issue. The Court consisted of five southerners and four northerners. Taney, then eighty, was racked with illness, but his mind was still luminous and bold.

Taney's decision in *Dred Scott v. Sandford* was the final blow struck by the slaveholding South before the clash of arms. And it was clearly, inescapably, and eternally wrong. There were three critical constitutional questions in the case. The most arguable of these was a question of jurisdiction—whether the Supreme Court had the right to decide the case at all. Taney and the majority (the decision was five to four) held that the Court did not have jurisdiction to hear and decide the case. But then, in utterly inconsistent and unheard of fashion, the majority went right ahead and did decide the case on the merits. (That portion of Taney's opinion which considers this jurisdictional question and which occupies thirty-two pages in the official report of the case has been omitted here, since it is a procedural matter.)

Secondly, Taney held that the specific clause in the Constitution giving Congress the power to regulate territories of the United States could not authorize the passage of the Missouri Compromise since this clause was meant by the framers of the Constitution to be limited to territories which the government possessed at the time of the adoption of the Constitution. Where was Marshall's "living Constitution"? If spirits can know anger, Marshall's soul must have been wrathful at such blasphemy. This holding, of course, could not and did not prevail. The Congress today governs the territories under the constitutional provision thus shunned.

Finally, Taney asserted that even if other constitutional provisions could be found which would authorize Congress to regulate territories, the Missouri Compromise was unconstitutional because in purporting to manumit slaves taken into "free territory," it deprived the owner of the slave of his property without compensation in violation of the Fifth Article of the Bill of Rights. Two simple present-day illustrations should suffice to demonstrate the error of this assertion. If a citizen of Nevada, where gambling is legal, should take his slot machine or other gambling paraphernalia into another state or a United States territory where gambling is prohibited, his property, now unlawful, could obviously be confiscated. Again, the lawful owner of whiskey subjects it to immediate confiscation if he takes it into a "dry" jurisdiction. Yet Taney said this species of control was unconstitutional—there was no way in which it could be accomplished. Yes, Taney's decision was wrong, unalterably wrong.

A durable and persuasive dissent was rendered by Justice Benjamin R. Curtis, a Fillmore appointee from Massachusetts. (I have excerpted only those portions of the Curtis opinion which meet the extracts from Taney's.) Next to the Chief Justice, Curtis was probably the most distinguished member of the Court as then constituted. By 1857, he had established a significant reputation through his court opinions, particularly his opinion in *Cooley v. Board of Wardens of the Port of Philadelphia,* 12 Howard 299, written in 1851, the year he was appointed to the

Court. Even today this opinion is second in importance only to Marshall's in *Gibbons v. Ogden* as a delineation of federal and state power under the commerce clause of the Constitution. Curtis had a younger brother, George Ticknor Curtis, who was a distinguished lawyer as well as a biographer and historian of the Supreme Court. George Curtis argued the Dred Scott case on behalf of Scott before his brother sitting on the Supreme Court.

Shortly after the Dred Scott decision, Benjamin Curtis resigned from the Court. He gave as his reason the inadequacy of the salary of a justice. It is now known, however, that he left because he felt that the Dred Scott decision descended to a purely political level and that the Court had thereby become so debased that it could no longer play its rightful role as an independent, co-ordinate branch of the federal government.

Historians of some years ago viewed the Dred Scott decision as the inciting cause of the Civil War. This view is now somewhat discounted, because it is realized that the schism over slavery in any event ran too deep to be healed. But the decision clearly did accelerate the tragic descent to war. The free North simply would not accept the proposition that slavery could be imposed upon free northern territories regardless of the wishes of the federal government and the people of those territories. The immediate traceable effect of the Dred Scott decision is perhaps even more significant. The holding in the case split the Democratic party in the election of 1860. And the divided Democratic vote, in turn, resulted in the election to the Presidency of Abraham Lincoln.

DRED SCOTT v. SANDFORD

Supreme Court of the United States, 1857, 19 Howard 393

Taney, C. J.:

The plaintiff was a negro slave, belonging to Dr. Emerson, who was a surgeon in the Army of the United States. In the year 1834, he took the plaintiff from the State of Missouri to the military post at Rock Island, in the State of Illinois, and held him there as a slave until the month of

April or May, 1836. At the time last mentioned, said Dr. Emerson removed the plaintiff from said military post at Rock Island to the military post at Fort Snelling, situate on the west bank of the Mississippi River, in the Territory known as Upper Louisiana, acquired by the United States of France, and situate north of the latitude of thirty-six degrees thirty minutes north, and north of the State of Missouri. Said Dr. Emerson held the plaintiff in slavery at said Fort Snelling, from said last mentioned date until the year 1838.

In the year 1835, Harriet, who is named in the second count of the plaintiff's declaration, was a negro slave of Major Taliaferro, who belonged to the Army of the United States. In that year, 1835, said Major Taliaferro took said Harriet to said Fort Snelling, a military post, situated as hereinbefore stated, and kept her there as a slave until the year 1836, and then sold and delivered her as a slave, at said Fort Snelling, unto the said Dr. Emerson hereinbefore named. Said Dr. Emerson held said Harriet in slavery at said Fort Snelling, until the year 1838.

In the year 1836, the plaintiff and Harriet intermarried, at Fort Snelling with the consent of Dr. Emerson, who then claimed to be their master and owner. Eliza and Lizzie, named in the third count of the plaintiff's declaration, are the fruit of that marriage. Eliza is about fourteen years old, and was born on board the steamboat Gipsey, north of the north line of the State of Missouri, and upon the River Mississippi. Lizzie is about seven years old, and was born in the State of Missouri, at the military post called Jefferson Barracks.

In the year 1838, said Dr. Emerson removed the plaintiff and said Harriet, and their said daughter Eliza, from said Fort Snelling, to the State of Missouri, where they have ever since resided.

Before the commencement of this suit, said Dr. Emerson sold and conveyed the plaintiff, and Harriet, Eliza, and Lizzie, to the defendant, as slaves, and the defendant has ever since claimed to hold them, and each of them, as slaves. . . .

The Act of Congress, upon which the plaintiff relies, declares that slavery and involuntary servitude, except as a punishment for crime, shall be forever prohibited in all that part of that territory ceded by France, under the name of Louisiana, which lies north of thirty-six degrees thirty minutes north latitude, and not included within the limits of Misscuri. And the difficulty which meets us at the threshold of this part of the inquiry is, whether Congress was authorized to pass this law under any of the powers granted to it by the Constitution; for if the authority is not given by that instrument, it is the duty of this court to declare it void and inoperative, and incapable of conferring freedom upon one who is held as a slave under the laws of any one of the States.

The counsel for the plaintiff has laid much stress upon that article in the Constitution which confers on Congress the power "to dispose of and make all needful rules and regulations respecting the territory or other property belonging to the United States;" but, in the judgment of the court, that provision has no bearing on the present controversy, and the power there given, whatever it may be, is confined, and was intended to be confined, to the territory which at that time belonged to, or was claimed by, the United States, and was within their boundaries as settled by the Treaty with Great Britain, and can have no influence upon a territory afterwards acquired from a foreign government. It was a special provision for a known and particular Territory, and to meet a present emergency, and nothing more. . . .

This brings us to examine by what provision of the Constitution the present Federal Government under its delegated and restricted powers, is authorized to acquire territory outside of the original limits of the United States, and what powers it may exercise therein over the person or property of a citizen of the United States, while it remains a territory, and until it shall be admitted as one of the States of the Union.

There is certainly no power given by the Constitution to the Federal Government to establish or maintain Colonies bordering on the United States or at a distance, to be ruled and governed at its own pleasure; nor to enlarge its territorial limits in any way, except by the admission of new States. That power is plainly given; and if a new State is admitted it needs no further legislation by Congress, because the Constitution itself defines the relative rights and powers and duties of the State, and the citizens of the State, and the Federal Government. But no power is given to acquire a Territory to be held and governed permanently in that character. . . .

It may be safely assumed that citizens of the United States who migrate to a territory belonging to the people of the United States, cannot be ruled as mere colonies, dependent upon the will of the general government, and to be governed by any laws it may think proper to impose. The principle upon which our governments rest, and upon which alone they continue to exist, is the union of States, sovereign and independent within their own limits in their internal and domestic concerns, and bound together as one people by a general government, possessing certain enumerated and restricted powers, delegated to it by the people of the several States, and exercising supreme authority within the scope of the powers granted to it, throughout the dominion of the United States. A power, therefore, in the general government to obtain and hold Colonies and dependent Territories, over which they might legislate without restriction, would be inconsistent with its own existence in its present form. Whatever it acquires, it acquires for the benefit of the people of the several States who created it. It is their trustee acting for them, and charged with the duty of promoting the interests of the whole people of the Union in the exercise of the powers specifically granted.

At the time when the Territory in question was obtained by cession from France it contained no population fit to be associated together and admitted as a State; and it therefore was absolutely necessary to hold possession of it as a Territory belonging to the United States until it was settled and inhabited by a civilized community capable of self-government, and in a condition to be admitted on equal terms with the other States as a member of the Union. But, as we have before said, it was acquired by the general government as the representative and trustee of the people of the United States, and it must, therefore, be held in that character for their common and equal benefit; for it was the people of the several States acting through their agent and representative, the Federal Government, who in fact acquired the territory in question, and the government holds it for their common use until it shall be associated with the other States as a member of the Union.

But until that time arrives, it is undoubtedly necessary that some government should be established, in order to organize society, and to protect the inhabitants in their persons and property; and as the people of the United States could act in this matter only through the government which represented them, and through which they spoke and acted when the territory was obtained, it was not only within the scope of its powers, but it was its duty to pass such laws and establish such a government as would enable those by whose authority they acted to reap the advantages anticipated from its acquisition, and to gather there a population which would enable it to assume the position to which it was destined among the States of the Union. The power to acquire, necessarily carries with it the power to preserve and apply to the purposes for which it was acquired. The form of government to be established necessarily rested in the discretion of Congress. It was their duty to establish the one that would be best suited for the protection and security of the citizens of the United States and other inhabitants who might be authorized to take up their abode there, and that must always depend upon the existing condition of the Territory, as to the number and character of its inhabitants, and the situation in the Territory. In some cases a government, consisting of persons appointed by the Federal Government, would best subserve the interests of the Territory, when the inhabitants were few and scattered, and new to one another. In other instances, it would be more advisable to commit the powers of self-government to the people who had settled in the territory, as being the most competent to determine what was best for their own interests. But some form of civil authority would be absolutely necessary to organize and preserve civilized society, and prepare it to become a state; and what is the best form must always depend on the condition of the territory at the time, and the choice of the mode must depend upon the exercise of a discretionary power by Congress acting within the scope of its constitutional authority, and not infringing upon the rights of persons or rights of property of the citizen who might go there to reside or for any other lawful purpose. It was acquired by the exercise of this discretion and it must be held and governed in like manner, until it is fitted to be a state.

But the power of Congress over the person or property of a citizen can never be a mere discretionary power under our Constitution and form of government. The powers of the government and the rights and privileges of the citizen are regulated and plainly defined by the Constitution itself. And when the territory becomes a part of the United States, the Federal Government enters into possession in the character impressed upon it by those who created it. It enters upon it with its powers over the citizen strictly defined, and limited by the Constitution, from which it derives its own existence, and by virtue of which alone it continues to exist and act as a government and sovereignty. It has no power of any kind beyond it; and it cannot, when it enters a territory of the United States, put off its character, and assume discretionary or despotic powers which the Constitution has denied to it. It cannot create for itself a new character separated from the citizens of the United States, and the duties it owes them under the provisions of the Constitution. The territory being a part of the United States, the government and the citizen both enter it under the authority of the Constitution, with their respective rights defined and marked out; and the Federal Government can exercise no power over his person or property, beyond what that instrument confers, nor lawfully deny any right which it has reserved.

A reference to a few of the provisions of the Constitution will illustrate this proposition.

For example, no one, we presume, will contend that Congress can make any law in a territory respecting the establishment of religion or the free exercise thereof, or abridging the freedom of speech or of the press, or the right of the people of the territory peaceably to assemble and to petition the government for the redress of grievances.

Nor can Congress deny to the people the right to keep and bear arms, nor the right to trial by jury, nor compel anyone to be a witness against himself in a criminal proceeding.

These powers, and others in relation to rights of person, which it is not necessary here to enumerate, are, in express and positive terms, denied to the general government; and the rights of private property have been guarded with equal care. Thus the rights of property are united with the rights of person, and placed on the same ground by the fifth amendment to the Constitution, which provides that no person shall be deprived of life, liberty and property, without due process of law. And an Act of Congress which deprives a citizen of the United States of his liberty or property, merely because he came himself or brought his property into a particular Territory of the United States, and who had committed no offense against the laws, could hardly be dignified with the name of due process of law.

So, too, it will hardly be contended that Congress could by law quarter a soldier in a house in a territory without the consent of the owner, in time of peace; nor in time of war, but in a manner prescribed by law. Nor could they by law forfeit the property of a citizen in a territory who was convicted of treason, for a longer period than the life of the person convicted; nor take private property for public use without just compensation.

The powers over person and property of which we speak are not only not granted to Congress, but are in express terms denied, and they are forbidden to exercise them. And this prohibition is not confined to the States, but the words are general, and extend to the whole territory over which the Constitution gives it power to legislate, including those portions of it remaining under territorial government, as well as that covered by States. It is a total absence of power everywhere within the dominion of the United States, and places the citizens of a territory, so far as these rights are concerned, on the same footing with citizens of the States, and guards them as firmly and plainly against any inroads which the general government might attempt, under the plea of implied or incidental powers. And if Congress itself cannot do this—if it is beyond the powers conferred on the Federal Government—it will be admitted, we presume, that it could not authorize a territorial government to exercise them. It could confer no power on any local government, established by its authority, to violate the provisions of the Constitution.

It seems, however, to be supposed, that there is a difference between property in a slave and other property, and that different rules may be applied to it in expounding the Constitution of the United States. And the laws and usages of nations, and the writings of eminent jurists upon the relation of master and slave and their mutual rights and duties, and the powers which governments may exercise over it, have been dwelt upon in the argument.

But in considering the question before us, it must be borne in mind that there is no law of nations standing between the people of the United States and their government and interfering with their relation to each other. The powers of the government, and the rights of the citizen under it, are positive and practical regulations plainly written down. The people of the United States have delegated to it certain enumerated powers, and forbidden it to exercise others. It has no power over the person or property of a citizen but what the citizens of the United States have granted. And no laws or usages of other nations, or reasoning of statesmen or jurists upon the relations of master and slave, can enlarge the powers of the government, or take from the citizens the rights they have reserved. And if the Constitution recognizes the right of property of the master in a slave, and makes no distinction between that description of property and other property owned by a citizen, no tribunal, acting under the authority of the United States, whether it be legislative, executive, or judicial, has a right to draw such a distinction, or deny to it the benefit of the provisions and guarantees which have been provided for the protection of private property against the encroachments of the governments. . . .

The right of property in a slave is distinctly and expressly affirmed in the Constitution. The right to traffic in it, like an ordinary article of merchandise and property, was guaranteed to the citizens of the United States, in every State that might desire it, for twenty years. And the government in express terms is pledged to protect it in all future time, if the slave escapes from his owner. This is done in plain words—too plain to be misunderstood. And no word can be found in the Constitution which gives Congress a greater power over slave property, or which entitles property of that kind to less protection than property of any other description. The only power conferred is the power coupled with the duty of guarding and protecting the owner in his rights.

Upon these considerations, it is the opinion of the court that the Act of Congress which prohibited a citizen from holding and owning property of this kind in the territory of the United States north of the line therein mentioned, is not warranted by the Constitution, and is therefore void; and that neither Dred Scott himself, nor any of his family, were made free by being carried into this territory; even if they had been carried there by the owner, with the intention of becoming a permanent resident. . . .

CURTIS, J., *dissenting*:

At the time of the adoption of the Constitution, the United States held a great tract of country northwest of the Ohio; another tract, then of unknown extent, ceded by South Carolina; and a confident expectation was then entertained, and afterwards realized, that they then were or would become the owners of other great tracts, claimed by North Carolina and Georgia. These ceded tracts lay within the limits of the United States, and out of the limits of any particular State; and the cessions embraced the civil and political jurisdiction, and so much of the soil as had not previously been granted to individuals.

These words, "territory belonging to the United States," were not used in the Constitution to describe an abstraction, but to identify and apply to these actual subjects, matter then existing and belonging to the United States, and other similar subjects which might afterwards be acquired; and this being so, all the essential qualities and incidents attending such actual subjects are embraced within the words "territory belonging to the United States," as fully as if each of those essential qualities and incidents had been specifically described. . . .

There is not, in my judgment, anything in the language, the history, or the subject matter of this article, which restricts its operation to territory owned by the United States when the Constitution was adopted. . . .

If, then, this clause does contain a power to legislate respecting the Territory, what are the limits of that power?

To this I answer, that, in common with all the other legislative powers of Congress, it finds limits in the express prohibitions on Congress not to do certain things; that, in the exercise of the legislative power, Congress cannot pass an ex post facto law or bill of attainder; and so in respect to each of the other prohibitions contained in the Constitution.

Besides this, the rules and regulations must be needful. But undoubtedly the question whether a particular rule or regulation be needful, must be finally determined by Congress itself. Whether a law be needful, is a legislative or political, not a judicial, question. Whatever Congress deems needful, is so, under the grant of power.

Nor am I aware that it has ever been questioned that laws providing for the temporary government of the settlers on the public lands are needful, not only to prepare them for admission to the Union as States, but even to enable the United States to dispose of the lands.

Without government and social order there can be no property; for without law, its ownership, its use and the power of disposing of it, cease to exist, in the sense in which those words are used and understood in all civilized States.

Since, then, this power was manifestly conferred to enable the United States to dispose of its public lands to settlers, and to admit them into the Union as States, when in the judgment of Congress they should be fitted therefor, since these were the needs provided for, since it is confessed that Government is indispensable to provide for those needs, and the power is, to make all needful rules and regulations respecting the Territory, I cannot doubt that this is a power to govern the inhabitants of the Territory, by such laws as Congress deems needful, until they obtain admission as States.

Whether they should be thus governed solely by laws enacted by Congress, or partly by laws enacted by legislative power conferred by Congress, is one of those questions which depend on the judgment of Congress—a question which of these is needful.

But it is insisted, that whatever other powers Congress may have respecting the Territory of the United States, the subject of negro slavery forms an exception.

The Constitution declares that Congress shall have power to make "all needful rules and regulations" respecting the Territory belonging to the United States.

The assertion is, though the Constitution says all, it does not mean all—though it says all, without qualification, it means all except such as allow or prohibit slavery. It cannot be doubted that it is incumbent on those who would thus introduce an exception not found in the language of the instrument, to exhibit some solid and satisfactory reason, drawn from the subject matter or the purposes and objects of the clause, the context, or from other provisions of the Constitution, showing that the words employed in this clause are not to be understood, according to their clear, plain, and natural signification.

The subject matter is the Territory of the United States out of the limits of every State, and consequently under the exclusive power of the people of the United States. Their will respecting it, manifested in the Constitution, can be subject to no restriction. The purposes and objects of the clause were the enactment of laws concerning the disposal of the public lands, and the temporary government of the settlers thereon, until new States should be formed. It will not be questioned that, when the Constitution of the United States was framed and adopted, the allowance and the prohibition of negro slavery were recognized subjects of municipal legislation; every State had in some measure acted thereon; and the only legislative Act concerning the Territory—the Ordinance of 1787, which had then so recently been passed—contained a prohibition of slavery....

I consider the passage of this law to have been an assertion by the first Congress of the power of the United States to prohibit slavery within this part of the Territory of the United States; for it clearly shows that slavery was thereafter to be prohibited there, and it could be prohibited only by an exertion of the power of the United States, under the Constitution; no other power being capable of operating within that Territory after the Constitution took effect....

Slavery being contrary to natural right, is created only by municipal law. This is not only plain in itself, and agreed by all writers on the subject, but is inferable from the Constitution, and has been explicity declared by this court. The Constitution refers to slaves as "persons held to service in one State, under the laws thereof." Nothing can more clearly describe a status created by municipal law. In *Prigg v. Pennsylvania,* 16 Pet. 611, this court said: "The state of slavery is deemed to be a mere municipal regulation, founded on and limited to the range of territorial laws." In *Rankin v. Lydia,* 2 A. K. Marsh, 470, the Supreme Court of Appeals of Kentucky said: "Slavery is sanctioned by the laws of this State, and the right to hold them under our municipal regulations is unquestionable. But we view this as a right existing by positive law of a municipal character, without foundation in the law of nature or the unwritten common law." I am not acquainted with any case or writer questioning the correctness of this doctrine....

Is it conceivable that the Constitution has conferred the right on every citizen to become a resident on the Territory of the United States with his slaves, and there to hold them as such, but has neither made nor provided for any municipal regulations which are essential to the existence of slavery?

Is it not more rational to conclude that they who framed and adopted the Constitution were aware that persons held to service under the laws of a State are property only to the extent and under the conditions fixed by those laws; that they must cease to be available as property, when their owners voluntarily place them permanently within another jurisdiction, where no municipal laws on the subject of slavery exist; and that, being aware of these principles, and having said nothing to interfere with or displace them, or compel Congress to legislate in any particular manner on the subject, and having empowered Congress to make all needful rules and regulations respecting the Territory of the United States, it was their intention to leave to the discretion of Congress what regulations, if any, should be made concerning slavery therein? Moreover, if the right exists, what are its limits, and what are its conditions? If citizens of the United States have the right to take their slaves to a Territory, and hold them there as slaves, without regard to the laws of the Territory, I suppose this right is not to be restricted to the citizens of slave-holding States. A citizen of a State which does not tolerate slavery can hardly be denied the power of doing the same thing. And what law of slavery does either take with him to the Territory? If it be said to be those laws respecting slavery which existed in the particular State from which each slave last came, what an anomaly is this? Where else can we find, under the law of any civilized country, the power to introduce and permanently continue diverse systems of foreign municipal law, for holding persons in slavery? ...

The assumption is, that the Territory ceded by France was acquired for the equal benefit of all the citizens of the United States. I agree to the position. But it was acquired for their benefit in their collective, not their individual, capacities. It was acquired for their benefit, as an organized political society, subsisting as "the people of the United States," under the Constitution of the United States; to be administered justly and impartially, and as nearly as possible for the equal benefit of every individual citizen, according to the best judgment and discretion of the Congress; to whose power, as the Legislature of the nation which acquired it, the people of United States have committed its administration. Whatever individual claims may be founded on local circumstances, or sectional differences of condition, cannot, in my opinion, be recognized in this court, without arrogating to the judicial branch of the government powers not committed to it; and which, with all the unaffected respect I feel for it, when acting in its proper sphere, I do not think it fitted to wield....

Chapter 2

"The highest honor of sovereignty is untarnished faith"

IN THE MALEVOLENT DAYS just before the outbreak of the war, the nation again beheld the spectacle of a state supreme court defying the jurisdiction of and a decision of the United States Supreme Court. The Supreme Court had in 1816 successfully met this challenge in *Martin v. Hunter's Lessee*. Could it do so again, in a setting of angry opposition to the Court engendered by the Dred Scott case less than two years before?

This time Wisconsin was the contumacious state. An abolitionist editor named Sherman Booth was found guilty in federal court of violation of the federal fugitive slave law. The Wisconsin Supreme Court found the federal law unconstitutional and directed that the prisoner be released, and then refused to acknowledge an order of appeal sent from the United States Supreme Court. Upon motion of the United States Attorney General, the United States Supreme Court nevertheless took jurisdiction of the delicate case.

To Taney's glory, his ablest and most powerful opinion is his answer to this Wisconsin defiance. Taney was then eighty-two, but never were his mental vigor and moral courage more clearly demonstrated. He established the United States Supreme Court as truly supreme, not because the federal government had made it so, and not because the states had made it so, but because the Constitution itself makes it so. Neither the winds of impending war nor the waves of present acrimony could overwhelm this essential principle. And this time the full Court was with him; the decision was unanimous.

Only the most rabid of northern Republicans criticized Taney for the Booth case. Cooler heads throughout the country realized that here was an immutable precept.

When the war did break, Taney remained loyal to the Union. He continued as Chief Justice until his death in 1864, although his health was such that he was unable to discharge his duties from 1863 on. As the years have passed, his decision in the Booth case and his earlier solid and perceptive work on the Court have taken some of the sting from his opinion in the Dred Scott case. Today, Taney is revered as a talented and eminent Chief Justice who made one arrant misstep.

ABLEMAN v. BOOTH

Supreme Court of the United States, 1859, 21 Howard 506

TANEY, C. J.

A judge of the Supreme Court of the State of Wisconsin, in the first of these cases, claimed and exercised the right to supervise and annul the proceedings of a commissioner of the United States, and to discharge a prisoner, who had been committed by the commissioner for an offense against the laws of this Government, and . . . this exercise of power by the judge was afterwards sanctioned and affirmed by the Supreme Court of the State.

In the second case the state court has gone a step further, and claimed and exercised jurisdiction over the proceedings and judgment of a District Court of the United States, and upon a summary and collateral proceedings, by *habeas corpus,* has set aside and annulled its judgment and discharged a prisoner, who had been tried and found guilty of an offense against the laws of the United States, and sentenced to imprisonment by the District Court.

And it further appears that the state court have not only claimed and exercised this jurisdiction, but have also determined that their decision is final and conclusive upon all the courts of the United States, and ordered their clerk to disregard and refuse obedience to the writ of error issued by this court, pursuant to the Act of Congress of 1789, to bring here for examination and revision the judgment of the state court. . . .

If the judicial power exercised in this instance has been reserved to the States, no offense against the laws of the United States can be punished by their own courts, without the permission and according to the judgment of the courts of the State in which the party happens to be imprisoned; for, if the Supreme Court of Wisconsin possessed the power it has exercised in relation to offenses against the Act of Congress in question, it necessarily follows that they must have the same judicial authority in relation to any other law of the United States; and, consequently, their supervising and controlling power would embrace the whole Criminal Code of the United States, and extend to offenses against our revenue laws, or any other laws intended to guard the different departments of the General Government from fraud or violence. And it would embrace all crimes, from the highest to the lowest; including felonies, which are punished with death, as well as misdemeanors, which are punished by imprisonment. And, moreover, if the power is possessed by the Supreme Court of the State of Wisconsin it must belong equally to every other State in the Union, when the prisoner is within its territorial limits; and it is very certain that the State courts would not always agree in opinion, and it would often happen, that an act which was admitted to be an offense, and justly punished, in one State, would be regarded as innocent and indeed praiseworthy, in another.

It would seem to be hardly necessary to do more than to state the result to which these decisions of the state courts must inevitably lead. It is, of itself, a sufficient and conclusive answer; for no one will suppose that a government which has now lasted nearly seventy years, enforcing its laws by its own tribunals, and preserving the union of the States, could have lasted a single year, or fulfilled the high trusts committed to it, if offenses against its laws could not have been punished without the consent of the State in which the culprit was found. . . .

Questions of this kind must always depend upon the Constitution and laws of the United States, and not of a State. The Constitution was not formed merely to guard the States against danger from foreign nations, but mainly to secure union and harmony at home; for if this object could be attained, there would be but little danger from abroad; and to accomplish this purpose, it was felt by the statesmen who framed the Constitution, and by the people who adopted it, that it was necessary that many of the rights of sovereignty which the States then possessed should be ceded to the General Government; and that, in the sphere of action assigned to it, it should be supreme and strong enough to execute its own laws by its own tribunals, without interruption from a State or from state authorities. And it was evident that anything short of this would be inadequate to the main objects for which the Government was established; and that local interest, local passions or prejudices, incited and fostered by individuals for sinister purposes, would lead to acts of aggression and injustice by one State upon the rights of another, which would ultimately terminate in violence and force, unless there was a common arbiter between them, armed with power enough to protect and guard the rights of all, by appropriate laws, to be carried into execution peacefully by its judicial tribunals.

The language of the Constitution, by which this power is granted, is too plain to admit of doubt or to need comment. It declares that "this Constitution, and the laws of the United States which shall be passed in pursuance thereof, and all treaties made, or which shall be made, under the authority of the United States, shall be the supreme law of the land, and the judges in every State shall be bound thereby, anything in the Constitution or laws of any State to the contrary nothwithstanding."

But the supremacy thus conferred on this Government could not peacefully be maintained, unless it was clothed with judicial power, equally paramount in authority to carry it into execution; for if left to the courts of justice in the several States, conflicting decisions would unavoidably take place, and the local tribunals could hardly be expected to be always free from the local influences of which we have spoken. And the Constitution and laws and treaties of the United States, and the powers granted to the Federal Government, would soon receive different interpretations in different States, and the Government of the United States would soon become one thing in one State and another thing in another. It was essential, therefore, to its very existence as a Government, that it should have the power of establishing courts of justice, altogether independent of state power, to carry into effect its own laws; and that a tribunal should be established in which all cases which might arise under the Constitution and laws and treaties of the United States, whether in a state court or a court of the United States, should be finally and conclusively decided. Without such a tribunal, it is obvious that there would be no uniformity of judicial decision; and that the supremacy (which is but another name for independence), so carefully provided in the clause of the Constitution above referred to, could not possibly be maintained peacefully, unless it was associated with this paramount judicial authority.

Accordingly, it was conferred on the General Government, in clear, precise and comprehensive terms. It is declared that its judicial power shall (among other subjects enumerated) extend to all cases in law and equity arising under the Constitution and laws of the United States, and that in such cases, as well as the others there enumerated, this court shall have appellate jurisdiction both as to law and fact, with such exceptions and under such regulations as Congress shall make. The appellate power, it will be observed, is conferred on this court in all cases or suits in which such a question shall arise. It is not confined to suits in the inferior courts of the United States, but extends to all cases where such a question arises, whether it be in a judicial tribunal of a State or of the United States. And it is manifest that this ultimate appellate power in a tribunal created by the Constitution itself was deemed essential to secure the independence and supremacy of the General Government in the sphere of action assigned to it, to make the Constitution and laws of the United States uniform, and the same in every State; and to guard against evils which would inevitably arise from conflicting opinions between the courts of a State and of the United States, if there was no common arbiter authorized to decide between them. . . .

The Constitution has accordingly provided, as far as human foresight could provide, against this danger. And in conferring judicial power upon the Federal Government, it declares that the jurisdiction of its courts shall extend to all cases arising under "this Constitution" and the laws of the United States—leaving out the words of restriction contained in the grant of legislative power which we have above noticed. The judicial power covers every legislative Act of Congress, whether it be made within the limits of its delegated powers, or be an assumption of power beyond the grants in the Constitution.

This judicial power was justly regarded as indispensable, not merely to maintain the supremacy of the laws of the United States, but also to guard the States from any encroachment upon their reserved rights by the General Government. And as the Constitution is the fundamental and supreme law, if it appears that an Act of Congress is not pursuant to and within the limits of the power assigned to the Federal Government, it is the duty of the courts of the United States to declare it unconstitutional and void. The grant of judicial power is not confined to the administration of laws passed in pursuance to the provisions of the Constitution, nor confined to the interpretation of such laws; but, by the very terms of the grant the Constitution is under their view when any Act of Congress is brought before them, and it is their duty to declare the law void, and refuse to execute it, if it is not pursuant to the legislative powers conferred upon Congress. And as the final appellate power in all such questions is given to this court, controversies as to the respective powers of the United States and the States, instead of being determined by military and physical force, are heard, investigated, and finally settled, with the calmness and deliberation of judicial inquiry. And no one can fail to see, that if such an arbiter had not been provided, in our complicated system of government, internal tranquillity could not have been preserved; and if such controversies were left to arbitrament of physical force, our Government, State and National, would soon cease to be Governments of laws, and revolutions by force of arms would take the place of courts of justice and judicial decisions.

In organizing such a tribunal, it is evident that every precaution was taken, which human wisdom could devise, to fit it for the high duty with which it was intrusted. It was not left to Congress to create it by law; for the States could hardly be expected to confide in the impartiality of a tribunal created exclusively by the General Government, without any participation on their part. And as the performance of its duty would sometimes come in conflict with individual ambition or interests, and powerful political combinations, an Act of Congress establishing such a tribunal might be repealed in order to establish another more subservient to the predominant political influences or excited passions of the day. This tribunal, therefore, was erected, and the powers of which we have spoken conferred upon it, not by the Federal Government, but by the people of the States, who formed and adopted that Government, and conferred upon it all the powers legislative, executive, and judicial, which it now possesses. And in order to secure its independence, and enable it faithfully and firmly to perform its duty, it engrafted it upon the Constitution itself, and declared that this court should have appellate power in all cases arising under the Constitution and laws of the United States. So long, therefore, as this Constitution shall endure, this tribunal must exist with it, deciding in the peaceful forms of judicial proceeding the angry and irritating controversies between sovereignties, which in other countries have been determined by the arbitrament of force. . . .

We do not question the authority of state court, or judge, who is authorized by the laws of the State to issue the writ of *habeas corpus,* to issue it in any case where the party is imprisoned within its territorial limits, provided it does not appear, when the application is made, that the person imprisoned is in custody under the authority of the United States. The court or judge has a right to inquire, in this mode of proceeding, for what cause and by what authority the prisoner is confined within the territorial limits of the state sovereignty. And it is the duty of the Marshal, or other person having the custody of the prisoner, to make known to the judge or court, by a proper return, the authority by which he holds him in custody. This right to inquire by process of *habeas corpus,* and the duty of the officer to make a return, grows, necessarily, out of the complex character of our Government, and the existence of two distinct and separate sovereignties within the same territorial space, each of them restricted in its powers, and each within its sphere of action, prescribed by the Constitution of the United States, independent of the other. But, after the return is made, and the state judge or court judicially apprised that the party is in custody under the authority of the United States, they can proceed no further. They then know that the prisoner is within the dominion and jurisdiction of another Government, and that neither the writ of *habeas corpus,* nor any other process issued under state authority, can pass over the line of division between the two sovereignties. He is then within the dominion and exclusive jurisdiction of the United States. If he has committed an offense against their laws, their tribunals alone can punish him. If he is wrongfully imprisoned, their judicial tribunals can release him and afford him redress. And although, as we have said, it is the duty of the Marshal, or other person holding him, to make known, by a proper return, the authority under which he detains him, it is at the same time imperatively his duty to obey the process of the United States, to hold the prisoner in custody under it, and to refuse obedience to the mandate or process of any other Government. And consequently it is his duty not to take the prisoner, nor suffer him to be taken, before a state judge or court upon a *habeas corpus* issued under state authority. No state judge or court, after they are judicially informed that the party is imprisoned under the authority of the United States, has any right to interfere with him, or to require him to be brought before them. And if the authority of a State in the form of judicial process or otherwise, should attempt to control the Marshal or other authorized officer or agent of the United States, in any respect, in the custody of his prisoner, it would be his duty to resist it, and to call to his aid any force that might be necessary to maintain the authority of law against illegal interference. No judicial process, whatever form it may assume, can have any lawful authority outside of the limits of the jurisdiction of the court or judge by whom it is issued; and an attempt to enforce it beyond these boundaries is nothing less than lawless violence.

Nor is there anything in this supremacy of the General Government, or the jurisdiction of its judicial tribunals, to awaken the jealousy or offend the natural and just pride of State sovereignty. Neither this Government, nor the powers of which we are speaking, were forced upon the States. The Constitution of the United States, with all the powers conferred by it on the General Government, and surrendered by the States, was the voluntary act of the people of the several states, deliberately done, for their own protection and safety against injustice from one another. And their anxiety to preserve it in full force, in all its powers, and to guard against resistance to or evasion of its authority, on the part of a State, is proved by the clause which requires that the members of the State Legislatures, and all executive and judicial officers of the several States (as well as those of the General Government), shall be bound, by oath or affirmation, to support this Constitution. This is the last and closing clause of the Constitution, and inserted when the whole frame of government, with the powers hereinbefore specified, had been adopted by the Convention; and it was in that form, and with these powers, that the Constitution was submitted to the people of the several States, for their consideration and decision.

Now, it certainly can be no humiliation to the citizen of a Republic to yield a ready obedience to the laws as administered by the constituted authorities. On the contrary, it is among his first and highest duties as a citizen, because free government cannot exist without it. Nor can it be inconsistent with the dignity of a sovereign State, to observe faithfully, and in the spirit of sincerity and truth, the compact into which it voluntarily entered when it became a State of this Union. On the contrary, the highest honor of sovereignty is untarnished faith. And certainly no faith could be more deliberately and solemnly pledged than that which every State has plighted to the other States to support the Constitution as it is, in all its provisions, until they shall be altered in the manner which the Constitution itself prescribes. In the emphatic language of the pledge required, it is to support this Constitution. And no power is more clearly conferred by the Constitution and laws of the United States, than the power of this court to decide, ultimately and finally, all cases arising under such constitution and laws; and for that purpose to bring here for revision, by writ of error, the judgment of a state court, where such questions have arisen, and the right claimed under them denied by the highest judicial tribunal in the State.

We are sensible that we have extended the examination of these decisions beyond the limits required by any intrinsic difficulty in the questions. But the decisions in question were made by the supreme judicial tribunal of the State; and when a court so elevated in its position has pronounced a judgment which, if it could be maintained, would subvert the very foundations of this Government, it seemed to be the duty of this court, when exercising its appellate power, to show plainly the grave errors into which the state court has fallen, and the consequences to which they would inevitably lead. . . .

If any argument was needed to show the wisdom and necessity of this appellate power, the cases before us sufficiently prove it, and at the same time emphatically call for its exercise.

Chapter 3

"It is no loose, unorganized insurrection"

CONSTITUTIONS do not make provision for civil war. The framers of everlasting documents do not contemplate that the validity of the entire structure may be challenged by force of arms. And yet if civil war does come, the basic document of government must provide the answers to the myriad problems which inevitably arise. Such was the challenge to the Supreme Court of the attack upon Fort Sumter and all the tragedy and bloodshed which followed.

The first constitutional issue of the Civil War was not long in arising. Just five days after the attack on Fort Sumter, Jefferson Davis, President of the Confederacy, issued an invitation to all those desiring to engage in privateering against United States shipping to obtain "letters of marque and reprisal" from the Confederate government.

Two days later, on April 19, 1861, President Lincoln made his countermove. He issued a proclamation blockading the Confederate ports. The constitutional validity of this northern blockade of the South was challenged in the *Prize Cases*, which arose out of the capture of privately owned vessels by ships of the United States Navy enforcing the blockade. The owners sued to recover their vessels and cargos, putting the lawfulness of the northern blockade in issue. Two serious constitutional issues were presented. First, there was the question whether the federal government could declare a blockade of the southern states in view of the accepted federal position that attempted secession was a nullity and those states remained part of the union. Second, Congress had not recognized that a war, even a civil war, had begun. In fact, Congress did not even convene until three months after hostilities became a reality. Thus, the question was whether the President had the power to declare a blockade in the absence of congressional declaration of war.

The validity of Lincoln's blockade was upheld by the Court in a sweeping and realistic opinion of Justice Robert C. Grier. Grier, a Pennsylvanian appointed by President Polk, was the only northern justice to concur with Chief Justice Taney's opinion in the Dred Scott case. Fortunately for his place in history he served with distinction on the Court for thirteen years after that decision, thus in large measure dispersing the cloud upon his career that the Dred Scott case created. He was a Democrat, but with the outbreak of the Civil War he immediately became an ardent supporter of the Union cause. Grier's eloquent opinion in the *Prize Cases* is a classic definition of governmental power in the face of armed rebellion.

PRIZE CASES

Supreme Court of the United States, 1863, 2 Black 635

GRIER, J.:

That a blockade *de facto* actually existed, and was formally declared and notified by the President . . . is an admitted fact in these cases.

That the President, as the Executive Chief of the Government and Commander-in-Chief of the Army and Navy, was the proper person to make such notification, has not been, and cannot be disputed.

The right of prize and capture has its origin in the *"jus belli,"* and is governed and adjudged under the law of nations. To legitimate the capture of a neutral vessel or property on the high seas, a war must exist *de facto*, and the neutral must have a knowledge or notice of the intention of one of the parties belligerent to use this mode of coercion against a port, city, or territory, in possession of the other.

Let us enquire whether, at the time this blockade was instituted, a state of war existed which would justify a resort to these means of subduing the hostile force.

War has been well defined to be, "That state in which a nation prosecutes its right by force."

The parties belligerent in a public war are independent nations. But it is not necessary to constitute war, that both parties should be acknowledged as independent nations or sovereign States. A war may exist where one of the belligerents claims sovereign rights as against the other.

Insurrection against a government may or may not culminate in an organized rebellion, but a civil war always begins by insurrection against the lawful authority of the Government. A civil war is never solemnly declared; it becomes such by its accidents—the number, power, and organization of the persons who originate and carry it on. When the party in rebellion occupy and hold in a hostile manner a certain portion of territory; have declared their independence; have cast off their allegiance; have organized armies; have commenced hostilities against their former sovereign, the world acknowledges them as belligerents, and the contest a *war. They* claim to be in arms to establish their liberty and independence, in order to become a sovereign State, while the sovereign party treats them as insurgents and rebels who owe allegiance and who should be punished with death for their treason.

The laws of war, as established among nations, have their foundation in reason, and all tend to mitigate the cruelties and misery produced by the scourge of war. Hence the parties to a civil war usually concede to each other belligerent rights. They exchange prisoners, and adopt the other courtesies and rules common to public or national wars.

"A civil war," says Vattel, "breaks the bands of society and government, or at least suspends their force and effect; it produces in the nation two independent parties who consider each other as enemies, and acknowledge no common judge. Those two parties, therefore, must necessarily be considered as constituting, at least for a time, two separate bodies, two distinct societies. Having no common superior to judge between them, they stand in precisely the same predicament as two nations who engage in a contest and have recourse to arms.

"This being the case, it is very evident that the common laws of war—those maxims of humanity, moderation, and honor—ought to be observed by both parties in every civil war. Should the sovereign conceive he has a right to hang up his prisoners as rebels, the opposite party will make reprisals, &c., &c.; the war will become cruel, horrible, and every day more destructive to the nation."

As a civil war is never publicly proclaimed, *eo nomine* against insurgents, its actual existence is a fact in our domestic history which the Court is bound to notice and to know.

The true test of its existence, as found in the writing of the sages of the common law, may be thus summarily stated: "When the regular course of justice is interrupted by revolt, rebellion, or insurrection, so that the Courts of Justice cannot be kept open, *civil war exists* and hostilities may be prosecuted on the same footing as if those opposing the Government were foreign enemies invading the land."

By the Constitution, Congress alone has the power to declare a national or foreign war. It cannot declare war against a State, or any number of States, by virtue of any clause in the Constitution. The Constitution confers on the President the whole Executive power. He is bound to take care that the laws be faithfully executed. He is Commander-in-Chief of the Army and Navy of the United States, and of the militia of the several States when called into the actual service of the United States. He has no power to initiate or declare a war either against a foreign nation or a domestic State. But by the Acts of Congress of February 28th, 1795, and 3d of March, 1807, he is authorized to call out the militia and use the military and naval forces of the United States in case of invasion by foreign nations, and to suppress insurrection against the government of a State or of the United States.

If a war be made by invasion of a foreign nation, the President is not only authorized but bound to resist force by force. He does not initiate the war, but is bound to accept the challenge without waiting for any special legislative authority. And whether the hostile party be a foreign invader, or States organized in rebellion, it is none the less a war, although the declaration of it be *"unilateral."* ...

This greatest of civil wars was not gradually developed by popular commotion, tumultuous assemblies, or local unorganized insurrections. However long may have been its previous conception, it nevertheless sprung forth suddenly from the parent brain, a Minerva in the full panoply of *war*. The President was bound to meet it in the shape it presented itself, without waiting for Congress to baptize it with a name; and no name given to it by him or them could change the fact.

It is not the less a civil war, with belligerent parties in hostile array, because it may be called an "insurrection" by one side, and the insurgents be considered as rebels or traitors. It is not necessary that the independence of the revolted province or State be acknowledged in order to constitute it a party belligerent in a war according to the law of nations. Foreign nations acknowledge it as war by a declaration of neutrality. The condition of neutrality cannot exist unless there be two belligerent parties. . . .

As soon as the news of the attack on Fort Sumter, and the organization of a government by the seceding States, assuming to act as belligerents, could become known in Europe, to wit, on the 13th day of May, 1861, the Queen of England issued her proclamation of neutrality, "recognizing hostilities as existing between the Government of the United States of America and *certain States* styling themselves the Confederate States of America." This was immediately followed by similar declarations or silent acquiescence by other nations.

After such an official recognition by the sovereign, a citizen of a foreign State is estopped to deny the existence of a war, with all its consequences as regards neutrals. They cannot ask a court to affect a technical ignorance of the existence of a war, which all the world acknowledges to be the greatest civil war known in the history of the human race, and thus cripple the arm of the Government and paralyze its power by subtle definitions and ingenious sophisms.

The law of nations is also called the law of nature; it is founded on the common consent as well as the common sense of the world. It contains no such anomalous doctrine as that which this Court are now for the first time desired to pronounce, to wit: That insurgents who have arisen in rebellion against their sovereign, expelled her Courts, established a revolutionary government, organized armies, and commenced hostilities, are not *enemies* because they are *traitors;* and a war levied on the Government by traitors, in order to dismember and destroy it, is not a *war* because it is an "insurrection."

Whether the President in fulfilling his duties, as Commander-in-Chief, in suppressing an insurrection, has met with such armed hostile resistance, and a civil war of such alarming proportions as will compel him to accord to them the character of belligerents, is a question to be decided *by him,* and this Court must be governed by the decisions and acts of the political department of the Government to which this power was entrusted. "He must determine what degree of force the crisis demands." The proclamation of blockade is itself official and conclusive evidence to the Court that a state of war existed which demanded and authorized a recourse to such a measure, under the circumstances peculiar to the case. . . .

If it were necessary to the technical existence of a war, that it should have a legislative sanction, we find it in almost every act passed at the extraordinary session of the Legislature of 1861, which was wholly employed in enacting laws to enable the Government to prosecute the war with vigor and efficiency. And finally, in 1861, we find Congress *"ex majore cautela"* and in anticipation of such astute objections, passing an act "approving, legalizing, and making valid all the acts, proclamations, and orders of the President, &c., as if they had been *issued and done under the previous express authority* and direction of the Congress of the United States." . . .

On this first question therefore we are of the opinion that the President had a right, *jure belli,* to institute a blockade of ports in possession of the States in rebellion, which neutrals are bound to regard.

We come now to the consideration of the second question. What is included in the term *"enemies' property"?*

Is the property of all persons residing within the territory of the States now in rebellion, captured on the high seas, to be treated as "enemies' property" whether the owner be in arms against the Government or not?

The right of one belligerent not only to coerce the other by direct force, but also to cripple his resources by the seizure or destruction of his property, is a necessary result of a state of war. Money and wealth, the products of agriculture and commerce, are said to be the sinews of war, and as necessary in its conduct as numbers and physical force. Hence it is, that the laws of war recognize the right of a belligerent to cut these sinews of the power of the enemy, by capturing his property on the high seas.

The appellants contend that the term "enemy" is properly applicable to those only who are subjects or citizens of a foreign State at war with our own. They quote from the pages of the common law, which say, "that persons who wage war against the King may be of two kinds, subjects or citizens. The former are not proper enemies, but rebels and traitors; the latter are those that come properly under the name of enemies."

They insist, moreover, that the President himself, in his proclamation, admits that great numbers of the persons residing within the territories in possession of the insurgent government, are loyal in their feelings, and forced by compulsion and the violence of the rebellious and revolutionary party and its "*de facto* government" to submit to their laws and assist in their scheme of revolution; that the acts of the usurping government cannot legally sever the bond of their allegiance; they have, therefore, a co-relative right to claim the protection of the government for their persons and property, and to be treated as loyal citizens, till legally convicted of having renounced their allegiance and made war against the Government by treasonably resisting its laws.

They contend, also, that insurrection is the act of individuals and not of a government or sovereignty; that the individuals engaged are subjects of law. That confiscation of their property can be effected only under a municipal law. That by the law of the land such confiscation cannot take place without the conviction of the owner of some offence, and finally that the secession ordinances are nullities and ineffectual to release any citizen from his allegiance to the national Government, and consequently that the Constitution and Laws of the United States are still operative over persons in all the States for punishment as well as protection.

This argument rests on the assumption of two propositions, each of which is without foundation on the established law of nations. It assumes that where a civil war exists, the party belligerent claiming to be sovereign, cannot, for some unknown reason, exercise the rights of belligerents, although the revolutionary party may. Being sovereign, he can exercise only sovereign rights over the other party. The insurgent may be killed on the battle-field or by the executioner; his property on land may be confiscated under the municipal law; but the commerce on the ocean, which supplies the rebels with means to support the war, cannot be made the subject of capture under the laws of war, because it is *"unconstitutional ! ! !"* Now, it is a proposition never doubted, that the belligerent party who claims to be sovereign, may exercise both belligerent and sovereign rights. Treating the other party as a belligerent and using only the milder modes of coercion which the law of nations has introduced to mitigate the rigors of war, cannot be a subject of complaint by the party to whom it is accorded as a grace or granted as a necessity. We have shown that a civil war such as that now waged between the Northern and Southern States is properly conducted according to the humane regulations of public law as regards capture on the ocean.

Under the very peculiar Constitution of this Government, although the citizens owe supreme allegiance to the Federal Government, they owe also a qualified allegiance to the State in which they are domiciled. Their persons and property are subject to its laws.

Hence, in organizing this rebellion, they have *acted as States* claiming to be sovereign over all persons and property within their respective limits, and asserting a right to absolve their citizens from their allegiance to the Federal Government. Several of these States have combined to form a new confederacy, claiming to be acknowledged by the world as a sovereign State. Their right to do so is now being decided by wager of battle. The ports and territory of each of these States are held in hostility to the General Government. It is no loose, unorganized insurrection, having no defined boundary or possession. It has a boundary marked by lines of bayonets, and which can be crossed only by force—south of this line is enemies' territory, because it is claimed and held in possession by an organized, hostile and belligerent power.

All persons residing within this territory whose property may be used to increase the revenues of the hostile power are, in this contest, liable to be treated as enemies, though not foreigners. They have cast off their allegiance and made war on their Government, and are none the less enemies because they are traitors. . . .

The produce of the soil of the hostile territory, as well as other property engaged in the commerce of the hostile power, as the source of its wealth and strength, are always regarded as legitimate prize, without regard to the domicil of the owner, and much more so if he reside and trade within their territory. . . .

Chapter 4

*"A law for rulers and people,
equally in war and in peace"*

LIBERTY IS IN PRECARIOUS BALANCE in time of war. The obvious necessity of victory is almost all-engulfing, even in a nation that cherishes human freedom. Yet even in such times there must be preserved a hard core of human rights, lest in fighting to save them, they are lost. The Civil War provided the opportunity for the Supreme Court to strike the telling blow for human liberty in perilous time of war.

The great legal process of human freedom is the writ of *habeas corpus*. It enables a person held in custody without lawful authority to obtain his release. Its importance is attested by the fact that the framers of the Constitution inserted in Article I, Section 9, a specific provision that *habeas corpus* cannot be suspended "unless when in Cases of Rebellion or Invasion the public safety may require it." Under specific congressional delegation of authority, President Lincoln, on September 15, 1863, suspended the writ of *habeas corpus* as to all prisoners held in military custody and charged with aiding and abetting the enemy, resisting the draft, or otherwise committing offenses against the military. The effect of this order seemingly was to compel military trial of such offenders, since the writ would not be available to free such persons from military custody.

A civilian named Milligan, an Indiana teacher, had been tried by a military court in Indiana, convicted of aiding the enemy, inciting insurrection, resisting the draft, and other similar offenses, and sentenced to hang. He petitioned for *habeas corpus* in the local federal court, claiming that the military tribunal which convicted him had no jurisdiction since he was a civilian and he was in an area where the regularly constituted civil courts were open and functioning. The federal court, being unsure it had power to hear Milligan's petition, sent the question to the United States Supreme Court under accepted procedure.

The Supreme Court held that the President had no power to provide for military trial in such circumstances. Milligan was freed. The Court did not specifically declare invalid Lincoln's order suspending the writ of *habeas corpus*, but it narrowed the applicability of the order to the holding of such prisoners as Milligan incommunicado for a period of time before trial. It insisted that the trial be held in the civil courts with all the usual constitutional procedural protections. Further, the Court established that the "suspension" of the writ of *habeas corpus* does not in fact wipe it out: the writ, commanding that the prisoner be brought before a court, is still issued, and at the hearing the court decides if the writ is validly suspended. This simply means that the court reserves the final power to decide if the executive or legislature acted with justification in suspending the writ. Thereby the protection of the individual against the overzealous political branches of the government is created.

The opinion of the Court was written by Justice David Davis, of Illinois. It is not very well written; it lives because of its substance. Davis had been elevated to the Court by President Lincoln in 1862. He was an intimate friend of Lincoln, even to the point of serving as the administrator of Lincoln's estate upon his assassination. Perhaps the fact that Lincoln was dead by the time the Milligan case came to decision made it easier for Davis to find the President's action unconstitutional. In any event, the commanding decision was made. Davis' reputation as a Supreme Court justice rests almost wholly upon the Milligan case. An inveterate politician, he was restless on the Court and finally resigned to be elected to the United States Senate from Illinois.

The Milligan decision was reached in the background of the rabid Reconstruction days immediately following the peace. The case played a role of major significance since it so devastatingly undermined the efforts of the Radical Republicans to impose complete military government upon the southern states. President Andrew Johnson, espousing the cause of moderation, relied heavily upon the case in resisting the proposals of the Reconstructionists. It was Johnson's resistance, bolstered by the Milligan case, that led to his impeachment and near conviction just a little over a year later. In this fashion did the Supreme Court provoke the only attempted removal of a President of the United States. But the incitement was a decision destined to endure for the ages as a memorable bulwark against military intrusion upon human freedom.

EX PARTE MILLIGAN
Supreme Court of the United States, 1866, 4 Wallace 2

DAVIS, J.:

The importance of the main question presented by this record cannot be overstated: for it involves the very framework of the government and the fundamental principles of American liberty.

During the late wicked Rebellion, the temper of the times did not allow that calmness in deliberation and discussion so necessary to a correct conclusion of a purely judicial question. Then, considerations of safety were mingled with the exercise of power; and feelings and interests prevailed which are happily terminated. Now that the public safety is assured, this question, as well as all others, can be discussed and decided without passion or the admixture of any element not required to form a legal judgment. We approach the investigation of this case, fully sensible of the magnitude of the inquiry and the necessity of full and cautious deliberation....

The controlling question in the case is this: Upon the facts stated in Milligan's petition, and the exhibits filed, had the Military Commission mentioned in it jurisdiction, legally, to try and sentence him? Milligan, not a resident of one of the rebellious States, or a prisoner of war, but a citizen of Indiana for twenty years past, and never in the military or naval service, is, while at his home, arrested by the military power of the United States, imprisoned and, on certain criminal charges preferred against him, tried, convicted and sentenced to be hanged by a military commission, organized under the direction of the military commander of the military district of Indiana. Had this tribunal the legal power and authority to punish this man?

No graver question was ever considered by this court, nor one which more nearly concerns the rights of the whole people; for it is the birthright of every American citizen when charged with crime, to be tried and punished according to law. The power of punishment is alone through the means which the laws have provided for that purpose, and if they are ineffectual, there is an immunity from punishment, no matter how great an offender the individual may be, or how much his crimes may have shocked the sense of justice of the country, or endangered its safety. By the protection of the law human rights are secured; withdraw that protection, and they are at the mercy of wicked rulers, or the clamor of an excited people. If there was law to justify this military trial, it is not our province to interfere; if there was not, it is our duty to declare the nullity of the whole proceedings. The decision of this question does not depend on argument or judicial precedents, numerous and highly illustrative as they are. These precedents inform us of the extent of the struggle to preserve liberty and to relieve those in civil life from military trials. The founders of our government were familiar with the history of that struggle; and secured in a written Constitution every right which the people had wrested from power during a contest of ages. By that Constitution and the laws authorized by it, this question must be determined. The provisions of that instrument on the administration of criminal justice are too plain and direct to leave room for misconstruction or doubt of their true meaning. Those applicable to this case are found in that clause of the original Constitution which says, "That the trial of all crimes, except in case of impeachment, shall be by jury;" and in the fourth, fifth and sixth articles of the amendments. The fourth proclaims the right to be secure in person and effects against unreasonable search and seizure; and directs that a judicial warrant shall not issue "without proof of probable cause supported by oath or affirmation." The fifth declares "that no person shall be held to answer for a capital or otherwise infamous crime unless on presentment by a grand jury, except in cases arising in the land or naval forces, or in the militia, when in actual service in time of war or public danger, nor be deprived of life, liberty, or property, without due process of law." And the sixth guarantees the right of trial by jury, in such manner and with such regulations that with upright judges, impartial juries, and an able bar, the innocent will be saved and the guilty punished. It is in these words: "In all criminal prosecutions the accused shall enjoy the right to a speedy and public trial by an impartial jury of the State and district wherein the crime shall have been committed, which district shall have been previously ascertained by law, and to be informed of the nature and cause of the accusation; to be confronted with the witnesses against him; to have compulsory process for obtaining witnesses in his favor, and to have the assistance of counsel for his defense." These securities for personal liberty thus embodied, were such as wisdom and experience had demonstrated to be necessary for the protection of those accused of crime. And so strong was the sense of the country of their importance, and so jealous were the people that these rights, highly prized, might be denied them by implication, that when the original Constitution was proposed for adoption it encountered severe opposition; and, but for the belief that it would be so amended as to embrace them, it would never have been ratified.

Time has proven the discernment of our ancestors; for even these provisions, expressed in such plain English words, that it would seem the ingenuity of man could not evade them, are now, after the lapse of more than seventy years, sought to be avoided. Those great and good men foresaw that troublous times would arise, when rulers and people would become restive under restraint, and seek by sharp and decisive measures to accomplish ends deemed just and proper; and that the principles of constitutional liberty would be in peril, unless established by irrepealable law. The history of the world had taught them that what was done in the past might be attempted in the future. The Constitution of the United States is a law for rulers and people, equally in war and in peace, and covers with the shield of its protection all classes of men, at all times, and under all circumstances. No doctrine, involving more pernicious consequences, was ever invented by the wit of man than that any of its provisions can be suspended during any of the great exigencies of government. Such a doctrine leads directly to anarchy or despotism, but the theory of necessity on which it is based is false; for the government, within the Constitution, has all the powers granted to it which are necessary to preserve its existence, as has been happily proved by the result of the great effort to throw off its just authority. . . .

It is claimed that martial law covers with its broad mantle the proceedings of this Military Commission. The proposition is this: that in a time of war the commander of an armed force (if in his opinion the exigencies of the country demand it, and of which he is to judge), has the power, within the lines of his military district, to suspend all civil rights and their remedies, and subject citizens as well as soldiers to the rule of his will; and in the exercise of his lawful authority cannot be restrained, except by his superior officer or the President of the United States.

If this position is sound to the extent claimed, then when war exists, foreign or domestic, and the country is subdivided into military departments for mere convenience, the commander of one of them can, if he chooses, within his limits, on the plea of necessity, with the approval of the Executive, substitute military force for and to the exclusion of the laws, and punish all persons, as he thinks right and proper, without fixed or certain rules.

The statement of this proposition shows its importance; for, if true, republican government is a failure, and there is an end of liberty regulated by law. Martial law, established on such a basis, destroys every guaranty of the Constitution, and effectually renders the "military independent of and superior to the civil power"—the attempt to do which by the King of Great Britain was deemed by our fathers such an offense, that they assigned it to the world as one of the causes which impelled them to declare their independence. Civil liberty and this kind of martial law cannot endure together; the antagonism is irreconcilable and, in the conflict, one or the other must perish.

This nation, as experience has proved, cannot always remain at peace, and has no right to expect that it will always have wise and humane rulers, sincerely attached to the principles of the Constitution. Wicked men, ambitious of power, with hatred of liberty and contempt of law, may fill the place once occupied by Washington and Lincoln; and if this right is conceded, and the calamities of war again befall us, the dangers to human liberty are frightful to contemplate. If our fathers had failed to provide for just such a contingency, they would have been false to the trust reposed in them. They knew—the history of the world told them—the nation they were founding, be its existence short or long, would be involved in war; how often or how long continued, human foresight could not tell; and that unlimited power, wherever lodged at such a time, was especially hazardous to freemen. For this, and other equally weighty reasons, they secured the inheritance they had fought to maintain, by incorporating in a written Constitution the safeguards which time had proved were essential to its preservation. Not one of these safeguards can the President or Congress or the Judiciary disturb, except the one concerning the writ of *habeas corpus*.

It is essential to the safety of every government that, in a great crisis, like the one we have just passed through, there should be a power somewhere of suspending the writ of *habeas corpus*. In every war, there are men of previously good character, wicked enough to counsel their fellow citizens to resist the measures deemed necessary by a good government to sustain its just authority and overthrow its enemies; and their influence may lead to dangerous combinations. In the emergency of the times, an immediate public investigation according to law may not be possible; and yet, the peril to the country may be too imminent to suffer such persons to go at large. Unquestionably, there is then an exigency which demands that the government, if it should see fit, in the exercise of a proper discretion, to make arrests, should not be required to produce the person arrested in answer to a writ of *habeas corpus*. The Constitution goes no further. It does not say after a writ of *habeas corpus* is denied a citizen, that he shall be tried otherwise than by the course of common law. If it had intended this result, it was easy by the use of direct words to have accomplished it. The illustrious men who framed that instrument were guarding the foundations of civil liberty against the abuses of unlimited power; they were full of wisdom and the lessons of history informed them that a trial by an established court, assisted by an impartial jury, was the only sure way of protecting the citizen against oppression and wrong. Knowing this, they limited the suspension to one great right, and left the rest to remain forever inviolable. But it is insisted that the safety of the country in time of war demands that this broad claim for martial law shall be sustained. If this were true, it could be well said that a country, preserved at the sacrifice of all the cardinal principles of liberty, is not worth the cost of preservation. Happily, it is not so. . . .

If, in foreign invasion or civil war, the courts are actually closed, and it is impossible to administer criminal justice according to law, then, on the theatre of active military operations, where war really prevails, there is a necessity to furnish a substitute for the civil authority, thus overthrown, to preserve the safety of the army and society; and as no power is left but the military, it is allowed to govern by martial rule until the laws can have their free course. As necessity creates the rule, so it limits its duration; for, if this government is continued after the courts are reinstated, it is a gross usurpation of power. Martial rule can never exist where the courts are open, and in the proper and unobstructed exercise of their jurisdiction. It is also confined to the locality of actual war. Because, during the late Rebellion it could have been enforced in Virginia, where the national authority was overturned and the courts driven out, it does not follow that it should obtain in Indiana, where that authority was never disputed, and justice was always administered. And so in the case of a foreign invasion, martial rule may become a necessity, in one State, when, in another, it would be "mere lawless violence."...

The suspension of the privilege of the writ of *habeas corpus* does not suspend the writ itself. The writ issues as a matter of course; and on the return made to it the court decides whether the party applying is denied the right of proceeding any further with it....

Chapter 5

"The Constitution deals with substance, not shadows"

OCCASIONALLY, a Supreme Court decision will so completely dispose of a constitutional issue that in a generation or two the decision itself is almost forgotten. Its complete effectiveness predestines its own oblivion. But then in a later era the constitutional issue is raised again by those who have forgotten the earlier conflict. There is a resurrection, and the old decision lives again. Such is the history of the Civil War case involving "test" or "loyalty" oaths.

The case, *Cummings v. Missouri,* was not lacking in notoriety when it was decided in the vortex of the bitter controversy over Reconstruction, nine months after the decision in *Ex parte Milligan* and one year before President Johnson's impeachment. The state of Missouri adopted a new constitution immediately upon the close of the Civil War. Contained in that constitution was a sweeping loyalty oath required of public officers, officers of corporations, teachers, lawyers, and clergymen. The oath required all such persons to swear not only that they had never been in armed hostility to the United States, but also that they had never "by act or word" manifested *adherence* to the cause of the enemy, or *desire* for its triumph, or *sympathy* for the rebels, or *disaffection* toward the United States government in its war with the South. Other provisions concerning avoidance of the draft and aiding southern guerrillas were also included.

The validity of this oath was challenged by Cummings, a Roman Catholic priest, who refused to swear to these matters. The United States Supreme Court held the oath requirement to be an unconstitutional bill of attainder and an *ex post facto* law. In a companion case the Court struck down a similar oath enacted by Congress and required of attorneys practicing before federal courts (*Ex parte Garland,* 4 Wallace 333). The opinions in both cases were written by Justice Stephen J. Field, of California, a Lincoln appointee. Justice Field, destined to serve on the Court thirty-four years (longer than any other justice up to the present time) was a distinguished man from a distinguished family. He was a man of consistency and power, completely unswayed by the varying winds of public opinion. Especially in his later years, he became somewhat arrogant in his views—as evidenced by his constant assertion in his opinions that God was on his side. Like a baseball umpire, he could not tolerate the thought that he might be wrong. His brother David Dudley Field was a leading constitutional lawyer of the time and argued a number of cases, including the Cummings case, before the Court. Another brother was Cyrus Field, the engineer-businessman who promoted the laying of the first Atlantic cable. A sister, Emilia, was the mother of Justice David Brewer, who was appointed to the Court in 1889, serving thus during the last eight years of his uncle's tenure.

Field's decision in the Cummings case, the object of vituperative criticism at the time, nevertheless won the day. The policy of evoking loyalty through test oaths disappeared. The case slumbered until the Communist threat following World War II brought forth a rash of similar oath requirements. The decision is now playing a vital role in testing the validity of these contemporary test oaths. The Cummings case stands at the flank of *Ex parte Milligan* as an additional rampart of the edifice of freedom.

CUMMINGS v. MISSOURI

Supreme Court of the United States, 1867, 4 Wallace 277

FIELD, J.:

The oath . . . required, is, for its severity, without any precedent that we can discover. In the first place, it is retrospective; it embraces all the past from this day; and, if taken years hence, it will also cover all the intervening period. In its retrospective feature we believe it is peculiar to this country. In England and France there have been test oaths, but they were always limited to an affirmation of present belief, or present disposition towards the government, and were never exacted with reference to particular instances of past misconduct. In the second place, the oath is directed not merely against overt and visible acts of hostility to the government, but is intended to reach words, desires, and sympathies also. And in the third place, it allows no distinction between acts springing from malignant enmity and acts which may have been prompted by charity, or affection or relationship. If one has ever expressed sympathy with any who were drawn into the rebellion, even if the recipients of that sympathy were connected by the closest ties of blood, he is as unable to subscribe to the oath as the most active and the most cruel of the rebels, and is equally debarred from the offices of honor or trust, and the positions and employment specified.

But, as it was observed by the learned counsel who appeared on behalf of the State of Missouri, this court cannot decide the case upon the justice or hardship of these provisions. Its duty is to determine whether they are in conflict with the Constitution of the United States. On behalf of Missouri, it is urged that they only prescribe a qualification for holding certain offices, and practicing certain callings, and that it is, therefore, within the power of the State to adopt them. On the other hand, it is contended that they are in conflict with that clause of the Constitution which forbids any State to pass a bill of attainder or an *ex post facto* law.

We admit the propositions of the counsel of Missouri, that the States which existed previous to the adoption of the Federal Constitution possessed originally all the attributes of sovereignty; and they still retain those attributes, except as they have been surrendered by the formation of the Constitution, and the amendments thereto; that the new States, upon their admission into the Union, became invested with equal rights, and were thereafter subject only to similar restrictions, and that among the rights reserved to the States is the right of each State to determine the qualifications for office, and the conditions upon which its citizens may exercise their various callings and pursuits within its jurisdiction.

These are general propositions, and involve principles of the highest moment. But it by no means follows that, under the form of creating a qualification or attaching a condition, the States can, in effect, inflict a punishment for a past act which was not punishable at the time it was committed. The question is not as to the existence of the power of the State over matters of internal police, but whether that power has been made in the present case an instrument for the infliction of punishment against the inhibition of the Constitution.

Qualifications relate to the fitness or capacity of the party for a particular pursuit or profession. Webster defines the term to mean "any natural endowment or any acquirement which fits a person for a place, office or employment, or enables him to sustain any character, with success." It is evident from the nature of the pursuits and professions of the parties, placed under disabilities by the Constitution of Missouri, that many of the acts, from the taint of which they must purge themselves, have no possible relation to their fitness for those pursuits and professions. There can be no connection between the fact that Mr. Cummings entered or left the State of Missouri to avoid enrollment or draft in the military service of the United States, and his fitness to teach the doctrines or administer the sacraments of his church; nor can a fact of this kind or the expression of words of sympathy, with some of the persons drawn into the Rebellion, constitute any evidence of the unfitness of the attorney or counselor to practice his profession; or of the professor to teach the ordinary branches of education; or of the want of business knowledge or business capacity in the manager of a corporation, or in any director or trustee. It is manifest upon the simple statement of many of the acts and of the professions and pursuits, that there is no such relation between them as to render a denial of the commission of the acts at all appropriate as a condition of allowing the exercise of the professions and pursuits. The oath could not, therefore, have been required as a means of ascertaining whether parties were qualified or not for their respective callings or the trusts with which they were charged. It was required in order to reach the person, not the calling. It was exacted, not from any notion that the several acts designated indicated unfitness for the callings, but because it was thought that the several acts deserved punishment, and that for many of them there was no way to inflict punishment except by depriving the parties who had committed them of some of the rights and privileges of the citizen.

The disabilities created by the Constitution of Missouri must be regarded as penalties—they constitute punishment. We do not agree with the counsel of Missouri that "to punish one is to deprive him of life, liberty or property, and that to take from him anything less than these is no punishment at all." The learned counsel does not use these terms—life, liberty, and property—as comprehending every right known to the law. He does not include under liberty freedom from outrage on the feelings as well as restraints on the person. He does not include under property those estates which one may acquire in professions, though they are often the source of the highest emoluments and honors. The deprivation of any rights, civil or political, previously enjoyed, may be punishment; the circumstances attending and the causes of the deprivation determining this fact. Disqualification from office may be punishment, as in cases of conviction upon impeachment. Disqualification from the pursuits of a lawful avocation, or from positions of trust, or from the privilege of appearing in the courts, or acting as an executor, administrator or guardian, may also, and often has been, imposed as punishment. . . .

The theory upon which our political institutions rest is, that all men have certain inalienable rights—that among these are life, liberty and the pursuit of happiness; and that in the pursuit of happiness all avocations, all honors, all positions, are alike open to everyone, and that in the protection of these rights all are equal before the law. Any deprivation or suspension of any of these rights for past conduct is punishment, and can be in no otherwise defined.

Punishment not being, therefore, restricted, as contended by counsel, to the deprivation of life, liberty or property, but also embracing de-

THE CIVIL WAR AND ITS AFTERMATH

privation or suspension of political or civil rights, and the disabilities prescribed by the provisions of the Missouri Constitution being, in effect, punishment, we proceed to consider whether there is any inhibition in the Constitution of the United States against their enforcement.

The counsel for Missouri closed his argument in this case by presenting a striking picture of the struggle for ascendency in that State during the recent Rebellion between the friends and the enemies of the Union, and of the fierce passions which that struggle aroused. It was in the midst of the struggle that the present Constitution was framed, although it was not adopted by the people until the war had closed. It would have been strange, therefore, had it not exhibited in its provisions some traces of the excitement amidst which the Convention held its deliberations.

It was against the excited action of the States, under such influences as these, that the framers of the Federal Constitution intended to guard. In *Fletcher v. Peck,* 6 Cranch, 137, Mr. Chief Justice Marshall, speaking of such action, uses this language: "Whatever respect might have been felt for the state sovereignties, it is not to be disguised that the framers of the Constitution viewed with some apprehension the violent acts which might grow out of the feelings of the moment; and that the people of the United States, in adopting that instrument, have manifested a determination to shield themselves and their property from the effects of those sudden and strong passions to which men are exposed. The restrictions on the legislative power of the States are obviously founded in this sentiment; and the Constitution of the United States contains what may be deemed a bill of rights for the people of each State."

" 'No State shall pass any bill of attainder, *ex post facto* law, or law impairing the obligation of contracts.' "

A bill of attainder is a legislative Act, which inflicts punishment without a judicial trial.

If the punishment be less than death, the Act is termed a bill of pains and penalties. Within the meaning of the Constitution, bills of attainder include bills of pains and penalties. In these cases the legislative body, in addition to its legitimate functions, exercises the powers and office of judge; it assumes, in the language of the text books, judicial magistracy; it pronounces upon the guilt of the party, without any of the forms or safeguards of trial; it determines the sufficiency of the proofs produced, whether conformable to the rules of evidence or otherwise; and it fixes the degree of punishment in accordance with its own notions of the enormity of the offense. . . .

If the clauses of the 2d article of the Constitution of Missouri, to which we have referred, had in terms declared that Mr. Cummings was guilty, or should be held guilty, of having been in armed hostility to the United States, or of having entered that State to avoid being enrolled or drafted into the military service of the United States and, therefore, should be deprived of the right to preach as a priest of the Catholic Church, or to teach in any institution of learning, there could be no question that the clauses would constitute a bill of attainder within the meaning of the Federal Constitution. If these clauses, instead of mentioning his name, had declared that all priests and clergymen within the State of Missouri were guilty of these acts, or should be held guilty of them, and hence be subjected to the like deprivation, the clauses would be equally open to objection. And, further, if these clauses had declared that all such priests and clergymen should be so held guilty, and be thus deprived, provided they did not, by a day designated, do certain specified acts, they would be no less within the inhibition of the Federal Constitution.

In all these cases there would be the legislative enactment creating the deprivation, without any of the ordinary forms and guards provided for the security of the citizen in the administration of justice by the established tribunals.

The results which would follow, from clauses of the character mentioned, do follow from the clauses actually adopted. The difference between the last case supposed and the case actually presented is one of form only, and not of substance. The existing clauses presume the guilt of the priests and clergymen, and adjudge the deprivation of their right to preach or teach unless the presumption be first removed by their expurgatory oath—in other words, they assume the guilt and adjudge the punishment conditionally. The clauses supposed differ only in that they declare the guilt instead of assuming it. The deprivation is effected with equal certainty in the one case as it would be in the other, but not with equal directness. The purpose of the law maker in the case supposed would be openly avowed; in the case existing it is only disguised. The legal result must be the same, for what cannot be done directly cannot be done indirectly. The Constitution deals with substance, not shadows. Its inhibition was leveled at the thing, not the name. It intended that the rights of the citizen should be secure against deprivation for past conduct by legislative enactment, under any form, however disguised. If the inhibition can be evaded by the form of the enactment, its insertion in the fundamental law was a vain and futile proceeding.

We proceed to consider the second clause of what Mr. Chief Justice Marshall terms a bill of rights for the people of each State—the clause which inhibits the passage of an *ex post facto* law.

By an *ex post facto* law is meant one which imposes a punishment for an act which is not punishable at the time it was committed; or imposes additional punishment to that then prescribed; or changes the rules of evidence by which less or different testimony is sufficient to convict than was then required. . . .

The clauses in the Missouri Constitution, which are the subject of consideration, do not, in terms, define any crimes, or declare that any punishment shall be inflicted; but they produce the same result upon the parties against whom they are directed, as though the crimes were defined and the punishment was declared. They assume that there are persons in Missouri who are guilty of some of the acts designated. They would have no meaning in the Constitution were not such the fact. They are aimed at past acts, and not future acts. They were intended especially to operate upon parties who, in some form or manner, by actions or words directly or indirectly, had aided or countenanced the Rebellion, or sympathized with parties engaged in the Rebellion, or had endeavored to escape the proper responsibilities and duties of a citizen in time of war; and they were intended to operate by depriving such persons of the right to hold certain offices and trusts, and to pursue their ordinary and regular avocations. This deprivation is punishment; nor is it any less so because a way is opened for escape from it by the expurgatory oath. The framers of the Constitution of Missouri knew at the time that whole classes of individuals would be unable to take the oath prescribed. To them there is no escape provided; to them the deprivation was intended to be and is, absolute and perpetual. To make the enjoyment of a right dependent upon an impossible condition is equivalent to an absolute denial of the right under any condition, and such denial, enforced for a past act, is nothing less than punishment imposed for that act. It is a misapplication of terms to call it anything else.

Now, some of the acts to which the expurgatory oath is directed were not offenses at the time they were committed. It was no offense against any law to enter or leave the State of Missouri for the purpose of avoiding enrollment or draft in the military service of the United States, however much the evasion of such service might be the subject of moral censure. Clauses which prescribe a penalty for an act of this nature are within the terms of the definition of an *ex post facto* law—"they impose a punishment for an act not punishable at the time it was committed."

Some of the acts at which the oath is directed constituted high offenses at the time they were committed, to which, upon conviction, fine and imprisonment, or other heavy penalties, were attached. The clauses which provide a further penalty for these acts are also within the definition of an *ex post facto* law—"they impose additional punishment to that prescribed when the act was committed."

And this is not all. The clauses in question subvert the presumptions of innocence, and alter the rules of evidence, which heretofore, under the universally recognized principles of the common law, have been supposed to be fundamental and unchangeable. They assume that the parties are guilty; they call upon the parties to establish their innocence; and they declare that such innocence can be shown only in one way—by an inquisition, in the form of an expurgatory oath, into the consciences of the parties. . . .

The judgment of the Supreme Court of Missouri must be reversed, and the cause remanded, with directions to enter a judgment reversing the judgment of the Circuit Court, and directing that court to discharge the defendant from imprisonment, and suffer him to depart without day.

Chapter 6

*"Government would be paralyzed
in the paralysis of the people"*

THE MOST ARDENT challenge of the federal powers wielded in winning the Civil War was the challenge directed at the government's fiscal policies. The Union financed its war effort by the issuance of paper money. To give this money the requisite backing to make it effective, the Legal Tender Acts were passed early in the war. These acts required creditors to accept the paper money, dollar for dollar, in discharge of debts. The issuance of paper currency, increasing the amount of money in circulation, debases the value of the dollar, or in modern vernacular, causes "inflation." This makes creditors exceedingly unhappy since debts are paid off with cheaper money than that the creditor originally loaned. Disgruntled creditors challenged the validity of the Legal Tender Acts. The issue thus posed was one that elicited great public fervor. And no matter which way the question was to be decided, large and vocal segments of the population would deplore the result—creditors if the acts were held valid, and debtors if the acts were void.

The Supreme Court managed to avoid passing upon the validity of the Legal Tender Acts during the Civil War and immediately following; in the cases which arose, it was able to hold that the basic decision could not be reached for procedural and jurisdictional reasons. Finally, in February, 1870, the Supreme Court held the Legal Tender Acts unconstitutional in the case of *Hepburn v. Griswold,* 8 Wallace 603. The justices split four to three; there were two vacancies on the Court. The decision intensified rather than quenched the fires of controversy.

On the very day the decision was handed down, President Grant sent to the Senate the names of William Strong and Joseph P. Bradley to fill the two vacancies on the Court. Their nominations were promptly confirmed. Four days later, the United States Attorney General asked the Court to reconsider Legal Tender. In a move which has been the subject of criticism to the present day, a bare majority of the Court as reconstituted agreed to the reconsideration. Certainly this decision was calculated to weaken the prestige of the Court and make it politically suspect. Yet, upon close analysis, the action would seem to be no worse than any court consideration of its own prior decisions, except for the peculiar coincidences which here occurred.

Decision was finally reached again in May, 1871, this time upholding the validity of the Acts. These *Legal Tender Cases,* grouped by the Court for purposes of decision and opinion, were *Knox v. Lee* and *Parker v. Davis.* In *Knox v. Lee,* a husband and wife, Hugh and Phoebe Lee, sued to recover the value of some sheep they owned which had been confiscated by the Confederate government and sold to the defendant, William B. Knox. There was no question but that the confiscation had been improper, that the defendant was liable. The only issue was whether the defendant could discharge his obligation by paying the Lees the dollar value of the sheep in the inflated currency which Congress had established as legal tender. Precisely the same kind of constitutional issue was presented in *Parker v. Davis,* which involved a simple contract for the sale and purchase of some timber land. The contract had been made before the Legal Tender Acts had been passed. The sole question was whether the buyer, George Davis, could pay the contract purchase price in the new, devalued currency in full discharge of his obligation. In both cases the debtor was held liable only for payment in the new, devalued currency. In this manner was a cardinal constitutional issue settled in cases between obscure private citizens.

With these holdings, President Grant was charged with "packing" the Court. The four justices who had constituted the majority in the earlier case now were dissenters. The three dissenters in that case were now joined in majority by Grant's new appointees, Justices Strong and Bradley. Further, and this can only be explained as inept Court administration, the two prevailing opinions were written by the two new appointees. Strong wrote the opinion of the Court, and Bradley wrote a special concurring opinion.

Yet latter-day historians acquit Grant of any intent to pack the Court. It now appears to be pure coincidence that Strong's and Bradley's nominations to the Court were made on the very day the Hepburn decision was announced. There is no indication that the Administration knew how the case would be decided nor that the decision would be handed down on that day. And historians can find no evidence that the appointment of Strong and Bradley was based upon their views on the Legal Tender question.

Bradley's was the more succinct and forcefully reasoned opinion, and is therefore chosen for printing here. Bradley, although without judicial experience prior to his appointment, was a lawyer and scholar of distinction. Worthy of particular mention is the fact that before donning judicial robes he was nationally known as a political essayist; his work on the Court reflected this background. His opinions are illuminating in their clarity, yet impellingly reasoned, and they are particularly rewarding to those persons not trained in the law.

Appended to the Bradley opinion in the *Legal Tender Cases* is the peroration of Justice Field's forty-seven-page dissenting opinion. It will be noted that Justice Field, as was his wont, aligned himself on the side of the Almighty.

LEGAL TENDER CASES

Supreme Court of the United States, 1871, 12 Wallace 457

BRADLEY, J., *concurring*:

The Constitution of the United States established a government, and not a league, compact, or partnership. It was constituted by the people. It is called a government. In the eighth section of Article I, it is declared that Congress shall have power to make all laws which shall be necessary and proper for carrying into execution the foregoing powers, and all other powers vested by this Constitution in *the government of the United States,* or in any department or office thereof. As a government it was invested with all the attributes of sovereignty. It is expressly declared in Article VI that the Constitution, and the laws of the United States made in pursuance thereof, and all treaties made under the authority of the United States, shall be the supreme law of the land.

The doctrine so long contended for, that the Federal Union was a mere compact of States, and that the States, if they chose, might annul or disregard the acts of the National legislature, or might secede from the Union at their pleasure, and that the General government had no power to coerce them into submission to the Constitution, should be regarded as definitely and forever overthrown. This has been finally effected by the National power, as it had often been before, by overwhelming argument.

The United States is not only a government, but it is a National government, and the only government in this country that has the character of nationality. It is invested with power over all the foreign relations of the country, war, peace, and negotiations and intercourse with other nations; all which are forbidden to the State governments. It has jurisdiction over all those general subjects of legislation and sovereignty which affect the interests of the whole people equally and alike, and which require uniformity of regulations and laws, such as the coinage, weights and measures, bankruptcies, the postal system, patent and copyright laws, the public lands, and interstate commerce; all which subjects are expressly or impliedly prohibited to the State governments. It has power to suppress insurrections, as well as to repel invasions, and to organize, arm, discipline, and call into service the militia of the whole country. The President is charged with the duty and invested with the power to take care that the laws be faithfully executed. The judiciary has jurisdiction to decide controversies between the States, and between their respective citizens, as well as questions of National concern; and the government is clothed with power to guarantee to every State a republican form of government, and to protect each of them against invasion and domestic violence. For the purpose of carrying into effect and executing these and the other powers conferred, and of providing for the common defense and general welfare, Congress is further invested with the taxing power in all its forms, except that of laying duties on exports, with the power to borrow money on the National credit, to punish crimes against the laws of the United States and of nations, to constitute courts, and to make all laws necessary and proper for carrying into execution the various powers vested in the government or any department or officer thereof.

Such being the character of the General government, it seems to be a self-evident proposition that it is invested with all those inherent and implied powers which, at the time of adopting the Constitution, were generally considered to belong to every government as such, and as being essential to the exercise of its functions. If this proposition be not true, it certainly is true that the government of the United States has express authority, in the clause last quoted, to make all such laws (usually regarded as inherent and implied) as may be necessary and proper for carrying on the government as constituted, and vindicating its authority and existence. . . .

I hold it to be the prerogative of every government not restrained by its Constitution to anticipate its resources by the issue of exchequer bills, bills of credit, bonds, stock, or a banking apparatus. Whether those issues shall or shall not be receivable in payment of private debts is an incidental matter in the discretion of such government unless restrained by constitutional prohibition.

This power is entirely distinct from that of coining money and regulating the value thereof. It is not only embraced in the power to make all necessary auxiliary laws, but it is incidental to the power of borrowing money. It is often a necessary means of anticipating and realizing promptly the national resources, when, perhaps, promptness is necessary to the national existence. It is not an attempt to coin money out of a valueless material, like the coinage of leather or ivory or kowrie shells. It is a pledge of the national credit. It is a promise by the government to pay dollars; it is not an attempt to make dollars. The standard of value is not changed. The government simply demands that its credit shall be accepted and received by public and private creditors during the pending exigency. Every government has a right to demand this when its existence is at stake. The interests of every citizen are bound up with the fate of the government. None can claim exemption. If they cannot trust their government in its time of trial they are not worthy to be its citizens.

But it is said, why not borrow money in the ordinary way? The answer is, the legislative department, being the nation itself, speaking by its representatives, has a choice of methods, and is the master of its own discretion. One mode of borrowing, it is true, is to issue the government bonds, and to invite capitalists to purchase them. But this is not the only mode. It is often too tardy and inefficient. In time of war or public danger, Congress, representing the sovereign power, by its right of eminent domain, may authorize the President to take private property for the public use and give government certificates therefor. This is largely done on such occasions. It is an indirect way of compelling the owner of property to lend to the government. He is forced to rely on the national credit.

Can the poor man's cattle, and horses, and corn be thus taken by the government when the public exigency requires it, and cannot the rich man's bonds and notes be in like manner taken to reach the same end? If the government enacts that the certificates of indebtedness which it gives to the farmer for his cattle and provender shall be receivable by the farmer's creditors in payment of his bonds and notes, is it anything more than transferring the government loan from the hands of one man to the hands of another—perhaps far more able to advance it? Is it anything more than putting the securities of the capitalist on the same platform as the farmer's stock?

No one supposes that these government certificates are never to be paid—that the day of specie payments is never to return. And it matters not in what form they are issued. The principle is still the same. Instead of certificates they may be treasury notes, or paper of any other form. And their payment may not be made directly in coin, but they may be first convertible into government bonds, or other government securities. Through whatever changes they pass, their ultimate destiny is *to be paid*. But it is prerogative of the legislative department to determine when the fit time for payment has come. It may be long delayed, perhaps many may think it too long after the exigency has passed. But the abuse of a power, if proven, is no argument against its existence. And the courts are not responsible therefor. Questions of political expediency belong to the legislative halls, not to the judicial forum. It might subserve the present good if we should declare the legal tender act unconstitutional, and a temporary public satisfaction might be the result. But what a miserable consideration would that be for a permanent loss of one of the just and necessary powers of the government; a power which, had Congress failed to exercise it when it did, we might have had no court here today to consider the question, nor a government or a country to make it important to do so. . . .

It is absolutely essential to independent national existence that government should have a firm hold on the two great sovereign instrumentalities of the *sword* and the *purse,* and the right to wield them without restriction on occasions of national peril. In certain emergencies government must have at its command, not only the personal services—the bodies and lives—of its citizens, but the lesser, though not less essential, power of absolute control over the resources of the country. Its armies must be filled, and its navies manned, by the citizens in person. Its material of war, its munitions, equipment, and commissary stores must come from the industry of the country. This can only be stimulated into activity by a proper financial system, especially as regards the currency.

A constitutional government, notwithstanding the right of eminent domain, cannot take physical and forcible possession of all that it may need to defend the country, and is reluctant to exercise such a power when it can be avoided. *It must purchase,* and by purchase command materials and supplies, products of manufacture, labor, service of every kind. The government cannot, by physical power, compel the workshops to turn out millions of dollars' worth of manufactures in leather, and cloth, and wood, and iron, which are the very first conditions of military equipment. It must stimulate and set in motion the industry of the country. In other words, it must *purchase*. But it cannot purchase with specie. That is soon exhausted, hidden, or exported. It must purchase by *credit*. It cannot force its citizens to take its bonds. It must be able to lay its hands on the currency—that great instrument of exchange by which the people transact all their own affairs with each other; that thing which they must have, and which lies at the foundation of all industrial effort and all business in the community. When the ordinary currency disappears, as it often does in time of war, when business begins to stagnate and general bankruptcy is imminent, then the government must have power at the same time to renovate its own resources and to revive the drooping energies of the nation by supplying it with a circulating medium. What that medium shall be, what its character and qualities, will depend upon the greatness of the exigency, and the degree of promptitude which it demands. These are legislative questions. The

LEGAL TENDER CASES

heart of the nation must not be crushed out. The people must be aided to pay their debts and meet their obligations. The debtor interest of the country represents its bone and sinew, and must be encouraged to pursue its avocations. If relief were not afforded universal bankruptcy would ensue, and industry would be stopped, and government would be paralyzed in the paralysis of the people. It is an undoubted fact that during the late civil war, the activity of the workshops and factories, mines and machinery, shipyards, railroads and canals of the loyal States, caused by the issue of the legal tender currency, constituted an inexhaustible fountain of strength to the National cause.

These views are exhibited, not for the purpose of showing that the power is a desirable one, and therefore ought to be assumed; much less for the purpose of giving judgment on the expediency of its exercise in any particular case; but for the purpose of showing that it is one of those vital and essential powers inhering in every national sovereignty and necessary to its self-preservation.

But the creditor interest will lose some of its gold! Is gold the one thing needful? Is it worse for the creditor to lose a little by depreciation than everything by the bankruptcy of his debtor? Nay, is it worse than to lose everything by the subversion of the government? What is it that protects him in the accumulation and possession of his wealth? Is it not the government and its laws? And can he not consent to trust that government for a brief period until it shall have vindicated its right to exist? All property and all rights, even those of liberty and life, are held subject to the fundamental condition of being liable to be impaired by providential calamities and national vicissitudes. Taxes impair my income or the value of my property. The condemnation of my homestead, or a valuable part of it for a public improvement, or public defence, will sometimes destroy its value to me; the conscription may deprive me of liberty and destroy my life. So with the power of government to borrow money, a power to be exercised by the consent of the lender, if possible, but to be exercised without his consent, if necessary. And when exercised in the form of legal tender notes or bills of credit, it may operate for the time being to compel the creditor to receive the *credit of the government* in place of the gold which he expected to receive from his debtor. All these are fundamental political conditions on which life, property, and money are respectively held and enjoyed under our system of government, nay, under any system of government. There are times when the exigencies of the state rightly absorb all subordinate considerations of private interest, convenience, or feeling; and at such times, the temporary though compulsory acceptance by a private creditor of the government credit, in lieu of his debtor's obligation to pay, is one of the slightest forms in which the necessary burdens of society can be sustained. Instead of being a violation of such obligation, it merely subjects it to one of those conditions under which it is held and enjoyed. ...

FIELD, J., *dissenting*:

I know that the measure, the validity of which I have called in question, was passed in the midst of a gigantic rebellion, when even the bravest hearts sometimes doubted the safety of the Republic, and that the patriotic men who adopted it did so under the conviction that it would increase the ability of the government to obtain funds and supplies, and thus advance the National cause. Were I to be governed by my appreciation of the character of those men, instead of my views of the requirements of the Constitution, I should readily assent to the views of the majority of the court. But, sitting as a judicial officer, and bound to compare every law enacted by Congress with the greater law enacted by the people, and being unable to reconcile the measure in question with that fundamental law, I cannot hesitate to pronounce it as being, in my judgment, unconstitutional and void.

In the discussions which have attended this subject of legal tender there has been at times what seemed to me to be a covert intimation, that opposition to the measure in question was the expression of a spirit not altogether favorable to the cause, in the interest of which that measure was adopted. All such intimations I repel with all the energy I can express. I do not yield to any one in honoring and reverencing the noble and patriotic men who were in the councils of the nation during the terrible struggle with the rebellion. To them belong the greatest of all glories in our history,—that of having saved the Union, and that of having emancipated a race. For these results they will be remembered and honored so long as the English language is spoken or read among men. But I do not admit that a blind approval of every measure which they may have thought essential to put down the rebellion is any evidence of loyalty to the country. The only loyalty which I can admit consists in obedience to the Constitution and laws made in pursuance of it. It is only by obedience that affection and reverence can be shown to a superior having a right to command. So thought our great Master when he said to his disciples: "If ye love me, keep my commandments."

Chapter 7

*"The natural and proper timidity and
delicacy which belongs to the female sex"*

A MOMENT'S DIGRESSION is in order since we are considering the work of Justice Bradley. No little amusement was occasioned in Washington by Bradley's opinion in *Bradwell v. Illinois*. Mrs. Bradwell insisted that she had a constitutional right to practice law under the newly adopted Fourteenth Amendment, since she was a United States citizen, and was entitled to pursue her chosen vocation without discrimination based upon her sex. Read the words of Justice Bradley reflecting the quaint views of another era on women's rights.

BRADWELL v. ILLINOIS

Supreme Court of the United States, 1873, 16 Wallace 130

BRADLEY, J., *concurring*:

The claim that, under the 14th Amendment of the Constitution, which declares that no State shall make or enforce any law which shall abridge the privileges and immunities of citizens of the United States, and the statute law of Illinois, or the common law prevailing in that State, can no longer be set up as a barrier against the right of females to pursue any lawful employment for a livelihood (the practice of law included), assumes that it is one of the privileges and immunities of women as citizens to engage in any and every profession, occupation or employment in civil life.

It certainly cannot be affirmed, as a historical fact, that this has ever been established as one of the fundamental privileges and immunities of the sex. On the contrary, the civil law, as well as nature herself, has always recognized a wide difference in the respective spheres and destinies of man and woman. Man is, or should be, woman's protector and defender. The natural and proper timidity and delicacy which belongs to the female sex evidently unfits it for many of the occupations of civil life. The constitution of the family organization, which is founded in the divine ordinance, as well as in the nature of things, indicates the domestic sphere as that which properly belongs to the domain and functions of womanhood. The harmony, not to say identity, of interests and views which belong or should belong to the family institution, is repugnant to the idea of a woman adopting a distinct and independent career from that of her husband. So firmly fixed was this sentiment in the founders of the common law that it became a maxim of that system of jurisprudence that a woman had no legal existence separate from her husband, who was regarded as her head and representative in the social state; and, notwithstanding some recent modifications of this civil *status,* many of the special rules of law flowing from and dependent upon this cardinal principle still exist in full force in most States. One of these is, that a married woman is incapable, without her husband's consent, of making contracts which shall be binding on her or him. This very incapacity was one circumstance which the Supreme Court of Illinois deemed important in rendering a married woman incompetent fully to perform the duties and trusts that belong to the office of an attorney and counselor.

It is true that many women are unmarried and not affected by any of the duties, complications, and incapacities arising out of the married state but these are exceptions to the general rule. The paramount destiny and mission of woman are to fulfill the noble and benign offices of wife and mother. This is the law of the Creator. And the rules of civil society must be adapted to the general constitution of things, and cannot be based upon exceptional cases.

The humane movements of modern society, which have for their object the multiplication of avenues for woman's advancement, and of occupations adapted to her condition and sex, have my heartiest concurrence. But I am not prepared to say that it is one of her fundamental rights and privileges to be admitted into every office and position, including those which require highly special qualifications and demanding special responsibilities. In the nature of things it is not every citizen of every age, sex, and condition that is qualified for every calling and position. It is the prerogative of the legislator to prescribe regulations founded on nature, reason, and experience for the due admission of qualified persons to professions and callings demanding special skill and confidence. This fairly belongs to the police power of the State; and, in my opinion, in view of the peculiar characteristics, destiny and mission of woman, it is within the province of the Legislature to ordain what offices, positions and callings shall be filled and discharged by men, and shall receive the benefit of those energies and responsibilities, and that decision and firmness which are presumed to predominate in the sterner sex.

For these reasons I think that the laws of Illinois now complained of are not obnoxious to the charge of abridging any of the privileges and immunities of citizens of the United States.

Chapter 8

"An indestructible Union, composed of indestructible States"

"THE CONSTITUTION, in all its provisions, looks to an indestructible Union, composed of indestructible States." With these words, Chief Justice Salmon P. Chase reunited a nation torn by secession and civil war. The case was *Texas v. White*. The state of Texas brought suit in the United States Supreme Court to have certain United States government bonds declared the property of the state, and to prevent the present holders of the bonds from collecting upon them. Texas had owned the bonds before the Civil War. As a means of financing during the war, while Texas was a member of the Confederacy, the bonds were sold. Texas now claimed that the sale was void and the bonds still belonged to the state.

The suit raised two formidable constitutional questions. First, Texas had brought suit directly in the Supreme Court. Under the Constitution, only a state may do this. These were the days of Reconstruction, and Texas had a military government; it did not yet have representatives in the United States Congress. Was Texas a state within the meaning of the Constitution so that it could bring this suit? Second, the bonds had been sold during the Civil War by the duly organized government. If Texas was at that time no longer a state of the Union in legal contemplation, then the sale was perfectly proper. If, on the other hand, Texas was legally a state, then its government during the Confederacy was a usurpation and its action was void. Was Texas legally a state of the Union during the Civil War?

Chief Justice Chase, speaking for the Supreme Court, answered both questions affirmatively. The Court ordered the bonds restored to Texas. The implication of this decision reached far beyond the precise legal question answered: the United States is one nation, and the ties uniting the states cannot be severed by any of them. And there was another implication, less important but still significant: the southern states were enabled to stand as states in the Union, and to assert their rights as states. The days of Reconstruction and Carpetbag Rule were numbered.

Texas v. White was Chief Justice Chase's most outstanding decision. Salmon P. Chase, appointed Taney's successor in 1864, served only slightly over eight years, dying in 1873. Over a longer span he might have been one of the great Chief Justices. When he was appointed he had had no judicial experience, had not even been a practicing lawyer for a number of years. However, he had built a remarkable career as a United States senator from Ohio, governor of Ohio, and then Secretary of the Treasury in Lincoln's cabinet. His appointment to the Court is to Lincoln's great honor. The two men were personally antagonistic because of Chase's imperious manner; yet, convinced that Chase had ability of the highest order, the President suppressed his personal predilections and made the appointment. It is possible that Lincoln was less concerned about his personal distaste for the man than about Chase's burning ambition to be President. But, in tribute to Chase, it can be said that there is no trace of political expediency in his work on the Court. He was the master, not the slave, of his ambition.

Two facets of Chase's term as Chief Justice are especially noteworthy. He presided at the impeachment trial of President Johnson in the Senate. His impartial and nonpolitical conduct in that sordid affair was a model of judiciousness and earned for him the accolades of historians. And particularly exceptional was the fact that he wrote the Court opinion in the first Legal Tender case and dissented in the second case that finally settled the validity of the Legal Tender Acts. As Secretary of the Treasury he had played a principal role in the enactment of the Legal Tender Laws. As Chief Justice he twice asserted their unconstitutionality.

Chase was challenged by the judicial role. And he grew and met the challenge.

TEXAS v. WHITE

Supreme Court of the United States, 1869, 7 Wallace 700

CHASE, C. J.:

The Union of the States never was a purely artificial and arbitrary relation. It began among the Colonies, and grew out of common origin, mutual sympathies, kindred principles, similar interests and geographical relations. It was confirmed and strengthened by the necessities of war, and received definite form, and character, and sanction from the Articles of Confederation. By these the Union was solemnly declared to "be perpetual." And when these articles were found to be inadequate to the exigencies of the country, the Constitution was ordained "to form a more perfect Union." It is difficult to convey the idea of indissoluble unity more clearly than by these words. What can be indissoluble if a perpetual Union, made more perfect, is not?

But the perpetuity and indissolubility of the Union by no means implies the loss of distinct and individual existence, or of the right of self-government by the States. Under the Articles of Confederation each State retained its sovereignty, freedom and independence, and every power, jurisdiction and right not expressly delegated to the United States. Under the Constitution, though the powers of the States were much restricted, still, all powers not delegated to the United States, nor prohibited to the States, are reserved to the States respectively, or to the people. And we have already had occasion to remark at this term, that "the people of each State compose a State, having its own government, and endowed with all the functions essential to separate and independent existence," and that "without the States in union, there could be no such political body as the United States." *Lane Co. v. Oregon.* Not only, therefore, can there be no loss of separate and independent autonomy to the States, through their union under the Constitution, but it may be not unreasonably said that the preservation of the States, and the maintenance of their governments, are as much within the design and care of the Constitution as the preservation of the Union and the maintenance of the National Government. The Constitution, in all its provisions, looks to an indestructible Union, composed of indestructible States.

When, therefore, Texas became one of the United States, she entered into an indissoluble relation. All the obligations of perpetual union, and all the guaranties of republican government in the Union, attached at once to the State. The Act which consummated her admission into the Union was something more than a compact; it was the incorporation of a new member into the political body. And it was final. The union betweeen Texas and the other States was as complete, as perpetual, and as indissoluble as the union between the original States. There was no place for reconsideration, or revocation, except through revolution, or through consent of the States.

Considered, therefore, as transactions under the Constitution, the Ordinance of Secession, adopted by the convention and ratified by a majority of the citizens of Texas, and all the Acts of her Legislature intended to give effect to that ordinance, were absolutely null. They were utterly without operation in law. The obligations of the State as a member of the Union, and of every citizen of the State, as a citizen of the United States, remained perfect and unimpaired. It certainly follows that the State did not cease to be a State, nor her citizens to be citizens of the Union. If this were otherwise, the State must have become foreign, and her citizens foreigners. The war must have ceased to be a war for the suppression of rebellion, and must have become a war for conquest and subjugation.

Our conclusion, therefore, is, that Texas continued to be a State, and a State of the Union, notwithstanding the transactions to which we have referred. And this conclusion, in our judgment, is not in conflict with any act or declaration of any department of the National Government, but entirely in accordance with the whole series of such acts and declarations since the first outbreak of the rebellion. . . .

Chapter 9

"The one pervading purpose"

THE CIVIL WAR, beyond question, had its origin in the slavery issue. But when the issue was joined in battle, much more was at stake. The defection of the southern states converted the war into a struggle for the preservation of the Union, and more specifically for the supremacy of national power over the power of the states. The war over, slavery was ended—and national sovereignty over asserted independence by the states was confirmed. During the war and through the days of Reconstruction the role played by the Supreme Court was predominately one of nationalism. The Union had come to fear the assertion of power by the states, since such an assertion had precipitated the conflict.

The Thirteenth, Fourteenth, and Fifteenth Amendments to the Constitution were adopted in the days of Reconstruction and in the climate of nationalism. The amendments were unquestionably intended, by the Reconstructionists who espoused them, to shift from the states to the national government the power and the obligation to preserve the fundamental constitutional rights of individuals. To take the clearest example, before the passage of the Fourteenth Amendment an individual could assert his freedom of speech in the United States Supreme Court only if that freedom was being impaired by the federal government. If infringement had its origin in a state, the person aggrieved had his only recourse under the state constitution and in the state supreme court. Similarly, all other aspects of individual liberty were under the protection of the states. The only exceptions were federal encroachments upon that liberty, and a few narrow protections contained in the body of the Constitution, such as that provision prohibiting *ex post facto* laws. The Civil War Amendments, particularly the Fourteenth Amendment, were meant to create a national protection of all freedoms as against state laws which impaired them. The Fourteenth Amendment has in large measure accomplished this objective. But, surprisingly, the Supreme Court for years denied it.

The first cases involving the Fourteenth Amendment to reach the Supreme Court were the *Slaughterhouse Cases*. The Reconstruction government of Louisiana had created a monopoly of the slaughtering business in the state. One company was licensed to own and operate all the state's abattoirs. Others who had been in the slaughtering business, and were now barred therefrom, brought suit to have the Louisiana law setting up the monopoly declared unconstitutional.

The Supreme Court placed the stamp of constitutional approval upon the Louisiana slaughterhouse monopoly. This holding, on the facts of the case, is sound constitutional law today. It is well established that states may rigidly control certain businesses in which the public is vitally concerned by making those businesses "public utilities." And this is all Louisiana had done with the slaughtering business.

But the reason the Court gave for its decision was remarkable. The Court in its opinion asserted that the kind of individual right which those who wished to engage in the slaughtering business were asserting was a matter for the state to define. The slaughterers could look only to the state constitution and the state courts to claim their right. This was a flat holding by the Court that the Fourteenth Amendment did not transfer to the national government the protection of individual liberty. Instead, the Court held that the role of the Fourteenth, as well as that of the other Civil War Amendments, was solely to give the Negro the status of citizenship and to protect him from discrimination because of his race.

The decision was close. Four of the nine justices, in dissent, asserted the broad construction of the Fourteenth Amendment which had been the intent of the framers. The following excerpts from the majority opinion by Justice Samuel F. Miller and the dissenting opinion by Justice Noah H. Swayne reveal the marked divergence of the theory. (Summaries of the careers and other opinions of these two justices appear in later pages.)

As we shall see, the rationale of the Court in the *Slaughterhouse Cases* was gradually to be abandoned. The Court was to begin to protect individual rights against state encroachment by finding that the state infringement of those rights was a deprivation of life, liberty, or property without due process of law, forbidden by the Fourteenth Amendment. But for the time being the *Slaughterhouse Cases* marked a major turn in direction: only eight years after the Civil War ended, the "Court of Nationalism and Reconstruction" became the "Court of States' Rights," and remained so for some years to come.

SLAUGHTERHOUSE CASES
Supreme Court of the United States, 1873, 16 Wallace 36

MILLER, J.:

Twelve articles of amendment were added to the Federal Constitution soon after the original organization of the government under it in 1789. Of these all but the last were adopted so soon afterwards as to justify the statement that they were practically contemporaneous with the adoption of the original; and the twelfth, adopted in eighteen hundred and three, was so nearly so as to have become, like all the others, historical and of another age. But within the last eight years three other articles of amendment of vast importance have been added, by the voice of the people, to that now venerable instrument.

The most cursory glance at these articles discloses a unity of purpose, when taken in connection with the history of the times, which cannot fail to have an important bearing on any question of doubt concerning their true meaning. Nor can such doubts, when any reasonably exist, be safely and rationally solved without a reference to that history; for in it is found the occasion and the necessity for recurring again to the great source of power in this country, the people of the States, for additional guaranties of human rights; additional powers to the Federal Government; additional restraints upon those of the States. Fortunately that history is fresh within the memory of us all, and its leading features, as they bear upon the matter before us, free from doubt.

The institution of African slavery, as it existed in about half the States of the Union, and the contests pervading the public mind for many years, between those who desired its curtailment and ultimate extinction and those who desired additional safeguards for its security and perpetuation, culminated in the effort, on the part of most of the States in which slavery existed, to separate from the Federal Government, and to resist its authority. This constituted the war of the rebellion, and whatever auxiliary causes may have contributed to bring about this war, undoubtedly the overshadowing and efficient cause was African slavery.

In that struggle slavery, as a legalized social relation, perished. It perished as a necessity of the bitterness and force of the conflict.... But the war being over, those who had succeeded in re-establishing the authority of the Federal Government were not content to permit this great act of emancipation to rest on the actual results of the contest or the Proclamation of the Executive, both of which might have been questioned in after times, and they determined to place this main and most valuable result in the Constitution of the restored Union as one of its fundamental articles. Hence the 13th article of amendment of that instrument....

The process of restoring to their proper relations with the Federal Government and with the other States those which had sided with the rebellion, undertaken under the Proclamation of President Johnson in 1865, and before the assembling of Congress, developed the fact that, notwithstanding the formal recognition by those States of the abolition of slavery, the condition of the slave race would, without further protection of the Federal Government, be almost as bad as it was before. Among the first Acts of legislation adopted by several of the states in the legislative bodies which claimed to be in their normal relations with the Federal Government, were laws which imposed upon the colored race onerous disabilities and burdens, and curtailed their rights in the pursuit of life, liberty and property, to such an extent that their freedom was of little value, while they had lost the protection which they had received from their former owners from motives both of interest and humanity....

These circumstances, whatever of falsehood or misconception may have been mingled with their presentation, forced upon the statesmen who had conducted the Federal Government in safety through the crisis of the rebellion, and who supposed that by the 13th article of amendment they had secured the result of their labors, the conviction that something more was necessary in the way of constitutional protection to the unfortunate race who had suffered so much. They accordingly passed through Congress the proposition for the 14th Amendment, and they declined to treat as restored to their full participation in the Government of the Union the States which had been in insurrection, until they ratified that article by a formal vote of their legislative bodies. . . .

A few years' experience satisfied the thoughtful men who had been the authors of the other two Amendments that, notwithstanding the restraints of those articles on the States, and the laws passed under the additional powers granted to Congress, these were inadequate for the protection of life, liberty and property, without which freedom to the slave was no boon. They were in all those States denied the right of suffrage. The laws were administered by the white man alone. It was urged that a race of men distinctively marked as was the negro, living in the midst of another and dominant race, could never be fully secured in their person and their property without the right of suffrage.

Hence the 15th Amendment. . . .

We repeat, then, in the light of this recapitulation of events, almost too recent to be called history, but which are familiar to us all; and on the most casual examination of the language of these amendments, no one can fail to be impressed with the one pervading purpose found in them all, lying at the foundation of each, and without which none of them would have been even suggested; we mean the freedom of the slave race, the security and firm establishment of that freedom, and the protection of the newly made freeman and citizen from the oppressions of those who had formerly exercised unlimited dominion over him. . . .

We do not say that no one else but the negro can share in this protection. Both the language and spirit of these articles are to have their fair and just weight in any question of construction. Undoubtedly, while negro slavery alone was in the mind of the Congress which proposed the 13th article, it forbids any other kind of slavery, now or hereafter. If Mexican peonage or the Chinese coolie labor system shall develop slavery of the Mexican or Chinese race within our territory, this Amendment may safely be trusted to make it void. And so, if other rights are assailed by the States which properly and necessarily fall within the protection of these articles, that protection will apply though the party interested may not be of African descent. But what we do say, and what we wish to be understood, is, that in any fair and just construction of any section or phrase of these amendments, it is necessary to look to the purpose which we have said was the pervading spirit of them all, the evil which they were designed to remedy, and the process of continued addition to the Constitution until that purpose was supposed to be accomplished, as far as constitutional law can accomplish it. . . .

In the early history of the organization of the government, its statesmen seem to have divided on the line which should separate the powers of the National Government from those of the state governments, and though this line has never been very well defined in public opinion, such a division has continued from that day to this.

The adoption of the first eleven amendments to the Constitution so soon after the original instrument was accepted, shows a prevailing sense of danger at that time from the federal power. And it cannot be denied that such a jealousy continued to exist with many patriotic men until the breaking out of the late civil war. It was then discovered that the true danger to the perpetuity of the Union was in the capacity of the state organizations to combine and concentrate all the powers of the State, and of contiguous States, for a determined resistance to the General Government.

Unquestionably this has given great force to the argument, and added largely to the number of those who believe in the necessity of a strong national government.

But, however pervading this sentiment, and however it may have contributed to the adoption of the Amendments we have been considering, we do not see in those Amendments any purpose to destroy the main features of the general system. Under the pressure of all the excited feeling growing out of the war, our statesmen have still believed that the existence of the States with powers for domestic and local government, including the regulation of civil rights, the rights of person and of property, was essential to the perfect working of our complex form of government, though they have thought proper to impose additional limitations on the States, and to confer additional power on that of the Nation.

But whatever fluctuations may be seen in the history of public opinion on this subject during the period of our national existence, we think it will be found that this court, so far as its functions required, has always held, with a steady and an even hand, the balance between state and federal power, and we trust that such may continue to be the history of its relation to that subject so long as it shall have duties to perform which demand of it a construction of the Constitution, or of any of its parts.

SWAYNE, J., *dissenting*:

The first eleven Amendments to the Constitution were intended to be checks and limitations upon the government which that instrument called into existence. They had their origin in a spirit of jealousy on the part of the States, which existed when the Constitution was adopted. The first ten were proposed in 1789 by the first Congress at its first session after the organization of the government. The eleventh was proposed in 1794, and the twelfth in 1803. The one last mentioned regulates the mode of electing the President and Vice-President. It neither increased nor diminished the power of the General Government, and may be said in that respect to occupy neutral ground. No further Amendments were made until 1865, a period of more than sixty years. The 13th Amendment was proposed by Congress on the 1st of February, 1865, the fourteenth on the 16th of June, 1866, and the fifteenth on the 27th of February, 1869. These Amendments are a new departure, and mark an important epoch in the constitutional history of the country. They trench directly upon the power of the States, and deeply affect those bodies. They are in this respect, at the opposite pole from the first eleven.

Fairly construed, these Amendments may be said to rise to the dignity of a new Magna Charta. . . .

These Amendments are all consequences of the late civil war. The prejudices and apprehension as to the central government which prevailed when the Constitution was adopted were dispelled by the light of experience. The public mind became satisfied that there was less danger of tyranny in the head than of anarchy and tyranny in the members. . . . [The Amendments] are a bulwark of defense, and can never be made an engine of oppression. The language employed is unqualified in its scope. There is no exception in its terms, and there can be properly none in their application. . . . No distinction is intimated on account of race or color. This court has no authority to interpolate a limitation that is neither expressed nor implied. Our duty is to execute the law, not to make it. The protection provided was not intended to be confined to those of any particular race or class, but to embrace equally all races, classes and conditions of men. It is objected that the power conferred is novel and large. The answer is that the novelty was known and the measure deliberately adopted. The power is beneficent in its nature, and cannot be abused. It is such as should exist in every well ordered system of polity. Where could it be more appropriately lodged than in the hands to which it is confided? It is necessary to enable the government of the Nation to secure to every one within its jurisdiction the rights and privileges enumerated, which, according to the plainest considerations of reason and justice and the fundamental principles of the social compact, all are entitled to enjoy. Without such authority any government claiming to be national is glaringly defective. The construction adopted by the majority of my brethren is, in my judgment, much too narrow. It defeats, by a limitation not anticipated, the intent of those by whom the instrument was framed and of those by whom it was adopted. To the extent of that limitation it turns, as it were, what was meant for bread into a stone. By the Constitution, as it stood before the war, ample protection was given against oppression by the Union, but little was given against wrong and oppression by the States. That want was intended to be supplied by this Amendment. Against the former this court has been called upon more than once to interpose. Authority of the same amplitude was intended to be conferred as to the latter. But this arm of our jurisdiction is, in these cases, stricken down by the judgment just given. Nowhere, than in this court, ought the will of the nation, as thus expressed, to be more liberally construed or more cordially executed. This determination of the majority seems to me to lie far in the other direction.

I earnestly hope that the consequences to follow may prove less serious and far-reaching than the minority fear they will be.

Chapter 10

"No man in this country is so high that he is above the law"

JUSTICE SAMUEL FREEMAN MILLER, of Iowa, the author of the majority opinion in the *Slaughterhouse Cases,* was appointed to the nation's highest tribunal by President Abraham Lincoln in 1862. A self-educated lawyer without prior judicial experience, he was nevertheless a giant on the Court. The most unusual aspect of Miller's career is that he had been a practicing physician for nearly ten years before he turned to the law. He was a man truly gifted, with a robust physique and an incisive, mighty mind. His opinions are strong, clear, and authoritative; when Miller was through, no one could doubt where he stood. He served on the Court for twenty-eight years, during which time he sat with such greats as Field, Bradley, Waite, and Harlan. But for sheer judgeship, Miller towered over them all.

It was Miller's own belief that his greatest opinion was the one he rendered for the Court in *United States v. Lee.* The son of General Robert E. Lee sued to recover the Custis-Lee estate, which had been confiscated during the Civil War by the Union and had been converted into the Arlington National Cemetery—just across the Potomac River from Washington, D. C. The case was exceedingly delicate in nature because it involved bringing suit against an officer of the government carrying out his official functions. It was felt by many that the government should not be subject to such a suit lest private citizens constantly harass and embarrass officials in the carrying out of their appointed tasks. But Miller and the Court refused to countenance this objection; Lee was awarded just compensation for the estate which the government had confiscated.

Miller's powerfully reasoned opinion is twenty-six pages long. Only the conclusion is printed here. These are the ringing words which establish the right of every citizen of the United States to be dealt with justly by his government.

UNITED STATES v. LEE

Supreme Court of the United States, 1882, 106 U. S. 196

MILLER, J.:

It appears that certain military officers, acting under the orders of the President, have seized this estate, and converted one part of it into a military fort and another into a cemetery.

It is not pretended, as the case now stands, that the President had any lawful authority to do this, or that the legislative body could give him any such authority except upon payment of just compensation. The defence stands here solely upon the absolute immunity from judicial inquiry of every one who *asserts* authority from the executive branch of the government, however clear it may be made that the executive possessed no such power. Not only no such power is given, but it is absolutely prohibited, both to the executive and the legislative, to deprive any one of life, liberty, or property without due process of law, or to take private property without just compensation....

No man in this country is so high that he is above the law. No officer of the law may set that law at defiance with impunity. All the officers of the government, from the highest to the lowest, are creatures of the law, and are bound to obey it.

It is the only supreme power in our system of government, and every man who by accepting office participates in its functions is only the more strongly bound to submit to that supremacy, and to observe the limitations which it imposes upon the exercise of the authority which it gives.

Courts of justice are established, not only to decide upon the controverted rights of the citizens as against each other, but also upon rights in controversy between them and the government; and the docket of this court is crowded with controversies of the latter class.

Shall it be said, in the face of all this, and of the acknowledged right of the judiciary to decide in proper cases, statutes which have been passed by both branches of Congress and approved by the President to be unconstitutional, that the courts cannot give a remedy when the citizen has been deprived of his property by force, his estate seized and converted to the use of the government without lawful authority, without process of law, and without compensation, because the President has ordered it and his officers are in possession?

If such be the law of this country, it sanctions a tyranny which has no existence in the monarchies of Europe, nor in any other government which has a just claim to well-regulated liberty and the protection of personal rights.

It cannot be, then, that when, in a suit between two citizens for the ownership of real estate, one of them has established his right to the possession of the property according to all the forms of judicial procedure, and by the verdict of a jury and the judgment of the court, the wrongful possessor can say successfully to the court, Stop here, I hold by order of the President, and the progress of justice must be stayed. That, though the nature of the controversy is one peculiarly appropriate to the judicial function, though the United States is no party to the suit, though one of the three great branches of the government to which by the Constitution this duty has been assigned has declared its judgment after a fair trial, the unsuccessful party can interpose an absolute veto upon that judgment by the production of an order of the Secretary of War, which that officer had no more authority to make than the humblest private citizen.

The evils supposed to grow out of the possible interference of judicial action with the exercise of powers of the government essential to some of its most important operations, will be seen to be small indeed compared to this evil, and much diminished, if they do not wholly disappear, upon a recurrence to a few considerations.

One of these, of no little significance, is, that during the existence of the government for now nearly a century under the present Constitution, with this principle and the practice under it well established, no injury from it has come to that government. During this time at least two wars, so serious as to call into exercise all the powers and all the resources of the government, have been conducted to a successful issue. One of these was a great civil war, such as the world has seldom known, which strained the powers of the national government to their utmost tension. In the course of this war persons hostile to the Union did not hesitate to invoke the powers of the courts for their protection as citizens, in order to cripple the exercise of the authority necessary to put down the rebellion; yet no improper interference with the exercise of that authority was permitted or attempted by the courts.

Another consideration is, that since the United States cannot be made a defendant to a suit concerning its property, and no judgment in any suit against an individual who has possession or control of such property can bind or conclude the government, the government is always at liberty, notwithstanding any such judgment, to avail itself of all the remedies which the law allows to every person, natural or artificial, for the vindication and assertion of its rights. Hence, taking the present case as an illustration, the United States may proceed by a bill in chancery to quiet its title, in aid of which, if a proper case is made, a writ of injunction may be obtained. Or it may bring an action of ejectment, in which, on a direct issue between the United States as plaintiff, and the present plaintiff as defendant, the title of the United States could be judicially determined. Or, if satisfied that its title has been shown to be invalid, and it still desires to use the property, or any part of it, for the purposes to which it is now devoted, it may purchase such property by fair negotiation, or condemn it by a judicial proceeding, in which a just compensation shall be ascertained and paid according to the Constitution....

While by the Constitution the judicial department is recognized as one of the three great branches among which all the powers and functions of the government are distributed, it is inherently the weakest of them all.

Dependent as its courts are for the enforcement of their judgments upon officers appointed by the executive and removable at his pleasure, with no patronage and no control of the purse or the sword, their power and influence rest solely upon the public sense of the necessity for the existence of a tribunal to which all may appeal for the assertion and protection of rights guaranteed by the Constitution and by the laws of the land, and on the confidence reposed in the soundness of their decisions and the purity of their motives.

From such a tribunal no well-founded fear can be entertained of injustice to the government, or of a purpose to obstruct or diminish its just authority.

Chapter 11

"The foundation of a republic is the virtue of its citizens"

ABRAHAM LINCOLN's first appointment to the United States Supreme Court was Justice Noah H. Swayne, of Ohio, who dissented in the *Slaughterhouse Cases*. Swayne was a noted practicing lawyer at the time of his appointment in 1862, but without judicial experience. He must be relegated to that group of justices who were competent but without the flair or force to lift them to the position of particular eminence. He was a confirmed nationalist, hence often a dissenter on a Court which was in a "states' rights" era. Historians view him largely as a lesser antagonist of Justice Miller in the area of commercial and business law. Most of Swayne's opinions were in this field. He espoused the position that the federal courts should make their own "common law" of commercial transactions, rather than follow the law of the states. This simply meant that a federal court should decide commercial cases by its own standards of the proper result rather than follow the decisions of the court of the state where the controversy arose. Swayne prevailed in his time over the regular dissent of Miller. But Miller won out posthumously; in 1938 the Supreme Court overruled the earlier doctrine and directed that henceforth the federal courts follow the state law of the state in which they sit, rather than create their own common law rules of decision.

Swayne's writing at times flashed to the highest pinnacles of eloquence. At other times he was unnecessarily obscure and complicated. At his best, as he was in his dissent in the *Slaughterhouse Cases* and in some paragraphs of *Trist v. Child,* he was the master of the short, lucid, yet easily flowing sentence, approaching in this the sparkling style of Justice Oliver Wendell Holmes of a later time. Admittedly some other portions of the opinion in *Trist v. Child* do not reflect this facile lucidity, but the discounted result is nevertheless a most impressive one. *Trist v. Child* involved the validity of a "lobbying" contract. Swayne held that any lobbying contract which contemplates personal solicitation of the members of Congress, as opposed to regular appearances before legislative committees, is void as contrary to public policy. While the holding is good law and the principle important, note how Swayne's opinion gives them added luster.

TRIST v. CHILD

Supreme Court of the United States, 1874, 21 Wallace 441

SWAYNE, J.:

Was the contract a valid one? It was, on the part of Child, to procure by lobby service, if possible, the passage of a bill providing for the payment of the claim. The aid asked by the younger Child of Trist, which indicated what he considered needful, and doubtless proposed to do and did do himself, is thus vividly pictured in his letter to Trist of the 20th February, 1871. After giving the names of several members of Congress, from whom he had received favorable assurances, he proceeds: "Please write to your friends to write to any member of Congress. Every vote tells, and a simple request may secure a vote, he not caring anything about it. Set every man you know at work. Even if he knows a page, for a page often gets a vote."

In the Roman law it was declared that "a promise made to effect a base purpose, as to commit homicide or sacrilege, is not binding." In our jurisprudence a contract may be illegal and void because it is contrary to a constitution or statute, or inconsistent with sound policy and good morals. Lord Mansfield said: "Many contracts which are not against morality, are still void as being against the maxims of sound policy." ...

Before considering the contract here in question, it may be well, by way of illustration, to advert to some of the cases presenting the subject in other phases, in which the principle has been adversely applied.

Within the condemned category are:

An agreement—to pay for supporting for election a candidate for sheriff; to pay for resigning a public position to make room for another; to pay for not bidding at a sheriff's sale of real property; to pay for not bidding for articles to be sold by the government at auction; to pay for not bidding for a contract to carry the mail on a specified route; to pay a person for his aid and influence in procuring an office, and for not being a candidate himself; to pay for procuring a contract from the government; to pay for procuring signatures to a petition to the governor for a pardon; to sell land to a particular person when the surrogate's order to sell should have been obtained; to pay for suppressing evidence and compounding a felony; to convey and assign a part of what should come from an ancestor by descent, devise, or distribution; to pay for promoting a marriage; to influence the disposition of property by will in a particular way.

The question now before us has been decided in four American cases. They were all ably considered, and in all of them the contract was held to be against public policy, and void. We entertain no doubt that in such cases, as under all other circumstances, an agreement express or implied for purely professional services is valid. Within this category are included, drafting the petition to set forth the claim, attending to the taking of testimony, collecting facts, preparing arguments, and submitting them orally or in writing, to a committee or other proper authority, and other services of like character. All these things are intended to reach only the reason of those sought to be influenced. They rest on the same principle of ethics as professional services rendered in a court of justice, and are no more exceptionable. But such services are separated by a broad line of demarcation from personal solicitation and the other means and appliances which the correspondence shows were resorted to in this case. There is no reason to believe that they involved anything corrupt or different from what is usually practiced by all paid lobbyists in the prosecution of their business.

The foundation of a republic is the virtue of its citizens. They are at once sovereigns and subjects. As the foundation is undermined, the structure is weakened. When it is destroyed, the fabric must fall. Such is the voice of universal history. The theory of our government is, that all public stations are trusts, and that those clothed with them are to be animated in the discharge of their duties solely by considerations of right, justice, and the public good. They are never to descend to a lower plane. But there is a correlative duty resting upon the citizen. In his intercourse with those in authority, whether executive or legislative, touching the performance of their functions, he is bound to exhibit truth, frankness, and integrity. Any departure from the line of rectitude in such cases, is not only bad in morals, but involves a public wrong. No people can have any higher public interest, except the preservation of their liberties, than integrity in the administration of their government in all its departments.

The agreement in the present case was for the sale of the influence and exertions of the lobby agent to bring about the passage of a law for the payment of a private claim, without reference to its merits, by means which, if not corrupt, were illegitimate, and considered in connection with the pecuniary interest of the agent at stake, contrary to the plainest principles of public policy. No one has a right, in such circumstances, to put himself in a position of temptation to do what is regarded as so pernicious in its character. The law forbids the inchoate step, and puts the seal of its reprobation upon the undertaking.

If any of the great corporations of the country were to hire adventurers who make market of themselves in this way, to procure the passage of a general law with a view to the promotion of their private interest, the moral sense of every right-minded man would instinctively denounce the employer and employed as steeped in corruption, and the employment as infamous.

If the instances were numerous, open, and tolerated, they would be regarded as measuring the decay of the public morals and the degeneracy of the times. No prophetic spirit would be needed to foretell the consequences near at hand. The same thing in lesser legislation, if not so prolific of alarming evils, is not less vicious in itself, nor less to be condemned. The vital principle of both is the same. The evils of the latter are of sufficient magnitude to invite the most serious consideration. The prohibition of the law rests upon a solid foundation. A private bill is apt to attract little attention. It involves no great public interest, and usually fails to excite much discussion. Not unfrequently the facts are whispered to those whose duty it is to investigate, vouched for by them, and the passage of the measure is thus secured. If the agent is truthful, and conceals nothing, all is well. If he uses nefarious means with success, the spring-head and the stream of legislation are polluted. To legalize the traffic of such service, would open a door at which fraud and falsehood would not fail to enter and make themselves felt at every accessible point. It would invite their presence and offer them a premium. If the tempted agent be corrupt himself, and disposed to corrupt others, the transition requires but a single step. He has the means in his hands, with every facility and a strong incentive to use them. The widespread suspicion which prevails, and charges openly made and hardly denied, lead to the conclusion that such events are not of rare occurrence. Where the avarice of the agent is inflamed by the hope of a reward contingent upon success, and to be graduated by a percentage upon the amount appropriated, the danger of tampering in its worst form is greatly increased.

It is by reason of these things that the law is as it is upon the subject. It will not allow either party to be led into temptation where the thing to be guarded against is so deleterious to private morals and so injurious to the public welfare. In expressing these views, we follow the lead of reason and authority.

We are aware of no case in English or American jurisprudence like the one here under consideration, where the agreement has not been adjudged to be illegal and void.

We have said that for professional services in this connection a just compensation may be recovered. But where they are blended and confused with those which are forbidden, the whole is a unit and indivisible. That which is bad destroys that which is good, and they perish together. Services of the latter character, gratuitously rendered, are not unlawful. The absence of motive to wrong is the foundation of the sanction. The tendency to mischief, if not wanting, is greatly lessened. The taint lies in the stipulation for pay. Where that exists, it affects fatally, in all its parts, the entire body of the contract. In all such cases, *protior conditio defendentis*. Where there is turpitude, the law will help neither party.

The elder agent in this case is represented to have been a lawyer of ability and high character. The appellee is said to be equally worthy. This can make no difference as to the legal principles we have considered, nor in their application to the case in hand. The law is no respecter of persons.

Chapter 12

"The gradual process of judicial inclusion and exclusion"

ONLY FOUR YEARS after the *Slaughterhouse Cases*, the Supreme Court began to take creeping steps away from the doctrine there enunciated. The change was hesitant and at snail's pace, yet it could be discerned. The Court was beginning to recognize that perhaps, after all, the Fourteenth Amendment did place some aspects of individual rights under the protecting wing of the national government, and especially of the Supreme Court.

It is an instructive exercise in the dynamics of government to see how the Supreme Court gradually and subtly assumed to itself the responsibility of enforcing the rights of the Fourteenth Amendment. The framers had not so intended; the fifth section of the Amendment gave to the Congress the power of enforcement. The Supreme Court knew this; in fact in one case the Court explicitly stated, "It is not said the *judicial power* of the general government shall extend to enforcing the prohibitions and to protecting the rights and immunities guaranteed [in the Fourteenth Amendment]. It is not said that branch of the government shall be authorized to declare void any action of a State in violation of the prohibitions. It is the power of Congress which has been enlarged. Congress is authorized to *enforce* the prohibitions by appropriate legislation." (Justice Strong in *Ex parte Virginia*, 1880, 100 U. S. 339.) Yet, as we shall see, three years later in the *Civil Rights Cases*, the Court sweepingly limited the power of Congress to enforce the Amendment by legislation.

But in the meantime cases continued to come to the Supreme Court based not upon Congressional enforcement legislation but upon the claim that the states had violated the provisions of the Amendment directly. It would have been an act of superhuman restraint for the Court to continue to decline to decide such cases, as it had done in the *Slaughterhouse Cases*. To decline would have been to refuse to assume a great new power offered to the Court for the taking. The Court showed reluctance; the Court was coy; but the Court, being a human institution, in the end acquiesced. The Court assumed the function of enforcing the Fourteenth Amendment—and still assumes it today.

The beginnings of this development are nowhere more clear than in Justice Miller's opinion in *Davidson v. New Orleans*. The case involved the validity of a Louisiana tax assessment. The Court upheld the constitutionality of the assessment, but the tone of Miller's words had changed from the *Slaughterhouse Cases*. True, he expressed concern over the number of suits being brought to the Court claiming violations of "due process of law." But there also is the admission, though reluctant, that perhaps a state could violate the Amendment and the Court would have to enforce it. These are the spring waters of the modern flow of cases in which the Supreme Court enforces the Fourteenth Amendment as a matter of course.

DAVIDSON v. NEW ORLEANS
Supreme Court of the United States, 1878, 96 U. S. 97

MILLER, J.:

The prohibition against depriving the citizen or subject of his life, liberty, or property without due process of law, is not new in the constitutional history of the English race. It is not new in the constitutional history of this country, and it was not new in the Constitution of the United States when it became a part of the fourteenth amendment, in the year 1866.

The equivalent of the phrase "due process of law," according to Lord Coke, is found in the words "law of the land," in the Great Charter, in connection with the writ of *habeas corpus,* the trial by jury, and other guarantees of the rights of the subject against the oppression of the crown. In the series of amendments to the Constitution of the United States, proposed and adopted immediately after the organization of the government, which were dictated by the jealousy of the States as further limitations upon the power of the Federal government, it is found in the fifth, in connection with other guarantees of personal rights of the same character. Among these are protection against prosecutions for crimes, unless sanctioned by a grand jury; against being twice tried for the same offence; against the accused being compelled, in a criminal case, to testify against himself; and against taking private property for public use without just compensation.

Most of these provisions, including the one under consideration, either in terms or in substance, have been embodied in the constitutions of the several States, and in one shape or another have been the subject of judicial construction.

It must be confessed, however, that the constitutional meaning or value of the phrase "due process of law," remains to-day without that satisfactory precision of definition which judicial decisions have given to nearly all the other guarantees of personal rights found in the constitutions of the several States and of the United States.

It is easy to see that when the great barons of England wrung from King John, at the point of the sword, the concession that neither their lives nor their property should be disposed of by the crown, except as provided by the law of the land, they meant by "law of the land" the ancient and customary laws of the English people, or laws enacted by the Parliament of which those barons were a controlling element. It was not in their minds, therefore, to protect themselves against the enactment of laws by the Parliament of England. But when, in the year of grace 1866, there is placed in the Constitution of the United States a declaration that "no State shall deprive any person of life, liberty, or property without due process of law," can a State make anything due process of law which, by its own legislation, it chooses to declare such? To affirm this is to hold that the prohibition of the States is of no avail, or has no application where the invasion of private rights is effected under the forms of State legislation. It seems to us that a statute which declares in terms, and without more, that the full and exclusive title of a described piece of land, which is now in A., shall be and is hereby vested in B., would, if effectual, deprive A. of his property without due process of law, within the meaning of the constitutional provision. . . .

It is not a little remarkable, that while this provision has been in the Constitution of the United States, as a restraint upon the authority of the Federal Government, for nearly a century, and while, during all that time, the manner in which the powers of that government have been exercised has been watched with jealousy, and subjected to the most rigid criticism in all its branches, this special limitation upon its powers has rarely been invoked in the judicial forum or the more enlarged theatre of public discussion. But while it has been a part of the Constitution, as a restraint upon the power of the States, only a very few years, the docket of this court is crowded with cases in which we are asked to hold that State courts and State legislatures have deprived their own citizens of life, liberty, or property without due process of law. There is here abundant evidence that there exists some strange misconception of the scope of this provision as found in the fourteenth amendment. In fact, it would seem, from the character of many of the cases before us, and the arguments made in them, that the clause under consideration is looked upon as a means of bringing to the test of the decision of this court the abstract opinions of every unsuccessful litigant in a State court of the justice of the decision against him, and of the merits of the legislation on which such a decision may be founded. If, therefore, it were possible to define what it is for a State to deprive a person of life, liberty, or property without due process of law, in terms which would cover every exercise of power thus forbidden to the State, and exclude those which are not, no more useful construction could be furnished by this or any other court to any part of the fundamental law.

But, apart from the imminent risk of a failure to give any definition which would be at once perspicuous, comprehensive, and satisfactory, there is wisdom, we think, in the ascertaining of the intent and application of such an important phrase in the Federal Constitution, by the gradual process of judicial inclusion and exclusion, as the cases presented for decision shall require, with the reasoning on which such decisions may be founded. This court is, after an experience of nearly a century, still engaged in defining the obligation of contracts, the regulation of commerce, and other powers conferred on the Federal government, or limitations imposed upon the States. . . .

Chapter 13

"It is State action that is prohibited"

THE POST-CIVIL WAR Congresses had undertaken to enforce civil rights throughout the United States by legislative fiat, under the enabling provisions of Section 5 of the Fourteenth Amendment. To this end they had passed a number of statutes, including the Civil Rights Act of 1875 that made it a criminal offense for any person to engage in racial discrimination upon public conveyances and in public places such as inns, restaurants, and theaters.

In the minds of the Reconstructionists, all of the Civil Rights Acts were clearly within the power of Congress under Section 5 of the Fourteenth Amendment. They conceived of that section as giving the power to define as well as enforce the rights established therein. Their goal, clearly, was to eliminate racial discrimination in every form throughout the United States, and in drafting the Amendment they had set out to accomplish this task.

But the pertinent words in the Fourteenth Amendment are, "nor shall any State deprive any person of life, liberty, or property, without due process of law." The wording indicates that a *state* must deprive the person of civil rights before there is a violation of the Amendment. If this be so, then a deprivation, such as racial discrimination, by a private citizen would not be prohibited. Only state laws or orders of state officials compelling racial discrimination would be constitutionally banned.

When the Civil Rights Act of 1875 was tested in the Supreme Court, it was held unconstitutional. The attempt to punish private citizens operating inns, theaters, restaurants, and conveyances for engaging in racial discrimination was beyond national power. The Court's answer to the broader motives of the Reconstructionists was that no matter what they intended in the passage of the Amendment, the words themselves did not accomplish their objective. The Court fastened upon the wording set forth above and held that infringement of a civil right violated the Constitution only when committed by a state, and not by a private citizen.

The *Civil Rights Cases* state the law as it is today. The national Constitution does not forbid a deprivation of life, liberty, or property by a private citizen; racial discrimination by private citizens is unaffected. All the cases we are cognizant of today are cases in which it is charged that a state is engaging in discrimination by requiring as a matter of law segregation of races in schools, on public transportation, and the like.

As previously mentioned, the net result of this holding was to deny to Congress any power to define the limits of the Fourteenth Amendment, leaving only the power to pass laws enforcing the provisions as defined by the Court. But since the Court could enforce the Amendment without enabling legislation by Congress, the seeming broad congressional power contained in the Amendment was reduced to insignificance. The Civil Rights Act is still on the statute books, but its only role today is to provide for criminal punishment for state and local officials who deprive persons of their constitutional rights.

We have already met Justice Bradley, the author of the majority opinion in the *Civil Rights Cases*. He is the political essayist turned judge; a man of clear thought and lucid expression. His theme that there must be "state action" before there can be a violation of the Fourteenth Amendment is probably his most noted single contribution to our constitutional scheme.

Justice Harlan's dissenting opinion deserves much more than passing mention. While Bradley followed the letter of the Amendment, Harlan sensed its spirit. His forceful and vibrant, though not crisply written, opinion leaves one not quite so sure that "state action" is required by the Amendment's wording. Losers of a contest can be great in defeat; Harlan's opinion is one of the greatest.

Justice John Marshall Harlan, of Kentucky, was appointed to the Court by President Hayes in 1877. By now it should be clear that the lack of significant judicial experience seems to play little or no part in assessing the potentialities of a prospective justice. With only one year's experience as a trial judge, but with eminence as a lawyer in Kentucky, Harlan assumed his Supreme Court judicial tasks at the age of forty-four. He quickly established himself as one of the powers of the Court and held his pre-eminence throughout his career. His opinions fairly shout the conviction and force of the man's personality.

CIVIL RIGHTS CASES

Supreme Court of the United States, 1883, 109 U. S. 3

BRADLEY, J.:

The essence of the law is, not to declare broadly that all persons shall be entitled to the full and equal enjoyment of the accommodations, advantages, facilities, and privileges of inns, public conveyances, and theatres; but that such enjoyment shall not be subject to any conditions applicable only to citizens of a particular race or color, or who had been in a previous condition of servitude. In other words, it is the purpose of the law to declare that, in the enjoyment of the accommodations and privileges of inns, public conveyances, theatres, and other places of public amusement, no distinction shall be made between citizens of different race or color, or between those who have, and those who have not, been slaves. Its effect is to declare, that in all inns, public conveyances, and places of amusement, colored citizens, whether formerly slaves or not, and citizens of other races, shall have the same accommodations and privileges in all inns, public conveyances, and places of amusement as are enjoyed by white citizens; and *vice versa*. The second section makes it a penal offence in any person to deny to any citizen of any race or color, regardless of previous servitude, any of the accommodations or privileges mentioned in the first section. . . .

The first section of the Fourteenth Amendment (which is the one relied on), after declaring who shall be citizens of the United States, and of the several States, is prohibitory in its character, and prohibitory upon the States. It declares that:

"No State shall make or enforce any law which shall abridge the privileges or immunities of citizens of the United States; nor shall any State deprive any person of life, liberty, or property without due process of law; nor deny to any person within its jurisdiction the equal protection of the laws."

It is State action of a particular character that is prohibited. Individual invasion of individual rights is not the subject-matter of the amendment. It has a deeper and broader scope. It nullifies and makes void all State legislation, and State action of every kind, which impairs the privileges and immunities of citizens of the United States, or which injures them in life, liberty or property without due process of law, or which denies to any of them the equal protection of the laws. It not only does this, but, in order that the national will, thus declared, may not be a mere *brutum fulmen*, the last section of the amendment invests Congress with power to enforce it by appropriate legislation. To enforce what? To enforce the prohibition. To adopt appropriate legislation for correcting the effects of such prohibited State laws and State acts, and thus to render them effectually null, void, and innocuous. This is the legislative power conferred upon Congress, and this is the whole of it. It does not invest Congress with power to legislate upon subjects which are within the domain of State legislation; but to provide modes of relief against State legislation, or State action, of the kind referred to. It does not authorize Congress to create a code of municipal law for the regulation of private rights; but to provide modes of redress against the operation of State laws, and the action of State officers executive or judicial, when these are subversive of the fundamental rights specified in the amendment. Positive rights and privileges are undoubtedly secured by the Fourteenth Amendment; but they are secured by way of prohibition against State laws and State proceedings affecting those rights and privileges, and by power given to Congress to legislate for the purpose of carrying such prohibition into effect; and such legislation must necessarily be predicated upon such supposed State laws or State proceedings, and be directed to the correction of their operation and effect. . . .

And so in the present case, until some State law has been passed, or some State action through its officers or agents has been taken, adverse to the rights of citizens sought to be protected by the Fourteenth Amendment, no legislation of the United States under said amendment, nor any proceeding under such legislation, can be called into activity; for the prohibitions of the amendment are against State laws and acts done under State authority. Of course, legislation may, and should be, provided in advance to meet the exigency when it arises; but it should be adapted to the mischief and wrong which the amendment was intended to provide against; and that is, State laws, or State action of some kind, adverse to the rights of the citizen secured by the amendment. Such legislation cannot properly cover the whole domain of rights appertaining to life, liberty, and property, defining them and providing for their vindication. That would be to establish a code of municipal law regulative of all private rights between man and man in society. It would be to make Congress take the place of the State legislatures and to supersede them. It is absurd to affirm that, because the rights of life, liberty, and property (which include all civil rights that men have) are by the amendment sought to be protected against invasion on the part of the State without due process of law, Congress may therefore provide due process of law for their vindication in every case; and that, because the denial by a State to any persons, of the equal protection of the laws, is prohibited by the amendment, therefore Congress may establish laws for their equal protection. In fine, the legislation which Congress is authorized to adopt in this behalf is not general legislation upon the rights of the citizen, but corrective legislation, that is, such as may be necessary and proper for counteracting such laws as the States may adopt or enforce, and which, by the amendment, they are prohibited from making or enforcing, or such acts and proceedings as the States may commit or take, and which, by the amendment, they are prohibited from committing or taking. . . .

If this legislation is appropriate for enforcing the prohibitions of the amendment, it is difficult to see where it is to stop. Why may not Congress with equal show of authority enact a code of laws for the enforcement and vindication of all rights of life, liberty, and property? If it is supposable that the States may deprive persons of life, liberty, and property without due process of law (and the amendment itself does suppose this), why should not Congress proceed at once to prescribe due process of law for the protection of every one of these fundamental rights, in every possible case, as well as to prescribe equal privileges in inns, public conveyances, and theatres? The truth is, that the implication of a power to legislate in this manner is based upon the assumption that if the States are forbidden to legislate or act in a particular way on a particular subject, and power is conferred upon Congress to enforce the prohibition, this gives Congress power to legislate generally upon the subject and not merely power to provide modes of redress against such State legislation or action. The assumption is certainly unsound. It is repugnant to the Tenth Amendment of the Constitution, which declares that powers not delegated to the United States by the Constitution, nor prohibited by it to the States, are reserved to the States respectively or to the people. . . .

Civil rights, such as are guaranteed by the Constitution against State aggression, cannot be impaired by the wrongful acts of individuals, unsupported by State authority in the shape of laws, customs, or judicial or executive proceedings. The wrongful act of an individual, unsupported by any such authority, is simply a private wrong, or a crime of that individual; an invasion of the rights of the injured party, it is true, whether they affect his person, his property, or his reputation; but if not sanctioned in some way by the State, or not done under State authority, his rights remain in full force, and may presumably be vindicated by resort to the laws of the State for redress. An individual cannot deprive a man of his right to vote, to hold property, to buy and sell, to sue in the courts, or to be a witness or a juror; he may, by force or fraud, interfere with the enjoyment of the right in a particular case; he may commit an assault against the person, or commit murder, or use ruffian violence at the polls, or slander the good name of a fellow citizen; but, unless protected in these wrongful acts by some shield of State law or State authority, he cannot destroy or injure the right; he will only render himself amenable to satisfaction or punishment; and amenable therefor to the laws of the State where the wrongful acts are committed. Hence, in all those cases where the Constitution seeks to protect the rights of the citizen against discriminative and unjust laws of the State by prohibiting such laws, it is not individual offences, but abrogation and denial of rights, which it denounces, and for which it clothes the Congress with power to provide a remedy. This abrogation and denial of rights, for which the States alone were or could be responsible, was the great seminal and fundamental wrong which was intended to be remedied. And the remedy to be provided must necessarily be predicated upon that wrong.

It must assume that in the cases provided for, the evil or wrong actually committed rests upon some State law or State authority for its excuse and perpetration. . . .

When a man has emerged from slavery, and by the aid of beneficent legislation has shaken off the inseparable concomitants of that state, there must be some stage in the progress of his elevation when he takes the rank of a mere citizen, and ceases to be the special favorite of the laws, and when his rights as a citizen, or a man, are to be protected in the ordinary modes by which other men's rights are protected. There were thousands of free colored people in this country before the abolition of slavery, enjoying all the essential rights of life, liberty, and property the same as white citizens; yet no one, at that time, thought that it was any invasion of his personal status as a freeman because he was not admitted to all the privileges enjoyed by white citizens, or because he was subjected to discriminations in the enjoyment of accommodations in inns, public conveyances and places of amusement. . . .

HARLAN, J., *dissenting*:

The opinion in these cases proceeds, it seems to me, upon grounds entirely too narrow and artificial. I cannot resist the conclusion that the substance and spirit of the recent amendments of the Constitution have been sacrificed by a subtle and ingenious verbal criticism. "It is not the words of the law but the internal sense of it that makes the law: the letter of the law is the body; the sense and reason of the law is the soul." Constitutional provisions, adopted in the interest of liberty, and for the purpose of securing, through national legislation, if need be, rights inhering in a state of freedom, and belonging to American citizenship, have been so construed as to defeat the ends the people desired to accomplish, which they attempted to accomplish, and which they supposed they had accomplished by changes in their fundamental law. By this I do not mean that the determination of these cases should have been materially controlled by considerations of mere expediency or policy. I mean only, in this form, to express an earnest conviction that the court has departed from the familiar rule requiring, in the interpretation of constitutional provisions, that full effect be given to the intent with which they were adopted. . . .

The opinion of the court proceeds upon the ground that the power of Congress to legislate for the protection of the rights and privileges secured by the Fourteenth Amendment cannot be brought into activity except with the view, and as it may become necessary, to correct and annul State laws and State proceedings in hostility to such rights and privileges. In the absence of State laws or State action adverse to such rights and privileges, the nation may not actively interfere for their protection and security, even against corporations and individuals exercising public or quasi public functions. Such I understand to be the position of my brethren. If the grant to colored citizens of the United States of citizenship in their respective States, imports exemption from race discrimination, in their States, in respect of such civil rights as belong to citizenship, then, to hold that the amendment remits that right to the States for their protection, primarily, and stays the hands of the nation, until it is assailed by State laws or State proceedings, is to adjudge that the amendment, so far from enlarging the powers of Congress—as we have heretofore said it did—not only curtails them, but reverses the policy which the general government has pursued from its very organization. Such an interpretation of the amendment is a denial to Congress of the power, by appropriate legislation, to enforce one of its provisions. In view of the circumstances under which the recent amendments were incorporated into the Constitution, and especially in view of the peculiar character of the new rights they created and secured, it ought not to be presumed that the general government has abdicated its authority, by national legislation, direct and primary in its character, to guard and protect privileges and immunities secured by that instrument. Such an interpretation of the Constitution ought not to be accepted if it be possible to avoid it. Its acceptance would lead to this anomalous result: that whereas, prior to the amendments, Congress, with the sanction of this court, passed the most stringent laws—operating directly and primarily upon States and their officers and agents, as well as upon individuals—in vindication of slavery and the right of the master, it may not now, by legislation of a like primary and direct character, guard, protect, and secure the freedom established, and the most essential right of the citizenship granted, by the constitutional amendments. With all respect for the opinion of others, I insist that the national legislature may, without transcending the limits of the Constitution, do for human liberty and the fundamental rights of American citizenship, what it did, with the sanction of this court, for the protection of slavery and the rights of the masters of fugitive slaves. If fugitive slave laws, providing modes and prescribing penalties, whereby the master could seize and recover his fugitive slave, were legitimate exercises of an implied power to protect and enforce a right recognized by the Constitution, why shall the hands of Congress be tied, so that—under an express power, by appropriate legislation, to enforce a constitutional provision granting citizenship—it may not, by means of direct legislation, bring the whole power of this nation to bear upon States and their officers, and upon such individuals and corporations exercising public functions as assume to abridge, impair, or deny rights confessedly secured by the supreme law of the land? . . .

It is said that any interpretation of the Fourteenth Amendment different from that adopted by the majority of the court, would imply that Congress had authority to enact a municipal code for all the States, covering every matter affecting the life, liberty, and property of the citizens of the several States. Not so. Prior to the adoption of that amendment the constitutions of the several States, without perhaps an exception, secured all *persons* against deprivation of life, liberty, or property, otherwise than by due process of law, and, in some form, recognized the right of all *persons* to the equal protection of the laws. Those rights, therefore, existed before that amendment was proposed or adopted, and were not created by it. If, by reason of that fact, it be assumed that protection in these rights of persons still rests primarily with the States, and that Congress may not interfere except to enforce, by means of corrective legislation, the prohibitions upon State laws or State proceedings inconsistent with those rights, it does not at all follow, that privileges which have been *granted by the nation,* may not be protected by primary legislation upon the part of Congress. The personal rights and immunities recognized in the prohibitive clauses of the amendment were, prior to its adoption, under the protection, primarily, of the States, while rights, created by or derived from the United States, have always been, and, in the nature of things, should always be, primarily, under the protection of the general government. Exemption from race discrimination in respect of the civil rights which are fundamental in *citizenship* in a republican government, is, as we have seen, a new right, created by the nation, with express power in Congress, by legislation, to enforce the constitutional provision from which it is derived. If, in some sense, such race discrimination is, within the letter of the last clause of the first section, a denial of that equal protection of the laws which is secured against State denial to all persons, whether citizens or not, it cannot be possible that a mere prohibition upon such State denial, or a prohibition upon State laws abridging the privileges and immunities of citizens of the United States, takes from the nation the power which it has uniformly exercised of protecting, by direct primary legislation, those privileges and immunities which existed under the Constitution before the adoption of the Fourteenth Amendment, or have been created by that amendment in behalf of those thereby made *citizens* of their respective States.

This construction does not in any degree intrench upon the just rights of the States in the control of their domestic affairs. It simply recognizes the enlarged powers conferred by the recent amendments upon the general government. In the view which I take of those amendments, the States possess the same authority which they have always had to define and regulate the civil rights which their own people, in virtue of State citizenship, may enjoy within their respective limits; except that its exercise is now subject to the expressly granted power of Congress, by legislation, to enforce the provisions of such amendment—a power which necessarily carries with it authority, by national legislation, to protect and secure the privileges and immunities which are created by or are derived from those amendments. That exemption of citizens from discrimination based on race or color, in respect of civil rights, is one of those privileges or immunities, can no longer be deemed an open question in this court.

It was said of the case of *Dred Scott v. Sandford,* that this court, there overruled the action of two generations, virtually inserted a new clause in the Constitution, changed its character, and made a new departure in the workings of the federal government. I may be permitted to say that if the recent amendments are so construed that Congress may not, in its own discretion, and independently of the action or non-action of the State, provide, by legislation of a direct character, for the security of rights created by the national Constitution; if it be adjudged that the obligation to protect the fundamental privileges and immunities granted by the Fourteenth Amendment to citizens residing in the several States, rests primarily, not on the nation, but on the States; if it be further adjudged that individuals and corporations, exercising public functions, or wielding power under public authority, may, without liability to direct primary legislation on the part of Congress, make the race of citizens the ground for denying them that equality of civil rights which the Constitution ordains as a principle of republican citizenship; then, not only the foundations upon which the national supremacy has always securely rested will be materially disturbed, but we shall enter upon an era of constitutional law, when the rights of freedom and American citizenship cannot receive from the nation that efficient protection which heretofore was unhesitatingly accorded to slavery and the rights of the master....

My brethren say, that when a man has emerged from slavery, and by the aid of beneficent legislation has shaken off the inseparable concomitants of that state, there must be some stage in the progress of his elevation when he takes the rank of a mere citizen, and ceases to be the special favorite of the laws, and when his rights as a citizen, or a man, are to be protected in the ordinary modes by which other men's rights are protected. It is, I submit, scarcely just to say that the colored race has been the special favorite of the laws. The statute of 1875, now adjudged to be unconstitutional, is for the benefit of citizens of every race and color. What the nation, through Congress, has sought to accomplish in reference to that race, is—what had already been done in every State of the Union for the white race—to secure and protect rights belonging to them as freemen and citizens; nothing more. It was not deemed enough "To help the feeble up, but to support him after." The one underlying purpose of congressional legislation has been to enable the black race to take the rank of mere citizens. The difficulty has been to compel a recognition of the legal right of the black race to take the rank of citizens, and to secure the enjoyment of privileges belonging, under the law, to them as a component part of the people for whose welfare and happiness government is ordained. At every step, in this direction, the nation has been confronted with class tyranny, which a contemporary English historian says is, of all tyrannies, the most intolerable, "for it is ubiquitous in its operation, and weighs, perhaps, most heavily on those whose obscurity or distance would withdraw them from the notice of a single despot." Today, it is the colored race which is denied, by corporations and individuals wielding public authority, rights fundamental in their freedom and citizenship. At some future time, it may be that some other race will fall under the ban of race discrimination. If the constitutional amendments be enforced, according to the intent with which, as I conceive, they were adopted, there cannot be, in this republic, any class of human beings in practical subjection to another class, with power in the latter to dole out to the former just such privileges as they may choose to grant. The supreme law of the land has decreed that no authority shall be exercised in this country upon the basis of discrimination, in respect of civil rights, against freemen and citizens because of their race, color, or previous condition of servitude. To that decree—for the due enforcement of which, by appropriate legislation, Congress has been invested with express power—every one must bow, whatever may have been, or whatever now are, his individual views as to the wisdom or policy, either of the recent changes in the fundamental law, or of the legislation which has been enacted to give them effect.

For the reasons stated I feel constrained to withhold my assent to the opinion of the court.

Chapter 14

"Their graves shall not remain unknown or unhonored"

THE CIVIL WAR was a devastating and almost mortal illness in the body of the nation. Recuperation was slow; even today evidence of the wastage is seen in our political life. But as with all great disasters, since suffering may generate compassion, serenity, and the love of life, compensations can be found. Out of the Civil War grew compassion for a wronged and abused race, serenity in the knowledge that the Union could endure and remain free, and an honest and patriotic love of American life.

If one stands today and looks across the fields of Gettysburg, it is impossible not to remember Lincoln's words spoken there. Here is a national shrine that has precious intrinsic and extrinsic meaning. When Congress moved to create the shrine by condemning the land for public use, private interests opposed, claiming that condemnation of land to preserve the battlefield was not a "public use" as required in the Fifth Amendment. But the Supreme Court caught the vision of what a national shrine could mean at Gettysburg.

Justice Peckham, speaking for the unanimous Court, held for the government: the creation of the national park at the battlefield was a constitutional exercise of the power of condemnation, since the use was truly public. Justice Rufus W. Peckham, of New York, a Cleveland appointee, was never a particularly outstanding member of the Court, despite his fifteen years of judicial experience on the highest court of the state of New York. He is best known for his uncompromising stand against government control of business, including the setting of maximum hours of labor in *Lochner v. New York* (see page 199), a stand that prevailed for a time but now garners no support in constitutional jurisprudence. But the Gettysburg case was not a matter of economic theory. Peckham's words are without the ageless sublimity of Abraham Lincoln's, yet they still may stand as a moving tribute, on behalf of the Supreme Court, to those embattled men who by their sacrifice snatched from the horror of war a strengthened and united nation.

UNITED STATES v. GETTYSBURG RAILWAY
Supreme Court of the United States, 1896, 160 U. S. 668

PECKHAM, J.:

The really important question to be determined in these proceedings is, whether the use to which the petitioner desires to put the land described in the petitions is of that kind of public use for which the government of the United States is authorized to condemn land. . . .

As just compensation, which is the full value of the property taken, is to be paid, and the amount must be raised by taxation where the land is taken by the government itself, there is not much ground to fear any abuse of the power. The responsibility of Congress to the people will generally, if not always, result in a most conservative exercise of the right. It is quite a different view of the question which courts will take when this power is delegated to a private corporation. In that case the presumption that the intended use for which the corporation proposes to take the land is public, is not so strong as where the government intends to use the land itself.

In examining an act of Congress it has been frequently said that every intendment is in favor of its constitutionality. Such act is presumed to be valid unless its invalidity is plain and apparent; no presumption of invalidity can be indulged in; it must be shown clearly and unmistakably. This rule has been stated and followed by this court from the foundation of the government.

Upon the question whether the proposed use of this land is a public one, we think there can be no well founded doubt. And also, in our judgment, the government has the constitutional power to condemn the land for the proposed use. It is, of course, not necessary that the power of condemnation for such purpose be expressly given by the Constitution. The right to condemn at all is not so given. It results from the powers that are given, and it is implied because of its necessity, or because it is appropriate in exercising those powers. Congress has power to declare war and to create and equip armies and navies. It has the great power of taxation to be exercised for the common defence and general welfare. Having such powers, it has such other and implied ones as are necessary and appropriate for the purpose of carrying the powers expressly given into effect. Any act of Congress which plainly and directly tends to enhance the respect and love of the citizen for the institutions of his country and to quicken and strengthen his motives to defend them, and which is germane to and intimately connected with and appropriate to the exercise of some one or all of the powers granted by Congress must be valid. This proposed use comes within such description. The provision comes within the rule laid down by Chief Justice Marshall, in *McCulloch v. Maryland,* 4 Wheat. 316, 421, in these words: "Let the end be legitimate, let it be within the scope of the Constitution, and all means which are appropriate, which are plainly adapted to that end, which are not prohibited but consist with the letter and spirit of the Constitution, are constitutional."

The end to be attained by this proposed use, as provided for by the act of Congress, is legitimate, and lies within the scope of the Constitution. The battle of Gettysburg was one of the great battles of the world. The numbers contained in the opposing armies were great; the sacrifice of life was dreadful; while the bravery and, indeed, heroism displayed by both the contending forces rank with the highest exhibition of those qualities ever made by man. The importance of the issue involved in the contest of which this great battle was a part cannot be overestimated. The existence of the government itself and the perpetuity of our institutions depended upon the result. Valuable lessons in the art of war can now be learned from an examination of this great battlefield in connection with the history of the events which there took place. Can it be that the government is without power to preserve the land, and properly mark out the various sites upon which this struggle took place? Can it not erect the monuments provided for by these acts of Congress, or even take possession of the field of battle in the name and for the benefit of all the citizens of the country for the present and for the future? Such a use seems necessarily not only a public use, but one so closely connected with the welfare of the republic itself as to be within the powers granted Congress by the Constitution for the purpose of protecting and preserving the whole country. It would be a great object lesson to all who looked upon the land thus cared for, and it would show a proper recognition of the great things that were done there on those momentous days. By this use the government manifests for the benefit of all its citizens the value put upon the services and exertions of the citizen soldiers of that period. Their successful effort to preserve the integrity and solidarity of the great republic of modern times is forcibly impressed upon every one who looks over the field. The value of the sacrifices then freely made is rendered plainer and more durable by the fact that the government of the United States, through its representatives in Congress assembled, appreciates and endeavors to perpetuate it by this most suitable recognition. Such action on the part of Congress touches the heart, and comes home to the imagination of every citizen, and greatly tends to enhance his love and respect for those institutions for which these heroic sacrifices were made. The greater the love of the citizen for the institutions of his country the greater is the dependence properly to be placed upon him for their defence in time of necessity, and it is to such men that the country must look for its safety. The institutions of our country which were saved at this enormous expenditure of life and property ought to and will be regarded with proportionate affection. Here upon this battlefield is one of the proofs of that expenditure, and the sacrifices are rendered more obvious and more easily appreciated when such a battlefield is preserved by the government at the public expense. The right to take land for cemeteries for the burial of the deceased soldiers of the country rests on the same footing and is connected with and springs from the same powers of the Constitution. It seems very clear that the government has the right to bury its own soldiers and to see to it that their graves shall not remain unknown or unhonored.

No narrow view of the character of this proposed use should be taken. Its national character and importance, we think, are plain. The power to condemn for this purpose need not be plainly and unmistakably deduced from any one of the particularly specified powers. Any number of those powers may be grouped together, and an inference from them all may be drawn that the power claimed has been conferred.

It is needless to enlarge upon the subject, and the determination is arrived at without hesitation that the use intended as set forth in the petition in this proceeding is of that public nature which comes within the constitutional power of Congress to provide for by the condemnation of land....

PART THREE

The Supreme Court Enters the Twentieth Century

THREE

Chapter 1

"Neagle fired two shots from his revolver"

THE UNITED STATES SUPREME COURT has its own crime thriller. One would hardly expect that august body to become involved in a violent episode of bloodshed and lust, but it did. True, the Court regularly considers a multitude of criminal cases in which the accused claims that his constitutional rights were infringed upon trial. But in the Neagle case the Court itself became involved in villainous events.

The story begins in California in 1883. A wealthy citizen of Nevada, William Sharon, brought suit in the federal court in California to have a document purporting to be a marriage contract between him and one Sarah Althea Hill declared a forgery and void. Sharon died before the decision, favorable to his suit, was rendered. Whether Miss Hill was an adventuress or a wronged woman is not clear, but it is certain that she was a woman of explosive and violent personality. Her attorney was Judge David S. Terry, a distinguished lawyer and a former chief justice of the California Supreme Court. Judge Terry and Miss Hill became enamored of each other during the course of the trial. With the death of Sharon, they married. The marriage did not tame Miss Hill. Instead, her violent nature became the smitten Judge Terry's also.

The decree of the court, ordering Miss Hill to surrender the purported marriage contract for cancellation, was never carried out. In 1888 the heir of William Sharon brought another suit in the federal court in California to revive the decree. At this hearing two local federal judges sat as members of the three-judge court, with Justice Stephen J. Field of the United States Supreme Court as presiding judge. (As had been customary since the Constitution was adopted, Supreme Court justices then sat for part of each year as trial judges in lower federal courts. In the twentieth century the custom has been generally abandoned, although it is still proper for a justice to serve on a lower federal court if he so desires.) Justice Field had formerly served as an associate justice of the California Supreme Court under Chief Justice Terry and had succeeded to the chief justiceship before his appointment to the United States Supreme Court. Thus were the lives of the major participants in this story of crime interwoven. Let the Supreme Court tell the rest of the story in the words of Justice Miller.

In re Neagle is not, however, just a paper-back story of violence and derring-do; it is a significant case in American constitutional jurisprudence. The Court held that a deputy United States marshal cannot be indicted and tried in a state court for actions taken while carrying out his official tasks. In this, the Court created additional significant underpinning to the doctrine that the national government is supreme and is free of state interference within its constitutionally defined sphere.

Our story, in the best tradition, has its never-solved mystery too. Was Judge Terry armed with a bowie knife? Did Mrs. Terry, when she knelt over her dying husband, remove and secrete a knife so that he would be found unarmed?

IN RE NEAGLE

Supreme Court of the United States, 1890, 135 U. S. 1

MILLER, J.:

The history of the incidents which led to the tragic event of the killing of Terry by the prisoner Neagle had its origin in a suit brought by William Sharon of Nevada, in the Circuit Court of the United States for the District of California, against Sarah Althea Hill, alleged to be a citizen of

California, for the purpose of obtaining a decree adjudging a certain instrument in writing, possessed and exhibited by her, purporting to be a declaration of marriage between them, under the code of California, to be a forgery, and to have it set aside and annulled. This suit, which was commenced October 3, 1883, was finally heard before Judge Sawyer, the Circuit Judge for that circuit, and Judge Deady, United States District Judge for Oregon, who had been duly appointed to assist in holding the Circuit Court for the District of California. The hearing was on September 29, 1885, and on the 15th of January, 1886, a decree was rendered granting the prayer of the bill. In that decree it was declared that the instrument purporting to be a declaration of marriage, set out and described in the bill of complaint, "Was not signed or executed at any time by William Sharon, the complainant; that it is not genuine; that it is false, counterfeited, fabricated, forged, and fraudulent, and as such, is utterly null and void. And it is further ordered and decreed that the respondent, Sarah Althea Hill, deliver up and deposit with the clerk of the court said instrument, to be endorsed 'cancelled,' and that the clerk write across it 'cancelled' and sign his name and affix his seal thereto."

The rendition of this decree was accompanied by two opinions, the principal one being written by Judge Deady and a concurring one by Judge Sawyer. They were very full in their statement of the fraud and forgery practised by Miss Hill, and stated that it was also accompanied by perjury. And inasmuch as Mr. Sharon had died between the hearing of the argument of the case on the 29th of September, 1885, and the time of rendering this decision, January 15, 1886, an order was made setting forth that fact, and declaring that the decree was entered as of the date of the hearing, *nunc pro tunc*.

Nothing was done under this decree. The defendant, Sarah Althea Hill, did not deliver up the instrument to the clerk to be cancelled, but she continued to insist upon its use in the state court. Under these circumstances, Frederick W. Sharon, as the executor of the will of his father, William Sharon, filed in the Circuit Court for the Northern District of California, on March 12, 1888, a bill of revivor, stating the circumstances of the decree, the death of his father, and that the decree had not been performed; alleging also the intermarriage of Miss Hill with David S. Terry, of the city of Stockton in California, and making the said Terry and wife parties to this bill of revivor. The defendants both demurred and answered resisting the prayer of the plaintiff and denying that the petitioner was entitled to any relief.

This case was argued in the Circuit Court before Field, Circuit Justice, Sawyer, Circuit Judge, and Sabin, District Judge. While the matter was held under advisement, Judge Sawyer, on returning from Los Angeles, in the Southern District of California, where he had been holding court, found himself on the train as it left Fresno, which is understood to have been the residence of Terry and wife, in a car in which he noticed that Mr. and Mrs. Terry were in a section behind him, on the same side. On this trip from Fresno to San Francisco, Mrs. Terry grossly insulted Judge Sawyer, and had her husband change seats so as to sit directly in front of the Judge, while she passed him with insolent remarks, and pulled his hair with a vicious jerk, and then, in an excited manner, taking her seat by her husband's side, said: "I will give him a taste of what he will get by and by. Let him render this decision if he dares,"—the decision being the one already mentioned, then under advisement. Terry then made some remark about too many witnesses being in the car, adding that "The best thing to do with him would be to take him out into the bay and drown him." These incidents were witnessed by two gentlemen who knew all the parties, and whose testimony is found in the record before us.

This was August 14, 1888. On the 3d of September, the court rendered its decision granting the prayer of the bill of revivor in the name of Frederick W. Sharon and against Sarah Althea Terry and her husband, David S. Terry. The opinion was delivered by Mr. Justice Field, and during its delivery a scene of great violence occurred in the court-room. It appears that shortly before the court opened on that day, both the defendants in the case came into the court-room, and took seats within the bar at the table next the clerk's desk, and almost immediately in front of the judges. Besides Mr. Justice Field there were present on the bench Judge Sawyer, and Judge Sabin of the District Court of the United States for the District of Nevada. The defendants had denied the jurisdiction of the court originally to render the decree sought to be revived, and the opinion of the court necessarily discussed this question without reaching the merits of the controversy. When allusion was made to this question Mrs. Terry rose from her seat, and addressing the justice who was delivering the opinion, asked in an excited manner whether he was going to order her to give up the marriage contract to be cancelled. Mr. Justice Field said: "Be seated, madam." She repeated the question, and was again told to be seated. She then said in a very excited and violent manner, that Justice Field had been bought, and wanted to know the price he had sold himself for; that he had got Newland's money for it, and everybody knew that he had got it, or words to that effect. Mr. Justice Field then directed the marshal to remove her from the court-room. She asserted that she would not go from the room, and that no one could take her from it.

Marshal Franks proceeded to carry out the order of the court by attempting to compel her to leave, when Terry, her husband, rose from his seat under great excitement, exclaiming that no man living should touch his wife, and struck the marshal a blow in his face so violent as to knock out a tooth. He then unbuttoned his coat, thrust his hand under his vest, apparently for the purpose of drawing a bowie-knife, when he was seized by persons present and forced down on his back. In the meantime Mrs. Terry was removed from the court-room by the marshal, and Terry was allowed to rise and was accompanied by officers to the door leading to the marshal's office. As he was about leaving the room, or immediately after being out of it, he succeeded in drawing a bowie-knife, when his arms were seized by a deputy marshal and others present to prevent him from using it, and they were able to wrench it from him only after a severe struggle. The most prominent person engaged in wresting the knife from Terry was Neagle, the prisoner now in court.

For this conduct both Terry and his wife were sentenced by the court to imprisonment for contempt, Mrs. Terry for one month and Terry for six months, and these sentences were immediately carried into effect. Both the judgment of the court on the petition for the revival of the decree in the case of Sharon against Hill and the judgment of the Circuit Court imprisoning Terry and wife for contempt have been brought to this court for review, and in both cases the judgments have been affirmed. The report of the cases may be found in *Ex parte Terry,* 128 U. S. 289, and *Terry v. Sharon,* 131 U. S. 40.

Terry and Mrs. Terry were separately indicted by the grand jury of the Circuit Court of the United States during the same term for their part in these transactions, and the cases were pending in said court at the time of Terry's death. It also appears that Mrs. Terry, during her part of this altercation in the court-room, was making efforts to open a small satchel which she had with her, but through her excitement she failed. This satchel, which was taken from her, was found to have in it a revolving pistol.

From that time until his death the denunciations by Terry and his wife of Mr. Justice Field were open, frequent, and of the most vindictive and malevolent character. While being transported from San Francisco to Alameda, where they were imprisoned, Mrs. Terry repeated a number of times that she would kill both Judge Field and Judge Sawyer. Terry, who was present, said nothing to restrain her, but added that *he* was not through with Judge Field yet; and, while in jail at Alemeda, Terry said that after he got out of jail he would horsewhip Judge Field; and that he did not believe he would ever return to California, but this earth was not large enough to keep him from finding Judge Field and horsewhipping him; and, in reply to a remark that this would be a dangerous thing to do, and that Judge Field would resent it, he said: "If Judge Field resents it I will kill him." And while in jail Mrs. Terry exhibited to a witness Terry's knife, at which he laughed, and said "Yes, I always carry that," and made a remark about judges and marshals that "they were all a lot of cowardly curs," and he would "see some of them in their graves yet." Mrs. Terry also said that she expected to kill Judge Field some day.

Perhaps the clearest expression of Terry's feelings and intentions in the matter was in a conversation with Mr. Thomas T. Williams, editor of one of the daily newspapers of California. This interview was brought about by a message from Terry requesting Williams to call and see him. In speaking of the occurrences in the court, he said that Justice Field had put a lie in the record about him, and when he met Field he would have to take that back, "and if he did not take it back and apologize for having lied about him, he would slap his face or pull his nose." "I said to him," said the witness, " 'Judge Terry, would not that be a dangerous thing to do? Justice Field is not a man who would permit any one to put a deadly insult upon him like that.' He said, 'Oh, Field won't fight.' I said, 'Well, Judge, I have found nearly all men will fight; nearly every man will fight when there is occasion for it, and Judge Field has had a character in this State of having the courage of his convictions, and being a brave man.' At the conclusion of that branch of the conversation, I said to him, 'Well, Judge Field is not your physical equal, and if any trouble should occur he would be very likely to use a weapon.' He said, 'Well, that's as good a thing as I want to get.' The whole impression conveyed to me by this conversation was, that he felt he had some cause of grievance against Judge Field; that he hoped they might meet, that he might have an opportunity to force a quarrel upon him, and he would get him into a fight." Mr. Williams says that after the return of Justice Field to California in the spring or summer of 1889, he had other conversations with Terry, in which the same vindictive feelings of hatred were manifested and expressed by him.

It is useless to go over the testimony on this subject more particularly. It is sufficient to say that the evidence is abundant that both Terry and wife contemplated some attack upon Judge Field during his official visit to California in the summer of 1889, which they intended should result in his death. Many of these matters were published in the newspapers, and the press of California was filled with conjectures of a probable attack by Terry on Justice Field, as soon as it became known that he was going to attend the Circuit Court in that year.

So much impressed were the friends of Judge Field, and of public justice, both in California and in Washington, with the fear that he would fall a sacrifice to the resentment of Terry and his wife, that application was made to the Attorney General of the United States suggesting the propriety of his furnishing some protection to the judge while in California. This resulted in a correspondence between the Attorney General of the United States, the District Attorney, and the marshal of the Northern District of California on that subject....

The result of this correspondence was that Marshal Franks appointed Mr. Neagle a deputy marshal for the Northern District of California, and gave him special instructions to attend upon Judge Field both in court and while going from one court to another, and protect him from any assault that might be attempted upon him by Terry and wife. Accordingly, when Judge Field went from San Francisco to Los Angeles to hold the Circuit Court of the United States at that place, Mr. Neagle accompanied him, remained with him for the few days that he was engaged in the business of that court, and returned with him to San Francisco.

It appears from the uncontradicted evidence in the case that while the sleeping car, in which were Justice Field and Mr. Neagle, stopped a moment in the early morning at Fresno, Terry and wife got on the train. The fact that they were on the train became known to Neagle, and he held a conversation with the conductor as to what peace officers could be found at Lathrop, where the train stopped for breakfast, and the conductor was requested to telegraph to the proper officers of that place to have a constable or some peace officer on the ground when the train should arrive, anticipating that there might be violence attempted by Terry upon Judge Field. It is sufficient to say that this resulted in no available aid to assist in keeping the peace. When the train arrived, Neagle informed Judge Field of the presence of Terry on the train, and advised him to remain and take his breakfast in the car. This the Judge refused to do, and he and Neagle got out of the car and went into the dining-room, and took seats beside each other in the place assigned them by the person in charge of the breakfast-room, and very shortly after this Terry and wife came into the room; and Mrs. Terry, recognizing Judge Field, turned and left in great haste, while Terry passed beyond where Judge Field and Neagle were and took his seat at another table. It was afterwards ascertained that Mrs. Terry went to the car, and took from it a satchel in which was a revolver. Before she returned to the eating-room, Terry arose from his seat, and, passing around the table in such a way as brought him behind Judge Field, who did not see him or notice him, came up where he was sitting with his feet under the table, and struck him a blow on the side of his face, which was repeated on the other side. He also had his arm drawn back and his fist doubled up, apparently to strike a third blow, when Neagle, who had been observing him all this time, arose from his seat with his revolver in his hand, and in a very loud voice shouted out: "Stop! Stop! I am an officer!" Upon this Terry turned his attention to Neagle, and, as Neagle testifies, seemed to recognize him, and immediately turned his hand to thrust it in his bosom, as Neagle felt sure, with the purpose of drawing a bowie-knife. At this instant Neagle fired two shots from his revolver into the body of Terry, who immediately sank down and died in a few minutes.

Mrs. Terry entered the room with the satchel in her hand just after Terry sank to the floor. She rushed up to the place where he was, threw herself upon his body, made loud exclamations and moans, and commenced inviting the spectators to avenge her wrong upon Field and Neagle. She appeared to be carried away by passion, and in a very earnest manner charged that Field and Neagle had murdered her husband intentionally, and shortly afterwards she appealed to the persons present to examine the body of Terry to see that he had no weapons. This she did once or twice. The satchel which she had, being taken from her, was found to contain a revolver.

These are the material circumstances produced in evidence before the Circuit Court on the hearing of this *habeas corpus* case. It is but a short sketch of a history which is given in over five hundred pages in the record, but we think it is sufficient to enable us to apply the law of the case to the question before us. Without a more minute discussion of this testimony, it produces upon us the conviction of a settled purpose on the part of Terry and his wife, amounting to a conspiracy, to murder Justice Field. And we are quite sure that if Neagle had been merely a brother or a friend of Judge Field, travelling with him, and aware of all the previous relations of Terry to the Judge,—as he was,—of his bitter animosity, his declared purpose to have revenge even to the point of killing him, he would have been justified in what he did in defence of Mr. Justice Field's life, and possibly of his own.

But such a justification would be a proper subject for consideration on a trial of the case for murder in the courts of the State of California, and there exists no authority in the courts of the United States to discharge the prisoner while held in custody by the State authorities for this offence, unless there be found in aid of the defence of the prisoner some element of power and authority asserted under the government of the United States.

This element is said to be found in the facts that Mr. Justice Field, when attacked, was in the immediate discharge of his duty as judge of the Circuit Courts of the United States within California; that the assault upon him grew out of the animosity of Terry and wife, arising out of the previous discharge of his duty as circuit justice in the case for which they were committed for contempt of court; and that the deputy marshal of the United States, who killed Terry in defence of Field's life, was charged with a duty under the law of the United States to protect Field from the violence which Terry was inflicting, and which was intended to lead to Field's death.

To the inquiry whether this proposition is sustained by law and the facts which we have recited, we now address ourselves.

Mr. Justice Field was a member of the Supreme Court of the United States, and had been a member of that court for over a quarter of a century, during which he had become venerable for his age and for his long and valuable service in that court. The business of the Supreme Court has become so exacting that for many years past the justices of it have been compelled to remain for the larger part of the year in Washington City, from whatever part of the country they may have been appointed. The term for each year, including the necessary travel and preparations to attend at its beginning, has generally lasted from eight to nine months.

But the justices of this court have imposed upon them other duties, the most important of which arise out of the fact that they are also judges of the Circuit Courts of the United States....

Justice Field had not only left Washington and travelled the three thousand miles or more which were necessary to reach his circuit, but he had entered upon the duties of that circuit, had held the court at San Francisco for some time; and, taking a short leave of that court, had gone down to Los Angeles, another place where a court was to be held, and sat as a judge there for several days, hearing cases and rendering decisions. It was in the necessary act of returning from Los Angeles to San Francisco, by the usual mode of travel between the two places, where his court was still in session, and where he was required to be, that he was assaulted by Terry in the manner which we have already described....

We have no doubt that Mr. Justice Field when attacked by Terry was engaged in the discharge of his duties as Circuit Justice of the Ninth Circuit, and was entitled to all the protection under those circumstances which the law could give him.

It is urged, however, that there exists no statute authorizing any such protection as that which Neagle was instructed to give Judge Field in the present case, and indeed no protection whatever against a vindictive or malicious assault growing out of the faithful discharge of his official duties....

In the view we take of the Constitution of the United States, any obligation fairly and properly inferrable from that instrument or any duty of the marshal to be derived from the general scope of his duties under the laws of the United States, is "a law" within the meaning of this phrase. It would be a great reproach to the system of government of the United States, declared to be within its sphere sovereign and supreme, if there is to be found within the domain of its powers no means of protecting the judges, in the conscientious and faithful discharge of their duties, from the malice and hatred of those upon whom their judgments may operate unfavorably.

It has in modern times become apparent that the physical health of the community is more efficiently promoted by hygienic and preventive means, than by the skill which is applied to the cure of disease after it has become fully developed. So also the law, which is intended to prevent crime, in its general spread among the community, by regulations, police organization, and otherwise, which are adapted for the protection of the lives and property of citizens, for the dispersion of mobs, for the arrest of thieves and assassins, for the watch which is kept over the community, as well as over this class of people, is more efficient than punishment of crimes after they have been committed.

If a person in the situation of Judge Field could have no other guarantee of his personal safety, while engaged in the conscientious discharge of a disagreeable duty, than the fact that if he was murdered his murderer would be subject to the laws of a State and by those laws could be punished, the security would be very insufficient. The plan which Terry and wife had in mind of insulting him and assaulting him and drawing him into a defensive physical contest, in the course of which they would slay him, shows the little value of such remedies. We do not believe that the government of the United States is thus inefficient, or that its Constitution and laws have left the high officers of the government so defenceless and unprotected....

That there is a peace of the United States; that a man assaulting a judge of the United States while in the discharge of his duties violates that peace; that in such case the marshal of the United States stands in the same relation to the peace of the United States which the sheriff of the county does to the peace of the State of California; are questions too clear to need argument to prove them. That it would be the duty of a sheriff, if one had been present at this assault by Terry upon Judge Field, to prevent this breach of the peace, to prevent this assault, to prevent the murder which was contemplated by it, cannot be doubted. And if, in performing this duty, it became necessary for the protection of Judge Field, or of himself, to kill Terry, in a case where, like this, it was evidently a question of the choice of who should be killed, the assailant and violator of the law and disturber of the peace, or the unoffending man who was in his power, there can be no question of the authority of the sheriff to have killed Terry. So the marshal of the United States, charged with the duty of protecting and guarding the judge of the United States court against this special assault upon his person and his life, being present at the critical moment, when prompt action was necessary, found it to be his duty, a duty which he had no liberty to refuse to perform, to take the steps which resulted in Terry's death. . . .

But all these questions being conceded, it is urged against the relief sought by this writ of *habeas corpus,* that the question of the guilt of the prisoner of the crime of murder is a question to be determined by the laws of California, and to be decided by its courts, and that there exists no power in the government of the United States to take away the prisoner from the custody of the proper authorities of the State of California and carry him before a judge of the court of the United States, and release him without a trial by jury according to the laws of the State of California. . . .

To the objection made in argument, that the prisoner is discharged by this writ from the power of the state court to try him for the whole offence, the reply is, that if the prisoner is held in the state court to answer for an act which he was authorized to do by the law of the United States, which it was his duty to do as marshal of the United States, and if in doing that act he did no more than what was necessary and proper for him to do, he *cannot* be guilty of a crime under the law of the State of California. When these things are shown, it is established that he is innocent of any crime against the laws of the State, or of any other authority whatever. There is no occasion for any further trial in the state court, or in any court. . . .

Chapter 2

"The settled law of income taxation"

THE AMERICAN Industrial Revolution took place in the latter half of the nineteenth century. These were the days of the "robber barons." Business monopoly reached full flower—and then the reaction set in. The people began to feel the necessity of controlling the economic power lodged in private hands. The Grange and Populist movements became significant political factors. The Democratic Party of Cleveland became the Democratic Party of Bryan.

This ground swell of popular opinion against the ruling "God of Money" began to be reflected in laws passed to curb unrestrained business practices. The Sherman Antitrust Act was passed in 1890. The Interstate Commerce Commission was created to control railroads. State governments were also active in passing similar regulatory measures under their "police power," including laws limiting the maximum hours of labor. The federal government levied an income tax. Although the rates were laughably small by today's standards, they were, nevertheless, progressive; the higher the income, the heavier the tax rate.

Cases challenging the constitutionality of these various governmental measures came into a Supreme Court thoroughly imbued with the laissez-faire economic philosophy—business must be free of governmental fetters. The Court set about the task of building into the Constitution this economic theory. The fact that doing so meant overruling constitutional doctrines that had been accepted ever since the Union was formed did not deter.

The theme of the Court was "freedom of contract." This meant that business was to be free to make any kind of contracts desired, without governmental interference—a contract to fix prices and monopolize an industry, or a contract to employ workmen for seventy hours a week. The only difficulty was that there is no provision in the Constitution referring to "freedom of contract." But the Court was ingenious. It held that to interfere with "freedom of contract" was a "deprivation of property without due process of law." With this step, interference with freedom of contract became a violation of the Fifth and Fourteenth Amendments.

In case after case, the Court at the turn of the century struck down both state and federal attempts to control business. We will not give much attention to these cases because they, having overruled past authority, have been in turn overruled in more recent times. Reasonable government restrictions upon the freedom to contract are the accepted pattern of today. These restrictions are called exercises of the "police power."

One case particularly indicative of the Court at this period was the suit involving the validity of the federal income tax. The Constitution requires that all *direct* taxes levied by the federal government must be apportioned according to population. This means that any direct tax of the federal government would have to be levied in precisely the same amount on every man, woman, and child in the United States. *Indirect* taxes, on the other hand, are not subject to this limitation; the Constitution only requires that they have geographical uniformity—that one state or region of the nation not be taxed at a higher rate than another.

The Court was faced with having to decide whether the income tax was a direct or indirect tax within the meaning of the Constitution. If indirect, the tax was valid, but if direct, it was clearly void because it was not apportioned on a population basis. The federal government had levied income taxes before, the most conspicuous instance being the tax levied during the Civil War. It had been accepted ever since the nation was formed that the income tax was an indirect tax and that the only direct taxes were those levied on persons or property as such—poll taxes or property taxes.

The income tax was held by the Court to be a direct tax and therefore unconstitutional. We shall not consider the lengthy, involved, and tortuous opinion of the Court since, as everyone knows, it was overruled by the people with the passage of the Sixteenth Amendment, finally ratified in 1913. The opinion was written by Chief Justice Melville W. Fuller, a delightful and winsome man, who is generally considered, nevertheless, to be the weakest judge ever to hold the position of Chief Justice.

We use here excerpts from the dissenting opinion of Justice Edward D. White, of Louisiana, a Cleveland appointee, as was Fuller. White later was appointed Chief Justice by President Taft, the first associate justice to be elevated to that position (Justice Harlan F. Stone was similarly elevated by President Franklin Roosevelt in 1941). White was a United States Senator at the time of his appointment to the Court. A genial and modest man, he was a highly popular figure throughout his judicial tenure. It is almost impossible to place his constitutional theories consistently. In the struggle within the Court between the laissez-faire philosophy and governmental regulation, White vacillated from side to side. Though not truly great, he was a sound and successful Chief Justice. His opinion in the income tax case is of particular interest because of the skillful and tactful way he admonishes the majority justices for their failure to sense the significance of what they were doing.

POLLOCK v. FARMERS' LOAN AND TRUST CO.

Supreme Court of the United States, 1895, 157 U. S. 429

WHITE, J., *dissenting*:

My brief judicial experience has convinced me that the custom of filing long dissenting opinions is one "more honored in the breach than in the observance." The only purpose which an elaborate dissent can accomplish, if any, is to weaken the effect of the opinion of the majority, and thus engender want of confidence in the conclusions of courts of last resort. This consideration would impel me to content myself with simply recording my dissent in the present case, were it not for the fact that I consider that the result of the opinion of the court just announced is to overthrow a long and consistent line of decisions, and to deny to the legislative department of the government the possession of a power conceded to it by universal consensus for one hundred years, and which has been recognized by repeated adjudications of this court. . . .

The facts . . . are briefly these: At the very birth of the government a contention arose as to the meaning of the word "direct." The controversy was determined by the legislative and executive departments of the government. Their action came to this court for review, and it was approved. Every judge of this court who expressed an opinion, made use of language which clearly showed that he thought the word "direct" in the Constitution applied only to capitation taxes and taxes directly on land. Thereafter the construction thus given was accepted everywhere as definitive. The matter came again and again to this court, and in every case the original ruling was adhered to. The suggestions made in the *Hylton* case were adopted here, and, in the last case here decided, reviewing all the others, this court said that direct taxes within the meaning of the Constitution were only taxes on land and capitation taxes. And now, after a hundred years, after long-continued action by other departments of the government, and after repeated adjudications of this court, this interpretation is overthrown, and the Congress is declared not to have a power of taxation which may at some time, as it has in the past, prove necessary to the very existence of the government. By what process of reasoning is this to be done? By resort to theories, in order to construe the word "direct" in its economic sense, instead of in accordance with its meaning in the Constitution, when the very result of the history which I have thus briefly recounted is to show that the economic construction of the word was repudiated by the framers themselves, and has been time and time again rejected by this court; by a resort to the language of the framers and a review of their opinions, although the facts plainly show that they themselves settled the question which the court now virtually unsettles. In view of all that has taken place and of the many decisions of this court, the matter at issue here ought to be regarded as closed forever.

The injustice and harm which must always result from overthrowing a long and settled practice sanctioned by the decisions of this court, could not be better illustrated than by the example which this case affords. Under the income tax laws which prevailed in the past for many years, and which covered every conceivable source of income, rentals from real estate, and everything else, vast sums were collected from the people of the United States. The decision here rendered announces that those sums were wrongfully taken, and thereby, it seems to me, creates a claim in equity and good conscience against the government for an enormous amount of money. Thus, from the change of view by this court, it happens that an act of Congress, passed for the purpose of raising revenue, in strict conformity with the practice of the government from the earliest time and in accordance with the oft-repeated decisions of this court, furnishes the occasion for creating a claim against the government for hundreds of millions of dollars; I say, creating a claim, because if the government be in good conscience bound to refund that which has been taken from the citizen in violation of the Constitution, although the technical right may have disappeared by lapse of time, or because the decisions of this court have misled the citizen to his grievous injury, the equity endures, and will present itself to the conscience of the government. This consequence shows how necessary it is that the court should not overthrow its past decisions. . . .

My inability to agree with the court in the conclusions which it has just expressed causes me much regret. Great as is my respect for any view by it announced, I cannot resist the conviction that its opinion and decree in this case virtually annuls its previous decisions in regard to the powers of Congress on the subject of taxation, and is therefore fraught with danger to the court, to each and every citizen, and to the republic. The conservation and orderly development of our institutions rests on our acceptance of the results of the past, and their use as lights to guide our steps in the future. Teach the lesson that settled principles may be overthrown at any time, and confusion and turmoil must ultimately result. In the discharge of its function of interpreting the Constitution, this court exercises an august power. It sits removed from the contentions of political parties and the animosities of factions. It seems to me that the accomplishment of its lofty mission can only be secured by the stability of its teachings and the sanctity which surrounds them. If the permanency of its conclusions is to depend upon the personal opinions of those who, from time to time, may make up its membership, it will inevitably become a theatre of political strife, and its action will be without coherence or consistency. There is no great principle of our constitutional law, such as the nature and extent of the commerce power, or the currency power, or other powers of the Federal government, which has not been ultimately defined by the adjudications of this court after long and earnest struggle. If we are to go back to the original sources of our political system, or are to appeal to the writings of the economists in order to unsettle all these great principles, everything is lost and nothing saved to the people. The rights of every individual are guaranteed by the safeguards which have been thrown around them by our adjudications. If these are to be assailed and overthrown, as is the settled law of income taxation by this opinion, as I understand it, the rights of property, so far as the Federal Constitution is concerned, are of little worth. My strong convictions forbid that I take part in a conclusion which seems to me so full of peril to the country. I am unwilling to do so, without reference to the question of what my personal opinion upon the subject might be if the question were a new one, and was thus unaffected by the action of the framers, the history of the government, and the long line of decisions by this court. The wisdom of our forefathers in adopting a written Constitution has often been impeached upon the theory that the interpretation of a written instrument did not afford as complete protection to liberty as would be enjoyed under a Constitution made up of the traditions of a free people. Writing, it has been said, does not insure greater stability than tradition does, while it destroys flexibility. The answer has always been that by the foresight of the fathers the construction of our written Constitution was ultimately confided to this body, which, from the nature of its judicial structure, could always be relied upon to act with perfect freedom from the influence of faction and to preserve the benefits of consistent interpretation. The fundamental conception of a judicial body is that of one hedged about by precedents which are binding on the court without regard to the personality of its members. Break down this belief in judicial continuity, and let it be felt that on great constitutional questions this court is to depart from the settled conclusions of its predecessors, and to determine them all according to the mere opinion of those who temporarily fill its bench, and our Constitution will, in my judgment, be bereft of value and become a most dangerous instrument to the rights and liberties of the people....

Chapter 3

"With better grace and greater cogency"

THE DEVELOPMENT of the concept of "freedom of contract," discussed in connection with the income tax case, did not occur all at once at the turn of the century. The Court grew into it. As late as 1898, the Court upheld the constitutionality of a Utah statute which limited the working hours of miners and employees of smelters and ore reduction works to eight hours a day, as a health and safety measure. The contention had been that the statute interfered with the "freedom of contract" of the laborer and his employer to establish a working day of as many hours as they wished. The Court refused to accept this assertion. But a harbinger of the future was the fact that two justices dissented.

The opinion of the Court in this case, *Holden v. Hardy,* constitutes the most significant work from the judicial pen of Justice Henry B. Brown, of Michigan, an appointee of President Harrison. Brown was the leading expert in the United States in the field of admiralty and maritime law. He came to the Court directly from fifteen years' experience as a lower federal court judge. Regrettably, his sound competence was somewhat obscured by a formal and pompous manner. His greatest contribution, the opinion in *Holden v. Hardy,* was destined to wither and seemingly die in a very short time, only to spring back to vigorous life in recent years.

Holden v. Hardy is an outstanding essay in constitutional law. Brown first succinctly explains why there are two "due process of law" clauses in the Constitution, the one in the Fifth Amendment being applicable only to the national government and the one in the Fourteenth Amendment applying to the states. Then he turns to a compelling exposition of the growth and modernization of the law—and the necessity for an interpretation of the Constitution broad enough to allow this growth. This is followed by an enlightening discussion of the meaning of "due process of law." Then, finally, he decides the case, stating his reasons in terms which live in the most modern decisions. Here is a most effective statement for the constitutional power of government to regulate business reasonably.

HOLDEN v. HARDY

Supreme Court of the United States, 1898, 169 U. S. 366

Brown, J.:

The validity of the statute in question is challenged upon the ground of an alleged violation of the Fourteenth Amendment to the Constitution of the United States, in that it abridges the privileges or immunities of citizens of the United States; deprives both the employer and the laborer of his property without due process of law, and denies to them the equal protection of the laws. As the three questions of abridging their immunities, depriving them of their property, and denying them the protection of the laws, are so connected that the authorities upon each are, to a greater or less extent, pertinent to the others, they may properly be considered together.

Prior to the adoption of the Fourteenth Amendment there was a similar provision against deprivation of life, liberty or property without due process of law incorporated in the Fifth Amendment; but as the first eight amendments to the Constitution were obligatory only upon Congress, the decisions of this court under this amendment have but a partial application to the Fourteenth Amendment, which operates only upon the action of the several States. The Fourteenth Amendment, which was finally adopted July 28, 1868, largely expanded the power of the Federal courts and Congress, and for the first time authorized the former to declare invalid all laws and judicial decisions of the States abridging the rights of citizens or denying them the benefit of due process of law. . . .

An examination of . . . cases under the Fourteenth Amendment will demonstrate that, in passing upon the validity of state legislation under that amendment, this court has not failed to recognize the fact that the law is, to a certain extent, a progressive science; that in some of the States methods of procedure, which at the time the Constitution was adopted were deemed essential to the protection and safety of the people, or to the liberty of the citizen, have been found to be no longer necessary; that restrictions which had formerly been laid upon the conduct of individuals, or of classes of individuals, had proved detrimental to their interests; while, upon the other hand, certain other classes of persons, particularly those engaged in dangerous or unhealthful employments, have been found to be in need of additional protection. Even before the adoption of the Constitution, much had been done toward mitigating the severity of the common law, particularly in the administration of its criminal branch. The number of capital crimes, in this country at least, had been largely decreased. Trial by ordeal and by battle had never existed here, and had fallen into disuse in England. The earlier practice of the common law, which denied the benefit of witnesses to a person accused of felony, had been abolished by statute, though so far as it deprived him of the assistance of counsel and compulsory process for the attendance of his witnesses, it had not been changed in England. But to the credit of her American colonies, let it be said that so oppressive a doctrine had never obtained a foothold there.

The present century has originated legal reforms of no less importance. The whole fabric of special pleading, once thought to be necessary to the elimination of the real issue between the parties, has crumbled to pieces. The ancient tenures of real estate have been largely swept away, and land is now transferred almost as easily and cheaply as personal property. Married women have been emancipated from the control of their husbands and placed upon a practical equality with them with respect to the acquisition, possession and transmission of property. Imprisonment for debt has been abolished. Exemptions from execution have been largely added to, and in most of the States homesteads are rendered incapable of seizure and sale upon forced process.

Witnesses are no longer incompetent by reason of interest, even though they be parties to the litigation. Indictments have been simplified, and an indictment for the most serious of crimes is now the simplest of all. In several of the States grand juries, formerly the only safeguard against a malicious prosecution, have been largely abolished, and in others the rule of unanimity, so far as applied to civil cases, has given way to verdicts rendered by a three-fourths majority. This case does not call for an expression of opinion as to the wisdom of these changes, or their validity under the Fourteenth Amendment. . . .

Of course, it is impossible to forecast the character or extent of these changes, but in view of the fact that from the day Magna Charta was signed to the present moment, amendments to the structure of the law have been made with increasing frequency, it is impossible to suppose that they will not continue, and the law be forced to adapt itself to new conditions of society, and, particularly, to the new relations between employers and employees as they arise. . . .

The same subject was also elaborately discussed by Mr. Justice Matthews in delivering the opinion of this court in *Hurtado v. California,* 110 U. S. 516, 530: "This flexibility and capacity for growth and adaptation is the peculiar boast and excellence of the common law. . . . The Constitution of the United States was ordained, it is true, by descendants of Englishmen, who inherited the traditions of English law and history; but it was made for an undefined and expanding future, and for a people gathered and to be gathered from many nations and of many tongues. And while we take just pride in the principles and institutions of common law, we are not to forget that in lands where other systems of jurisprudence prevail, the ideas and processes of civil justice are also not unknown. Due process of law, in spite of the absolutism of continental governments, is not alien to that code which survived the Roman Empire as the foundation of modern civilization in Europe, and which has given us that fundamental maxim of distributive justice —*suum cuique tribuere*. There is nothing in Magna Charta, rightly construed as a broad charter of public right and law, which ought to exclude the best ideas of all systems and of every age; and as it was the characteristic principle of the common law to draw its inspiration from every fountain of justice, we are not to assume that the sources of its supply have been exhausted. On the contrary, we should expect that the new and various experiences of our own situation and system will mould and shape it into new and not less useful forms." We have seen no reason to doubt the soundness of these views. In the future growth of the nation, as heretofore, it is not impossible that Congress may see fit to annex territories whose jurisprudence is that of the civil law. One of the considerations moving to such annexation might be the very fact that the territory so annexed should enter the Union with its traditions, laws and systems of administration unchanged. It would be a narrow construction of the Constitution to require them to abandon these, or to substitute for a system, which represented the growth of generations of inhabitants, a jurisprudence with which they had had no previous acquaintance or sympathy.

We do not wish, however, to be understood as holding that this power is unlimited. While the people of each State may doubtless adopt such systems of laws as best conform to their own traditions and customs, the people of the entire country have laid down in the Constitution of the United States certain fundamental principles to which each member of the Union is bound to accede as a condition of its admission as a State. Thus, the United States are bound to guarantee to each State a republican form of government, and the tenth section of the first article contains certain other specified limitations upon the power of the several States, the object of which was to secure to Congress paramount authority with respect to matters of universal concern. In addition, the Fourteenth Amendment contains a sweeping provision forbidding the States from abridging the privileges and immunities of citizens of the United States, and denying them the benefit of due process or equal protection of the laws.

This court has never attempted to define with precision the words, "due process of law," nor is it necessary to do so in this case. It is sufficient to say that there are certain immutable principles of justice which inhere in the very idea of free government which no member of the Union may disregard, as that no man shall be condemned in his person or property without due notice and an opportunity of being heard in his defence. What shall constitute due process of law was perhaps as well stated by Mr. Justice Curtis in *Murray's Lessees v. Hoboken Land Co.*, 18 How. 272, 276, as anywhere. He said. "The Constitution contains no description of those processes which it was intended to allow or forbid. It does not even declare what principles are to be applied to ascertain whether it be due process. It is manifest that it was not left to the legislative power to enact any process which might be devised. The article is a restraint on the legislative as well as on the executive and judicial powers of the Government, and cannot be so construed as to leave Congress free to make any process 'due process of law,' by its mere will. To what principles, then, are we to resort to ascertain whether this process, enacted by Congress, is due process? To this the answer must be twofold. We must examine the Constitution itself, to see whether this process be in conflict with any of its provisions. If not found to be so, we must look to those settled usages and modes of proceeding existing in the common and statute law of England, before the emigration of our ancestors, and which are shown not to have been unsuited to their civil and political condition by having been acted on by them after the settlement of this country." . . .

While the business of mining coal and manufacturing iron began in Pennsylvania as early as 1716, and in Virginia, North Carolina and Massachusetts even earlier than this, both mining and manufacturing were carried on in such a limited way and by such primitive methods that no special laws were considered necessary, prior to the adoption of the Constitution, for the protection of the operatives; but, in the vast proportions which these industries have since assumed, it has been found that they can no longer be carried on with due regard to the safety and health of those engaged in them, without special protection against the dangers necessarily incident to these employments. In consequence of this, laws have been enacted in most of the States designed to meet these exigencies and to secure the safety of persons peculiarly exposed to these dangers. Within this general category are ordinances providing for fire escapes for hotels, theatres, factories and other large buildings, a municipal inspection of boilers, and appliances designed to secure passengers upon railways and steamboats against the dangers necessarily incident to these methods of transportation. In States where manufacturing is carried on to a large extent, provision is made for the protection of dangerous machinery against accidental contact, for the cleanliness and ventilation of working rooms, for guarding of well holes, stairways, elevator shafts and for the employment of sanitary appliances. In others, where mining is the principal industry, special provision is made for the shoring up of dangerous walls, for ventilation shafts, bore holes, escapement shafts, means of signalling the surface, for the supply of fresh air and the elimination, as far as possible, of dangerous gases, for safe means of hoisting and lowering cages, for a limitation upon the number of persons permitted to enter a cage, that cages shall be covered, and that there shall be fences and gates around the top of shafts, besides other similar precautions. . . .

If it be within the power of a legislature to adopt such means for the protection of the lives of its citizens, it is difficult to see why precautions may not also be adopted for the protection of their health and morals. It is as much for the interest of the State that the public health should be preserved as that life should be made secure. With this end in view quarantine laws have been enacted in most if not all of the States; insane asylums, public hospitals and institutions for the care and education of the blind established, and special measures taken for the exclusion of infected cattle, rags and decayed fruit. In other States laws have been enacted limiting the hours during which women and children shall be employed in factories; and while their constitutionality, at least as applied to women, has been doubted in some of the States, they have been generally upheld. . . .

Upon the principles above stated, we think the act in question may be sustained as a valid exercise of the police power of the State. The enactment does not profess to limit the hours of all workmen, but merely those who are employed in underground mines, or in the smelting, reduction or refining of ores or metals. These employments, when too long pursued, the legislature has judged to be detrimental to the health of the employees, and, so long as there are reasonable grounds for believing that this is so, its decision upon this subject cannot be reviewed by the Federal courts.

While the general experience of mankind may justify us in believing that men may engage in ordinary employments more than eight hours per day without injury to their health, it does not follow that labor for the same length of time is innocuous when carried on beneath the surface of the earth, where the operative is deprived of fresh air and sunlight, and is frequently subjected to foul atmosphere and a very high temperature, or to the influence of noxious gases, generated by the processes of refining or smelting. . . .

The legislature has recognized the fact, which the experience of legislators in many States has corroborated, that the proprietors of these establishments and their operatives do not stand upon an equality, and that their interests are, to a certain extent, conflicting. The former naturally desire to obtain as much labor as possible from their employees, while the latter are often induced by the fear of discharge to conform to regulations which their judgment, fairly exercised, would pronounce to be detrimental to their health or strength. In other words, the proprietors lay down the rules and the laborers are practically constrained to obey them. In such cases self-interest is often an unsafe guide, and the legislature may properly interpose its authority.

It may not be improper to suggest in this connection that although the prosecution in this case was against the employer of labor, who apparently under the statute is the only one liable, his defence is not so much that his right to contract has been infringed upon, but that the act works a peculiar hardship to his employees, whose right to labor as long as they please is alleged to be thereby violated. The argument would certainly come with better grace and greater cogency from the latter class. But the fact that both parties are of full age and competent to contract does not necessarily deprive the State of the power to interfere where the parties do not stand upon an equality, or where the public health demands that one party to the contract shall be protected against himself. "The State still retains an interest in his welfare, however reckless he may be. The whole is no greater than the sum of all the parts, and when the individual health, safety and welfare are sacrificed or neglected, the State must suffer."

We have no disposition to criticise the many authorities which hold that state statutes restricting the hours of labor are unconstitutional. Indeed, we are not called upon to express an opinion upon this subject. It is sufficient to say of them, that they have no application to cases where the legislature had adjudged that a limitation is necessary for the preservation of the health of employees, and there are reasonable grounds for believing that such determination is supported by the facts. The question in each case is whether the legislature has adopted the statute in exercise of a reasonable discretion, or whether its action be a mere excuse for an unjust discrimination, or the oppression, or spoliation of a particular class. . . .

Chapter 4

"The 14th Amendment does not enact Mr. Herbert Spencer's Social Statics"

THE "FREEDOM OF CONTRACT" constitutional theory, created by the Court, achieved its full growth and maturity in a decision seven years after *Holden v. Hardy*. In varying strength, the concept was destined to rule for thirty years. The principles so effectively asserted in the Holden case were abandoned.

The decision was *Lochner v. New York*. It involved the validity of a New York statute limiting the work day of bakers to ten hours and the work week to sixty hours. The Court held the statute to be unconstitutional interference with freedom of contract. The author of the opinion was Justice Rufus W. Peckham, the archadvocate of a laissez-faire economic theory built into the Constitution. Just two sentences from his opinion serve to give its essence: "Clean and wholesome bread does not depend upon whether the baker works but ten hours per day or only sixty hours a week.... We think that there can be no fair doubt that the trade of a baker, in and of itself, is not an unhealthy one to that degree which would authorize the legislature to interfere with the right to labor, and with the right of free contract on the part of the individual, either as employer or employee."

The decision was exceedingly controversial since it gave promise, later fulfilled, of holdings invalidating great segments of the then current laws directed at economic and social reform. It evoked challenging threats to limit the Court's power of judicial review of legislation—threats by President Theodore Roosevelt and the Progressive Party, in the election of 1912.

The opponents of the holding had their champion, a newcomer to the Supreme Bench, Justice Oliver Wendell Holmes. His opinion in the Lochner case is magnificently clear, precise, and above all completely frank in stating the issue without judicial obfuscation. It was a trumpet call played by a master—brief, loud, ringingly clear, and perfectly executed.

It must be stressed that Holmes was not advocating the maximum hour law and the economic theory of government regulation which he wished to uphold. Every indication from his career is that he himself was a believer in laissez-faire economics (though we cannot draw that conclusion as a sure thing). But he was eternally adamantine on the proposition that, regardless of his personal feelings, if the *people* wanted to adopt some economic theory other than laissez-faire, it was their business, and the Constitution did not stop them. In this, throughout his long tenure on the Supreme Court, he became the Great Dissenter—the nagging conscience of the "freedom of contract" Court.

More detailed consideration of the career of this matchless jurist will follow in Part Four. For the present let us say that Holmes towers among the greatest judges of all history. Meet him through his flashing dissent in the Lochner case. There is no abridgment; it is printed in its entirety.

LOCHNER v. NEW YORK

Supreme Court of the United States, 1905, 198 U. S. 45

HOLMES, J., *dissenting*:

I regret sincerely that I am unable to agree with the judgment in this case, and that I think it my duty to express my dissent.

This case is decided upon an economic theory which a large part of the country does not entertain. If it were a question whether I agreed with that theory, I should desire to study it further and long before making up my mind. But I do not conceive that to be my duty, because I strongly believe that my agreement or disagreement has nothing to do with the right of a majority to embody their opinions in law. It is settled by various decisions of this court that state constitutions and state laws may regulate life in many ways which we as legislators might think as injudicious, or if you like as tyrannical, as this, and which, equally with this, interfere with the liberty to contract. Sunday laws and usury laws are ancient examples. A more modern one is the prohibition of lotteries. The liberty of the citizen to do as he likes so long as he does not interfere with the liberty of others to do the same, which has been a shibboleth for some well-known writers, is interfered with by school laws, by the Postoffice, by every state or municipal institution which takes his money for purposes thought desirable, whether he likes it or not. The 14th Amendment does not enact Mr. Herbert Spencer's Social Statics. The other day we sustained the Massachusetts vaccination law. *Jacobson v. Massachusetts,* 197 U. S. 11. United States and state statutes and decisions cutting down the liberty to contract by way of combination are familiar to this court. *Northern Securities Co. v. United States,* 193 U. S. 197. Two years ago we upheld the prohibition of sales of stock on margins, or for future delivery, in the Constitution of California. *Otis v. Parker,* 187 U. S. 606. The decision sustaining an eight-hour law for miners is still recent. *Holden v. Hardy,* 169 U. S. 366. Some of these laws embody convictions or prejudices which judges are likely to share. Some may not. But a Constitution is not intended to embody a particular economic theory, whether of paternalism and the organic relation of the citizen to the state or of *laissez faire.* It is made for people of fundamentally differing views, and the accident of our finding certain opinions natural and familiar, or novel, and even shocking, ought not to conclude our judgment upon the question whether statutes embodying them conflict with the Constitution of the United States.

General propositions do not decide concrete cases. The decision will depend on a judgment or intuition more subtle than any articulate major premise. But I think that the proposition just stated, if it is accepted, will carry us far toward the end. Every opinion tends to become a law. I think that the word "liberty," in the 14th Amendment, is perverted when it is held to prevent the natural outcome of a dominant opinion, unless it can be said that a rational and fair man necessarily would admit that the statute proposed would infringe fundamental principles as they have been understood by the traditions of our people and our law. It does not need research to show that no such sweeping condemnation can be passed upon the statute before us. A reasonable man might think it a proper measure on the score of health. Men whom I certainly could not pronounce unreasonable would uphold it as a first instalment of a general regulation of the hours of work. Whether in the latter aspect it would be open to the charge of inequality I think it unnecessary to discuss.

PART FOUR

The Era of Holmes

FOUR

Chapter 1

*"The ultimate good desired is better
reached by free trade in ideas"*

THE YEARS from 1905 to 1932 must be called the Supreme Court's "Era of Holmes." Although Holmes served under four Chief Justices, he was clearly the dominant figure of the Court. From his Lochner dissent in 1905 to his retirement in 1932, the work of the Court revolved around him. Yet he was the Great Dissenter. Never in all history has so great a judge had so little influence upon the immediate decisions of the Court of which he was a member. In his own time he was the nagging conscience; in our time he is a foremost creator of constitutional law.

We shall take significant notice of two other great jurists of this time, Justice Brandeis, who was Holmes' intimate companion in the law, and Chief Justice Taft. But the theme must be Justice Oliver Wendell Holmes. Holmes made two major contributions to constitutional doctrine; they are both contributions of surpassing significance in the present day. One of these was presaged by his dissent in the Lochner case, already considered. The principles there set forth concerning reasonable governmental power to regulate our economic life are now accepted beyond cavil. The other contribution is of even greater import. To Holmes we owe the modern constitutional law of the most fundamental of all human liberties—freedom of speech. But before we turn our attention to this latter contribution, we should know something of the man.

THE ERA OF HOLMES

Oliver Wendell Holmes, Jr., was the son of the "Autocrat of the Breakfast Table," Dr. Oliver Wendell Holmes, distinguished physician, poet, and essayist, who was the center of the cultural and intellectual life of Boston in the years immediately preceding the Civil War. The future jurist grew up in this atmosphere of stimulation and ferment. One of the major impacts on the personality and character of Oliver Wendell Holmes, Jr., was his service in the Civil War. He volunteered immediately upon the outbreak of the War, just as he finished his work as an undergraduate at Harvard. Although he did not participate in the Battle of Gettysburg, he was in the thick of the fighting elsewhere and was seriously wounded three times.

Holmes is probably the only Supreme Court justice in history who actually bent his entire career toward becoming a judge. Immediately upon his release from the army, he entered Harvard Law School. Upon graduation he began the practice of law in a Boston firm. He rose rapidly in the ranks of practicing attorneys, meanwhile consistently working and writing in the field of legal philosophy and legal history. He also taught part time at the Harvard Law School; later, when he accepted a full-time position on the Harvard Law faculty he expressly stipulated that his contract should not bind him in case a judgeship was offered.

The selection of Holmes to deliver the series of Lowell Lectures at Harvard in 1880 was a principal turn in his career. These lectures, on the topic "The Common Law," published in book form, probably constitute the most significant essay in legal history and jurisprudence from the pen of an American. In them he created the foundation of his legal philosophy, a philosophy destined to have an immeasurable impact upon American law.

Holmes taught less than one year as a full-time member of the Harvard faculty. At the age of forty-one, in 1882, he was appointed a justice of the Supreme Judicial Court of Massachusetts. He served on this court with distinction for twenty years, the last three years as chief justice. In 1902 President Theodore Roosevelt designated him an associate justice of the United States Supreme Court. Holmes was sixty-one; yet there he was to serve for thirty years.

These are the raw materials that went into the makings of Oliver Wendell Holmes, Jr., justice of the United States Supreme Court and probably the greatest jurist in all American history. Only John Marshall might be his equal, but it must be observed that Marshall was in a sense a product of the times as well as a product of his own ability. Marshall was challenged by an overriding necessity to create a system of government.

Holmes achieved his stature without such a spur. Indeed, Holmes' greatness stands largely on opinions which were dissents—nullities in the eyes of the law at the time they were written. An incredible, almost bizarre circumstance! Yet there he stands as magnificent as any, and to many the greatest of them all.

In the last few years there has been a widespread and concerted attempt to belittle Justice Holmes and the greatness of his career. The attacks have been oblique. The judgeship of Holmes has not been assailed, rather the assaults have been against his legal philosophy, upon which his opinions, of course, are based. Epithets such as "authoritarian," "totalitarian," "undemocratic," and "un-American" have been directed at him. As we shall see, in so far as his judicial opinions reflect his philosophy of law, these charges are utterly fantastic. Where could one find a more loyal and patriotic American, and a more fervent defender of the cherished political and civil freedoms of Americans? Then what is this disparagement all about? The reader should be cautioned that any attempted answer in a short space cannot paint the entire picture. Those sincerely interested in the merits of this debate on Holmes' philosophy should partially discount the writings of columnists and others in the popular press of the day. They should go to the nearest law library and read an exchange of articles by Professors Howe and Hart of the Harvard Law Faculty in 64 *Harvard Law Review,* pages 529, 929, 937 (1951). Both sides are there presented in honest, unemotional, and readable fashion. But for an understanding of Holmes and his philosophy, the fundamentals of this controversy should be known, and they are sketched below.

Holmes was a skeptic, and this is reflected in his legal philosophy. He could not abide the thought that "the law" in a given case is simply the application of immutable principles established either by religious belief or the laws of nature. To him, the decision in a particular case was not the statement of a law which was already silently in existence. Rather the decision actually made the law which it declared. A statement from one of Holmes' Supreme Court opinions constitutes an excellent summary of this position. Although directed at another issue it serves the purpose well. Holmes said: "The common law is not a brooding omnipresence in the sky, but the articulate voice of some sovereign." The law is not a series of immutable principles waiting to be applied to the facts of a given lawsuit, but the law is actually created by the decision in that lawsuit.

The next step is, since case law as well as statutory law reflect the attitudes of the people at a given time, the law is a growing and changing thing adaptable to the circumstances of the present. While this belief may concededly tend to weaken the role formal religious precepts play in our law, it is certainly the complete antithesis of "totalitarianism" or an "undemocratic" faith. In the Holmes philosophy, the people themselves through their own governmental institutions make their own law. To him the only sources of the law are the Constitution, case and statutory law, and what the people want—the people and the instruments they create for their own government.

Beyond question, Holmes had a greater impact upon American law than any other human being in all history. The whole body of American law underwent a reorientation as the direct result of his teachings. No longer was antiquity alone enough to justify a particular rule of law; to be accepted, the rule had to have sufficient merit to justify its existence in the present. No longer could judges retire behind a rationalization that they had no control over the right or wrong of a rule of law since they only declared what was the one "true rule"; judges had to face up to the fact that they were making law and they had to assume a responsibility to decide which was the better rule. In short, there was no right or wrong in any absolute abstract sense; the law was not a black or white choice but a shading between better and worse with good and bad on both sides. And the good and bad were determined by practical considerations of usefulness and worth in society. Holmes was the father of this philosophy, and the dominant forces in molding the law followed him.

But what is the role of "ethics" and "morality" in all this? Does the Holmes philosophy divorce law from moral precepts and leave law to be controlled only by expedience? Holmes' attackers answer "yes" to this latter question and view him as a dangerous subverter of moral principles. The primary object of their attack is a lecture Holmes prepared for a group of law students, a lecture he called "The Path of the Law." In it Holmes told his audience that students of the law must recognize a fundamental distinction between law and morality. He added that it obscures clear analysis to think of law in terms of ethical principles of right and wrong. Rather, for the student to analyze and understand, law should be thought of as simply an informed and prophetic prediction of how a court will decide a given case.

Taken alone these words surely do indicate a divorcing of law from morals and ethics. But they do not stand alone, even within this same lecture. In relying upon these assertions, Holmes' detractors are guilty of the sin of quotation out of context. Holmes made it completely clear at the very beginning of the lecture that he was doing no more than offering law students a practical and useful means of analyzing court decisions. He specifically warned his listeners not to take his remarks more broadly in these words: "I take it for granted that no hearer of mine will misinterpret what I have to say in the language of cynicism. The law is the witness and external deposit of our moral life. Its history is the history of the moral development of the race.... When I emphasize the difference between law and morals I do so with reference to a single end, that of learning and understanding the law. For that purpose ... I ask you for the moment to imagine yourselves indifferent to other and greater things."

And this is not all. In the concluding portion of the same lecture he expanded on the theme that the law "is the witness and external deposit of our moral life." He firmly recognized that law has its foundations in ethical and moral judgments. To Holmes, these judgments were the judgments of society. Thus, Holmes returned to his fundamental theme: the right and wrong, the ethics and morals of a given situation are to be determined by what is best for the society in which we now live. The present-day applicability of ancient abstract moral precepts depends upon their present-day usefulness; their applicability today is not justified on the *sole* ground that they exist.

This, in brief, is the Holmes philosophy and the source of the current assault upon the man and his work. Of course reasonable and honest men can and do differ with the Holmes thesis. But this is a philosophical argument, which offers no justification for personal, vicious, epithetical attacks upon the man. Although Holmes himself was an agnostic, there is absolutely nothing in his philosophy of the law which cannot be accepted by those of deep religious persuasion, at least in the area of modern liberal Protestantism—which, in fact, owes much of its own self-searching and re-evaluation of dogma to Holmes and his followers. Admittedly, some other religious persuasions cannot accept Holmes. And he would be the first to insist that they should have their say. But again it must be stressed that this is a matter of religious and philosophical belief.

Agree or disagree with the Holmes philosophy as you will; disagreement cannot alter the fact that Holmes stands as the most significant legal philosopher in American history and, perhaps with Marshall, the greatest American judge. He was of unimpeachable loyalty and patriotism to America, a believer in free enterprise and the American way of life. But above all he was a believer in the people, in democracy, and a champion of human dignity and human liberty.

In spite of criticism, the Holmes philosophy permeates the law today. The critics, at least at present, are a relatively small but quite vocal minority. Lawyers and judges are following Holmes day in and day out. Future philosophical development may well reveal fallacies in his theses —no philosophy is perfect. But it is almost inconceivable that the role of Holmes in our law will dwindle to insignificance. As long as our Constitution endures, the people, in molding our institutions, and judges, in reaching their decisions, will be beholden in great measure to Holmes.

Oliver Wendell Holmes was a fanatic believer in democracy. But democracy cannot exist without civil and political rights. To Holmes' obvious satisfaction, he was to play the dominant role in forging the modern constitutional law preserving these rights. Holmes elevated human freedom to a preferred place in our constitutional scheme. He did it largely through his inspiring opinions defining and undergirding the right of free speech. He asserted the proposition that speech could be circumscribed only if it created "a clear and present danger" that it would bring about evils which the state had a right to prevent.

Holmes created this test in a case, *Schenck v. United States,* which involved intense agitation against the draft laws of World War I, agitation advocating defiance of those laws. Holmes, writing the opinion of the unanimous Court, held in that case that the test had been met, that is, the words did create a *clear* and *present* danger of defiance of the draft laws. Thus the speech was not constitutionally protected.

But after this case, the Court refused to follow the Holmes test. Just eight months later the Court decided another free speech case, *Abrams v. United States,* and Holmes dissented. This case involved flamboyant pamphleteering protests against the allied military expedition into Russia at the time of the Russian Revolution. The Court held the publication of these pamphlets not privileged as free speech, and the conviction of Abrams under the wartime Espionage Act was upheld.

Holmes dissented, joined by Justice Brandeis. He could not see any clear and present danger to the United States in this totally footless effort. His opinion is a brief and effective exposition of the role of free speech in our constitutional system. He recognizes that allowing free speech takes courage. But it is the way of freedom.

A word of caution in reading this and other Holmes opinions. Holmes writes excitingly and well. But he must be read with deliberation. For most writers each Holmesian sentence would form the theme of an entire paragraph, with elaboration and example. Holmes depended upon his readers to do this. So each sentence should be savored. Like a small portion of extraordinarily rich food, Holmes can be appreciated through tiny bites, not through great gulps.

ABRAMS v. UNITED STATES
Supreme Court of the United States, 1919, 250 U. S. 616

HOLMES, J., *dissenting:*

In this case sentences of twenty years imprisonment have been imposed for the publishing of two leaflets that I believe the defendants had as much right to publish as the Government has to publish the Constitution of the United States now vainly invoked by them. Even if I am technically wrong and enough can be squeezed from these poor and puny anonymities to turn the color of legal litmus paper . . . the most nominal punishment seems to me all that possibly could be inflicted, unless the defendants are to be made to suffer not for what the indictment alleges but for the creed that they avow—a creed that I believe to be the creed of ignorance and immaturity when honestly held, as I see no reason to doubt that it was held here, but which, although made the subject of examination at the trial, no one has a right even to consider in dealing with the charges before the Court.

Persecution for the expression of opinions seems to me perfectly logical. If you have no doubt of your premises or your power and want a certain result with all your heart you naturally express your wishes in law and sweep away all opposition. To allow opposition by speech seems to indicate that you think the speech impotent, as when a man says that he has squared the circle, or that you do not care whole-heartedly for the result, or that you doubt either your power or your premises. But when men have realized that time has upset many fighting faiths, they may come to believe even more than they believe the very foundations of their own conduct that the ultimate good desired is better reached by free trade in ideas—that the best test of truth is the power of the thought to get itself accepted in the competition of the market, and that truth is the only ground upon which their wishes safely can be carried out. That at any rate is the theory of our Constitution. It is an experiment, as all life is an experiment. Every year if not every day we have to wager our salvation upon some prophecy based upon imperfect knowledge. While that experiment is part of our system I think we should be eternally vigilant against attempts to check the expression of opinions that we loathe and believe to be fraught with death, unless they so imminently threaten immediate interference with the lawful and pressing purposes of the law that an immediate check is required to save the country. I wholly disagree with the argument of the Government that the First Amendment left the common law as to seditious libel in force. History seems to me against the notion. I had conceived that the United States through many years had shown its repentance for the Sedition Act of 1798, by repaying fines that it imposed. Only the emergency that makes it immediately dangerous to leave the correction of evil counsels to time warrants making any exception to the sweeping command, "Congress shall make no law . . . abridging the freedom of speech." Of course I am speaking only of expressions of opinion and exhortations, which were all that were uttered here, but I regret that I cannot put into more impressive words my belief that in their conviction upon this indictment the defendants were deprived of their rights under the Constitution of the United States.

Chapter 2

"Every idea is an incitement"

SIX YEARS after the Abrams decision, the Court had before it the case of *Gitlow v. New York*. Gitlow had been tried and convicted in the New York courts for the offense of criminal anarchy. This conviction was based upon the publication of a pamphlet called "The Left Wing Manifesto," in which Gitlow wrote of proletarian dictatorship, political strikes, and the like. He concluded with these words, "The Communist International calls the proletariat of the world to the final struggle!"

It should be noted that Gitlow was charged with nothing but the circulation of this pamphlet—there were no overt acts directed at overthrow of the government. So the case presented the narrow issue of whether such political agitation by words alone was constitutionally privileged. The Court held that it was not. In reaching this result, the Court perverted the Holmes "clear and present danger" test by stating that it was not the business of the Court to decide whether there was a clear and present danger that the words would bring about the result, but that this was a matter for the determination of the legislature in passing the criminal anarchy statute.

Holmes again dissented; Brandeis again joined. Since this was an alleged infringement of free speech by a state rather than by the federal government, Holmes first pointed out that free speech is not specifically protected from state encroachment in the Constitution since the First

Amendment is applicable only to the federal government. But the "due process of law" clause of the Fourteenth Amendment, as we have already seen, is a broad protection of human freedoms. Holmes, as well as the majority of the Court, recognized this and, in effect, "read into" that clause of the Fourteenth Amendment the protections of the First Amendment.

Then Holmes turned to the problem of defining the areas of free speech. Again he was brief, incisive, and courageous. It is hard for anyone to tolerate the publication of such propaganda. But if we do not so tolerate, how can we preserve our own liberty to speak our minds? The message of Holmes is that to preserve freedom there must be freedom to differ about things that are important; our freedom to differ must not be limited to insignificancies.

GITLOW v. NEW YORK

Supreme Court of the United States, 1925, 268 U. S. 652

HOLMES, J., *dissenting*:

MR. JUSTICE BRANDEIS and I are of the opinion that this judgment should be reversed. The general principle of free speech, it seems to me, must be taken to be included in the Fourteenth Amendment, in view of the scope that has been given to the word "liberty" as there used, although perhaps it may be accepted with a somewhat larger latitude of interpretation than is allowed to Congress by the sweeping language that governs or ought to govern the laws of the United States. If I am right, then I think that the criterion sanctioned by the full Court in *Schenck v. United States,* 249 U. S. 47, 52 applies. "The question in every case is whether the words used are used in such circumstances and are of such a nature as to create a clear and present danger that they will bring about the substantive evils that [the State] has a right to prevent." It is true that in my opinion this criterion was departed from in *Abrams v. United States,* 250 U. S. 616, but the convictions that I expressed in that case are too deep for it to be possible for me as yet to believe that it and *Schaefer v. United States,* 251 U. S. 466, have settled the law. If what I think the correct test is applied, it is manifest that there was no present danger of an attempt to overthrow the government by force on the part of the admittedly small minority who shared the defendant's views. It is said that this manifesto was more than a theory, that it was an incitement. Every idea is an incitement. It offers itself for belief and if believed it is acted on unless some other belief outweighs it or some failure of energy stifles the movement at its birth. The only difference between the expression of an opinion and an incitement in the narrower sense is the speaker's enthusiasm for the result. Eloquence may set fire to reason. But whatever may be thought of the redundant discourse before us it had no chance of starting a present conflagration. If in the long run the beliefs expressed in proletarian dictatorship are destined to be accepted by the dominant forces of the community, the only meaning of free speech is that they should be given their chance and have their way.

If the publication of this document had been laid as an attempt to induce an uprising against government at once and not at some indefinite time in the future it would have presented a different question. The object would have been one with which the law might deal, subject to the doubt whether there was any danger that the publication could produce any result; or in other words, whether it was not futile and too remote from possible consequences. But the indictment alleges the publication and nothing more.

Chapter 3

"Those who won our independence by revolution were not cowards"

THOUGH JUSTICE HOLMES created our modern law of free speech, his concise and almost cryptic opinions left the principles skeletal. Someone was needed to give flesh to the Holmesian framework. One of those happy historical fortuities supplied that man—Justice Louis D. Brandeis.

Justice Brandeis, a noted Boston lawyer, was appointed to the Court in 1916 by President Wilson. The appointment was confirmed by the Senate only after the bitterest fight in the history of the Court. The opposition largely flowed from conservative lawyers and financiers, but unhappily there was also some undercurrent of objection on a racial basis. Until Brandeis' appointment, no Jew had ever served upon the Supreme Court.

The confirmation hearings took the form of a five-month running "trial" before the Senate Judiciary Committee and its subcommittee, and in the public press. The opponents of Brandeis' confirmation hired a New York lawyer, Austen W. Fox, to present their "case." All of Brandeis' famous legal battles were reviewed in minute detail by the committee. Brandeis was called a radical, a reformer of nonjudicial temperament, a duplicitous lawyer, and more. Among those who publicly excoriated him were former President William Howard Taft, President Lowell of Harvard, Elihu Root, Charles Francis Adams, and Senator Henry Cabot Lodge of Brandeis' home state.

The Brandeis forces were able to show that almost every one of his bitterest opponents had some personal reason for his position. Brandeis had bested many of the lawyers in racking court battles. The financiers had felt the sting of his eloquent hostility to some of the practices of big business. Paradoxically, there was also an attempt to establish that he was too closely allied with big business. In the course of his large and variegated practice Brandeis had often represented powerful financial interests as well as fought them. Senator Borah opposed him throughout because of this business clientele. Yet Senator La Follette, another noted liberal Republican, was one of Brandeis' most fervent supporters.

There never was much doubt of a clear Senate vote for Brandeis if the matter ever came to the floor. The Judiciary Committee was the key to confirmation. After five months of grueling debate, with pressure and counterpressure, the conservative Democrats upon the committee were whipped into line. The Committee recommended confirmation by a 10–8 vote, splitting on strict party lines. The Senate vote for confirmation, 47–22, was anticlimactic.

Louis D. Brandeis was born in Louisville, Kentucky, and attended the public schools there. After study in Europe, he took his law degree at Harvard. He practiced law for a short time in St. Louis and then returned to Boston, where he engaged in the practice of law until his appointment to the Supreme Court. Brandeis was a leader of the Boston Bar, but he was also much more than that. Throughout his life, he evidenced his broad social outlook by assuming dominant roles in the areas of law reform, the professional responsibilities of lawyers, social legislation, and the Zionist movements. Many of these activities were the source of opposition to his confirmation. Lawyers know him particularly for being the creator of the "Brandeis Brief," a type of law brief that gathers and presents to the court great masses of factual data designed to educate the court and aid it in reaching its decision. This Brandeis contribution was a major advance in legal advocacy.

Holmes and Brandeis grew to be stanch and intimate friends on the Court. They complemented each other to perfection. Holmes was a scholar, but only in broad philosophical terms. He abhorred detailed research. He thought rather than sought. Brandeis certainly had much of the broad approach, but in addition he was a meticulous scholar. He wanted to know everything, including the minutiae. And he had the disposition and zeal to accompany his restless mind. A Brandeis opinion is a step-by-step description of the road traveled in reaching the result. Yet this is no dull travelogue. Brandeis wrote with finesse and charm, and when aroused he achieved moving eloquence. Nowhere are these attributes more revealingly shown than in his concurring opinion in the free speech case of *Whitney v. California*.

Elizabeth Whitney, of the famous Field family and a "renegade" niece of Justice Stephen Field, assisted in the organization of the Communist Labor Party in California. She was tried and convicted of a felony, under the California Criminal Syndicalism Law, for engaging in these acts. The Supreme Court upheld the conviction upon the same rationale as that of the majority in the Gitlow case. Since the party advocated overthrow of the government at some time in the future, participation in the activities of advocacy were not constitutionally privileged. The Court did not require a showing of clear and present danger that overthrow of the government would be achieved.

Justices Brandeis and Holmes concurred in the upholding of Miss Whitney's conviction, but dissented from the reasoning of the majority. They concurred in the result because Miss Whitney had not put the question of clear and present danger properly in issue, and also there was evidence that the party had a program of *present* acts of defiance against lawful authority. Though these acts were far short of attempting to overthrow the government, they were nevertheless acts of illegal defiance. But Brandeis and Holmes were steadfast in their belief that the advocacy of overthrow of the government at some indefinite time in the future was constitutionally privileged free speech under the clear and present danger test.

Brandeis wrote the concurring opinion. Note how he spells out in masterful detail the application of the clear and present danger test. The Holmes sentence becomes the Brandeis paragraph; and the subject is illuminated as never before. Holmes must bow to Brandeis. This is surely the greatest court opinion on freedom of speech ever written.

WHITNEY v. CALIFORNIA

Supreme Court of the United States, 1927, 274 U. S. 357

BRANDEIS, J., *concurring*:

  Miss Whitney was convicted of the felony of assisting in organizing, in the year 1919, the Communist Labor Party of California, of being a member of it, and of assembling with it. These acts are held to constitute a crime, because the party was formed to teach criminal syndicalism. The statute which made these acts a crime restricted the right of free speech and of assembly theretofore existing. The claim is that the statute, as applied, denied to Miss Whitney the liberty guaranteed by the Fourteenth Amendment.

The felony which the statute created is a crime very unlike the old felony of conspiracy or the old misdemeanor of unlawful assembly. The mere act of assisting in forming a society for teaching syndicalism, of becoming a member of it, or of assembling with others for that purpose is given the dynamic quality of crime. There is guilt although the society may not contemplate immediate promulgation of the doctrine. Thus the accused is to be punished, not for contempt, incitement or conspiracy, but for a step in preparation, which, if it threatens the public order at all, does so only remotely. The novelty in the prohibition introduced is that the statute aims, not at the practice of criminal syndicalism, nor even directly at the preaching of it, but at association with those who propose to preach it. . . .

All fundamental rights comprised within the term liberty are protected by the Federal Constitution from invasion by the States. The right of free speech, the right to teach and the right of assembly are, of course, fundamental rights. . . . These may not be denied or abridged. But, although the rights of free speech and assembly are fundamental, they are not in their nature absolute. Their exercise is subject to restriction, if the particular restriction proposed is required in order to protect the State from destruction or from serious injury, political, economic or moral. That the necessity which is essential to a valid restriction does not exist unless speech would produce, or is intended to produce, a clear and imminent danger of some substantive evil which the State constitutionally may seek to prevent has been settled. See *Schenck v. United States,* 249 U. S. 47, 52.

It is said to be the function of the legislature to determine whether at a particular time and under the particular circumstances the formation of, or assembly with, a society organized to advocate criminal syndicalism constitutes a clear and present danger of substantive evil; and that by enacting the law here in question the legislature of California determined that question in the affirmative. Compare *Gitlow v. New York,* 268 U. S. 652, 668–671. The legislature must obviously decide, in the first instance, whether a danger exists which calls for a particular protective measure. But where a statute is valid only in case certain conditions exist, the enactment of the statute cannot alone establish the facts which are essential to its validity. . . . The power of the courts to strike down an offending law is no less when the interests involved are not property rights, but the fundamental personal rights of free speech and assembly.

This Court has not yet fixed the standard by which to determine when a danger shall be deemed clear; how remote the danger may be and yet be deemed present; and what degree of evil shall be deemed sufficiently substantial to justify resort to abridgment of free speech and assembly as the means of protection. To reach sound conclusions on these matters, we must bear in mind why a State is, ordinarily, denied the power to prohibit dissemination of social, economic and political doctrine which a vast majority of its citizens believes to be false and fraught with evil consequence.

Those who won our independence believed that the final end of the State was to make men free to develop their faculties; and that in its government the deliberative forces should prevail over the arbitrary. They valued liberty both as an end and as a means. They believed liberty to be the secret of happiness and courage to be the secret of liberty. They believed that freedom to think as you will and to speak as you think are means indispensable to the discovery and spread of political truth; that without free speech and assembly discussion would be futile; that with them, discussion affords ordinarily adequate protection against the dissemination of noxious doctrine; that the greatest menace to freedom is an inert people; that public discussion is a political duty; and that this should be a fundamental principle of the American government.[1] They recognized the risks to which all human institutions are subject. But they knew that order cannot be secured merely through fear of punishment for its infraction; that it is hazardous to discourage thought, hope and imagination; that fear breeds repression; that repression breeds hate; that hate menaces stable government; that the path of safety lies in the opportunity to discuss freely supposed grievances and proposed remedies; and that the fitting remedy for evil counsels is good ones. Believing in the power of reason as applied through public discussion, they eschewed silence coerced by law—the argument of force in its worst form. Recognizing the occasional tyrannies of governing majorities, they amended the Constitution so that free speech and assembly should be guaranteed.

Fear of serious injury cannot alone justify suppression of free speech and assembly. Men feared witches and burnt women. It is the function of speech to free men from the bondage of irrational fears. To justify suppression of free speech there must be reasonable ground to fear that serious evil will result if free speech is practiced. There must be reasonable ground to believe that the danger apprehended is imminent. There must be reasonable ground to believe that the evil to be prevented is a serious one. Every denunciation of existing law tends in some measure to increase the probability that there will be violation of it. Condonation of a breach enhances the probability. Expressions of approval add to the probability. Propagation of the criminal state of mind by teaching syndicalism increases it. Advocacy of law-breaking heightens it still further. But even advocacy of violation, however reprehensible morally, is not a justification for denying free speech where the advocacy falls short of incitement and there is nothing to indicate that the advocacy would be immediately acted on. The wide difference between advocacy and in-

---

[1] Compare Thomas Jefferson: "We have nothing to fear from the demoralizing reasonings of some, if others are left free to demonstrate their errors and especially when the law stands ready to punish the first criminal act produced by the false reasonings; these are safer corrections than the conscience of the judge." Quoted by Charles A. Beard, *The Nation,* July 7, 1926, vol. 123, p. 8. Also in first Inaugural Address: "If there be any among us who would wish to dissolve this union or change its republican form, let them stand undisturbed as monuments of the safety with which error of opinion may be tolerated where reason is left free to combat it." [Footnote by Justice Brandeis.]

citement, between preparation and attempt, between assembling and conspiracy, must be borne in mind. In order to support a finding of clear and present danger it must be shown either that immediate serious violence was to be expected or was advocated, or that the past conduct furnished reason to believe that such advocacy was then contemplated.

Those who won our independence by revolution were not cowards. They did not fear political change. They did not exalt order at the cost of liberty. To courageous, self-reliant men, with confidence in the power of free and fearless reasoning applied through the processes of popular government, no danger flowing from speech can be deemed clear and present, unless the incidence of the evil apprehended is so imminent that it may befall before there is opportunity for full discussion. If there be time to expose through discussion the falsehood and fallacies, to avert the evil by the processes of education, the remedy to be applied is more speech, not enforced silence. Only an emergency can justify repression. Such must be the rule if authority is to be reconciled with freedom. Such, in my opinion, is the command of the Constitution. It is therefore always open to Americans to challenge a law abridging free speech and assembly by showing that there was no emergency justifying it.

Moreover, even imminent danger cannot justify resort to prohibition of these functions essential to effective democracy, unless the evil apprehended is relatively serious. Prohibition of free speech and assembly is a measure so stringent that it would be inappropriate as the means for averting a relatively trivial harm to society. A police measure may be unconstitutional merely because the remedy, although effective as a means of protection, is unduly harsh or oppressive. Thus, a State might, in the exercise of its police power, make any trespass upon the land of another a crime, regardless of the results or of the intent or purpose of the trespasser. It might, also, punish an attempt, a conspiracy, or an incitement to commit the trespass. But it is hardly conceivable that this Court would hold constitutional a statute which punished as a felony the mere voluntary assembly with a society formed to teach that pedestrians had the moral right to cross unenclosed, unposted, waste lands and to advocate their doing so, even if there was imminent danger that advocacy would lead to a trespass. The fact that speech is likely to result in some violence or in destruction of property is not enough to justify its suppression. There must be the probability of serious injury to the

State. Among free men, the deterrents ordinarily to be applied to prevent crime are education and punishment for violations of the law, not abridgment of the rights of free speech and assembly. . . .

Whether in 1919, when Miss Whitney did the things complained of, there was in California such clear and present danger of serious evil, might have been made the important issue in the case. She might have required that the issue be determined either by the court or the jury. She claimed below that the statute as applied to her violated the Federal Constitution; but she did not claim that it was void because there was no clear and present danger of serious evil, nor did she request that the existence of these conditions of a valid measure thus restricting the rights of free speech and assembly be passed upon by the court or a jury. On the other hand, there was evidence on which the court or jury might have found that such danger existed. I am unable to assent to the suggestion in the opinion of the Court that assembling with a political party, formed to advocate the desirability of a proletarian revolution by mass action at some date necessarily far in the future, is not a right within the protection of the Fourteenth Amendment. In the present case, however, there was other testimony which tended to establish the existence of a conspiracy, on the part of members of the International Workers of the World, to commit present serious crimes; and likewise to show that such a conspiracy would be furthered by the activity of the society of which Miss Whitney was a member. Under these circumstances the judgment of the state court cannot be disturbed. . . .

MR. JUSTICE HOLMES joins in this opinion.

Chapter 4

*"The greatest dangers to liberty lurk in
insidious encroachment by men of zeal"*

JUSTICE BRANDEIS need yield to no man as a civil libertarian. Time and time again he and Holmes joined in dissenting when they felt that the Court was shirking its responsibility to uphold human freedom. One such case, of particular relevance in this day, is *Olmstead v. United States*. Olmstead was convicted of violation of the National Prohibition Act upon evidence obtained by wire-tapping. The Supreme Court affirmed the conviction, holding that wire-tapping was not an unreasonable search and seizure within the meaning of the Fourth Amendment and was not compulsory self-incrimination within the meaning of the Fifth Amendment. Justices Brandeis, Holmes, Stone, and Butler dissented. Brandeis wrote the outstanding dissenting opinion, an impassioned and ringing plea for the sanctity of human privacy against the prying ears of government.

This dissent has not prevailed. The constitutional rule is still to the effect that wire-tapping is not forbidden, although in 1934 Congress enacted a statute which made wire-tapping unlawful. However, the federal agency charged with enforcing federal law, the Federal Bureau of Investigation, has made no attempt to enforce it—in fact, the FBI itself has publicly admitted that it regularly engages in wire-tapping. The stirring warning of Justice Brandeis contained in the last paragraph of his opinion in the Olmstead case has not been heeded. The framers of our Constitution could not prophesy wire-tapping. But did they so build the fortress of human liberty in the Bill of Rights that this invasion should be repelled? Here is the answer of Justice Brandeis.

OLMSTEAD v. UNITED STATES
Supreme Court of the United States, 1928, 277 U. S. 438

BRANDEIS, J., *dissenting*:

The defendants were convicted of conspiring to violate the National Prohibition Act. Before any of the persons now charged had been arrested or indicted, the telephones by means of which they habitually communicated with one another and with others had been tapped by federal officers. To this end, a lineman of long experience in wire-tapping was employed, on behalf of the Government and at its expense. He tapped eight telephones, some in the homes of the persons charged, some in their offices. Acting on behalf of the Government and in their official capacity, at least six other prohibition agents listened over the tapped wires and reported the messages taken. Their operations extended over a period of nearly five months. The typewritten record of the notes of conversations overheard occupies 775 typewritten pages. By objections seasonably made and persistently renewed, the defendants objected to the admission of the evidence obtained by wire-tapping, on the ground that the Government's wire-tapping constituted an unreasonable search and seizure, in violation of the Fourth Amendment; and that the use as evidence of the conversations overheard compelled the defendants to be witnesses against themselves, in violation of the Fifth Amendment.

The Government makes no attempt to defend the methods employed by its officers. Indeed, it concedes that if wire-tapping can be deemed a search and seizure within the Fourth Amendment, such wire-tapping as was practiced in the case at bar was an unreasonable search and seizure, and that the evidence thus obtained was inadmissible. But it relies on the language of the Amendment; and it claims that the protection given thereby cannot properly be held to include a telephone conversation.

"We must never forget," said Mr. Chief Justice Marshall in *McCulloch v. Maryland,* 4 Wheat. 316, 407, "that it is a constitution we are expounding." Since then, this Court has repeatedly sustained the exercise of power by Congress, under various clauses of that instrument, over objects of which the Fathers could not have dreamed. . . . Clauses guaranteeing to the individual protection against specific abuses of power, must have a . . . capacity of adaption to a changing world. It was with reference to such a clause that this Court said in *Weems v. United States,* 217 U. S. 349, 373: "Legislation, both statutory and constitutional, is enacted, it is true, from an experience of evils, but its general language should not, therefore, be necessarily confined to the form the evil had theretofore taken. Time works changes, brings into existence new conditions and purposes. Therefore a principle to be vital must be capable of wider application than the mischief which gave it birth. This is peculiarly true of constitutions. They are not ephemeral enactments, designed to meet passing occasions. They are, to use the words of Chief Justice Marshall 'designed to approach immortality as nearly as human institutions can approach it.' The future is their care and provision for events of good and bad tendencies of which no prophecy can be made. In the application of a constitution, therefore, our contemplation cannot be only of what has been but of what may be. Under any other rule a constitution would indeed be as easy of application as it would be deficient in efficacy and power. Its general principles would have little value and be converted by precedent into impotent and lifeless formulas. Rights declared in words might be lost in reality."

When the Fourth and Fifth Amendments were adopted, "the form that evil had therefore taken," had been necessarily simple. Force and violence were then the only means known to man by which a Government could directly effect self-incrimination. It could compel the individual to testify—a compulsion effected, if need be, by torture. It could secure possession of his papers and other articles incident to his private life—a seizure effected, if need be, by breaking and entry. Protection against such invasion of "the sanctities of a man's home and the privacies of life" was provided in the Fourth and Fifth Amendments by specific language. *Boyd v. United States,* 116 U. S. 616, 630. But "time works changes, brings into existence new conditions and purposes." Subtler and more far-reaching means of invading privacy have become available to the Government. Discovery and invention have made it possible for the Government, by means far more effective than stretching upon the rack, to obtain disclosure in court of what is whispered in the closet.

Moreover, "in the application of a constitution, our contemplation cannot be only of what has been but of what may be." The progress of science in furnishing the Government with means of espionage is not likely to stop with wire-tapping. Ways may some day be developed by which the Government, without removing papers from secret drawers, can reproduce them in court, and by which it will be enabled to expose to a jury the most intimate occurrences of the home. Advances in the psychic and related sciences may bring means of exploring unexpressed beliefs, thoughts and emotions. "That places the liberty of every man in the hands of every petty officer" was said by James Otis of much lesser intrusions than these. To Lord Camden, a far slighter intrusion seemed "subversive of all the comforts of society." Can it be that the Constitution affords no protection against such invasions of individual security?

A sufficient answer is found in *Boyd v. United States,* 116 U. S. 616, 627–630, a case that will be remembered as long as civil liberty lives in the United States. This Court there reviewed the history that lay behind the Fourth and Fifth Amendments. We said with reference to Lord Camden's judgment in *Entick v. Carrington,* 19 Howell's State Trials, 1030: "The principles laid down in this opinion affect the very essence of constitutional liberty and security. They reach farther than the concrete form of the case there before the court, with its adventitious circumstances; they apply to all invasions on the part of the Government and its employes of the sanctities of a man's home and the privacies of life. It is not the breaking of his doors, and the rummaging of his drawers, that constitutes the essence of the offence; but it is the invasion of his indefeasible right of personal security, personal liberty and private property, where that right has never been forfeited by his conviction of some public offence,—it is the invasion of this sacred right which underlies and constitutes the essence of Lord Camden's judgment. Breaking into a house and opening boxes and drawers are circumstances of aggravation; but any forcible and compulsory extortion of a man's own testimony or of his private papers to be used as evidence of a crime or to forfeit his goods, is within the condemnation of that judgment. In this regard the Fourth and Fifth Amendments run almost into each other." . . .

The evil incident to invasion of the privacy of the telephone is far greater than that involved in tampering with the mails. Whenever a telephone line is tapped, the privacy of the persons at both ends of the line is invaded and all conversations between them upon any subject, and although proper, confidential and privileged, may be overheard. Moreover, the tapping of one man's telephone line involves the tapping of the telephone of every other person whom he may call or who may call him. As a means of espionage, writs of assistance and general warrants are but puny instruments of tyranny and oppression when compared with wire-tapping. . . .

The makers of our Constitution undertook to secure conditions favorable to the pursuit of happiness. They recognized the significance of man's spiritual nature, of his feelings and of his intellect. They knew that only a part of the pain, pleasure and satisfactions of life are to be found in material things. They sought to protect Americans in their beliefs, their thoughts, their emotions and their sensations. They conferred, as against the Government, the right to be let alone—the most comprehensive of rights and the right most valued by civilized men. To protect that right, every unjustifiable intrusion by the Government upon the privacy of the individual, whatever the means employed, must be deemed a violation of the Fourth Amendment. And the use, as evidence in a criminal proceeding, of facts ascertained by such intrusion must be deemed a violation of the Fifth.

Applying to the Fourth and Fifth Amendments the established rule of construction, the defendants' objections to the evidence obtained by wire-tapping must, in my opinion, be sustained. It is, of course, immaterial where the physical connection with the telephone wires leading into the defendant's premises was made. And it is also immaterial that the intrusion was in aid of law enforcement. Experience should teach us to be most on our guard to protect liberty when the Government's purposes are beneficent. Men born to freedom are naturally alert to repel invasion of their liberty by evil-minded rulers. The greatest dangers to liberty lurk in insidious encroachment by men of zeal, well-meaning but without understanding. . . .

By the laws of Washington [the state], wire-tapping is a crime. . . .

Here the evidence obtained by crime was obtained at the Government's expense, by its officers, while acting on its behalf; the officers who committed these crimes are the same officers who were charged with the enforcement of the Prohibition Act; the crimes of these officers were committed for the purpose of securing evidence with which to obtain an indictment and to secure a conviction. The evidence so obtained constitutes the warp and woof of the Government's case. . . .

Decency, security, and liberty alike demand that government officials shall be subjected to the same rules of conduct that are commands to the citizen. In a government of laws, existence of the government will be imperiled if it fails to observe the law scrupulously. Our Government is the potent, the omnipresent teacher. For good or for ill, it teaches the whole people by its example. Crime is contagious. If the Government becomes a lawbreaker, it breeds contempt for law; it invites every man to become a law unto himself; it invites anarchy. To declare that in the administration of the criminal law the end justifies the means—to declare that the Government may commit crimes in order to secure the conviction of a private criminal—would bring terrible retribution. Against that pernicious doctrine this court should resolutely set its face.

Chapter 5

"Not a universal, inexorable command"

A MATTER OF CONTINUING MOMENT in the work of the Supreme Court, and any court for that matter, is the extent to which the Court should feel bound by its own prior decisions. How free should the Court be to make new constitutional law when the establishment of the new principle requires the overruling of prior decisions? The most thorough Supreme Court opinion on this question is one by Justice Brandeis, whose work on the Court we are now considering.

First, it is essential that two different doctrines involving the force of prior decisions be strictly distinguished. The theory of *res judicata,* as lawyers call it, is the theory that after a given case is decided and appeals are exhausted, that case is final and binding, once and for all. Hence, the literal meaning of the words, "the thing has been adjudged." This principle is universally followed by all courts. Once the courts have decided the question, *that case* is over forever, no matter how wrong it may later appear the decision has been. Otherwise there would never be an end to a lawsuit.

On the other hand, the doctrine of *stare decisis,* "to stand by decided cases," has to do with the binding effect of prior decisions when *new* cases arise. Stated in another way, the question is: to what extent are prior decisions on the same question binding as precedent? Whereas *res judicata* is a doctrine of unswerving application, *stare decisis* is not.

Courts usually follow past decisions, but it has always been accepted in the United States that courts can overrule earlier cases and strike out upon new paths. The only critical question is, how free should a court feel in this overruling? The two following opinions present well the competing points of view.

The Brandeis opinion in the Coronado case is a dissenting opinion in which he is urging that an earlier decision, relied upon by the majority of the Court, should be overruled. His circumspect consideration of the *stare decisis* doctrine is of great utility. In footnotes to the opinion he listed approximately forty Supreme Court decisions on constitutional issues which had been partially or completely overruled by later decisions. We have already considered one decision which overruled a former decision of only a year previously—the *Legal Tender Cases.*

In sharp contrast is the dissenting opinion of Justice Owen J. Roberts in *Smith v. Allwright.* Justice Roberts, whose career we will consider later, stresses the wisdom of the past in his protest against the overruling of cases. One would conclude that Justice Roberts was set surely against overruling prior constitutional decisions.

BURNET v. CORONADO OIL & GAS CO.
Supreme Court of the United States, 1932, 285 U. S. 393

BRANDEIS, J., *dissenting*:

Under the rule of *Gillespie v. Oklahoma,* vast private incomes are being given immunity from state and federal taxation. . . . That case was wrongly decided and should now be frankly overruled. . . .

Stare decisis is not, like the rule of *res judicata,* a universal, inexorable command. "The rule of *stare decisis,* though one tending to consistency and uniformity of decision, is not inflexible. Whether it shall be followed or departed from is a question entirely within the discretion of the court, which is again called upon to consider a question once decided." *Hertz v. Woodman,* 218 U.S. 205, 212. *Stare decisis* is usually the wise policy, because in most matters it is more important that the applicable rule of law be settled than that it be settled right. . . . This is commonly true even where the error is a matter of serious concern, provided correction can be had by legislation. But in cases involving the Federal Constitution, where correction through legislative action is practically impossible, this Court has often overruled its earlier decisions. The Court bows to the lessons of experience and the force of better reasoning, recognizing that the process of trial and error, so fruitful in the physical sciences, is appropriate also in the judicial function. . . . Recently, it overruled several leading cases, when it concluded that the States should not have been permitted to exercise powers of taxation which it had theretofore repeatedly sanctioned. In cases involving the Federal Constitution the position of this Court is unlike that of the highest court of England, where the policy of *stare decisis* was formulated and is strictly applied to all classes of cases. Parliament is free to correct any judicial error; and the remedy may be promptly invoked.

The reasons why this Court should refuse to follow an earlier constitutional decision which it deems erroneous are particularly strong where the question presented is one of applying, as distinguished from what may accurately be called interpreting, the Constitution. In the cases which now come before us there is seldom any dispute as to the interpretation of any provision. The controversy is usually over the application to existing conditions of some well-recognized constitutional limitation. This is strikingly true of cases under the due process clause when the question is whether a statute is unreasonable, arbitrary or capricious; of cases under the equal protection clause when the question is whether there is any reasonable basis for the classification made by a statute; and of cases under the commerce clause when the question is whether an admitted burden laid by a statute upon interstate commerce is so substantial as to be deemed direct. These issues resemble, fundamentally, that of reasonable care in negligence cases, the determination of which is ordinarily left to the verdict of the jury. In every such case the decision, in the first instance, is dependent upon the determination of what in legal parlance is called a fact, as distinguished from the declaration of a rule of law. When the underlying fact has been found, the legal result follows inevitably. The circumstance that the decision of that fact is made by a court, instead of by a jury, should not be allowed to obscure its real character.

The issue presented by the case at bar is of the character of those discussed above. Here, also, the applicable provision of law is beyond dispute. Confessedly, the United States may not, by a tax, interfere substantially with the functions of a State. The question at issue is, whether as a practical matter, it does so interfere by a statute which includes among the items on which its general income tax is laid, the profits derived by the taxpayer from operating some of the State's school lands under a lease. . . . The question whether it would interfere substantially with the functions of the state government to permit the general income tax of the United States to include profits derived from the lease involves primarily the determination of a fact, not the decision of a proposition of law.

The doctrine of *res judicata* demands that a decision made by the highest court whether it be a determination of a fact or a declaration of a rule of law, shall be accepted as a final disposition of the particular controversy, even if confessedly wrong. But the decision of the Court, if, in essence, merely the determination of a fact, is not entitled, in later controversies between other parties, to that sanction which, under the policy of *stare decisis,* is accorded to the decision of a proposition purely of law. For not only may the decision of the fact have been rendered upon an inadequate presentation of then existing conditions, but the conditions may have changed meanwhile. . . . Moreover, the judgment of the Court in the earlier decision may have been influenced by prevailing views as to economic or social policy which have since been abandoned. In cases involving constitutional issues of the character discussed, this Court must, in order to reach sound conclusions, feel free to bring its opinions into agreement with experience and with facts newly ascertained, so that its judicial authority may, as Mr. Chief Justice Taney said, "depend altogether on the force of the reasoning by which it is supported."

SMITH v. ALLWRIGHT

Supreme Court of the United States, 1944, 321 U. S. 649

ROBERTS, J., *dissenting*:

In *Mahnich v. Southern Steamship Co.*, 321 U. S. 96, 105, I have expressed my views with respect to the present policy of the court freely to disregard and to overrule considered decisions and the rules of law announced in them. This tendency, it seems to me, indicates an intolerance for what those who have composed this court in the past have conscientiously and deliberately concluded, and involves an assumption that knowledge and wisdom reside in us which was denied to our predecessors. . . .

The reason for my concern is that the instant decision, overruling that announced about nine years ago, tends to bring adjudications of this tribunal into the same class as a restricted railroad ticket, good for this day and train only. I have no assurance, in view of current decisions, that the opinion announced today may not shortly be repudiated and overruled by justices who deem they have new light on the subject. In the present term the court has overruled three cases. . . .

It is suggested that *Grovey v. Townsend* [the case here overruled] was overruled *sub silentio* in *United States v. Classic,* 313 U. S. 299. If so, the situation is even worse than that exhibited by the outright repudiation of an earlier decision. . . .

If this court's opinion in the *Classic* case discloses its method of overruling earlier decisions, I can only protest that, in fairness, it should rather have adopted the open and frank way of saying what it was doing than, after the event, characterize its past action as overruling *Grovey v. Townsend* though those less sapient never realized the fact.

It is regrettable that in an era marked by doubt and confusion, an era whose greatest need is steadfastness of thought and purpose, this court, which has been looked to as exhibiting consistency in adjudication, and a steadiness which would hold the balance even in the face of temporary ebbs and flows of opinion, should now itself become the breeder of fresh doubt and confusion in the public mind as to the stability of our institutions.

ADDENDUM: Justice Roberts, the author of this opinion, was on the Court at the time of the decision in the Coronado case—and he joined in Justice Brandeis' dissenting opinion! Supreme Court justices are human. When they feel a prior decision is correct, they rely impregnably upon the doctrine of *stare decisis*. But when they are convinced that the earlier decision is wrong, *stare decisis* yields gracefully to new constitutional law. Thus does our Constitution adapt and grow to meet the challenges of each new day.

Chapter 6

"A strong public desire is not enough"

THE GOVERNMENTAL POWER to condemn private property so that it may be applied to a public use, which lawyers call "the power of eminent domain," was considered in the Gettysburg case. There the question was whether the preservation of a famous battlefield as a public park was a "public use," and the Court held that it was. Another phase of this governmental power of eminent domain raises a perplexing constitutional issue. What constitutes a "taking" of property, and thereby constitutionally requires the government to pay just compensation?

This problem can be most easily understood by assuming a practical situation. Suppose that a city enacts a zoning law restricting certain areas to residential use only. The owner of a plot of ground in that restricted area might have wished to build a factory or oil refinery upon his land. If such a use were allowed, the property would be worth a great deal more than its worth for residential purposes. The zoning law has caused him a great loss in the value of his property. Is this a "taking" of his property for which the government must pay compensation? The courts regularly answer, "No." The property has lost substantial value, but this is just one of the uncompensated losses common to all laws passed in our society. All laws to some extent restrict the freedoms of large numbers of citizens. A random consideration of laws of many types reveals this fundamental truth. Traffic regulations, proration of oil production, public utility rate regulation, pure food and drug acts, all of these, for instance, restrict freedom in the use of property or the personal freedom of some persons for the good of society as a whole. If we forced the government to pay for all these restrictions, no laws could be passed. The cost of paying compensation to all those damaged by the laws would be incalculable.

There must come a point, however, where the governmental regulation so interferes with the use of property that a "taking" within the meaning of the Constitution has occurred, and government must pay compensation. If the government decides to build a public structure on your property, obviously your property has been "taken" and the government must pay you. In the area between this obvious case of a "taking" of property and the situations mentioned in the preceding paragraph, cases arise in which a clear line is difficult to draw.

The leading Supreme Court decision drawing this line between permissible governmental regulation and the taking of property for which compensation must be paid is *Pennsylvania Coal Company v. Mahon*. In 1920 and 1921 the city of Scranton, Pennsylvania, suddenly awoke to the disheartening realization that it was in imminent danger of being swallowed up by the good earth. Coal mining in shafts honeycombing beneath the city had become so extensive that subsidence of the surface was beginning. A law was rushed through the state legislature by unanimous vote. It prohibited the mining of coal so as to cause subsidence of the surface. No compensation to the mining companies was provided.

Such a law might seem eminently reasonable, yet the mining companies protested its constitutionality. They protested because in earlier years when they had sold the surface of the land to private purchasers, and also to the city of Scranton for streets, parks, and other public uses, they had specifically limited their sales to the surface of the land only. The right of *surface support* was not sold to the surface owners. Since the newly enacted law prevented them from mining coal which they had previously had a right to mine, the mining companies asserted that their property had been "taken" in the constitutional sense. It followed that the statute was invalid since no just compensation had been provided.

The United States Supreme Court agreed with the assertion of the mining companies and held the statute unconstitutional. The opinion of the Court was written by Justice Holmes. His opinion is noteworthy because it provides at least a partial answer to those who charge him with subverting the constitutional protections of property. Here Holmes upheld the property right against the unanimous vote of the Pennsylvania legislature.

But the opinion has larger significance than this. It is one of the most outstanding examples of Holmes' openly pragmatic approach to the law. Holmes doesn't engage in the sophistry of making it a question of black or white. He candidly says it is purely a question of degree. Government can take some values in property without having to pay compensation, but if it takes too much, it has to pay. This viewing of the law in shadings of degree is accepted as elementary today. But until Holmes cast his light on this musty corner of jurisprudence, courts rarely talked in these straightforward terms. Holmes shook courts free from their polite and sterile language.

PENNSYLVANIA COAL COMPANY v. MAHON
Supreme Court of the United States, 1922, 260 U. S. 393

HOLMES, J.:

This is a bill in equity brought by the defendants in error to prevent the Pennsylvania Coal Company from mining under their property in such way as to remove the supports and cause a subsidence of the surface and of their house. The bill sets out a deed executed by the Coal Company in 1878, under which the plaintiffs claim. The deed conveys the surface, but in express terms reserves the right to remove all the coal under the same, and the grantee takes the premises with the risk, and waives all claim for damages that may arise from mining out the coal. But the plaintiffs say that whatever may have been the Coal Company's rights, they were taken away by an Act of Pennsylvania, approved May 27, 1921, P. L. 1198, commonly known there as the Kohler Act. . . .

The statute forbids the mining of anthracite coal in such way as to cause the subsidence of, among other things, any structure used as a human habitation, with certain exceptions, including among them land where the surface is owned by the owner of the underlying coal and is distant more than one hundred and fifty feet from any improved property belonging to any other person. As applied to this case the statute is admitted to destroy previously existing rights of property and contract. The question is whether the police power can be stretched so far.

Government hardly could go on if to some extent values incident to property could not be diminished without paying for every such change in the general law. As long recognized, some values are enjoyed under an implied limitation and must yield to the police power. But obviously the implied limitation must have its limits, or the contract and due process clauses are gone. One fact for consideration in determining such limits is the extent of the diminution. When it reaches a certain magnitude, in most if not in all cases there must be an exercise of eminent domain and compensation to sustain the act. So the question depends upon the particular facts. The greatest weight is given to the judgment of the legislature, but it always is open to interested parties to contend that the legislature has gone beyond its constitutional power. . . .

It is our opinion that the act cannot be sustained as an exercise of the police power, so far as it affects the mining of coal under streets or cities in places where the right to mine such coal has been reserved. As said in a Pennsylvania case, "For practical purposes, the right to coal consists in the right to mine it." *Commonwealth v. Clearview Coal Co.,* 256 Pa. St. 328, 331. What makes the right to mine coal valuable is that it can be exercised with profit. To make it commercially impracticable to mine certain coal has very nearly the same effect for constitutional purposes as appropriating or destroying it. This we think that we are warranted in assuming that the statute does. . . .

The rights of the public in a street purchased or laid out by eminent domain are those that it has paid for. If in any case its representatives have been so short sighted as to acquire only surface rights without the right of support, we see no more authority for supplying the latter without compensation than there was for taking the right of way in the first place, and refusing to pay for it because the public wanted it very much. The protection of private property in the Fifth Amendment presupposes that it is wanted for public use, but provides that it shall not be taken for such use without compensation. A similar assumption is made in the decisions upon the Fourteenth Amendment. When this seemingly absolute protection is found to be qualified by the police power, the natural tendency of human nature is to extend the qualification more and more until at last private property disappears. But that cannot be accomplished in this way under the Constitution of the United States.

The general rule, at least, is that while property may be regulated to a certain extent, if regulation goes too far it will be recognized as a taking. It may be doubted how far exceptional cases, like the blowing up of a house to stop a conflagration, go—and if they go beyond the general rule, whether they do not stand as much upon tradition as upon principle. In general it is not plain that a man's misfortunes or necessities will justify his shifting the damages to his neighbor's shoulders. We are in danger of forgetting that a strong public desire to improve the public condition is not enough to warrant achieving the desire by a shorter cut than the constitutional way of paying for the change. As we already have said, this is a question of degree—and therefore cannot be disposed of by general propositions. But we regard this as going beyond any of the cases decided by this Court. . . .

We assume, of course, that the statute was passed upon the conviction that an exigency existed that would warrant it, and we assume that an exigency exists that would warrant the exercise of eminent domain. But the question at bottom is upon whom the loss of the changes desired should fall. So far as private persons or communities have seen fit to take the risk of acquiring only surface rights, we cannot see that the fact that their risk has become a danger warrants the giving to them greater rights than they bought.

Chapter 7

"I do not believe in such apologies"

JUSTICE HOLMES wrote all of his opinions in longhand while standing at a high table. He once said when he began to get tired, he knew he was writing too much. This may be one reason for his terseness. His unique ability to say much with few words is surely another. Before we take leave of the man, let us read three more of the brief and remarkable constitutional documents which flowed from his pen.

The first opinion, his dissent in *Tyson & Brother v. Banton,* reiterates his belief that the Constitution does not forbid general governmental control of business. In this, its consideration is particularly apposite with the Mahon case. The suit challenged the constitutionality of a New York law which limited to fifty cents the mark-up of a theater ticket agency over the list price of the tickets which it sold. In modern parlance, the law was designed to eliminate "ticket scalping." The Supreme Court held the statute unconstitutional as a taking of property without due process of law.

The Holmes dissent is here printed in its entirety, except for one sentence containing a technical allusion to another field of the law. The case has since been specifically overruled, and the Holmes dissent states the law of today.

TYSON & BROTHER v. BANTON
Supreme Court of the United States, 1927, 273 U. S. 418

HOLMES, J., *dissenting*:

We fear to grant power and are unwilling to recognize it when it exists.... When legislatures are held to be authorized to do anything considerably affecting public welfare it is covered by apologetic phrases like the police power, or the statement that the business concerned has been dedicated to a public use. The former expression is convenient, to be sure, to conciliate the mind to something that needs explanation; the fact that the constitutional requirement of compensation when property is taken cannot be pressed to its grammatical extreme; that property rights may be taken for public purposes without pay if you do not take too much; that some play must be allowed to the joints if the machine is to work. But police power often is used in a wide sense to cover and, as I said, to apologize for the general power of the legislature to make a part of the community uncomfortable by a change.

I do not believe in such apologies. I think the proper course is to recognize that a state legislature can do whatever it sees fit to do unless it is restrained by some express prohibition in the Constitution of the United States or of the State, and that Courts should be careful not to extend such prohibitions beyond their obvious meaning by reading into them conceptions of public policy that the particular Court may happen to entertain. Coming down to the case before us, I think that the notion that a business is clothed with a public interest and has been devoted to the public use is little more than a fiction intended to beautify what is disagreeable to the sufferers. The truth seems to me to be that, subject to compensation when compensation is due, the legislature may forbid or restrict any business when it has a sufficient force of public opinion behind it. Lotteries were thought useful adjuncts of the State a century or so ago; now they are believed to be immoral and they have been stopped. Wine has been thought good for man from the time of the Apostles until recent years. But when public opinion changed it did not need the Eighteenth Amendment, nothwithstanding the Fourteenth, to enable a State to say that the business should end. What has happened to lotteries and wine might happen to theatres in some moral storm of the future, not because theatres were devoted to a public use, but because people had come to think that way.

But if we are to yield to fashionable conventions, it seems to me that theatres are as much devoted to public use as anything well can be. We have not that respect for art that is one of the glories of France. But to many people the superfluous is the necessary, and it seems to me that Government does not go beyond its sphere in attempting to make life livable for them. I am far from saying that I think this particular law a wise and rational provision. That is not my affair. But if the people of the State of New York speaking by their authorized voice say that they want it, I see nothing in the Constitution of the United States to prevent their having their will.

Chapter 8

*"Because they believe more than some of us do
in the teachings of the Sermon on the Mount"*

ONE OF HOLMES' MOST DEVASTATING dissenting opinions was that in *United States v. Schwimmer*. Mrs. Schwimmer, of Hungarian birth, made application to become a naturalized citizen of the United States. She was an extreme pacifist. Since she would not swear to "bear arms to defend the Constitution," she was denied citizenship under the Naturalization Act. The United States Supreme Court affirmed.

The dissent is here printed in its entirety. The leitmotif of the fundamental dignity of the human spirit is heard throughout, completely antithetical to the charges of "totalitarianism" and "authoritarianism" sung by Holmes' detractors.

UNITED STATES v. SCHWIMMER
Supreme Court of the United States, 1929, 279 U. S. 644

HOLMES, J., *dissenting*:

The applicant seems to be a woman of superior character and intelligence, obviously more than ordinarily desirable as a citizen of the

UNITED STATES V. SCHWIMMER

United States. It is agreed that she is qualified for citizenship except so far as the views set forth in a statement of facts "may show that the applicant is not attached to the principles of the Constitution of the United States and well disposed to the good order and happiness of the same, and except in so far as the same may show that she cannot take the oath of allegiance without a mental reservation." The views referred to are an extreme opinion in favor of pacifism and a statement that she would not bear arms to defend the Constitution. So far as the adequacy of her oath is concerned I hardly can see how that is affected by the statement, inasmuch as she is a woman over fifty years of age, and would not be allowed to bear arms if she wanted to. And as to the opinion, the whole examination of the applicant shows that she holds none of the now-dreaded creeds, but thoroughly believes in organized government and prefers that of the United States to any other in the world. Surely it cannot show lack of attachment to the principles of the Constitution that she thinks that it can be improved. I suppose that most intelligent people think that it might be. Her particular improvement looking to the abolition of war seems to me not materially different in its bearing on this case from a wish to establish cabinet government as in England, or a single house, or one term of seven years for the President. To touch a more burning question, only a judge mad with partisanship would exclude because the applicant thought that the Eighteenth Amendment should be repealed.

Of course, the fear is that if a war came the applicant would exert activities such as were dealt with in *Schenck v. United States,* 249 U. S. 47. But that seems to me unfounded. Her position and motives are wholly different from those of Schenck. She is an optimist and states in strong and, I do not doubt, sincere words her belief that war will disappear and that the impending destiny of mankind is to unite in peaceful leagues. I do not share that optimism nor do I think that a philosophic view of the world would regard war as absurd. But most people who have known it regard it with horror, as a last resort, and even if not yet ready for cosmopolitan efforts, would welcome any practicable combinations that would increase the power on the side of peace. The notion that the applicant's optimistic anticipation would make her a worse citizen is sufficiently answered by her examination, which seems to me a better argument for her admission than any that I can offer.

Some of her answers might excite popular prejudice, but if there is any principle of the Constitution that more imperatively calls for attachment than any other it is the principle of free thought—not free thought for those who agree with us but freedom for the thought that we hate. I think that we should adhere to that principle with regard to admission into, as well as to life within, this country. And recurring to the opinion that bars this applicant's way, I would suggest that the Quakers have done their share to make the country what it is, that many citizens agree with the applicant's belief, and that I had not supposed hitherto that we regretted our inability to expel them because they believe more than some of us do in the teachings of the Sermon on the Mount.

Chapter 9

"And that is enough"

MAJORITY OPINIONS of the Supreme Court normally spin an intricate web of legalism. There is iteration and reiteration, and all the byways are explored in meticulous detail. When Holmes wrote for the majority he had to be more prolix than was characteristically his style. He was writing for the other justices as well, and they had to be satisfied. But even then he still said more in fewer words than any judge in the history of the Supreme Court, and probably of any court.

One of the great examples in our literature of economy in writing is his opinion for the unanimous Court in *Herbert v. Shanley Co.* Yet there isn't a dull phrase in it; this is brevity with the sparkling touch of a master. Victor Herbert brought suit for copyright infringement claiming that the defendant hotel was in violation of the copyright law for having an orchestra in its dining room play Herbert's music without paying him for that privilege. The copyright statute prohibited the playing without permission of copyrighted music "for profit." The hotel defended by asserting that the music was not being played for profit since no admission was charged. Except for the omission of the statement of facts which all majority opinions must have, this is Holmes' answer in its entirety—clear, definite, complete, and final. Here is our last look at the workings of that magnificent legal mind.

247

HERBERT v. SHANLEY CO.
Supreme Court of the United States, 1917, 242 U. S. 591

HOLMES, J.:

If the rights under the copyright are infringed only by a performance where money is taken at the door, they are very imperfectly protected. Performances not different in kind from those of the defendants could be given that might compete with and even destroy the success of the monopoly that the law intends the plaintiffs to have. It is enough to say that there is no need to construe the statute so narrowly. The defendants' performances are not eleemosynary. They are part of a total for which the public pays, and the fact that the price of the whole is attributed to a particular item which those present are expected to order is not important. It is true that the music is not the sole object, but neither is the food, which probably could be got cheaper elsewhere. The object is a repast in surroundings that to people having limited powers of conversation, or disliking the rival noise, give a luxurious pleasure not to be had from eating a silent meal. If music did not pay, it would be given up. If it pays, it pays out of the public's pocket. Whether it pays or not, the purpose of employing it is profit, and that is enough.

Chapter 10

*"The stockyards are but a throat
through which the current flows"*

THE CONSTITUTION of the United States lives and grows. The federal government today exercises powers which it did not have in earlier times. The clearest example of this change is the great mass of legislation which the federal government now bases upon its power to regulate interstate commerce. Most of these regulations would not have been within the constitutional power of Congress in the earlier days of our government. Yet the words of the Constitution have not changed. How, then, does this increase of power take place? The answer to this question contains the secret of immortality in our splendid charter of government.

Let us pursue an example. In this century the national government has engaged in the detailed regulation of stockyards and slaughterhouses. If the First Congress, in 1789, had enacted such controls, they would surely have been unconstitutional. But from 1789 to the twentieth century, a great change has taken place in the business of selling meat. The development of transportation and refrigeration makes it possible today for a resident of New York City to eat fresh meat which has its origin on a ranch in Montana. The stockyards and slaughterhouses are an integral link in a nationwide pattern of commerce in livestock and meat products. Without modern transportation and refrigeration, preparing meat for use as food had to be a small local business. The livestock was obtained from nearby, and the meat sold in a narrow area. Scientific developments have changed a local business to a tremendous multi-state enterprise. Local commerce has become interstate commerce. Thus, the Constitution itself has not changed, but conditions have changed, and through that change dormant constitutional power is awakened. One hundred and fifty years ago Congress could not regulate the stockyard and slaughtering businesses because they were not interstate commerce. The businesses have now become interstate commerce, and Congress now has the power.

The case of *Stafford v. Wallace* exemplifies this growth of constitutional power necessary to stay abreast of changing needs. In 1921 Congress passed the Packers and Stockyards Act. Included within its provisions were detailed controls of the business practices of all stockyards having an area greater than 20,000 square feet. The unconstitutionality of this statute was asserted upon the ground that federal regulation was not within the national power over interstate commerce. The United States Supreme Court upheld the exertion of federal power. The unanimous decision was written by Chief Justice Taft. His specific recognition that the Constitution adapts itself to changing times is the core of his case.

Former President William Howard Taft was appointed Chief Justice by President Harding in 1921. This unique career could hardly have been foreseen in Taft's years of growth. Jovial, and rather indolent and a procrastinator, he was viewed by his illustrious family as somewhat of a wastrel in his earlier years. Taft seemed to find himself, however, when he was appointed to fill an unexpired term on the superior court of Ohio in 1887. After three years on this court he served two years as Solicitor General of the United States (the government's head trial lawyer), and was then named a federal circuit court judge by President Harrison. After eight years of this service, Taft resigned in 1900 to head the Philippine Commission, under the designation of President McKinley. In 1904 he returned to this country to become the Secretary of War in the cabinet of President Theodore Roosevelt.

In 1908, as Roosevelt's hand-picked successor, Taft was elected the twenty-seventh President of the United States. Taft's leanings were as deeply conservative as Roosevelt's were liberal. As soon as he left the role of servant and became the master, his conservatism rose to the forefront. Roosevelt abandoned his protégé, and in 1912 opposed him by running for President on the Bull Moose ticket. The resulting split of the Republican vote led to the election of President Woodrow Wilson.

After Taft left the Presidency, he became professor of constitutional law at the Yale Law School. During the First World War he served as chairman of the National War Labor Board. With his appointment as the ninth Chief Justice of the United States, he became truly unique— the only former President to sit on the Supreme Court Bench.

Taft was the most winsome of men, and an excellent administrator. The inspiring temple of justice that is the Supreme Court building in Washington was Taft's vision; he inaugurated the congressional action for its construction. As a judge, Taft displayed some indicia of mediocrity—he was unduly verbose, and his tendency to indolence and procrastination plagued him. But these are merely surface signs. If this veil is brushed aside, one finds a strong and thoroughly competent judge. He was much less willing to broaden the constitutional protections of individual freedom than were Holmes and Brandeis, but he was a stanch defender of national power. His opinion in *Stafford v. Wallace* reveals this latter bent.

STAFFORD v. WALLACE

Supreme Court of the United States, 1922, 258 U. S. 495

TAFT, C.J.:

The stockyards are not a place of rest or final destination. Thousands of head of live stock arrive daily by carload and trainload lots, and must be promptly sold and disposed of and moved out to give place to the constantly flowing traffic that presses behind. The stockyards are but a throat through which the current flows, and the transactions which occur therein are only incident to this current from the West to the East, and from one State to another. Such transactions can not be separated from the movement to which they contribute, and necessarily take on its character. The commission men are essential in making the sales without which the flow of the current would be obstructed, and this, whether they are made to packers or dealers. The dealers are essential to the sales to the stock farmers and feeders. The sales are not in this aspect merely local transactions. They create a local change of title, it is true, but they do not stop the flow; they merely change the private interest in the subject of the current, not interfering with, but, on the contrary, being indispensable to its continuity. The origin of the live stock is in the West, its ultimate destination known to, and intended by, all engaged in the business, is in the Middle West and East, either as meat products or stock for feeding and fattening. This is the definite and well-understood course of business. The stockyards and the sales are necessary factors in the middle of this current of commerce.

The act, therefore, treats the various stockyards of the country as great national public utilities to promote the flow of commerce from the ranges and farms of the West to the consumers in the East. It assumes that they conduct a business affected by a public use of a national character and subject to national regulation. That it is a business within the power of regulation by legislative action needs no discussion. That has been settled since the case of *Munn v. Illinois,* 94 U. S. 113. Nor is there any doubt that in the receipt of live stock by rail, and in their delivery by rail, the stockyards are an interstate commerce agency. *United States v. Union Stock Yard Co.,* 226 U. S. 286. The only question here is whether the business done in the stockyards between the receipt of the live stock in the yards and the shipment of them therefrom is a part of interstate commerce, or is so associated with it as to bring it within the power of national regulation. A similar question has been before this court and had great consideration in *Swift & Co. v. United States,* 196 U. S. 375. The judgment in that case gives a clear and comprehensive exposition which leaves to us in this case little but the obvious application of the principles there declared. . . .

"Commerce among the States is not a technical legal conception, but a practical one, drawn from the course of business. When cattle are sent for sale from a place in one State, with the expectation that they will end their transit, after purchase, in another, and when in effect they do so, with only the interruption necessary to find a purchaser at the stockyards, and when this is a typical, constantly recurring course, the current thus existing is a current of commerce among the States, and the purchase of the cattle is a part and incident of such commerce. What we say is true, at least, of such a purchase by residents in another State from that of the seller and of the cattle."

The application of the commerce clause of the Constitution in the *Swift Case* was the result of the natural development of interstate commerce under modern conditions. It was the inevitable recognition of the great central fact that such streams of commerce from one part of the country to another, which are ever flowing, are, in their very essence, the commerce among the States and with foreign nations which historically it was one of the chief purposes of the Constitution to bring under national protection and control. This court declined to defeat this purpose in respect of such a stream, and take it out of complete national regulation by a nice and technical inquiry into the non-interstate character of some of its necessary incidents and facilities when considered alone and without reference to their association with the movement of which they were an essential but subordinate part.

The principles of the *Swift Case* have become a fixed rule of this court in the construction and application of the commerce clause. . . .

Of course, what we are considering here is not a bill in equity or an indictment charging conspiracy to obstruct interstate commerce, but a law. The language of the law shows that what Congress had in mind primarily was to prevent such conspiracies by supervision of the agencies which would be likely to be employed in it. If Congress could provide for punishment or restraint of such conspiracies after their formation through the Anti-Trust Law, as in the *Swift Case,* certainly it may provide regulation to prevent their formation. The reasonable fear by Congress that such acts, usually lawful, and affecting only intrastate commerce when considered alone, will probably and more or less constantly be used in conspiracies against interstate commerce, or constitute a direct and undue burden on it, expressed in this remedial legislation, serves the same purpose as the intent charged in the Swift indictment to bring acts of a similar character into the current of interstate commerce for federal restraint. Whatever amounts to more or less constant practice, and threatens to obstruct or unduly to burden the freedom of interstate commerce, is within the regulatory power of Congress under the commerce clause, and it is primarily for Congress to consider and decide the fact of the danger and meet it. This court will certainly not substitute its judgment for that of Congress in such a matter unless the relation of the subject to interstate commerce and its effect upon it are clearly non-existent. . . .

As already noted, the word "commerce," when used in the act, is defined to be interstate and foreign commerce. Its provisions are carefully drawn to apply only to those practices and obstructions which, in the judgment of Congress, are likely to affect interstate commerce prejudicially. Thus construed and applied, we think the act clearly within congressional power and valid....

Chapter 11

"The strike became a lawful instrument in a lawful economic struggle"

TAFT CAME to the Supreme Court marked as a man unfriendly to labor. During his service as a federal circuit court judge from 1892 to 1900, his lot had been to decide a number of labor cases. These decisions form a definite antilabor pattern, but no more so than the vast majority of court decisions of that time. This was the heyday of the labor injunction, and Taft only conformed to the contemporaneous pattern. Nevertheless these antilabor decisions were used as ammunition against him in the presidential campaigns of 1908 and 1912.

Taft's "labor record" while he was Chief Justice certainly cannot be characterized as prolabor. On the other hand, he did dispel any thought that he was more antilabor than the general tenor of the times. And one of his labor opinions is cited today as embodying the classic Court statement justifying the forming of labor unions by workingmen. The case, *American Steel Foundries v. Tri-City Central Trades Council*, involved a more or less typical strike situation of the time. The employees were striking to force the employer to recognize and bargain with their union. Other union men in the community, not employees of the struck plant, were aiding in the picketing of the plant. The strikers were picketing in substantial numbers, and there had been some violence and abuse on the picket line. The company sued for an injunction prohibiting all picketing of the plant and, failing this, for an order prohibiting all men not employees of the company from participating in the picketing.

The Supreme Court unanimously refused to grant the relief asked. They did uphold an injunction against mass picketing and violent and unlawful acts. To prevent the picketing from getting out of hand the Court limited the number of pickets to one at each entrance of the plant. But the decision allowing some picketing to continue was a substantial advance for labor. Up to this case, courts had regularly prohibited all picketing once any violence on the picket line had occurred. As to the actions of the sympathetic union members aiding in the strike, the Court held flatly for the workers and against the company. The portion of Taft's opinion deciding this issue contains his memorable justification of labor unions.

Here is Taft at his honest, straightforward, and temperate best.

AMERICAN STEEL FOUNDRIES v. TRI-CITY CENTRAL TRADES COUNCIL

Supreme Court of the United States, 1921, 257 U. S. 184.

TAFT, C. J.:

The American Steel Foundries is a New Jersey corporation operating a large plant for the manufacture of steel products in Granite City, Illinois. In May, 1914, it filed a bill in the District Court for the Southern District of Illinois to enjoin the defendants, the Tri-City Central Trades Council, and fourteen individual defendants, some of them officers of the Council, all of them citizens of other States than New Jersey, from carrying on a conspiracy to prevent complainant from retaining and obtaining skilled laborers to operate its plant. The bill charged that the conspiracy was being executed by organized picketing, accompanied by threats, intimidation and violence toward persons employed or seeking employment there. The defendants in their answer admitted that the Central Trades Council had established a picket upon streets leading to the plant, with instructions to notify all persons entering it that a strike had been called because of reduction of wages, and to use all honorable means to persuade such persons not to take the places of the men on the strike; admitted the participation of individual defendants in the picketing, but denied threats of injury or violence or responsibility for the violence that admittedly had occurred....

It is clear from the evidence that, from the outset, violent methods were pursued from time to time in such a way as to characterize the attitude of the picketers as continuously threatening. A number of employees, sometimes fifteen or more, slept in the plant for a week during the trouble, because they could not safely go to their homes. The result of the campaign was to put employees and would-be employees in such fear that many abandoned work, and this seriously interfered with the complainant in operating the plant until the issue of the restraining order....

How far may men go in persuasion and communication and still not violate the right of those whom they would influence? In going to and from work, men have a right to as free a passage without obstruction as the streets afford, consistent with the right of others to enjoy the same privilege. We are a social people, and the accosting by one of another in an inoffensive way, and an offer by one to communicate and discuss information with a view to influencing the other's action, are not regarded as aggression or a violation of that other's rights. If, however, the offer is declined, as it may rightfully be, then persistence, importunity, following and dogging become unjustifiable annoyance and obstruction which is likely soon to savor of intimidation. From all of this the person sought to be influenced has a right to be free, and his employer has a right to have him free.

The nearer this importunate intercepting of employees or would-be employees is to the place of business, the greater the obstruction and interference with the business, and especially with the property right of access of the employer. Attempted discussion and argument of this kind in such proximity is certain to attract attention and congregation of the curious, or, it may be, interested bystanders, and thus to increase the obstruction as well as the aspect of intimidation which the situation quickly assumes. In the present case the three or four groups of picketers were made up of from four to twelve in a group. They constituted the picket lines. Each union interested, electricians, cranemen, machinists and blacksmiths, had several representatives on the picket line, and assaults and violence ensued. They began early and continued from time to time during the three weeks of the strike after the picketing began. All information tendered, all arguments advanced, and all persuasion used under such circumstances were intimidation. They could not be otherwise. It is idle to talk of peaceful communication in such a place and under such conditions. The numbers of the pickets in the groups constituted intimidation. The name "picket" indicated a militant purpose, inconsistent with peaceable persuasion. The crowds they drew made the passage of the employees to and from the place of work one of running the gauntlet. Persuasion or communication attempted in such a presence and under such conditions was anything but peaceable and lawful. When one or more assaults or disturbances ensued, they characterized the whole campaign, which became effective because of its intimidating character, in spite of the admonitions given by the leaders to their followers as to lawful methods to be pursued, however sincere. Our conclusion is that picketing thus instituted is unlawful and can not be peaceable, and may be properly enjoined by the specific term because its meaning is clearly understood in the sphere of the controversy by those who are parties to it. . . .

A restraining order against picketing will advise earnest advocates of labor's cause that the law does not look with favor on an enforced discussion of the merits of the issue between individuals who wish to work, and groups of those who do not, under conditions which subject the individuals who wish to work to a severe test of their nerve and physical strength and courage. But while this is so, we must have every regard to the congressional intention manifested in the act and to the principle of existing law which it declared, that ex-employees and others properly acting with them shall have an opportunity, so far as is consistent with peace and law, to observe who are still working for the employer, to communicate with them, and to persuade them to join the ranks of his opponents in a lawful economic struggle. Regarding as primary the

AMERICAN STEEL V. TRI-CITY CENTRAL TRADES COUNCIL

rights of the employees to work for whom they will, and, undisturbed by annoying importunity or intimidation of numbers, to go freely to and from their place of labor, and keeping in mind the right of the employer, incident to his property and business, to free access of such employees, what can be done to reconcile the conflicting interests?

Each case must turn on its own circumstances. It is a case for the flexible remedial power of a court of equity, which may try one mode of restraint, and if it fails or proves to be too drastic, may change it. We think that the strikers and their sympathizers engaged in the economic struggle should be limited to one representative for each point of ingress and egress in the plant or place of business, and that all others be enjoined from congregating or loitering at the plant or in the neighboring streets by which access is had to the plant; that such representatives should have the right of observation, communication and persuasion but with special admonition that their communication, arguments and appeals shall not be abusive, libelous or threatening, and that they shall not approach individuals together, but singly, and shall not, in their single efforts at communication or persuasion, obstruct an unwilling listener by importunate following or dogging his steps. This is not laid down as a rigid rule, but only as one which should apply to this case under the circumstances disclosed by the evidence, and which may be varied in other cases. It becomes a question for the judgment of the Chancellor, who has heard the witnesses, familiarized himself with the *locus in quo,* and observed the tendencies to disturbance and conflict. The purpose should be to prevent the inevitable intimidation of the presence of groups of pickets, but to allow missionaries. . . .

The second important question in the case is as to the form of decree against the Tri-City Trades Council and the other defendants. What has been said as to picketing applies to them, of course, as fully as to the ex-employees, but how as to the injunction against persuasion?

The argument made on behalf of the American Foundries in support of enjoining persuasion is that the Tri-City Central Trades Council and the other defendants, being neither employees nor strikers, were intruders into the controversy, and were engaged without excuse in an unlawful conspiracy to injure the American Foundries by enticing its employees, and, therefore, should be enjoined.

It is to be noted, that while there was only one member of the unions of the Trades Council who went out in the strike, the number of skilled employees then engaged by the Foundries was not one-quarter of the whole number of men who would be engaged when it was in full operation. The works manager said that eighty or ninety per cent of the employees were old men and that he assumed these men were members of various organizations. Other witnesses, members of the unions, testified that they had been employees of complainant in the previous fall. It is thus probable that members of the local unions were looking forward to employment when complainant should resume full operation, and even though they were not ex-employees within the Clayton Act, they were directly interested in the wages which were to be paid.

Is interference of a labor organization by persuasion and appeal to induce a strike against low wages, under such circumstances, without lawful excuse and malicious? We think not. Labor unions are recognized by the Clayton Act as legal when instituted for mutual help and lawfully carrying out their legitimate objects. They have long been thus recognized by the courts. They were organized out of the necessities of the situation. A single employee was helpless in dealing with an employer. He was dependent ordinarily on his daily wage for the maintenance of himself and family. If the employer refused to pay him the wages that he thought fair, he was nevertheless unable to leave the employ and to resist arbitrary and unfair treatment. Union was essential to give laborers opportunity to deal on equality with their employer. They united to exert influence upon him and to leave him in a body, in order, by this inconvenience, to induce him to make better terms with them. They were withholding their labor of economic value to make him pay what they thought it was worth. The right to combine for such a lawful purpose has in many years not been denied by any court. The strike became a lawful instrument in a lawful economic struggle or competition between employer and employees as to the share or division between them of the joint product of labor and capital. To render this combination at all effective, employees must make their combination extend beyond one shop. It is helpful to have as many as may be in the same trade in the same community united, because in the competition between employers they are bound to be affected by the standard of wages of their trade in the neighborhood. Therefore, they may use all lawful propaganda to enlarge their membership, and especially among those whose labor at lower wages will injure their whole guild. It is impossible to hold such persuasion and propaganda, without more, to be without excuse and malicious. The principle of the unlawfulness of maliciously enticing laborers still remains, and action may be maintained therefor in proper cases; but to make it applicable to local labor unions, in such a case as this, seems to us to be unreasonable. . . .

PART FIVE

Chief Justice Hughes and the Court
of the "Nine Old Men"

FIVE

Chapter 1

"A growth from the seeds which the fathers planted"

THE GREAT DEPRESSION struck. And government moved to counter its devastation. The New Deal, with its National Industrial Recovery Act and other stringent business controls, pushed federal power far beyond any previous uses. Nor were the states idle; desperate and novel measures streamed from state legislatures to stop the descent into an economic void. Broadside constitutional attack upon this panoply of governmental regulation was inevitable. A whirlwind of constitutional cases roared into the Supreme Court—the Court of the "Nine Old Men," as it later came to be called.

Before we can understand what happened in these cases, a few words of analysis are necessary. Almost all constitutional questions fall into two fundamental classifications. One classification consists of the questions involving governmental control of the freedoms of the individual. Here the Constitution defines a broad area which preserves human freedom against the encroachment of either the federal government or the governments of the states. This is the area of freedom of speech and religion, of freedom from unreasonable searches and seizures, and freedom from unfair judicial process. In general, this is the area we have already referred to as "due process of law"—the freedom of the individual to live, own property, and move about without undue governmental restriction. Both federal and state governments are forbidden intrusion on this sacred ground.

The other fundamental classification of constitutional questions is applicable only to a federal system of government. Here are the questions that have to do with the apportionment of power between the federal government and the states—hard and intricate questions in our scheme of government. They are nonexistent in unitary governments like those of Great Britain and most of the other countries of the world. Note particularly that these questions never arise unless the "due process" issues in a case have been resolved in favor of constitutionality—because if a law violates individual liberties it is of no moment which government, state or federal, passed the law. The law fails in either case. It is only when a law can validly be enacted by one of the two governments, federal or state, that the question arises as to which of those two governments has the power. And the constitutional principle is that the states have all the power that is not specifically delegated to the federal government by the Constitution.

The significance of these two classifications is revealed in the clearly defined pattern of Supreme Court decisions involving the validity of the depression-countering measures. Generally speaking, in the earlier days of the New Deal the Court upheld the validity of those statutes challenged as infringements of individual liberty. The decisions were close, nearly all of them five to four, but nevertheless most of these measures were upheld. On the other hand, the decisions which involved the second category, the power of the federal government as against state power, almost universally held against federal regulation. Here the decisions were usually close also, the vote being typically five to four, occasionally six to three.

Thus, a bare majority of the Court created a general pattern upholding state attempts to fight depression and striking down federal controls. Yet, as one of those peculiarities which counting of votes can cause, only one of the nine justices actually was in agreement with this pattern of constitutional decision. Four of the nine voted regularly to strike down both state and federal measures. The other four voted almost as regularly to uphold the federal as well as the state laws. The ninth justice, Owen J. Roberts, usually determined the decisions by voting in favor of state control and against federal. He was truly the "swing man."

With a reminder once again that the cases involving *state* depression-countering measures were cases concerned with the impact of governmental control upon individual freedom, let us consider the "Mortgage Moratorium Case." In the depths of the depression most states enacted laws postponing the foreclosure of mortgages for failure to meet payments. Economic conditions were so ominous that much of the mortgaged residential and business property in the United States would have been foreclosed without these laws. However, there was a vital constitutional issue posed by their enactment. Article I, Section 10 of the Constitution provides, "No State shall... pass any... Law impairing the Obligation of Contracts." A mortgage is, of course, a contract. Further, it is clear that the framers of the Constitution inserted this provision specifically to prevent states' easing the obligations of debtors in times of depression.

The challenge in the Supreme Court directed at the Minnesota Mortgage Moratorium (*Home Building & Loan Association v. Blaisdell*) raised a tense issue in troublous times. The Court held in a five–four decision that the act was constitutional. Chief Justice Hughes wrote the opinion. The legal dilemma posed by the constitutional words set forth above was resolved by a finding that all contracts are impliedly limited by governmental power to protect the health, welfare, and safety of citizens—the "police power." This principle has its roots in ancient common law—a contract contrary to "public policy" is unenforceable. However, the Court did not give legislatures carte blanche to subvert all contract obligations. There was clear inference that this doctrine would not countenance a wiping out of the mortgage debts. Rather, the opinion stressed that the statutes were far short of *releasing* the obligations secured by mortgage: the obligations were only *postponed*. Further, during the interim period, the rights of the creditor were adequately preserved by requiring a fair rental to be paid him. The net result was a reasonable reconciliation of the conflicting interests.

The author of the Mortgage Moratorium opinion, Chief Justice Hughes, was the very prototype for a Chief Justice of the United States, not only in his career but in his appearance. With his flowing white beard, dignified and austere manner, he was the picture of the great statesman. And he was a great statesman. For variety in statecraft, his career is unrivaled by that of any other man who ever served upon the Court.

Charles Evans Hughes was born and reared in New York. He did his undergraduate work at Brown University and received his law degree from Columbia Law School. He taught law at Cornell for two years and then practiced in New York City. The prominence he gained as special prosecutor in a New York political scandal led to his election in 1906 as governor of New York. He was re-elected in 1908; in 1910 he resigned to accept President Taft's appointment as an associate justice of the

United States Supreme Court. Upon his nomination in 1916 for President of the United States, he resigned from the Court. President Wilson, running for re-election, defeated him by the narrowest of margins. Hughes then returned to law practice in New York City until he was designated Secretary of State by President Harding in 1921; after Harding's death, he continued to serve under Coolidge until 1925. From 1926 to 1930, Hughes was probably the leading diplomat of the world. A delegate to all important international conclaves, he also served as a member of the Permanent Court of Arbitration (an international tribunal) and as a justice of the Permanent Court of International Justice.

In 1930 Charles Evans Hughes returned to the Court which he had left in 1916, named Chief Justice by President Hoover. There he served for eleven dramatic and perilous years. As Chief Justice, he was not only a sound administrator but a great leader. The breadth of his leadership will be the subject of later consideration. As a judge, Hughes was powerful and compelling. Neither liberal nor conservative, he was often found with the dissenting justices when the Court, in the earlier days of the New Deal, struck down federal laws as beyond the national power. His opinions are formal, restrained, and somewhat heavy. They read as polished official state documents, as indeed they are.

HOME BUILDING & LOAN ASSOCIATION v. BLAISDELL

Supreme Court of the United States, 1934, 290 U. S. 398

HUGHES, C. J.:

In determining whether the provision for this temporary and conditional relief exceeds the power of the State by reason of the clause in the Federal Constitution prohibiting impairment of the obligations of contracts, we must consider the relation of emergency to constitutional power, the historical setting of the contract clause, the development of the jurisprudence of this Court in the construction of that clause, and the principles of construction which we may consider to be established.

Emergency does not create power. Emergency does not increase granted power or remove or diminish the restrictions imposed upon power granted or reserved. The Constitution was adopted in a period of grave emergency. Its grants of power to the Federal Government and its limitations of the power of the States were determined in the light of emergency, and they are not altered by emergency. What power was thus granted and what limitations were thus imposed are questions which have always been, and always will be, the subject of close examination under our constitutional system.

While emergency does not create power, emergency may furnish the occasion for the exercise of power. "Although an emergency may not call into life a power which has never lived, nevertheless emergency may afford a reason for the exertion of a living power already enjoyed." *Wilson v. New,* 243 U. S. 332, 348. The constitutional question presented in the light of an emergency is whether the power possessed embraces the particular exercise of it in response to particular conditions. Thus, the war power of the Federal Government is not created by the emergency of war, but it is a power given to meet that emergency. It is a power to wage war successfully, and thus it permits the harnessing of the entire energies of the people in a supreme cooperative effort to preserve the nation. But even the war power does not remove constitutional limitations safeguarding essential liberties. When the provisions of the Constitution, in grant or restriction, are specific, so particularized as not to admit of construction, no question is presented. Thus, emergency would not permit a State to have more than two Senators in the Congress, or permit the election of President by a general popular vote without regard to the number of electors to which the States are respectively entitled, or permit the States to "coin money" or to "make anything but gold and silver coin a tender in payment of debts." But where constitutional grants and limitations of power are set forth in general clauses, which afford a broad outline, the process of construction is essential to fill in the details. That is true of the contract clause....

The reservation of essential attributes of sovereign power is also read into contracts as a postulate of the legal order. The policy of protecting contracts against impairment presupposes the maintenance of a government by virtue of which contractual relations are worthwhile,— a government which retains adequate authority to secure the peace and good order of society. This principle of harmonizing the constitutional prohibition with the necessary residuum of state power has had progressive recognition in the decisions of this Court....

The legislature cannot "bargain away the public health or the public morals." Thus, the constitutional provision against the impairment of contracts was held not to be violated by an amendment of the state constitution which put an end to a lottery theretofore authorized by the legislature. *Stone v. Mississippi,* 101 U. S. 814, 819. The lottery was a valid enterprise when established under express state authority, but the legislature in the public interest could put a stop to it. A similar rule has been applied to the control by the State of the sale of intoxicating liquors. *Boston Beer Co. v. Massachusetts,* 97 U. S. 25, 32, 33. The States retain adequate power to protect the public health against the maintenance of nuisances despite insistence upon existing contracts. *Northwestern Fertilizing Co. v. Hyde Park,* 97 U. S. 659, 667. Legislation to protect the public safety comes within the same category of reserved power....

The economic interests of the State may justify the exercise of its continuing and dominant protective power notwithstanding interference with contracts. In *Manigault v. Springs,* 199 U. S. 473, riparian owners in South Carolina had made a contract for a clear passage through a creek by the removal of existing obstructions. Later, the legislature of the State, by virtue of its broad authority to make public improvements, and in order to increase the taxable value of the lowlands which would be drained, authorized the construction of a dam across the creek. The Court sustained the statute upon the ground that the private interests were subservient to the public right. The Court said (id., p. 480): "It is the settled law of this court that the interdiction of statutes impairing the obligation of contracts does not prevent the State from exercising such powers as are vested in it for the promotion of the common weal, or are necessary for the general good of the public, though contracts previously entered into between individuals may thereby be affected. This power, which in its various ramifications is known as the police power, is an exercise of the sovereign right of the Government to protect the lives, health, morals, comfort and general welfare of the people, and is paramount to any rights under contracts between individuals." A statute of New Jersey prohibiting the transportation of water of the

State into any other State was sustained against the objection that the statute impaired the obligation of contracts which had been made for furnishing such water to persons without the State. *Hudson Water Co. v. McCarter,* 209 U. S. 349. Said the Court, by Mr. Justice Holmes (id., p. 357): "One whose rights, such as they are, are subject to state restriction, cannot remove them from the power of the State by making a contract about them. The contract will carry with it the infirmity of the subject matter." ...

Undoubtedly, whatever is reserved of state power must be consistent with the fair intent of the constitutional limitation of that power. The reserved power cannot be construed so as to destroy the limitation, nor is the limitation to be construed to destroy the reserved power in its essential aspects. They must be construed in harmony with each other. This principle precludes a construction which would permit the State to adopt as its policy the repudiation of debts or the destruction of contracts or the denial of means to enforce them. But it does not follow that conditions may not arise in which a temporary restraint of enforcement may be consistent with the spirit and purpose of the constitutional provision and thus be found to be within the range of the reserved power of the State to protect the vital interests of the community. It cannot be maintained that the constitutional prohibition should be so construed as to prevent limited and temporary interpositions with respect to the enforcement of contracts if made necessary by a great public calamity such as fire, flood, or earthquake. See *American Land Co. v. Zeiss,* 219 U. S. 47. The reservation of state power appropriate to such extraordinary conditions may be deemed to be as much a part of all contracts, as is the reservation of state power to protect the public interest in the other situations to which we have referred. And if state power exists to give temporary relief from the enforcement of contracts in the presence of disasters due to physical causes such as fire, flood or earthquake, that power cannot be said to be non-existent when the urgent public need demanding such relief is produced by other and economic causes. ...

It is manifest from this review of our decisions that there has been a growing appreciation of public needs and of the necessity of finding ground for a rational compromise between individual rights and public welfare. The settlement and consequent contraction of the public domain, the pressure of a constantly increasing density of population, the interrelation of the activities of our people and the complexity of our economic interests, have inevitably led to an increased use of the organization of society in order to protect the very bases of individual opportunity. Where, in earlier days, it was thought that only the concerns of individuals or of classes were involved, and that those of the State itself were touched only remotely, it has later been found that the fundamental interests of the State are directly affected; and that the question is no longer merely that of one party to a contract as against another, but of the use of reasonable means to safeguard the economic structure upon which the good of all depends.

It is no answer to say that this public need was not apprehended a century ago, or to insist that what the provision of the Constitution meant to the vision of that day it must mean to the vision of our time. If by the statement that what the Constitution meant at the time of its adoption it means today, it is intended to say that the great clauses of the Constitution must be confined to the interpretation which the framers, with the conditions and outlook of their time, would have placed upon them, the statement carries its own refutation. It was to guard against such a narrow conception that Chief Justice Marshall uttered the memorable warning—"We must never forget that it is a constitution we are expounding" (*McCulloch v. Maryland,* 4 Wheat. 316, 407)—"a constitution intended to endure for ages to come, and consequently, to be adapted to the various crises of human affairs." Id., p. 415. When we are dealing with the words of the Constitution, said this Court in *Missouri v. Holland,* 252 U. S. 416, 433, "we must realize that they have called into life a being the development of which could not have been foreseen completely by the most gifted of its begetters. . . . The case before us must be considered in the light of our whole experience and not merely in that of what was said a hundred years ago."

Nor is it helpful to attempt to draw a fine distinction between the intended meaning of the words of the Constitution and their intended application. When we consider the contract clause and the decisions which have expounded it in harmony with the essential reserved power of the States to protect the security of their peoples, we find no warrant for the conclusion that the clause has been warped by these decisions from its proper significance or that the founders of our Government would have interpreted the clause differently had they had occasion to assume that responsibility in the conditions of the later day. The vast body of law which has been developed was unknown to the fathers, but it is believed to have preserved the essential content and the spirit of the Constitution. With a growing recognition of public needs and the relation of individual right to public security, the court has sought to prevent the perversion of the clause through its use as an instrument to throttle the capacity of the States to protect their fundamental interests. This development is a growth from the seeds which the fathers planted. . . . The principle of this development is, as we have seen, that the reservation of the reasonable exercise of the protective power of the State is read into all contracts. . . .

Applying the criteria established by our decisions, we conclude:

1. An emergency existed in Minnesota which furnished a proper occasion for the exercise of the reserved power of the State to protect the vital interests of the community. . . .

2. The legislation was addressed to a legitimate end; that is, the legislation was not for the mere advantage of particular individuals but for the protection of a basic interest of society.

3. In view of the nature of the contracts in question—mortgages of unquestionable validity—the relief afforded and justified by the emergency, in order not to contravene the constitutional provision, could only be of a character appropriate to that emergency, and could be granted only upon reasonable conditions.

4. The conditions . . . do not appear to be unreasonable. . . . The integrity of the mortgage indebtedness is not impaired; interest continues to run. . . . The mortgagor . . . must pay the rental value of the premises as ascertained in judicial proceedings and this amount is applied to the carrying of the property and to interest upon the indebtedness. . . .

5. The legislation is temporary in operation. It is limited to the exigency which called it forth. . . .

We are of the opinion that the Minnesota statute as here applied does not violate the contract clause of the Federal Constitution. Whether the legislation is wise or unwise as a matter of policy is a question with which we are not concerned. . . .

Chapter 2

"For adequate reason"

THE TERM "PHILADELPHIA LAWYER" originated in Colonial days, stemming from the high reputation of the Philadelphia Bar. Recently it has come to be used disparagingly; but in its earlier sense Justice Owen J. Roberts was its personification. Born and reared in the City of Brotherly Love, he took his undergraduate and law degrees at the University of Pennsylvania, then taught at the University Law School until his rapidly burgeoning practice forced him to abandon teaching. He was soon a leader of the Philadelphia Bar. In 1924 President Coolidge appointed him a special prosecutor in the Teapot Dome oil scandal, and his outstanding success here led to national renown. Busy and successful practice of the law continued until President Hoover named him to the Supreme Court in 1930.

During Roberts' tenure on the Court he headed an unusual and difficult mission. President Franklin Roosevelt named him to lead an investigation of the Pearl Harbor tragedy, and Roberts took leave from the Court for the task. The unbiased and exhaustive report resulting from the investigation is an invalauble historical document. In 1945 Roberts retired from the Court, still vigorous and alert at the age of seventy. He then devoted himself to the cause of world peace, and also to his beloved alma mater, where he served as dean of the Law School from 1948 to 1952. He died in the spring of 1955, at the age of eighty.

The opportune role which Justice Roberts played in the early New Deal days has already been mentioned. It was the Roberts vote that usually swung the Court toward upholding state depression legislation, where the question was one of governmental power against individual freedom, and swung the Court against upholding federal power, where the question was whether the federal government or the states could control.

In many ways Chief Justice Hughes and Justice Roberts were alike in their judicial roles. Roberts was a man of dignified bearing and forceful personality. Kindly and warm in the intimacy of close friendship, his public appearance as a judge was one of solemnity and poise. His opinions are without flair, but they sound of firmness and authority.

The most significant opinion in Roberts' career is the one he wrote for the five-man majority in *Nebbia v. New York*. As a depression measure, New York embarked upon a program of governmental fixing of milk prices. Constitutional challenge of the validity of this program was grounded upon the "freedom of contract" concept. Under the Court's prior decisions, the assertion of unconstitutionality would appear to have been well taken. Recall that regularly in the earlier years of this century the Court struck down business controls. Justice Holmes and Brandeis constantly attacked these holdings in dissent, but without success. It remained for Roberts to abandon the older cases and strike out anew upon the path which Holmes and Brandeis had charted.

The Nebbia case is truly the turning point in this constitutional area. Before this decision, only the narrow class of businesses historically classified as "public utilities" were held subject to any substantial governmental control by either the states or the nation. Roberts swept away this restrictive limitation and held that any business, "for adequate reason, is subject to control for the public good." Since the Nebbia case, governmental control of business has become so ingrained in our thinking that constitutional challenge rarely occurs. Justice Brandeis, still on the Court, concurred in this vindication of his own prior dissents. Justice Holmes, retired and a venerable ninety-three years of age, must have sighed with satisfaction and muttered, "It had to come."

NEBBIA v. NEW YORK

Supreme Court of the United States, 1934, 291 U. S. 502

ROBERTS, J.:

Under our form of government the use of property and the making of contracts are normally matters of private and not of public concern. The general rule is that both shall be free of governmental interference. But neither property rights nor contract rights are absolute; for government cannot exist if the citizen may at will use his property to the detriment of his fellows, or exercise his freedom of contract to work them harm. Equally fundamental with the private right is that of the public to regulate it in the common interest. . . .

This court from the early days [has] affirmed that the power to promote the general welfare is inherent in government. Touching the matters committed to it by the Constitution, the United States possesses the power, as do the states in their sovereign capacity touching all subjects jurisdiction of which is not surrendered to the federal government. . . . These correlative rights, that of the citizen to exercise exclusive dominion over property and freely to contract about his affairs, and that of the state to regulate the use of property and the conduct of business, are always in collision. No exercise of the private right can be imagined which will not in some respect, however slight, affect the public; no exercise of the legislative prerogative to regulate the conduct of the citizen which will not to some extent abridge his liberty or affect his property. But subject only to constitutional restraint the private right must yield to the public need.

The Fifth Amendment, in the field of federal activity, and the Fourteenth, as respects state action, do not prohibit governmental regulation for the public welfare. They merely condition the exertion of the admitted power, by securing that the end shall be accomplished by methods consistent with due process. And the guaranty of due process, as has often been held, demands only that the law shall not be unreasonable, arbitrary or capricious, and that the means selected shall have a real and substantial relation to the object sought to be attained. It results that a regulation valid for one sort of business, or in given circumstances, may be invalid for another sort, or for the same business under other circumstances, because the reasonableness of each regulation depends upon the relevant facts.

The reports of our decisions abound with cases in which the citizen, individual or corporate, has vainly invoked the Fourteenth Amendment in resistance to necessary and appropriate exertion of the police power.

The court has repeatedly sustained curtailment of enjoyment of private property, in the public interest. The owner's rights may be subordinated to the needs of other private owners whose pursuits are vital to the paramount interests of the community. The state may control the use of property in various ways; may prohibit advertising bill boards except of a prescribed size and location, or their use for certain kinds of advertising; may in certain circumstances authorize encroachments by party walls in cities; may fix the height of buildings, the character of materials, and methods of construction, the adjoining area which must be left open, and may exclude from residential sections offensive trades, industries and structures likely injuriously to affect the public health or safety; or may establish zones within which certain types of buildings or businesses are permitted and others excluded. And although the Fourteenth Amendment extends protection to aliens as well as citizens, a state may for adequate reasons of policy exclude aliens altogether from the use and occupancy of land.

Laws passed for the suppression of immorality, in the interest of health, to secure fair trade practices, and to safeguard the interests of depositors in banks, have been found consistent with due process. These measures not only affected the use of private property, but also interfered with the right of private contract. Other instances are numerous where valid regulation has restricted the right of contract, while less directly affecting property rights.

The Constitution does not guarantee the unrestricted privilege to engage in a business or to conduct it as one pleases. Certain kinds of business may be prohibited; and the right to conduct a business, or to pursue a calling, may be conditioned. Regulation of a business to prevent waste of the state's resources may be justified. And statutes prescribing the terms upon which those conducting certain businesses may contract, or imposing terms if they do enter into agreements, are within the state's competency.

Legislation concerning sales of goods, and incidentally affecting prices, has repeatedly been held valid. In this class fall laws forbidding unfair competition by the charging of lower prices in one locality than those exacted in another, by giving trade inducements to purchasers, and by other forms of price discrimination. The public policy with respect to free competition has engendered state and federal statutes prohibiting monopolies, which have been upheld. On the other hand, where the policy of the state dictated that a monopoly should be granted, statutes having that effect have been held inoffensive to the constitutional guarantees. Moreover, the state or a municipality may itself enter into business in competition with private proprietors, and thus effectively although indirectly control the prices charged by them.

The milk industry in New York has been the subject of long-standing and drastic regulation in the public interest. The legislative investigation of 1932 was persuasive of the fact that for this and other reasons unrestricted competition aggravated existing evils, and the normal law of supply and demand was insufficient to correct maladjustments detrimental to the community. The inquiry disclosed destructive and demoralizing competitive conditions and unfair trade practices which resulted in retail price-cutting and reduced the income of the farmer below the cost of production. We do not understand the appellant to deny that in these circumstances the legislature might reasonably consider further regulation and control desirable for protection of the industry and the consuming public. That body believed conditions could be improved by preventing destructive price-cutting by stores which, due to the flood of surplus milk, were able to buy at much lower prices than the larger distributors and to sell without incurring the delivery costs of the latter. In the order of which complaint is made the Milk Control Board fixed a price of ten cents per quart for sales by a distributor to a consumer, and nine cents by a store to a consumer, thus recognizing the lower costs of the store, and endeavoring to establish a differential which would be just to both. In the light of the facts the order appears not to be unreasonable or arbitrary, or without relation to the purpose to prevent ruthless competition from destroying the wholesale price structure on which the farmer depends for his livelihood, and the community for an assured supply of milk.

But we are told that because the law essays to control prices it denies due process. Notwithstanding the admitted power to correct existing economic ills by appropriate regulation of business, even though an indirect result may be a restriction of the freedom of contract or a modification of charges for services or the price of commodities, the appellant urges that direct fixation of prices is a type of regulation absolutely forbidden. His position is that the Fourteenth Amendment requires us to hold the challenged statute void for this reason alone. The argument runs that the public control of rates or prices is *per se* unreasonable and unconstitutional, save as applied to businesses affected with a public interest; that a business so affected is one in which property is devoted to an enterprise of a sort which the public itself might appropriately undertake, or one whose owner relies on a public grant or franchise for the right to conduct the business, or in which he is bound to serve all who apply; in short, such as is commonly called a public utility; or a business in its nature a monopoly. The milk industry, it is said, possesses none of these characteristics, and, therefore, not being affected with a public interest, its charges may not be controlled by the state. Upon the soundness of this contention the appellant's case against the statute depends.

We may as well say at once that the dairy industry is not, in the accepted sense of the phrase, a public utility. We think the appellant is also right in asserting that there is in this case no suggestion of any monopoly or monopolistic practice. It goes without saying that those engaged in the business are in no way dependent upon public grants or franchises for the privilege of conducting their activities. But if, as must be conceded, the industry is subject to regulation in the public interest, what constitutional principle bars the state from correcting existing maladjustments by legislation touching prices? We think there is no such principle. The due process clause makes no mention of sales or of prices any more than it speaks of business or contracts or buildings or other incidents of property. The thought seems nevertheless to have persisted that there is something peculiarly sacrosanct about the price one may charge for what he makes or sells, and that, however able to regulate other elements of manufacture or trade, with incidental effect upon price, the state is incapable of directly controlling the price itself. This view was negatived many years ago. *Munn v. Illinois,* 94 U. S. 113. The appellant's claim is, however, that this court, in there sustaining a statutory prescription of charges for storage by the proprietors of a grain elevator, limited permissible legislation of that type to businesses affected with a public interest, and he says no business is so affected except it have one or more of the characteristics he enumerates. But this is a misconception. Munn and Scott held no franchise from the state. They owned the property upon which their elevator was situated and conducted their business as private citizens. No doubt they felt at liberty to deal with whom they pleased and on such terms as they might deem just to themselves. Their enterprise could not fairly be called a monopoly, although it was referred to in the decision as a "virtual monopoly." This meant only that their elevator was strategically situated and that a large portion of the public found it highly inconvenient to deal with others. This court concluded the circumstances justified the legislation as an exercise of the governmental right to control the business in the public interest; that is, as an exercise of the police power. . . .

It is clear that there is no closed class or category of businesses affected with a public interest, and the function of courts in the application of the Fifth and Fourteenth Amendments is to determine in each case whether circumstances vindicate the challenged regulation as a reasonable exertion of governmental authority or condemn it as arbitrary or discriminatory. The phrase "affected with a public interest" can, in the nature of things, mean no more than that an industry, for adequate reason, is subject to control for the public good. In several of the decisions of this court wherein the expressions, "affected with a public interest," and "clothed with a public use," have been brought forward as the criteria of the validity of price control, it has been admitted that they are not susceptible of definition and form an unsatisfactory test of the constitutionality of legislation directed at business practices or prices. These decisions must rest, finally, upon the basis that the requirements of due process were not met because the laws were found arbitrary in their operation and effect. But there can be no doubt that upon proper occasion and by appropriate measures the state may regulate a business in any of its aspects, including the prices to be charged for the products or commodities it sells.

So far as the requirement of due process is concerned, and in the absence of other constitutional restriction, a state is free to adopt whatever economic policy may reasonably be deemed to promote public welfare, and to enforce that policy by legislation adapted to its purpose. The courts are without authority either to declare such policy, or, when it is declared by the legislature, to override it. If the laws passed are seen to have a reasonable relation to a proper legislative purpose, and are neither arbitrary nor discriminatory, the requirements of due process are satisfied, and judicial determination to that effect renders a court *functus officio.* "Whether the free operation of the normal laws of competition is a wise and wholesome rule for trade and commerce is an economic question which this court need not consider or determine." *Northern Securities Co. v. United States,* 193 U. S. 197, 337–8. And it is equally clear that if the legislative policy be to curb unrestrained and harmful competition by measures which are not arbitrary or discriminatory it does not lie with the courts to determine that the rule is unwise. With the wisdom of the policy adopted, with the adequacy or practicability of the law enacted to forward it, the courts are both incompetent and unauthorized to deal. The course of decision in this court exhibits a firm adherence to these principles. Times without number we have said that the legislature is primarily the judge of the necessity of such an enactment, that every possible presumption is in favor of its validity, and that though the court may hold views inconsistent with the wisdom of the law, it may not be annulled unless palpably in excess of legislative power.

The law-making bodies have in the past endeavored to promote free competition by laws aimed at trusts and monopolies. The consequent interference with private property and freedom of contract has not availed with the courts to set these enactments aside as denying due process. Where the public interest was deemed to require the fixing of minimum prices, that expedient has been sustained. If the law-making body within its sphere of government concludes that the conditions or practices in an industry make unrestricted competition an inadequate safeguard of the consumer's interests, produce waste harmful to the public, threaten ultimately to cut off the supply of a commodity needed by the public, or portend the destruction of the industry itself, appropriate statutes passed in an honest effort to correct the threatened consequences may not be set aside because the regulation adopted fixes prices reasonably deemed by the legislature to be fair to those engaged in the industry and to the consuming public. And this is especially so where, as here, the economic maladjustment is one of price, which threatens harm to the producer at one end of the series and the consumer at the other. The Constitution does not secure to anyone liberty to conduct his business in such fashion as to inflict injury upon the public at large, or upon any substantial group of the people. Price control, like any other form of regulation, is unconstitutional only if arbitrary, discriminatory, or demonstrably irrelevant to the policy the legislature is free to adopt, and hence an unnecessary and unwarranted interference with individual liberty. . . .

Chapter 3

"Frank recognition that language may mean what it says"

IN THE SPRING OF 1935 the Supreme Court began a two-year vendetta against the major measures of President Franklin Roosevelt's New Deal. In May of that year the Court decided *Schechter Poultry Corp. v. United States,* 295 U. S. 495. The basic New Deal statute, the National Industrial Recovery Act, was held unconstitutional in a sweeping, unanimous decision. The Court found that the national power to regulate interstate commerce did not justify rigid control of all businesses, no matter how small, in the United States—in effect, a control that the NIRA had attempted to maintain. Other more technical grounds for the failure of the statute were also asserted. This was the first of the three major decisions which excised the heart of the New Deal program.

The second such decision held unconstitutional the first Agricultural Adjustment Act. This was *United States v. Butler,* 297 U. S. 1, announced in January of 1936. The Court split six to three in this case.

Then in May of 1936 the Court held unconstitutional the Bituminous Coal Conservation Act, which was a governmental attempt to rescue the decidedly sick bituminous coal industry. This was *Carter v. Carter Coal Company,* 298 U. S. 238. Here the Court was arrayed five to four. As in the Schechter case, the Court held that the national commerce power was not broad enough to justify control of the bituminous coal industry.

These three cases merit only scant attention per se. They were the product of a two-year era. As the era has passed, so have they. Not one has been specifically overruled, yet they are gone as surely as the earlier cases which held that government could not fix minimum wages, maximum hours, and prices. If in some future time and by some future Supreme Court the powers of the federal government are narrowed to the limits of these cases, it will be new constitutional law, not a continuation of the old.

The Butler case, however, the second of the three, is worthy of our attention because of an impassioned dissenting opinion by a man not given to passion in judicial affairs, Justice Harlan Fiske Stone. A brief description of the constitutional issue in the case is necessary to an understanding of his opinion. Congress did not ground the first Agricultural Adjustment Act upon its power over interstate commerce, as had been done with the other New Deal measures. Rather, the law was based upon the federal power to spend money "for the general welfare." In brief, the statutory scheme was to levy a tax upon agricultural products and use the money thus obtained to make contracts with farmers in which they agreed to restrict production in return for compensating money payments. The goal was to raise farm prices by reducing surpluses.

The majority of the Court held that this plan was unconstitutional because conditioning the money payments to the farmers upon agreement to restrict production was a means of buying federal control over agriculture. The insurmountable difficulty with this result was that there were a number of significant past decisions of the Court which upheld conditional gifts of money to those whom the national government could not directly control. There is no need to enter this issue with more particularity here because Justice Stone does so thoroughly in his opinion.

Justice Harlan Fiske Stone, a New Englander by birth, was President Coolidge's lone Supreme Court appointment. Stone's undergraduate work was done at Amherst College, and his law degree was obtained at Columbia Law School. Following graduation, he taught part time at Columbia while he practiced law in New York City. After four years he gave up the teaching to devote his entire time to practice. But the pulls of law teaching were strong: five more years of practice, and then Stone returned to Columbia as dean of the Law School. This was in 1910. He continued as dean until his resignation in 1923 to become a member of a leading law firm in New York City. The interregnum of practice was destined to be brief, however. In 1924 President Coolidge named Stone the Attorney General of the United States, and a year later an associate justice of the United States Supreme Court.

Stone's opinions reveal him to have been a careful and deliberate artificer of the law. His principal forte was his ability to take a seemingly conflicting mass of past cases and mold them into a consistent structure. This is the idiom of the great judges of the common law. Thus his opinions, impassive and meticulous, usually have appeal only for those trained in the law.

But not so his dissent in the Butler case. Here one can see that he was moved and moved deeply. Stone could sense that the Court was allowing its opposition to the New Deal to color its requisite objectivity in constitutional affairs. The Court was not just checking an expansion of federal power here, instead it was narrowing power to less than previously accepted limits.

The opinion is the more remarkable because we know that Stone personally believed the Agricultural Adjustment Act to be ill-considered and unwise governmental policy. He was a conservative Republican. In fact, confirmation of his appointment to the Court had been opposed in the Senate by liberal members of his own party. But he was in the great tradition of constitutional judges. He had the objectivity to see that unwisdom and unconstitutionality are not synonymous. The people must be free to legislate in ways the judges may think foolish, so long as the Constitution is not transcended.

Stone's self-denying objectivity brought later reward. In 1941 President Franklin Roosevelt raised him to the position of Chief Justice. This appointment is to the undying honor of President Roosevelt. True, Stone had, while on the Court, voted to uphold the validity of most New Deal measures. But he had been on the other side, too. He was a Republican, and he was beholden to no man. Yet Roosevelt passed over members of his own party, those subservient to his own political philosophy, and appointed Harlan Fiske Stone, a man of high and proven ability, of independence and unimpeachable integrity.

In 1946 Chief Justice Stone collapsed while announcing an opinion from the bench. He died a few hours later. Thus passed a great judge, the eleventh Chief Justice of the United States, an honored man of the law.

UNITED STATES v. BUTLER

Supreme Court of the United States, 1936, 297 U. S. 1

STONE, J., *dissenting*:

The present stress of widely held and strongly expressed differences of opinion of the wisdom of the Agricultural Adjustment Act makes it important, in the interest of clear thinking and sound result, to emphasize at the outset certain propositions which should have controlling influence in determining the validity of the Act. They are:

1. The power of courts to declare a statute unconstitutional is subject to two guiding principles of decision which ought never to be absent from judicial consciousness. One is that courts are concerned only with the power to enact statutes, not with their wisdom. The other is that while unconstitutional exercise of power by the executive and legislative branches of the government is subject to judicial restraint, the only check upon our own exercise of power is our own sense of self-restraint. For the removal of unwise laws from the statute books appeal lies, not to the courts, but to the ballot and to the processes of democratic government.

2. The constitutional power of Congress to levy an excise tax upon the processing of agricultural products is not questioned. The present levy is held invalid, not for any want of power in Congress to lay such a tax to defray public expenditures, including those for the general welfare, but because the use to which its proceeds are put is disapproved.

3. As the present depressed state of agriculture is nation wide in its extent and effects, there is no basis for saying that the expenditure of public money in aid of farmers is not within the specifically granted power of Congress to levy taxes to "provide for the . . . general welfare." The opinion of the Court does not declare otherwise. . . .

It is with these preliminary and hardly controverted matters in mind that we should direct our attention to the pivot on which the decision of the Court is made to turn. It is that a levy unquestionably within the taxing power of Congress may be treated as invalid because it is a step in a plan to regulate agricultural production and is thus a forbidden infringement of state power. The levy is not any the less an exercise of taxing power because it is intended to defray an expenditure for the general welfare rather than for some other support of government. Nor is the levy and collection of the tax pointed to as effecting the regulation. While all federal taxes inevitably have some influence on the internal economy of the states, it is not contended that the levy of a processing tax upon manufacturers using agricultural products as raw material has any perceptible regulatory effect upon either their production or manufacture.... Here regulation, if any there be, is accomplished not by the tax but by the method by which its proceeds are expended, and would equally be accomplished by any like use of public funds, regardless of their source.

The method may be simply stated. Out of the available fund payments are made to such farmers as are willing to curtail their productive acreage, who in fact do so and who in advance have filed their written undertaking to do so with the Secretary of Agriculture. In saying that this method of spending public moneys is an invasion of the reserved powers of the states, the Court does not assert that the expenditure of public funds to promote the general welfare is not a substantive power specifically delegated to the national government, as Hamilton and Story pronounced it to be. It does not deny that the expenditure of funds for the benefit of farmers and in aid of a program of curtailment of production of agricultural products, and thus of a supposedly better ordered national economy, is within the specifically granted power. But it is declared that state power is nevertheless infringed by the expenditure of the proceeds of the tax to compensate farmers for the curtailment of their cotton acreage. Although the farmer is placed under no legal compulsion to reduce acreage, it is said that the mere offer of compensation for so doing is a species of economic coercion which operates with the same legal force and effect as though the curtailment were made mandatory by Act of Congress. In any event it is insisted that even though not coercive the expenditure of public funds to induce the recipients to curtail production is itself an infringement of state power, since the federal government cannot invade the domain of the states by the "purchase" of performance of acts which it has no power to compel.

Of the assertion that the payments to farmers are coercive, it is enough to say that no such contention is pressed by the taxpayer, and no such consequences were to be anticipated or appear to have resulted from the administration of the Act. The suggestion of coercion finds no support in the record or in any data showing the actual operation of the Act. Threat of loss, not hope of gain, is the essence of economic coercion. Members of a long depressed industry have undoubtedly been tempted to curtail acreage by the hope of resulting better prices and by the preferred opportunity to obtain needed ready money. But there is nothing to indicate that those who accepted benefits were impelled by fear of lower prices if they did not accept, or that at any stage in the operation of the plan a farmer could say whether, apart from the certainty of cash payments at specified times, the advantage would lie with curtailment of production plus compensation, rather than with the same or increased acreage plus the expected rise in prices which actually occurred. . . .

It is upon the contention that state power is infringed by purchased regulation of agricultural production that chief reliance is placed. It is insisted that, while the Constitution gives to Congress, in specific and unambiguous terms, the power to tax and spend, the power is subject to limitations which do not find their origin in any express provision of the Constitution and to which other expressly delegated powers are not subject.

The Constitution requires that public funds shall be spent for a defined purpose, the promotion of the general welfare. Their expenditure usually involves payment on terms which will insure use by the selected recipients within the limits of the constitutional purpose. Expenditures would fail of their purpose and thus lose their constitutional sanction if the terms of payment were not such that by their influence on the action of the recipients the permitted end would be attained. The power of Congress to spend is inseparable from persuasion to action over which Congress has no legislative control. Congress may not command that the science of agriculture be taught in state universities. But if it would aid the teaching of that science by grants to state institutions, it is appropriate, if not necessary, that the grant be on the condition, incorporated in the Morrill Act, 12 Stat. 503, 26 Stat. 417, that it be used for the intended purpose. Similarly it would seem to be compliance with the Constitution, not violation of it, for the government to take and the university to give a contract that the grant would be so used. It makes no difference that there is a promise to do an act which the condition is calculated to induce. Condition and promise are alike valid since both are in furtherance of the national purpose for which the money is appropriated.

These effects upon individual action, which are but incidents of the authorized expenditure of government money, are pronounced to be themselves a limitation upon the granted power, and so the time-honored principle of constitutional interpretation that the granted power includes all those which are incident to it is reversed. "Let the end be legitimate," said the great Chief Justice, "let it be within the scope of the Constitution, and all means which are appropriate, which are plainly adapted to that end, which are not prohibited, but consist with the letter and spirit of the Constitution, are constitutional." *McCulloch v. Maryland,* 4 Wheat. 316, 421. This cardinal guide to constitutional exposition must now be re-phrased so far as the spending power of the federal government is concerned. Let the expenditure be to promote the general welfare, still, if it is needful in order to insure its use for the intended purpose to influence any action which Congress cannot command because within the sphere of state government, the expenditure is unconstitutional. And taxes otherwise lawfully levied are likewise unconstitutional if they are appropriated to the expenditure whose incident is condemned. . . .

The spending power of Congress is in addition to the legislative power and not subordinate to it. This independent grant of the power of the purse, and its very nature, involving in its exercise the duty to insure expenditure within the granted power, presuppose freedom of selection among divers ends and aims, and the capacity to impose such conditions as will render the choice effective. It is a contradiction in terms to say that there is power to spend for the national welfare, while rejecting any power to impose conditions reasonably adapted to the attainment of the end which alone would justify the expenditure.

The limitation now sanctioned must lead to absurd consequences. The government may give seeds to farmers, but may not condition the gift upon their being planted in places where they are most needed or even planted at all. The government may give money to the unemployed, but may not ask that those who get it shall give labor in return, or even use it to support their families. It may give money to sufferers from earthquake, fire, tornado, pestilence or flood, but may not impose conditions—health precautions designed to prevent the spread of disease, or induce the movement of population to safer or more sanitary areas. All that, because it is purchased regulation infringing state powers, must be left for the states, who are unable or unwilling to supply the necessary relief. The government may spend its money for vocational rehabilitation, 48 Stat. 389, but it may not, with the consent of all concerned, supervise the process which it undertakes to aid. It may spend its money for the suppression of the boll weevil, but may not compensate the farmers for suspending the growth of cotton in the infected areas. It may aid state reforestation and forest fire prevention agencies, 43 Stat. 653, but may not be permitted to supervise their conduct. It may support rural schools, 39 Stat. 929, 45 Stat. 1151, 48 Stat. 792, but may not condition its grant by the requirement that certain standards be maintained. It may appropriate moneys to be expended by the Reconstruction Finance Corporation "to aid in financing agriculture, commerce and industry," and to facilitate "the exportation of agricultural and other products." Do all its activities collapse because, in order to effect the permissible purpose in myriad ways the money is paid out upon terms and conditions which influence action of the recipients within the states, which Congress cannot command? The answer would seem plain. If the expenditure is for a national public purpose, that purpose will not be thwarted because payment is on condition which will advance that purpose. The action which Congress induces by payments of money to promote the general welfare, but which it does not command or coerce, is but an incident to a specifically granted power, but a permissible means to a legitimate end. If appropriation in aid of a program of curtailment of agricultural production is constitutional, and it is not denied that it is, payment to farmers on condition that they reduce their crop acreage is constitutional. It is not any the less so because the farmer at his own option promises to fulfill the condition.

That the governmental power of the purse is a great one is not now for the first time announced. Every student of the history of government and economics is aware of its magnitude and of its existence in every civilized government. Both were well understood by the framers of the Constitution when they sanctioned the grant of the spending power to the federal government, and both were recognized by Hamilton and

Story, whose views of the spending power as standing on a parity with the other powers specifically granted, have hitherto been generally accepted.

The suggestion that it must now be curtailed by judicial fiat because it may be abused by unwise use hardly rises to the dignity of argument. So may judicial power be abused. "The power to tax is the power to destroy," but we do not, for that reason, doubt its existence, or hold that its efficacy is to be restricted by its incidental or collateral effects upon the states. The power to tax and spend is not without constitutional restraints. One restriction is that the purpose must be truly national. Another is that it may not be used to coerce action left to state control. Another is the conscience and patriotism of Congress and the Executive. "It must be remembered that legislators are the ultimate guardians of the liberties and welfare of the people in quite as great a degree as the courts." Justice Holmes, in *Missouri, Kansas and Texas Ry. Co. v. May*, 194 U. S. 267, 270.

A tortured construction of the Constitution is not to be justified by recourse to extreme examples of reckless congressional spending which might occur if courts could not prevent expenditures which, even if they could be thought to effect any national purpose, would be possible only by action of a legislature lost to all sense of public responsibility. Such suppositions are addressed to the mind accustomed to believe that it is the business of courts to sit in judgment on the wisdom of legislative action. Courts are not the only agency of government that must be assumed to have capacity to govern. Congress and the courts both unhappily may falter or be mistaken in the performance of their constitutional duty. But interpretation of our great charter of government which proceeds on any assumption that the responsibility for the preservation of our institutions is the exclusive concern of any one of the three branches of government, or that it alone can save them from destruction is far more likely, in the long run, "to obliterate the constituent members" of "an indestructible union of indestructible states" than the frank recognition that language, even of a constitution, may mean what it says: That the power to tax and spend includes the power to relieve a nationwide economic maladjustment by conditional gifts of money.

Chapter 4

*"We are asked to shut our eyes to the
plainest facts of our national life"*

FRANKLIN ROOSEVELT was re-elected President in 1936 by the largest electoral majority, save one, in the history of contested presidential elections. The lone exception is the re-election of President James Monroe in 1820. It seemed that everyone was behind Roosevelt and his New Deal policies except Maine and Vermont—and the Supreme Court, the Court of the "Nine Old Men." At this time the average age of the members of the Court was seventy-one. Of the hard core of "conservatives," Van Devanter was seventy-seven, McReynolds seventy-four, Sutherland seventy-four, and Butler seventy. These four voted regularly against sustaining both state and federal measures for business control; their dual themes were "freedom of contract" and "no federal power." The "liberals," who were then voting regularly to uphold the state and federal measures, were Brandeis, who was eighty, Stone sixty-four, and Cardozo sixty-six. These three were now being joined with some regularity by Chief Justice Hughes, who was seventy-four. The "swing man" on the Court, Justice Roberts, was also the junior member at sixty-one.

President Roosevelt apparently viewed his overwhelming re-election not only as a mandate for his program but as a mandate to do something about the obstruction of that program by the Supreme Court. Accordingly, on February 5, 1937, he made his proposal to "pack" the Court.

The plan provided for the appointment of an additional justice, up to a total of fifteen, for each justice who did not retire when he reached the age of seventy. Of course, appointments would be immediately available to "match" every justice then on the Court who was over seventy and did not retire forthwith. The President openly stated as justification for this proposal that old judges, in their cloistered existence, lose touch with the people and the spirit of the times.

A bitter and vituperative battle broke out in the Congress and, indeed, throughout the nation. Many of the President's strongest supporters opposed this measure. They agreed that the legislative program should not be thwarted but abjured the means. Instead, they proposed various constitutional amendments to grant the states and federal government the powers the Court was denying.

Then the bombshell exploded. In a series of ten important cases between March 29, 1937, and May 24, 1937, during the height of the controversy over the packing plan, the Supreme Court abandoned the constitutional theories which had been blocking business control. Minimum wage legislation was upheld against a claim of "freedom of contract." Thus fell the last vestige of the doctrine that the Nebbia case had earlier so weakened. But more significant was the upholding of federal regulation of manufacturing enterprises under the constitutional delegation of power over interstate commerce. This effected a reversal of the doctrines of the Schechter case and the Carter case. Next, the federal power to tax and spend for the general welfare was vindicated in cases upholding the Social Security program. Here was an abandonment of the philosophy of the Butler case. The cause for the proposed packing plan was removed. The plan became moot and died away without enactment.

Inaccurate memory of historical facts has led many in recent years to believe that this abrupt about-face by the Court was occasioned by a shift in the majority brought about by Roosevelt appointees to the Court. But Roosevelt's first appointment, that of Justice Hugo Black, was not made until August, 1937. By then, all of these cases had been decided. The modern constitutional law of broad federal power under the commerce clause of the Constitution, and of broad governmental power, federal and state, to control business and property reasonably is a creature of the Court of the "Nine Old Men." The later so-called Roosevelt Court had absolutely nothing to do with it, nor did any Roosevelt Court appointee.

How did this prodigious shift in constitutional doctrine come about?

Just one justice changed sides. Justice Roberts, the "swing man," abandoned Justices Van Devanter, McReynolds, Sutherland, and Butler and joined Chief Justice Hughes and Justices Stone, Brandeis, and Cardozo. One man changed his mind, and the whole course of constitutional law was altered. Thus is the fabric of history woven.

By contrasting two cases the extent of the constitutional mutation is revealed. In May, 1936, as previously mentioned, the Court held unconstitutional the Bituminous Coal Conservation Act in *Carter v. Carter Coal Company*. The reason given for the holding was that Congress had no power to control the business of manufacturing under its power to regulate interstate commerce, no matter how great the effect of manufacturing upon commerce. Justice Sutherland wrote the majority opinion in the five-four decision. Less than a year later, in April, 1937, the Court upheld the constitutionality of the National Labor Relations Act, which controlled labor relations in manufacturing enterprises, under the federal power to regulate interstate commerce. Chief Justice Hughes wrote the majority opinion in this, the Jones and Laughlin Steel Corporation case, also a five-four decision. Only one member of the nine-man Court was on the majority in both cases—Justice Roberts. Whether Justice Roberts simply changed his mind or whether he was persuaded by Chief Justice Hughes, as unconfirmed rumor would have it, no one really knows.

Justice George Sutherland, the author of the majority opinion in the Carter case, was a Republican from Utah, appointed by Harding in 1922. A native of Great Britain, he was brought to this country at an early age and was educated in the Utah schools. He had neither college nor law degree, although he attended the Michigan Law School for one year. He began his practice of law in 1883, later served one term in the Utah Legislature, one term in the United States House of Representatives and two terms in the Senate. In spite of his firm alignment with the "conservatives" in the Court's battle with the New Deal, he was a stanch defender of civil liberties, and in the area of federal power over *international* as opposed to *domestic* matters his opinions gave a breadth to federal power which has never been exceeded. He is generally considered to have been the strongest of the four "conservatives" of the Court of the "Nine Old Men."

Since the Carter case is no longer of significance, only an excerpt is given sufficient to dramatize the contrast with Chief Justice Hughes' opinion in the Jones and Laughlin case. Particularly note how Justice Sutherland draws a qualitative rather than quantitative line—manufacturing cannot be controlled under the commerce power, no matter how overwhelming its impact upon commerce, and the degree of impact upon commerce is irrelevant. The opinion by Hughes is completely antithetic. To him the question is solely one of degree. If the manufacturing enterprise has a substantial quantitative impact upon commerce, it is within the federal sphere of control.

The Jones and Laughlin case is the great modern case on the scope of federal power over interstate commerce. Other cases involving much smaller businesses were decided the same day with the same result. The way was open for general control of business by the federal government if the people so wished. The panoramic view of the Jones and Laughlin case emerges: the United States consists no longer of forty-eight separate economic entities. Economically we are one nation, and accordingly, in economic matters we stand or fall together. The Great Depression taught us this, and the Court of the "Nine Old Men" confirmed it.

CARTER v. CARTER COAL COMPANY

Supreme Court of the United States, 1936, 298 U. S. 238

SUTHERLAND, J.:

That the production of every commodity intended for interstate sale and transportation has some effect upon interstate commerce may be, if it has not already been, freely granted; and we are brought to the final and decisive inquiry, whether here that effect is direct . . . or indirect. The distinction is not formal, but substantial in the highest degree. . . .

Whether the effect of a given activity or condition is direct or indirect is not always easy to determine. The word "direct" implies that the activity or condition invoked or blamed shall operate proximately—not mediately, remotely, or collaterally—to produce the effect. It connotes the absence of an efficient intervening agency or condition. And the extent of the effect bears no logical relation to its character. The distinction between a direct and an indirect effect turns, not upon the magnitude of either the cause or the effect, but entirely upon the manner in which the effect has been brought about. If the production by one man of a single ton of coal intended for interstate sale and shipment, and actually so sold and shipped, affects interstate commerce indirectly, the effect does not become direct by multiplying the tonnage, or increasing the number of men employed, or adding to the expense or complexities of the business, or by all combined. It is quite true that rules of law are sometimes qualified by considerations of degree, as the government argues. But the matter of degree has no bearing upon the question here, since that question is not—What is the *extent* of the local activity or condition, or the *extent* of the effect produced upon interstate commerce? but—What is the *relation* between the activity or condition and the effect? . . .

The controversies and evils, which it is the object of the act to regulate and minimize, are local controversies and evils affecting local work undertaken to accomplish that local result. Such effect as they may have upon commerce, however extensive it may be, is secondary and indirect. An increase in the greatness of the effect adds to its importance. It does not alter its character. . . .

NATIONAL LABOR RELATIONS BOARD v. JONES & LAUGHLIN STEEL CORP.

Supreme Court of the United States, 1937, 301 U. S. 1

HUGHES, C. J.:

In a proceeding under the National Labor Relations Act of 1935, the National Labor Relations Board found that the respondent, Jones & Laughlin Steel Corporation, had violated the Act by engaging in unfair labor practices affecting commerce. The proceeding was instituted by the Beaver Valley Lodge No. 200, affiliated with the Amalgamated Association of Iron, Steel and Tin Workers of America, a labor organization. The unfair labor practices charged were that the corporation was discriminating against members of the union with regard to hire and tenure of employment, and was coercing and intimidating its employees in order to interfere with their self-organization. The discriminatory and coercive action alleged was the discharge of certain employees. . . .

The facts as to the nature and scope of the business of the Jones & Laughlin Steel Corporation have been found by the Labor Board and, so far as they are essential to the determination of this controversy, they are not in dispute. The Labor Board has found: The corporation is organized under the laws of Pennsylvania and has its principal office at Pittsburgh. It is engaged in the business of manufacturing iron and steel in plants situated in Pittsburgh and nearby Aliquippa, Pennsylvania. It manufactures and distributes a widely diversified line of steel and pig iron, being the fourth largest producer of steel in the United States. With its subsidiaries—nineteen in number—it is a completely integrated enterprise, owning and operating ore, coal and limestone properties, lake and river transportation facilities and terminal railroads located at its manufacturing plants. It owns or controls mines in Michigan and Minnesota. It operates four ore steamships on the Great Lakes, used in the transportation of ore to its factories. It owns coal mines in Pennsylvania. It operates towboats and steam barges used in carrying coal to its factories. It owns limestone properties in various places in Pennsylvania and West Virginia. It owns the Monongahela connecting railroad which connects the plants of the Pittsburgh works and forms an interconnection with the Pennsylvania, New York Central and Baltimore and Ohio Railroad systems. It owns the Aliquippa and Southern Railroad Company which connects the Aliquippa works with the Pittsburgh and Lake Erie, part of the New York Central system. Much of its product is shipped to its warehouses in Chicago, Detroit, Cincinnati and Memphis,—to the last two places by means of its own barges and transportation equipment. In Long Island City, New York, and in New Orleans it operates structural steel fabricating shops in connection with the warehousing of semi-finished materials sent from its works. Through one of its wholly-owned subsidiaries it owns, leases and operates stores, warehouses and yards for the distribution of equipment and supplies for drilling and operating oil and gas wells and for pipe lines, refineries and pumping stations. It has sales offices in twenty cities in the United States and a wholly-owned subsidiary which is devoted exclusively to distributing its product in Canada. Approximately 75 per cent of its product is shipped out of Pennsylvania.

Summarizing these operations, the Labor Board concluded that the works in Pittsburgh and Aliquippa "might be likened to the heart of a self-contained, highly integrated body. They draw in the raw materials from Michigan, Minnesota, West Virginia, Pennsylvania in part through arteries and by means controlled by the respondent; they transform the materials and then pump them out to all parts of the nation through the vast mechanism which the respondent has elaborated."

To carry on the activities of the entire steel industry, 33,000 men mine ore, 44,000 men mine coal, 4,000 men quarry limestone, 16,000 men manufacture coke, 343,000 men manufacture steel, and 83,000 men transport its product. Respondent has about 10,000 employees in its Aliquippa plant, which is located in a community of about 30,000 persons.

Respondent points to evidence that the Aliquippa plant, in which the discharged men were employed, contains complete facilities for the production of finished and semi-finished iron and steel products from raw materials; that its works consist primarily of a by-product coke plant for the production of coke; blast furnaces for the production of pig iron; open hearth furnaces and Bessemer converters for the production of steel; blooming mills for the reduction of steel ingots into smaller shapes; and a number of finishing mills such as structural mills, rod mills, wire mills and the like. In addition there are other buildings, structures and equipment, storage yards, docks and an intra-plant storage system. Respondent's operations at these works are carried on in two distinct stages, the first being the conversion of raw materials into pig iron and the second being the manufacture of semi-finished and finished iron and steel products; . . . the operations result in substantially changing the character, utility and value of the materials wrought upon, which is apparent from the nature and extent of the processes to which they are subjected and which respondent fully describes. Respondent also directs attention to the fact that the iron ore which is procured from mines in Minnesota and Michigan and transported to respondent's plant is stored in stock piles for future use, the amount of ore in storage varying with the season but usually being enough to maintain operations from nine to ten months; that the coal which is procured from the mines of a subsidiary located in Pennsylvania and taken to the plant at Aliquippa is there, like ore, stored for future use, approximately two to three months' supply of coal being always on hand; and that the limestone which is obtained in Pennsylvania and West Virginia is also stored in amounts usually adequate to run the blast furnaces for a few weeks. Various details of operation, transportation, and distribution are also mentioned which for the present purpose it is not necessary to detail. . . .

The statute goes no further than to safeguard the right of employees to self-organization and to select representatives of their own choosing for collective bargaining or other mutual protection without restraint or coercion by their employer.

That is a fundamental right. Employees have as clear a right to organize and select their representatives for lawful purposes as the respondent has to organize its business and select its own officers and agents. Discrimination and coercion to prevent the free exercise of the right of employees to self-organization and representation is a proper subject for condemnation by competent legislative authority. Long ago we stated the reason for labor organizations. We said that they were organized out of the necessities of the situation; that a single employee was helpless in dealing with an employer; that he was dependent ordinarily on his daily wage for the maintenance of himself and family; that if the employer refused to pay him the wages that he thought fair, he was nevertheless unable to leave the employ and resist arbitrary and unfair treatment; that union was essential to give laborers opportunity to deal on an equality with their employer. *American Steel Foundries v. Tri-City Central Trades Council,* 257 U. S. 184, 209. We reiterated these views when we had under consideration the Railway Labor Act of 1926. Fully recognizing the legality of collective action on the part of employees in order to safeguard their proper interests, we said that Congress was not required to ignore this right but could safeguard it. Congress could seek to make appropriate collective action of employees an instrument of peace rather than of strife. We said that such collective action would be a mockery if representation were made futile by interference with freedom of choice. Hence the prohibition by Congress of interference with the selection of representatives for the purpose of negotiation and conference between employers and employees, "instead of being an invasion of the constitutional right of either, was based on the recognition of the rights of both." *Texas & N.O.R. Co. v. Railway Clerks,* 281 U. S. 548....

Respondent says that whatever may be said of employees engaged in interstate commerce, the industrial relations and activities in the manufacturing department of respondent's enterprise are not subject to federal regulation. The argument rests upon the proposition that manufacturing in itself is not commerce. . . . [Citing a number of cases including the Schechter and Carter cases.]

The Government distinguishes these cases. The various parts of respondent's enterprise are described as interdependent and as thus involving "a great movement of iron ore, coal and limestone along well-defined paths to the steel mills, thence through them, and thence in the form of steel products into the consuming centers of the country—a definite and well-understood course of business." It is urged that these activities constitute a "stream" or "flow" of commerce, of which the Aliquippa manufacturing plant is the focal point, and that industrial strife at that point would cripple the entire movement. . . .

We do not find it necessary to determine whether these features of defendant's business dispose of the asserted analogy to the "stream of commerce" cases. The instances in which that metaphor has been used are but particular, and not exclusive, illustrations of the protective power which the Government invokes in support of the present Act. The congressional authority to protect interstate commerce from burdens and obstructions is not limited to transactions which can be deemed to be an essential part of a "flow" of interstate or foreign commerce. Burdens and obstructions may be due to injurious action springing from other sources. The fundamental principle is that the power to regulate commerce is the power to enact "all appropriate legislation" for "its protection and advancement" (*The Daniel Ball,* 10 Wall. 557, 564); to adopt measures "to promote its growth and insure its safety" (*Mobile County v. Kimball,* 102 U. S. 691, 696, 697); "to foster, protect, control and restrain." (*Second Employers' Liability Cases,* 223 U. S. 1, 47.) That power is plenary and may be exerted to protect interstate commerce "no matter what the source of the dangers which threaten it." (*Second Employers' Liability Cases,* p. 51.) Although activities may be intrastate in character when separately considered, if they have such a close and substantial relation to interstate commerce that their control is essential or appropriate to protect that commerce from burdens and obstructions, Congress cannot be denied the power to exercise that control. Undoubtedly the scope of this power must be considered in the light of our dual system of government and may not be extended so as to embrace effects upon interstate commerce so indirect and remote that to embrace them, in view of our complex society, would effectually obliterate the distinction between what is national and what is local and create a completely centralized government. The question is necessarily one of degree. As the Court said in *Chicago Board of Trade v. Olsen,* 262 U. S. 1, 37: "Whatever amounts to more or less constant practice, and threatens to obstruct or unduly to burden the freedom of interstate commerce is within the regulatory power of Congress under the commerce clause, and it is primarily for Congress to consider and decide the fact of the danger and meet it." . . .

Giving full weight to respondent's contention with respect to a break in the complete continuity of the "stream of commerce" by reason of respondent's manufacturing operations, the fact remains that the stoppage of those operations by industrial strife would have a most serious effect upon interstate commerce. In view of respondent's far-flung activities, it is idle to say that the effect would be indirect or remote. It is obvious that it would be immediate and might be catastrophic. We are asked to shut our eyes to the plainest facts of our national life and to deal with the question of direct and indirect effects in an intellectual vacuum. Because there may be but indirect and remote effects upon interstate commerce in connection with a host of local enterprises throughout the country, it does not follow that other industrial activities do not have such a close and intimate relation to interstate commerce as to make the presence of industrial strife a matter of the most urgent national concern. When industries organize themselves on a national scale, making their relation to interstate commerce the dominant factor in their activities, how can it be maintained that their industrial labor relations constitute a forbidden field into which Congress may not enter when it is necessary to protect interstate commerce from the paralyzing consequences of industrial war? We have often said that intersate commerce itself is a practical conception. It is equally true that interferences with that commerce must be appraised by a judgment that does not ignore actual experience.

Experience has abundantly demonstrated that the recognition of the right of employees to self-organization and to have representatives of their own choosing for the purpose of collective bargaining is often an essential condition of industrial peace. Refusal to confer and negotiate has been one of the most prolific causes of strife. This is such an outstanding fact in the history of labor disturbances that it is a proper subject of judicial notice and requires no citation of instances. The opinion in the case of *Virginian Railway Co. v. System Federation, No. 40,* 300 U. S. 515, points out that, in the case of carriers, experience has shown that before the amendment, of 1934, of the Railway Labor Act, "when there was no dispute as to the organizations authorized to represent the employees and when there was a willingness of the employer to meet such representative for a discussion of their grievances, amicable adjustment of differences had generally followed and strikes had been avoided." That, on the other hand, "a prolific source of dispute had been the maintenance by the railroad of company unions and the denial by railway management of the authority of representatives chosen by their employees." The opinion in that case also points to the large measure of success of the labor policy embodied in the Railway Labor Act. But with respect to the appropriateness of the recognition of self-organization and representation in the promotion of peace, the question is not essentially different in the case of employees in industries of such a character that interstate commerce is put in jeopardy from the case of employees of transportation companies. And of what avail is it to protect the facility of transportation, if interstate commerce is throttled with respect to the commodities to be transported!

These questions have frequently engaged the attention of Congress and have been the subject of many inquiries. The steel industry is one of the great basic industries of the United States, with ramifying activities affecting interstate commerce at every point. The Government aptly refers to the steel strike of 1919–1920 with its far-reaching consequences. The fact that there appears to have been no major disturbance in that industry in the more recent period did not dispose of the possibilities of future and like dangers to interstate commerce which Congress was entitled to foresee and to exercise its protective power to forestall. It is not necessary again to detail the facts as to respondent's enterprise. Instead of being beyond the pale, we think that it presents in a most striking way the close and intimate relation which a manufacturing industry may have to interstate commerce and we have no doubt that Congress had constitutional authority to safeguard the right of respondent's employees to self-organization and freedom in the choice of representatives for collective bargaining....

Chapter 5

"The haunting fear when journey's end is near"

BARELY A MONTH after the decision in the Jones and Laughlin case, the Court upheld in two cases the validity of the Social Security program in both its unemployment compensation and its old age pension aspects. This legislation was based upon the federal power to spend money for the general welfare, the power narrowed by the Butler case in declaring unconstitutional the Agricultural Adjustment Act.

One case considered the unemployment compensation phase of the program and the other, printed here, the old age pension provisions. Both majority opinions were written by Justice Cardozo. Each decision was by a five to four majority. Justice Roberts, who had written the prevailing opinion in the Butler case, joined with the majority in these two cases. Especially noteworthy in Justice Cardozo's opinion is his recognition of the economic unity of the nation, thus making explicit the previously mentioned broader impact of the Jones and Laughlin case.

Cardozo's opinion is included for another reason, too. Yielding only perhaps to Holmes, Cardozo is the greatest literary stylist the Court has ever known. Many rank him even greater than Holmes because the beauty and eloquence of his words are not accompanied by the Great Dissenter's cryptic manner. The comparison of the two men is particularly apt because Cardozo replaced Holmes on the Court when the latter retired; and the similarity runs more deeply than mere literary style.

Both men came to the Court from long and distinguished service on the highest courts of their respective states. Further, they had almost identical constitutional views. Finally, together they are the two greatest legal philosophers ever to grace the Supreme Court.

Justice Benjamin Nathan Cardozo, a Democrat from New York, was appointed to the Court by President Hoover. Born and reared in New York City, Cardozo did both his undergraduate and law work at Columbia University. He then practiced law in New York until 1913 when he was elected to the state supreme court. In 1914 he became a judge of the New York Court of Appeals (the highest court in New York). Here he served, the last five years as chief judge, until his appointment to the United States Supreme Court in 1932.

Cardozo leaves a heritage of more than his opinions. His four short books on legal philosophy* reveal much of the man and his thought. And they glow with the precision and beauty of his writing. Cardozo was a man of quiet and gentle temperament, an introspective genius of the law.

HELVERING v. DAVIS

Supreme Court of the United States, 1937, 301 U. S. 619

CARDOZO, J.:

Congress may spend money in aid of the "general welfare." Constitution, Art. I, section 8; *United States v. Butler,* 297 U. S. 1, 65. . . . There have been great statesmen in our history who have stood for other views. We will not resurrect the contest. It is now settled by decision. . . . Yet difficulties are left when the power is conceded. The line must still be drawn between one welfare and another, between particular and general. Where this shall be placed cannot be known through a formula in advance of the event. There is a middle ground or certainly a penumbra

* *The Nature of the Judicial Process,* Yale University Press, 1921; *The Growth of the Law,* Yale University Press, 1924; *The Paradoxes of Legal Science,* Columbia University Press, 1928; *Law and Literature and Other Essays,* Harcourt, Brace and Company, Inc., 1931.

in which discretion is at large. The discretion, however, is not confided to the courts. The discretion belongs to Congress, unless the choice is clearly wrong, a display of arbitrary power, not an exercise of judgment. This is now familiar law. "When such a contention comes here we naturally require a showing that by no reasonable possibility can the challenged legislation fall within the wide range of discretion permitted to the Congress." *United States v. Butler,* supra, p. 67. . . . Nor is the concept of the general welfare static. Needs that were narrow or parochial a century ago may be interwoven in our day with the well-being of the Nation. What is critical or urgent changes with the times.

The purge of nation-wide calamity that began in 1929 has taught us many lessons. Not the least is the solidarity of interests that may once have seemed to be divided. Unemployment spreads from State to State, the hinterland now settled that in pioneer days gave an avenue of escape. . . . Spreading from State to State, unemployment is an ill not particular but general, which may be checked, if Congress so determines, by the resources of the Nation. . . . But the ill is all one, or at least not greatly different, whether men are thrown out of work because there is no longer work to do or because the disabilities of age make them incapable of doing it. Rescue becomes necessary irrespective of the cause. The hope behind this statute is to save men and women from the rigors of the poor house as well as from the haunting fear that such a lot awaits them when journey's end is near.

Congress did not improvise a judgment when it found that the award of old age benefits would be conducive to the general welfare. The President's Committee on Economic Security made an investigation and report, aided by a research staff of Government officers and employees, and by an Advisory Council and seven other advisory groups. Extensive hearings followed before the House Committee on Ways and Means, and the Senate Committee on Finance. A great mass of evidence was brought together supporting the policy which finds expression in the act. Among the relevant facts are these: The number of persons in the United States 65 years of age or over is increasing proportionately as well as absolutely. What is even more important the number of such persons unable to take care of themselves is growing at a threatening pace. More and more our population is becoming urban and industrial instead of rural and agricultural. The evidence is impressive that among industrial workers the younger men and women are preferred over the older. In times of retrenchment the older are commonly the first to go, and even if retained, their wages are likely to be lowered. The plight of men and women at so low an age as 40 is hard, almost hopeless, when they are driven to seek for reemployment. . . . In 1930, out of 224 American factories investigated, 71, or almost one third, had fixed maximum hiring age limits; in 4 plants the limit was under 40; in 41 it was under 46. In the other 153 plants there were no fixed limits, but in practice few were hired if they were over 50 years of age. With the loss of savings inevitable in periods of idleness, the fate of workers over 65, when thrown out of work, is little less than desperate. A recent study of the Social Security Board informs us that "one-fifth of the aged in the United States were receiving old-age assistance, emergency relief, institutional care, employment under the works program, or some other form of aid from public or private funds; two-fifths to one-half were dependent on friends and relatives, one-eighth had some income from earnings; and possibly one-sixth had some savings or property. Approximately three out of four persons 65 or over were probably dependent wholly or partially on others for support." . . .

The problem is plainly national in area and dimensions. Moreover, laws of the separate states cannot deal with it effectively. Congress, at least, had a basis for that belief. States and local governments are often lacking in the resources that are necessary to finance an adequate program of security for the aged. This is brought out with a wealth of illustration in recent studies of the problem. Apart from the failure of resources, states and local governments are at times reluctant to increase so heavily the burden of taxation to be borne by their residents for fear of placing themselves in a position of economic disadvantage as compared with neighbors or competitors. . . . A system of old age pensions has special dangers of its own, if put in force in one state and rejected in another. The existence of such a system is a bait to the needy and dependent elsewhere, encouraging them to migrate and seek a haven of repose. Only a power that is national can serve the interests of all.

Whether wisdom or unwisdom resides in the scheme of benefits set forth in Title II, it is not for us to say. The answer to such inquiries must come from Congress, not the courts. Our concern here, as often, is with power, not with wisdom. Counsel for respondent has recalled to us the virtues of self-reliance and frugality. There is a possibility, he says, that aid from a paternal government may sap those sturdy virtues and breed a race of weaklings. If Massachusetts so believes and shapes her laws in that conviction, must her breed of sons be changed, he asks, because some other philosophy of government finds favor in the halls of Congress? But the answer is not doubtful. One might ask with equal reason whether the system of protective tariffs is to be set aside at will in one state or another whenever local policy prefers the rule of *laissez faire*. The issue is a closed one. It was fought out long ago.

When money is spent to promote the general welfare, the concept of welfare or the opposite is shaped by Congress, not the states. So the concept be not arbitrary, the locality must yield....

Chapter 6

"We are to keep the balance true"

THE GRIST MUST CONTINUE to grind through the legal mills. Great cases and notorious political battles must not stay the regular day in and day out settlement of legal issues. During all the period of the Court battle, which we have been considering, the Court went about its work of deciding the multitude of controversies which are its usual stock in trade. There were free-speech cases, cases involving the fairness of criminal trials, cases involving the interpretation of federal statutes, and cases involving the many other matters within the Court's jurisdiction.

We take note of two of these cases, both of them in the area of fair criminal trial procedure. The opinions in both were written by Justice Cardozo, a sufficient reason alone for them to be read. One of them, *Palko v. Connecticut,* is of major significance in the field of civil liberties. The role of the "due process of law" clause of the Fourteenth Amendment in protecting these individual rights has been previously mentioned (see page 213). In effect, some of the rights specifically detailed in the Bill of Rights are "read into" the due process of law clause to protect them from state encroachment. This process of accretion was necessary if there was to be any protection in the United States Constitution against state infringement of these freedoms. The necessity arose because of the early holding that the Bill of Rights was applicable only to the national government and not to the states.

But not all of the rights protected from federal encroachment are read into the Fourteenth Amendment. For example, states are not limited to indictment by grand jury, and states have a wider latitude to alter the nature of a jury trial than does the federal government.

Cardozo's opinion in the Palko case explains these differences and also articulates the rationalizing principle upon which they are based. The case itself involved the scope of the constitutional prohibition against "double jeopardy." This is the principle that, in its broadest aspect, forbids the retrial of a person for a crime for which he has been acquitted. Its overt purpose is to prevent the government from trying an accused over and over again until a jury is found which will convict. The legal result of the principle is broader; it means that the government may not appeal the verdict in a criminal trial, even though the trial court committed error favorable to the accused. This is the universal rule in the federal courts and in all but two states. Connecticut and Vermont, by state constitution and statute, permit the government to appeal a criminal case when it is asserted that the trial court committed error favorable to the accused. The Palko case challenged the constitutionality of this appeal by the state in criminal cases. The Court held Connecticut's procedure not in violation of the Fourteenth Amendment.

The other case, *Snyder v. Massachusetts,* is somewhat in the same pattern, but narrower in scope. The Constitution requires as a fundamental aspect of due process of law that an accused be allowed to be present at his trial. But what is the "trial"? The question is easily answered in most instances, but not always. During the course of what we commonly know as a trial, juries are sometimes taken to the scene of the crime so that they may more clearly picture and understand the descriptions of the witnesses. Lawyers call this a "view" by the jury. "Views" are often also taken by juries in civil cases, as well as criminal; for example, the jury often leaves the courthouse to look at the scene of an automobile accident. The Snyder case involves a jury "view" of the scene of the alleged crime with which Snyder was charged. Snyder was not taken along on this "view." Thus the question was whether it was a part of the trial, within the constitutional guarantee that an accused must be allowed to be present during his trial. Cardozo, speaking for the Court, held that the trial for purposes of the constitutional provision does not include the jury "view."

These two opinions reveal how Cardozo's matchless writing could make even technical legal issues come to life.

PALKO v. CONNECTICUT
Supreme Court of the United States, 1937, 302 U. S. 319

CARDOZO, J.:

A statute of Connecticut permitting appeals in criminal cases to be taken by the state is challenged by appellant as an infringement of the Fourteenth Amendment of the Constitution of the United States. Whether the challenge should be upheld is now to be determined.

Appellant was indicted in Fairfield County, Connecticut, for the crime of murder in the first degree. A jury found him guilty of murder in the second degree, and he was sentenced to confinement in the state prison for life. Thereafter the State of Connecticut, with the permission of the judge presiding at the trial, gave notice of appeal to the Supreme Court of Errors. . . . Upon such appeal, the Supreme Court of Errors reversed the judgment and ordered a new trial. It found that there had been error of law to the prejudice of the state (1) in excluding testimony as to a confession by defendant; (2) in excluding testimony upon cross-examination of defendant to impeach his credibility; and (3) in the instruction to the jury as to the difference between first and second degree murder.

Pursuant to the mandate of the Supreme Court of Errors, defendant was brought to trial again. . . . The jury returned a verdict of murder in the first degree, and the court sentenced the defendant to the punishment of death. . . .

The argument for appellant is that whatever is forbidden by the Fifth Amendment is forbidden by the Fourteenth also. The Fifth Amendment, which is not directed to the states, but solely to the Federal Government, creates immunity from double jeopardy. No person shall be "subject for the same offense to be twice put in jeopardy of life or limb." The Fourteenth Amendment ordains, "nor shall any State deprive any person of life, liberty, or property, without due process of law." To retry a defendant, though under one indictment and only one, subjects him, it is said, to double jeopardy in violation of the Fifth Amendment, if the prosecution is one on behalf of the United States. From this the consequence is said to follow that there is a denial of life or liberty without due process of law, if the prosecution is one on behalf of the People of a State. . . .

We do not find it profitable to mark the precise limits of the prohibition of double jeopardy in federal prosecutions. The subject was much considered in *Kepner v. United States,* 195 U. S. 100, decided in 1904 by a closely divided court. The view was there expressed for a majority of the court that the prohibition was not confined to jeopardy in a new and independent case. It forbade jeopardy in the same case if the new trial was at the instance of the government and not upon defendant's motion. All this may be assumed for the purpose of the case at hand, though the dissenting opinions show how much was to be said in favor of a different ruling. Right-minded men, as we learn from those opinions, could reasonably, even if mistakenly, believe that a second trial was lawful in prosecutions subject to the Fifth Amendment, if it was all in the same case. Even more plainly, right-minded men could reasonably believe that in espousing that conclusion they were not favoring a practice repugnant to the conscience of mankind. Is double jeopardy in such circumstances, if double jeopardy it must be called, a denial of due process forbidden to the states? The tyranny of labels, *Snyder v. Massachusetts,* 291 U. S. 97, 114, must not lead us to leap to a conclusion that a word which in one set of facts may stand for oppression or enormity is of like effect in every other.

We have said that in appellant's view the Fourteenth Amendment is to be taken as embodying the prohibitions of the Fifth. His thesis is even broader. Whatever would be a violation of the original bill of rights (Amendments I to VIII) if done by the federal government is now equally unlawful by force of the Fourteenth Amendment if done by a state. There is no such general rule.

The Fifth Amendment provides, among other things, that no person shall be held to answer for a capital or otherwise infamous crime unless on presentment or indictment of a grand jury. This court has held that, in prosecutions by a state, presentment or indictment by a grand jury may give way to informations at the instance of a public officer. *Hurtado v. California,* 110 U. S. 516; *Gaines v. Washington,* 277 U. S. 81, 86. The Fifth Amendment provides also that no person shall be compelled in any criminal case to be a witness against himself. This court has said that, in prosecutions by a state, the exemption will fail if the state elects to end it. The Sixth Amendment calls for a jury trial in criminal cases and the Seventh for a jury trial in civil cases at common law where the value in controversy shall exceed twenty dollars. This court has ruled that consistently with those amendments trial by jury may be modified by a state or abolished altogether....

On the other hand, the due process clause of the Fourteenth Amendment may make it unlawful for a state to abridge by its statutes the freedom of speech which the First Amendment safeguards against encroachment by the Congress, *De Jonge v. Oregon,* 299 U.S. 353, 364; *Herndon v. Lowry,* 301 U. S. 242, 259; or the like freedom of the press, *Grosjean v. American Press Co.,* 297 U. S. 233; *Near v. Minnesota ex rel. Olson,* 283 U. S. 697, 707; or the free exercise of religion, *Hamilton v. Regents,* 293 U. S. 245, 262; cf. *Grosjean v. American Press Co.,* supra; *Pierce v. Society of Sisters,* 268 U. S. 510; or the right of peaceable assembly, without which speech would be unduly trammeled, *De Jonge v. Oregon,* supra; *Herndon v. Lowry,* supra; or the right of one accused of crime to the benefit of counsel, *Powell v. Alabama,* 287 U. S. 45. In these and other situations immunities that are valid as against the federal government by force of the specific pledges of particular amendments have been found to be implicit in the concept of ordered liberty, and thus, through the Fourteenth Amendment, become valid as against the states.

The line of division may seem to be wavering and broken if there is a hasty catalogue of the cases on the one side and the other. Reflection and analysis will induce a different view. There emerges the perception of a rationalizing principle which gives to discrete instances a proper order and coherence. The right to trial by jury and the immunity from prosecution except as the result of an indictment may have value and importance. Even so, they are not of the very essence of a scheme of ordered liberty. To abolish them is not to violate a "principle of justice so rooted in the traditions and conscience of our people as to be ranked as fundamental." *Snyder v. Massachusetts,* supra, p. 105. Few would be so narrow or provincial as to maintain that a fair and enlightened system of justice would be impossible without them. What is true of jury trials and indictments is true also, as the cases show, of the immunity from compulsory self-incrimination. This too might be lost, and justice still be done. Indeed, today as in the past there are students of our penal system who look upon the immunity as a mischief rather than a benefit, and who would limit its scope, or destroy it altogether. No doubt there would remain the need to give protection against torture, physical or mental. Justice, however, would not perish if the accused were subject to a duty to respond to orderly inquiry. The exclusion of these immunities and privileges from the privileges and immunities protected against the action of the states has not been arbitrary or casual. It has been dictated by a study and appreciation of the meaning, the essential implications, of liberty itself.

We reach a different plane of social and moral values when we pass to the privileges and immunities that have been taken over from the earlier articles of the federal bill of rights and brought within the Fourteenth Amendment by the process of absorption. These in their origin were effective against the federal government alone. If the Fourteenth Amendment has absorbed them, the process of absorption has had its source in the belief that neither liberty nor justice would exist if they were sacrificed. This is true, for illustration, of freedom of thought, and speech. Of that freedom one may say that it is the matrix, the indispensable condition, of nearly every other form of freedom. With rare aberrations a pervasive recognition of that truth can be traced in our history, political and legal. So it has come about that the domain of liberty, withdrawn by the Fourteenth Amendment from encroachment by the states, has been enlarged by latter-day judgment to include liberty of the mind as well as liberty of action. The extension became, indeed, a logical imperative when once it was recognized, as long ago it was, that liberty is something more than exemption from physical restraint, and that even in the field of substantive rights and duties the legislative judgment, if oppressive and arbitrary, may be overridden by the courts. Fundamental too in the concept of due process, and so in that of liberty, is the thought that condemnation shall be rendered only after trial. *Scott v. McNeal,* 154 U. S. 34; *Blackmer v. United States,* 284 U. S. 421. The hearing, moreover, must be a real one, not a sham or a pretense. *Moore v. Dempsey,* 261 U. S. 86; *Mooney v. Holohan,* 294 U. S. 103. For that reason, ignorant defendants in a capital case were held to have been condemned unlawfully when in truth, though not in form, they were refused the aid of counsel. *Powell v. Alabama,* supra, pp. 67, 68. The decision did not turn upon the fact that the benefit of counsel would have been guaranteed to the defendants by the provisions of the Sixth Amendment if they had been prosecuted in a federal court. The decision turned upon the fact that in the particular situation laid before us in the evidence the benefit of counsel was essential to the substance of a hearing.

Our survey of the cases serves, we think, to justify the statement that the dividing line between them, if not unfaltering throughout its course, has been true for the most part to a unifying principle. On which side of the line the case made out by the appellant has appropriate location must be the next inquiry and the final one. Is that kind of double jeopardy to which the statute has subjected him a hardship so acute and shocking that our polity will not endure it? Does it violate those "fundamental principles of liberty and justice which lie at the base of all our civil and political institutions"? The answer surely must be "no." What the answer would have to be if the state were permitted after a trial free from error to try the accused over again or to bring another case against him, we have no occasion to consider. We deal with the statute before us and no other. The state is not attempting to wear the accused out by a multitude of cases with accumulated trials. It asks no more than this, that the case against him shall go on until there shall be a trial free from the corrosion of substantial legal error. This is not cruelty at all, nor even vexation in any immoderate degree. If the trial had been infected with error adverse to the accused, there might have been review at his instance, and as often as necessary to purge the vicious taint. A reciprocal privilege, subject at all times to the discretion of the presiding judge, has now been granted to the state. There is here no seismic innovation. The edifice of justice stands, its symmetry, to many, greater than before. . . .

SNYDER v. COMMONWEALTH OF MASSACHUSETTS
Supreme Court of the United States, 1934, 291 U. S. 97

CARDOZO, J.:

A fertile source of perversion in constitutional theory is the tyranny of labels. Out of the vague precepts of the Fourteenth Amendment a court frames a rule which is general in form, though it has been wrought under the pressure of particular situations. Forthwith another situation is placed under the rule because it is fitted to the words, though related faintly, if at all, to the reasons that brought the rule into existence. A defendant in a criminal case must be present at a trial when evidence is offered, for the opportunity must be his to advise with his counsel and cross-examine his accusers. Let the words "evidence" and "trial" be extended but a little, and the privilege will apply to stages of the cause at which the function of counsel is mechanical or formal and at which a scene and not a witness is to deliver up its message. In such circumstances the solution of the problem is not to be found in dictionary definitions of evidence or trials. It is not to be found in judgments of the courts that at other times or in other circumstances the presence of a defendant is a postulate of justice. There can be no sound solution without an answer to the question whether in the particular conditions exhibited by the record the enforced absence of the defendant is so flagrantly unjust that the Constitution of the United States steps in to forbid it. What we are subjecting to revision is not the action of a legislature excluding a defendant from a view at all times or in all conditions. What is here for revision is the action of the judicial department of a state excluding the defendant in a particular set of circumstances, and the justice or injustice of that exclusion must be determined in the light of the whole record. Discretion has not been abdicated. To the contrary, the record makes it clear that discretion has been exercised. . . .

True, indeed, it is that constitutional privileges or immunities may be conferred so explicitly as to leave no room for an inquiry whether prejudice to a defendant has been wrought through their denial. . . . If the defendant in a federal court were to be denied the opportunity to be confronted with the "witnesses against him," the denial of the privilege would not be overlooked as immaterial because the evidence thus procured was persuasive of the defendant's guilt. In the same way, privileges, even though not explicit, may be so obviously fundamental as to bring us to the same result. A defendant who has been denied an opportunity to be heard in his defense has lost something indispensable, however convincing the *ex parte* showing. But here, in the case at hand, the privilege, if it exists, is not explicitly conferred, nor has the defendant been denied an opportunity to answer and defend. The Fourteenth Amendment has not said in so many words that he must be present every second or minute or even every hour of the trial. If words so inflexible are to be taken as implied, it is only because they are put there by a court, and not because they are there already, in advance of the decision. Due process of law requires that the proceedings shall be fair, but fairness is a relative, not an absolute concept. It is fairness with reference to particular conditions or particular results. . . .

We find it of no moment that the judge in this case described the view as evidence. The Supreme Judicial Court of Massachusetts has said of a view that "its chief purpose is to enable the jury to understand better the testimony which has or may be introduced." . . . To say that the defendant may be excluded from the scene if the court tells the jury that the view has no other function than to give them understanding of the evidence, but that there is an impairment of the constitutional privileges of a defendant thus excluded if the court tells the jury that the view is part of the evidence—to make the securities of the constitution depend upon such quiddities is to cheapen and degrade them.

The law, as we have seen, is sedulous in maintaining for a defendant charged with crime whatever forms of procedure are of the essence of an opportunity to defend. Privileges so fundamental as to be inherent in every concept of a fair trial that could be acceptable to the thought of reasonable men will be kept inviolate and inviolable, however crushing may be the pressure of incriminating proof. But justice, though due to the accused, is due to the accuser also. The concept of fairness must not be strained till it is narrowed to a filament. We are to keep the balance true.

The constitution and statutes and judicial decisions of the Commonwealth of Massachusetts are the authentic forms through which the sense of justice of the People of that Commonwealth expresses itself in law. We are not to supersede them on the ground that they deny the essentials of a trial because opinions may differ as to their policy or fairness. Not all the precepts of conduct precious to the hearts of many of us are immutable principles of justice, acknowledged *semper ubique et ab omnibus* (*Otis v. Parker,* 187 U. S. 606, 609), wherever the good life is a subject of concern. There is danger that the criminal law will be brought into contempt—that discredit will even touch the great immunities assured by the Fourteenth Amendment—if gossamer possibilities of prejudice to a defendant are to nullify a sentence pronounced by a court of competent jurisdiction in obedience to local law, and set the guilty free.

PART SIX

The Modern Supreme Court

SIX

Chapter 1

"The compulsion is to bear false witness to his religion"

THE WORK of the Supreme Court since the 1940's has exhibited a salient change from that of the Court of the "Nine Old Men." The justices have been little concerned with questions of the scope of federal power to control the economy, or with "due process" limitations upon governmental power to regulate business. The decisions of the spring of 1937 settled these issues. The Court has not been disposed to resurrect them.

Analysis of the Supreme Court's docket in the current years reveals that in general the cases fall into three categories. First in quantity are those cases which involve matters of statutory interpretation. The broad federal programs regulating business, agriculture, labor relations, food and drugs, patents, and the like are constantly raising legal issues concerning the meaning and application of the laws designed to carry them out. These are not constitutional questions at all since they involve only statutes. They are, therefore, outside the scope of this book.

A second category of current litigation will also not be considered at length here, but for a somewhat different reason. This includes the cases concerned with the rights of states to engage in various sorts of commercial, business, health, and safety regulation in fields where Congress is also actually regulating or has the power to do so. Here there is possible conflict between state and federal regulation. Whenever this conflict does occur, the federal power prevails by virtue of Article VI (second paragraph) of the Constitution—the "Supremacy Clause." Chief Justice Marshall's decision in *Gibbons v. Ogden* was precisely of this nature. As we have seen, the conclusion of that opinion demonstrated that the role of the Court in such a case is to decide whether the state statute conflicts with federal policy. It is properly said that these cases do present a constitutional issue since they are based upon the Supremacy Clause. But they are decided as matters of statutory interpretation, because the question is whether the state statute conflicts with federal *law*—not whether there is conflict with the Constitution. A further factor lessens the permanency of these cases; Congress may (as it has done a number of times) reverse a Court decision by specifically authorizing the state law to apply. It follows that these cases are important only in a transitory sense; they do not involve constitutional issues other than federal supremacy.

It is in the third group of cases that the currently significant constitutional work of the Court is found. Here are the questions concerning human freedom and civil rights; and these cases will occupy our attention almost exclusively in Part Six. The constitutional law of religious freedom is largely a product of the fifteen years since 1940. In addition, freedom of speech issues constantly recur and must receive attention, and racial problems further swell the stream of decision. (Another aspect of civil liberty, the fairness of criminal trial procedure, bulks large in current constitutional litigation, but these cases are not presented here because of their technical nature.)

One final introductory word to Part Six. As in earlier portions of this book, there is no attempt to offer a representative opinion of each justice. The special milieu of some of the justices is the area of statutory interpretation and application, and so their opinions concern the cases we are not considering. Further, as before, opinions have been chosen that will have particular appeal and utility to the reader not trained in the law. As a result some of the opinions most cogent to the lawyer are not included.

The preliminaries now aside, civil liberties of the modern day assume the stage. We begin with the Gobitis case, one of the cases concerning the scope of freedom of religion.

Members of the Jehovah's Witnesses, a religious sect, refuse to salute the flag of the United States because they apply literally the Biblical commandment that one shall not bow down to any "graven image." The refusal to salute the flag came in conflict with a daily ritual commonly required of children in the public schools. The Jehovah's Witnesses challenged the constitutionality of the required flag salute on the ground that their religious freedom was thus interfered with.

In several cases the Supreme Court had upheld the power of the state to require the flag salute even when in contravention of religious belief. These holdings were almost casual in that lower court decisions were simply affirmed without even assigning enough dignity to the question to write opinions. Finally, in the Gobitis case, the Court was goaded to more meticulous consideration of the issue by the decision of a lower federal court holding the compulsory flag salute unconstitutional. Reassessment did not change the view of the Court, however; the constitutionality of forcing a person contrary to his religious belief to salute the flag was again upheld. Justice Frankfurter wrote the opinion of the Court.

Justice Stone was alone in dissent. His dissenting opinion is printed here because it was destined to play a more vital role than the majority opinion, as we shall see. The opinion is typical of Justice Stone, quiet, firm, and carefully reasoned, but without eloquence almost to the point of stolidity. The strength of his position seethes beneath the surface of his unemotional words.

MINERSVILLE DISTRICT v. GOBITIS
Supreme Court of the United States, 1940, 310 U. S. 586

STONE, J., *dissenting*:

Two youths, now fifteen and sixteen years of age, are by the judgment of this Court held liable to expulsion from the public schools and to denial of all publicly supported educational privileges because of their refusal to yield to the compulsion of a law which commands their participation in a school ceremony contrary to their religious convictions. They and their father are citizens and have not exhibited by any action or statement of opinion, any disloyalty to the Government of the United States. They are ready and willing to obey all its laws which do not conflict with what they sincerely believe to be the higher commandments of God. It is not doubted that these convictions are religious, that they are genuine, or that the refusal to yield to the compulsion of the law is in good faith and with all sincerity. It would be a denial of their faith as well as the teachings of most religions to say that children of their age could not have religious convictions.

The law which is thus sustained is unique in the history of Anglo-American legislation. It does more than suppress freedom of speech and more than prohibit the free exercise of religion, which concededly are forbidden by the First Amendment and are violations of the liberty guaranteed by the Fourteenth. For by this law the state seeks to coerce these children to express a sentiment which, as they interpret it, they do not entertain, and which violates their deepest religious convictions. It is not denied that such compulsion is a prohibited infringement of personal liberty, freedom of speech and religion, guaranteed by the Bill of Rights, except in so far as it may be justified and supported as a proper exercise of the state's power over public education. Since the state, in competition with parents, may through teaching in the public schools indoctrinate the minds of the young, it is said that in aid of its undertaking to inspire loyalty and devotion to constituted authority and the flag which symbolizes it, it may coerce the pupil to make affirmation contrary to his belief and in violation of his religious faith. And, finally, it is said that since the Minersville School Board and others are of the opinion that the country will be better served by conformity than by the observance of religious liberty which the Constitution prescribes, the courts are not free to pass judgment on the Board's choice.

Concededly the constitutional guaranties of personal liberty are not always absolutes. Government has a right to survive and powers conferred upon it are not necessarily set at naught by the express prohibitions of the Bill of Rights. It may make war and raise armies. To that end it may compel citizens to give military service, *Selective Draft Law Cases,* 245 U. S. 366, and subject them to military training despite their religious objections. *Hamilton v. Regents,* 293 U. S. 245. It may suppress religious practices dangerous to morals, and presumably those also which are inimical to public safety, health and good order. *Davis v. Beason,* 133 U. S. 333. But it is a long step, and one which I am unable to take, to the position that government may, as a supposed educational measure and as a means of disciplining the young, compel public affirmations which violate their religious conscience.

The very fact that we have constitutional guaranties of civil liberties and the specificity of their command where freedom of speech and of religion are concerned require some accommodation of the powers which government normally exercises, when no question of civil liberty is involved, to the constitutional demand that those liberties be protected against the action of government itself. The state concededly has power to require and control the education of its citizens, but it cannot by a general law compelling attendance at public schools preclude attendance at a private school adequate in its instruction, where the parent seeks to secure for the child the benefits of religious instruction not provided by the public school. *Pierce v. Society of Sisters,* 268 U. S. 510. And only recently we have held that the state's authority to control its public streets by generally applicable regulations is not an absolute to which free speech must yield, and cannot be made the medium of its suppression, *Hague v. Committee for Industrial Organization,* 307 U. S. 496, 514, et seq., any more than can its authority to penalize littering of the streets by a general law be used to suppress the distribution of handbills as a means of communicating ideas to their recipients. *Schneider v. State,* 308 U. S. 147.

In these cases it was pointed out that where there are competing demands of the interests of government and of liberty under the Constitution, and where the performance of governmental functions is brought into conflict with specific constitutional restrictions, there must, when that is possible, be reasonable accommodation between them so as to preserve the essentials of both and that it is the function of courts to determine whether such accommodation is reasonably possible. In the cases just mentioned the Court was of opinion that there were ways enough to secure the legitimate state end without infringing the asserted immunity, or that the inconvenience caused by the inability to secure that end satisfactorily through other means, did not outweigh freedom of speech or religion. So here, even if we believe that such compulsions will contribute to national unity, there are other ways to teach loyalty and patriotism which are the sources of national unity, than by compelling the pupil to affirm that which he does not believe and by commanding a form of affirmance which violates his religious convictions. Without recourse to such compulsion the state is free to compel attendance at school and require teaching by instruction and study of all in our history and in the structure and organization of our government, including the guaranties of civil liberty which tend to inspire patriotism and love of country. I cannot say that government here is deprived of any interest or function which it is entitled to maintain at the expense of the protection of civil liberties by requiring it to resort to the alternatives which do not coerce an affirmation of belief.

The guaranties of civil liberty are but guaranties of freedom of the human mind and spirit and of reasonable freedom and opportunity to express them. They presuppose the right of the individual to hold such opinions as he will and to give them reasonably free expression, and his freedom, and that of the state as well, to teach and persuade others by the communication of ideas. The very essence of the liberty which they guaranty is the freedom of the individual from compulsion as to what he shall think and what he shall say, at least where the compulsion is to bear false witness to his religion. If these guaranties are to have any meaning they must, I think, be deemed to withhold from the state any authority to compel belief or the expression of it where that expression violates religious convictions, whatever may be the legislative view of the desirability of such compulsion.

History teaches us that there have been but few infringements of personal liberty by the state which have not been justified, as they are here, in the name of righteousness and the public good, and few which have not been directed, as they are now, at politically helpless minorities. The framers were not unaware that under the system which they created most governmental curtailments of personal liberty would have the support of a legislative judgment that the public interest would be better served by its curtailment than by its constitutional protection. I cannot conceive that in prescribing, as limitations upon the powers of government, the freedom of the mind and spirit secured by the explicit guaranties of freedom of speech and religion, they intended or rightly could have left any latitude for a legislative judgment that the compulsory expression of belief which violates religious convictions would better serve the public interest than their protection. The Constitution may well elicit expressions of loyalty to it and to the government which it created, but it does not command such expressions or otherwise give any indication that compulsory expressions of loyalty play any such part in our scheme of government as to override the constitutional protection of freedom of speech and religion. And while such expressions of loyalty, when voluntarily given, may promote national unity, it is quite another matter to say that their compulsory expression by children in violation of their own and their parents' religious convictions can be regarded as playing so important a part in our national unity as to leave school boards free to exact it despite the constitutional guarantee of freedom of religion. The very terms of the Bill of Rights preclude, it seems to me, any reconciliation of such compulsions with the constitutional guaranties by a legislative declaration that they are more important to the public welfare than the Bill of Rights.

But even if this view be rejected and it is considered that there is some scope for the determination by legislatures whether the citizen shall be compelled to give public expression of such sentiments contrary to his religion, I am not persuaded that we should refrain from passing upon the legislative judgment "as long as the remedial channels of the democratic process remain open and unobstructed." This seems to me no less than the surrender of the constitutional protection of the liberty of small minorities to the popular will. We have previously pointed to the importance of a searching judicial inquiry into the legislative judgment in situations where prejudice against discrete and insular minorities may tend to curtail the operation of those political processes ordinarily to be relied on to protect minorities. See *United States v. Carolene Products Co.*, 304 U. S. 144, 152, note 4. And until now we have not hesitated similarly to scrutinize legislation restricting the civil liberty of racial and religious minorities although no political process was affected. *Meyer v. Nebraska*, 262 U. S. 390. Here we have such a small minority entertaining in good faith a religious belief, which is such a departure from the usual course of human conduct, that most persons are disposed to regard it with little toleration or concern. In such circumstances careful scrutiny of legislative efforts to secure conformity of belief and opinion by a compulsory affirmation of the desired belief, is especially needful if civil rights are to receive any protection. Tested by this standard, I am not prepared to say that the right of this small and helpless minority, including children having a strong religious conviction, whether they understand its nature or not, to refrain from an expression obnoxious to their religion, is to be overborne by the interest of the state in maintaining discipline in the schools.

The Constitution expresses more than the conviction of the people that democratic processes must be preserved at all costs. It is also an expression of faith and a command that freedom of mind and spirit must be preserved, which government must obey, if it is to adhere to that justice and moderation without which no free government can exist. For this reason it would seem that legislation which operates to repress the religious freedom of small minorities, which is admittedly within the scope of the protection of the Bill of Rights, must at least be subject to the same judicial scrutiny as legislation which we have recently held to infringe the constitutional liberty of religious and racial minorities.

With such scrutiny I cannot say that the inconveniences which may attend some sensible adjustment of school discipline in order that the religious convictions of these children may be spared, presents a problem so momentous or pressing as to outweigh the freedom from compulsory violation of religious faith which has been thought worthy of constitutional protection.

Chapter 2

*"Compulsory unification of opinion achieves
only the unanimity of the graveyard"*

JUSTICE STONE'S was a lone and lonesome dissent. But it was precursory to one of the most outstanding personal triumphs ever achieved by a justice of the Supreme Court. Just three years later, in the Barnette case, the Court reversed itself and held the compulsory flag salute unconstitutional. The reversal had been foreshadowed a year before. In an opinion not involving the flag salute issue, three justices publicly recanted their alignment with the majority in the Gobitis case. This unusual move by Justices Black, Douglas, and Murphy, together with two new Court appointments, revived the constitutional issue. And Justice Stone's lone dissent became a majority of six.

The Barnette case is one of the great American constitutional decisions. The majority opinion by Justice Jackson and the dissenting opinion by Justice Frankfurter are both magnificent public documents. Justice Jackson is eloquent in the truest and noblest sense—a raging fire yet under complete control. Justice Frankfurter, while not so eloquent, is in the grand manner of judging. The poignant first sentence of his opinion shows unmistakably that his sympathies lie with the minority group here, yet as a judge he cannot bring himself to believe that theirs is a constitutional right in this case.

Thus again is posed that ageless constitutional dilemma. We are a democracy, and yet we are not. An absolute democracy would allow the majority to run roughshod over all minorities. But the majority is not always right in our system. We withdraw from majority control the human freedoms, and we insist that no matter how drastically outnumbered a person may be he is entitled to those basic liberties. All justices at all times have recognized this. But the difficult and ever-continuing question is setting the boundaries of this protected field of individual liberty. In the Barnette case, Justice Jackson and the majority of the Court believed that a compulsory flag salute invades this field. The determinative guide offered was that of Justice Holmes—the basic human freedoms cannot be assailed by the government unless their assertion constitutes a "clear and present danger to a substantial interest of the state." Justice Frankfurter, in dissent, refused this test by ignoring it. Rather, he offered a test of the "rationality" of the government's control and presented a truly excellent essay upon the Court's requisite self-restraint in striking down governmental exertions of power in the sensitive civil liberties area. Together, the opinions offer a stirring education on the meaning of liberty in a nation which wants its people free.

The author of the majority opinion in the Barnette case, Justice Robert H. Jackson, a Democrat of New York, was appointed to the Court by President Franklin Roosevelt in 1941. Justice Jackson came to the Court via the route of government service. After studying law at the Albany Law School, he practiced in Jamestown, New York. In 1934 he entered government service as general counsel of the Bureau of Internal Revenue. Two years later he was appointed an assistant attorney general of the United States, and in another two years Solicitor General. In 1940 he became United States Attorney General and served in this capacity for eighteen months, until his elevation to the Supreme Court. He gained additional fame by taking leave from the Court in 1945 to serve as the chief prosecutor for the United States in the Nazi War Crime Trials in Germany. He died of a heart attack in Washington in 1954. His place upon the Court was taken in 1955 by John Marshall Harlan, grandson and namesake of the illustrious Justice Harlan, the powerful dissenter in the Civil Rights Cases of 1883.

In Jackson's work on the Court, he was an individualist among individualists. He was unquestionably the finest literary stylist of the Court during his tenure; and, as well, his stylistic peers among all the justices in Supreme Court history can probably be counted on the fingers of one hand. He did not have the serene flow of Cardozo's literary charm; he ran the entire gamut from the loftiness and nobleness of the Barnette case to a sarcasm and vindictiveness that led some to say he talked down to the other members of the Court. But, whatever his mood, his opinions are exciting and pungent reading. A Jackson opinion is like a bird in free flight, swooping and diving, then soaring almost motionless, only to break into headlong flight again.

Justice Felix Frankfurter, the Barnette dissenter, came to the Court as a political independent from Massachusetts. He was appointed by President Roosevelt in 1939, directly from the faculty of the Harvard Law School. Frankfurter, a native of Vienna, came to the United States at the age of fourteen. His undergraduate college training was taken at City College of New York, his law degree from Harvard. After a period spent in law practice and as an assistant United States attorney in New York, he joined the Harvard Law School faculty in 1914. During the First World War he served in various capacities associated with the government's wartime labor program, but, except for various specific public projects, his full-time membership of the Harvard Law faculty was his real pre-Court career. Through his young protégés who graduated from Harvard Law, he is credited with wielding substantial influence in the formulation of the New Deal policies in the early days of the Roosevelt administration.

Frankfurter's obeisance to Justice Holmes was a marked aspect of his pre-Court days. However, many Holmesians have been disappointed in his work on the Court, because he appears to have headed off on trails of his own. He delights in procedural and technical matters. He is the most prolific writer of opinions on the Court. Even though he agrees with a decision, he often feels that the justice writing the opinion hasn't disposed of the matter quite to his liking, so he appends his own concurring opinion. Frankfurter writes well, but a studied effort to say things in new and different ways not infrequently obscures meaning. The grand manner of Holmes is not quite there; it yields to the Frankfurter meticulousness.

Here are both sides of the compulsory flag salute controversy. As you will be asked several times in Part Six—who has the better of it?

WEST VIRGINIA BOARD OF EDUCATION v. BARNETTE
Supreme Court of the United States, 1943, 319 U. S. 624

JACKSON, J.:

This case calls upon us to reconsider a precedent decision, as the Court throughout its history often has been required to do. Before turning to the *Gobitis* case, however, it is desirable to notice certain characteristics by which this controversy is distinguished.

The freedom asserted by these appellees does not bring them into collision with rights asserted by any other individual. It is such conflicts which most frequently require intervention of the State to determine where the rights of one end and those of another begin. But the refusal of these persons to participate in the ceremony does not interfere with or deny rights of others to do so. Nor is there any question in this case that their behavior is peaceable and orderly. The sole conflict is between authority and rights of the individual. The State asserts power to condition access to public education on making a prescribed sign and profession and at the same time to coerce attendance by punishing both parent and child. The latter stand on a right of self-determination in matters that touch individual opinion and personal attitude.

As the present Chief Justice [Stone] said in dissent in the *Gobitis* case, the State may "require teaching by instruction and study of all in our history and in the structure and organization of our government, including the guaranties of civil liberty which tend to inspire patriotism and love of country." Here, however, we are dealing with a compulsion of students to declare a belief. They are not merely made acquainted with the flag salute so that they may be informed as to what it is or even what it means. The issue here is whether this slow and easily neglected route to aroused loyalties constitutionally may be short-cut by substituting a compulsory salute and slogan. . . .

There is no doubt that, in connection with the pledges, the flag salute is a form of utterance. Symbolism is a primitive but effective way of communicating ideas. The use of an emblem or flag to symbolize some system, idea, institution, or personality, is a short cut from mind to mind. Causes and nations, political parties, lodges and ecclesiastical groups seek to knit the loyalty of their followings to a flag or banner, a color or design. The State announces rank, function, and authority through crowns and maces, uniforms and black robes; the church speaks through the Cross, the Crucifix, the altar and shrine, and clerical raiment. Symbols of State often convey political ideas just as religious symbols come to convey theological ones. Associated with many of these symbols are appropriate gestures of acceptance or respect: a salute, a bowed or bared head, a bended knee. A person gets from a symbol the meaning he puts into it, and what is one man's comfort and inspiration is another's jest and scorn....

It is also to be noted that the compulsory flag salute and pledge requires affirmation of a belief and an attitude of mind. It is not clear whether the regulation contemplates that pupils forego any contrary convictions of their own and become unwilling converts to the prescribed ceremony or whether it will be acceptable if they stimulate assent by words without belief and by a gesture barren of meaning. It is now a commonplace that censorship or suppression of expression of opinion is tolerated by our Constitution only when the expression presents a clear and present danger of action of a kind the State is empowered to prevent and punish. It would seem that involuntary affirmation could be commanded only on even more immediate and urgent grounds than silence. But here the power of compulsion is invoked without any allegation that remaining passive during a flag salute ritual creates a clear and present danger that would justify an effort even to muffle expression. To sustain the compulsory flag salute we are required to say that a Bill of Rights which guards the individual's right to speak his own mind, left it open to public authorities to compel him to utter what is not in his mind.

Whether the First Amendment to the Constitution will permit officials to order observance of ritual of this nature does not depend upon whether as a voluntary exercise we would think it to be good, bad or merely innocuous. Any credo of nationalism is likely to include what some disapprove or to omit what others think essential, and to give off different overtones as it takes on different accents or interpretations. If official power exists to coerce acceptance of any patriotic creed, what it shall contain cannot be decided by courts, but must be largely discretionary with the ordaining authority, whose power to prescribe would no doubt include power to amend. Hence validity of the asserted power to force an American citizen publicly to profess any statement or belief or to engage in any ceremony of assent to one presents questions of power that must be considered independently of any idea we may have as to the utility of the ceremony in question.

Nor does the issue as we see it turn on one's possession of particular religious views or the sincerity with which they are held. While religion supplies appellees' motive for enduring the discomforts of making the issue in this case, many citizens who do not share these religious views hold such a compulsory rite to infringe constitutional liberty of the individual. It is not necessary to inquire whether non-conformist beliefs will exempt from the duty to salute unless we first find power to make the salute a legal duty.

The *Gobitis* decision, however, *assumed,* as did the argument in that case and in this, that power exists in the State to impose the flag salute discipline upon school children in general. The Court only examined and rejected a claim based on religious beliefs of immunity from an unquestioned general rule. The question which underlies the flag salute controversy is whether such a ceremony so touching matters of opinion and political attitude may be imposed upon the individual by official authority under powers committed to any political organization under our Constitution. We examine rather than assume existence of this power and, against this broader definition of issues in this case, re-examine specific grounds assigned for the *Gobitis* decision.

1. It was said that the flag-salute controversy confronted the Court with "the problem which Lincoln cast in memorable dilemma: 'Must a government of necessity be too strong for the liberties of its people, or too weak to maintain its own existence?'" and that the answer must be in favor of strength.

We think these issues may be examined free of pressure or restraint growing out of such considerations.

It may be doubted whether Mr. Lincoln would have thought that the strength of government to maintain itself would be impressively vindicated by our confirming power of the State to expel a handful of children from school. Such oversimplification, so handy in political debate, often lacks the precision necessary to postulates of judicial reasoning. If validly applied to this problem, the utterance cited would resolve every issue of power in favor of those in authority and would require us to override every liberty thought to weaken or delay execution of their policies.

Government of limited power need not be anemic government. Assurance that rights are secure tends to diminish fear and jealousy of strong government, and by making us feel safe to live under it makes for its better support. Without promise of a limiting Bill of Rights it is doubtful if our Constitution could have mustered enough strength to enable its ratification. To enforce those rights today is not to choose weak government over strong government. It is only to adhere as a means of strength to individual freedom of mind in preference to officially disciplined uniformity for which history indicates a disappointing and disastrous end.

The subject now before us exemplifies this principle. Free public education, if faithful to the ideal of secular instruction and political neutrality, will not be partisan or enemy of any class, creed, party, or faction. If it is to impose any ideological discipline, however, each party or denomination must seek to control, or failing that, to weaken the influence of the educational system. Observance of the limitations of the Constitution will not weaken government in the field appropriate for its exercise.

2. It was also considered in the *Gobitis* case that functions of educational officers in states, counties and school districts were such that to interfere with their authority "would in effect make us the school board for the country."

The Fourteenth Amendment, as now applied to the States, protects the citizen against the State itself and all of its creatures—Boards of Education not excepted. These have, of course, important, delicate, and highly discretionary functions, but none that they may not perform within the limits of the Bill of Rights. That they are educating the young for citizenship is reason for scrupulous protection of constitutional freedoms of the individual, if we are not to strangle the free mind at its source and teach youth to discount important principles of our government as mere platitudes.

Such Boards are numerous and their territorial jurisdiction often small. But small and local authority may feel less sense of responsibility to the Constitution, and agencies of publicity may be less vigilant in calling it to account. The action of Congress in making flag observance voluntary and respecting the conscience of the objector in a matter so vital as raising the Army contrasts sharply with these local regulations in matters relatively trivial to the welfare of the nation. There are village tyrants as well as village Hampdens, but none who acts under color of law is beyond reach of the Constitution.

3. The *Gobitis* opinion reasoned that this is a field "where courts possess no marked and certainly no controlling competence," that it is committed to the legislatures as well as the courts to guard cherished liberties and that it is constitutionally appropriate to "fight out the wise use of legislative authority in the forum of public opinion and before legislative assemblies rather than to transfer such a contest to the judicial arena," since all the "effective means of inducing political changes are left free."

The very purpose of a Bill of Rights was to withdraw certain subjects from the vicissitudes of political controversy, to place them beyond the reach of majorities and officials and to establish them as legal principles to be applied by the courts. One's right to life, liberty, and property, to free speech, a free press, freedom of worship and assembly, and other fundamental rights may not be submitted to vote; they depend on the outcome of no elections.

In weighing arguments of the parties it is important to distinguish between the due process clause of the Fourteenth Amendment as an instrument for transmitting the principles of the First Amendment and those cases in which it is applied for its own sake. The test of legislation which collides with the Fourteenth Amendment, because it also collides with the principles of the First, is much more definite than the test when only the Fourteenth is involved. Much of the vagueness of the due process clause disappears when the specific prohibitions of the First become its standard. The right of a State to regulate, for example, a public utility may well include, so far as the due process test is concerned, power to impose all of the restrictions which a legislature may have a "rational basis" for adopting. But freedoms of speech and of press, of assembly, and of worship may not be infringed on such slender grounds. They are susceptible to restriction only to prevent grave and immediate danger to interests which the State may lawfully protect. It is important to note that while it is the Fourteenth Amendment which bears directly upon the State it is the more specific limiting principles of the First Amendment that finally govern this case.

Nor does our duty to apply the Bill of Rights to assertions of official authority depend upon our possession of marked competence in the field where the invasion of rights occurs. True, the task of translating the majestic generalities of the Bill of Rights, conceived as part of the pattern of liberal government in the eighteenth century, into concrete restraints on officials dealing with the problems of the twentieth century, is one to disturb self-confidence. These principles grew in soil which also produced a philosophy that the individual was the center of society, that his liberty was attainable through mere absence of governmental restraints, and that government should be entrusted with few controls and only the mildest supervision over men's affairs. We must transplant these rights to a soil in which the *laissez-faire* concept or principle of non-interference has withered at least as to economic affairs, and social advancements are increasingly sought through closer integration of society and through expanded and strengthened governmental controls. These changed conditions often deprive precedents of reliability and cast us more than we would choose upon our own judgment. But we act in these matters not by authority of our competence but by force of our commissions. We cannot, because of modest estimates of our competence in such specialties as public education, withhold the judgment that history authenticates as the function of this Court when liberty is infringed.

4. Lastly, and this is the very heart of the *Gobitis* opinion, it reasons that "National unity is the basis of national security," that the authorities have "the right to select appropriate means for its attainment," and hence reaches the conclusion that such compulsory measures toward "national unity" are constitutional. Upon the verity of this assumption depends our answer in this case.

National unity as an end which officials may foster by persuasion and example is not in question. The problem is whether under our Constitution compulsion as here employed is a permissible means for its achievement.

Struggles to coerce uniformity of sentiment in support of some end thought essential to their time and country have been waged by many good as well as by evil men. Nationalism is a relatively recent phenomenon but at other times and places the ends have been racial or territorial security, support of a dynasty or regime, and particular plans for saving souls. As first and moderate methods to attain unity have failed, those bent on its accomplishment must resort to an ever-increasing severity. As governmental pressure toward unity becomes greater, so strife becomes more bitter as to whose unity it shall be. Probably no deeper division of our people could proceed from any provocation than from finding it necessary to choose what doctrine and whose program public educational officials shall compel youth to unite in embracing. Ultimate futility of such attempts to compel coherence is the lesson of every such effort from the Roman drive to stamp out Christianity as a disturber of its pagan unity, the Inquisition, as a means to religious and dynastic unity, the Siberian exiles as a means to Russian unity, down to the fast failing efforts of our present totalitarian enemies. Those who begin coercive elimination of dissent soon find themselves exterminating dissenters. Compulsory unification of opinion achieves only the unanimity of the graveyard.

It seems trite but necessary to say that the First Amendment to our Constitution was designed to avoid these ends by avoiding these beginnings. There is no mysticism in the American concept of the State or of the nature or origin of its authority. We set up government by consent of the governed, and the Bill of Rights denies those in power any legal opportunity to coerce that consent. Authority here is to be controlled by public opinion, not public opinion by authority.

The case is made difficult not because the principles of its decision are obscure but because the flag involved is our own. Nevertheless, we apply the limitations of the Constitution with no fear that freedom to be intellectually and spiritually diverse or even contrary will disintegrate the social organization. To believe that patriotism will not flourish if patriotic ceremonies are voluntary and spontaneous instead of a compulsory routine is to make an unflattering estimate of the appeal of our institutions to free minds. We can have intellectual individualism and the rich cultural diversities that we owe to exceptional minds only at the price of occasional eccentricity and abnormal attitudes. When they are so harmless to others or to the State as those we deal with here, the price is not too great. But freedom to differ is not limited to things that do not matter much. That would be a mere shadow of freedom. The test of its substance is the right to differ as to things that touch the heart of the existing order.

If there is any fixed star in our constitutional constellation, it is that no official, high or petty, can prescribe what shall be orthodox in politics, nationalism, religion, or other matters of opinion or force citizens to confess by word or act their faith therein. If there are any circumstances which permit an exception, they do not now occur to us.

We think the action of the local authorities in compelling the flag salute and pledge transcends constitutional limitations on their power and invades the sphere of intellect and spirit which it is the purpose of the First Amendment to our Constitution to reserve from all official control.

The decision of this Court in *Minersville School District v. Gobitis* and the holdings of those few per curiam decisions which proceeded and foreshadowed it are overruled, and the judgment enjoining enforcement of the West Virginia Regulation is affirmed.

FRANKFURTER, J., *dissenting*:

One who belongs to the most vilified and persecuted minority in history is not likely to be insensible to the freedoms guaranteed by our Constitution. Were my purely personal attitude relevant I should wholeheartedly associate myself with the general libertarian views in the Court's opinion, representing as they do the thought and action of a lifetime. But as judges we are neither Jew nor Gentile, neither Catholic nor agnostic. We owe equal attachment to the Constitution and are equally bound by our judicial obligations whether we derive our citizenship from the earliest or the latest immigrants to these shores. As a member of this Court I am not justified in writing my private notions of policy into the Constitution, no matter how deeply I may cherish them or how mischievous I may deem their disregard. The duty of a judge who must decide which of two claims before the Court shall prevail, that of a State to enact and enforce laws within its general competence or that of an individual to refuse obedience because of the demands of his conscience, is not that of the ordinary person. It can never be emphasized too much that one's own opinion about the wisdom or evil of a law should be excluded altogether when one is doing one's duty on the bench. The only opinion of our own even looking in that direction that is material is our opinion whether legislators could in reason have enacted such a law. In the light of all the circumstances, including the history of this question in this Court, it would require more daring than I possess to deny that reasonable legislators could have taken the action which is before us for review. Most unwillingly, therefore, I must differ from my brethren with regard to legislation like this. I cannot bring my mind to believe that the "liberty" secured by the Due Process Clause gives this Court authority to deny to the State of West Virginia the attainment of that which we all recognize as a legitimate legislative end, namely, the promotion of good citizenship, by employment of the means here chosen. . . .

The reason why from the beginning even the narrow judicial authority to nullify legislation has been viewed with a jealous eye is that it serves to prevent the full play of the democratic process. The fact that it may be an undemocratic aspect of our scheme of government does not call for its rejection or its disuse. But it is the best of reasons, as this Court has frequently recognized, for the greatest caution in its use.

The precise scope of the question before us defines the limits of the constitutional power that is in issue. The State of West Virginia requires all pupils to share in the salute to the flag as part of school training in citizenship. The present action is one to enjoin the enforcement of this requirement by those in school attendance. We have not before us any attempt by the State to punish disobedient children or visit penal consequences on their parents. All that is in question is the right of the State to compel participation in this exercise by those who choose to attend the public schools.

We are not reviewing merely the action of a local school board. The flag salute requirement in this case comes before us with the full authority of the State of West Virginia. We are in fact passing judgment on "the power of the State as a whole." *Rippey v. Texas,* 193 U. S. 504, 509. Practically we are passing upon the political power of each of the forty-eight states. . . . To suggest that we are here concerned with the heedless action of some village tyrants is to distort the augustness of the constitutional issue and the reach of the consequences of our decision.

Under our constitutional system the legislature is charged solely with civil concerns of society. If the avowed or intrinsic legislative purpose is either to promote or to discourage some religious community or creed, it is clearly within the constitutional restrictions imposed on legislatures and cannot stand. But it by no means follows that legislative power is wanting whenever a general non-discriminatory civil regulation in fact touches conscientious scruples or religious beliefs of an individual or a group. Regard for such scruples or beliefs undoubtedly presents one of the most reasonable claims for the exertion of legislative accommodation. It is, of course, beyond our power to rewrite the state's requirement, by providing exemptions for those who do not wish to participate in the flag salute or by making some other accommodations to meet their scruples. That wisdom might suggest the making of such accommodations and that school administration would not find it too difficult to make them and yet maintain the ceremony for those not refusing to conform, is outside our province to suggest. Tact, respect, and generosity toward variant views will always commend themselves to those charged with the duties of legislation so as to achieve a maximum of good will and to require a minimum of unwilling submission to a general law. But the real question is, who is to make such accommodations, the courts or the legislature?

This is no dry, technical matter. It cuts deep into one's conception of the democratic process—it concerns no less the practical differences between the means for making these accommodations that are open to courts and to legislatures. A court can only strike down. It can only say "This or that law is void." It cannot modify or qualify, it cannot make exceptions to a general requirement. And it strikes down not merely for a day. At least the finding of unconstitutionality ought not to have ephemeral significance unless the Constitution is to be reduced to the fugitive importance of mere legislation. When we are dealing with the Constitution of the United States, and more particularly with the great safeguards of the Bill of Rights, we are dealing with principles of liberty and justice "so rooted in the traditions and conscience of our people as to be ranked as fundamental"—something without which "a fair and enlightened system of justice would be impossible." *Palko v. Connecticut,* 302 U. S. 319, 325. If the function of this Court is to be essentially no different from that of a legislature, if the considerations governing constitutional construction are to be substantially those that underlie legislation, then indeed judges should not have life tenure and they should be made directly responsible to the electorate. There have been many but unsuccessful proposals in the last sixty years to amend the Constitution to that end. See Sen. Doc. No. 91, 75th Cong., 1st Sess., pp. 248-51.

Conscientious scruples, all would admit, cannot stand against every legislative compulsion to do positive acts in conflict with such scruples. We have been told that such compulsions override religious scruples only as to major concerns of the state. But the determination of what is major and what is minor itself raises questions of policy. For the way in which men equally guided by reason appraise importance goes to the very heart of policy. Judges should be very diffident in setting their judgment against that of a state in determining what is and what is not a major concern, what means are appropriate to proper ends, and what is the total social cost in striking the balance of imponderables.

What one can say with assurance is that the history out of which grew constitutional provisions for religious equality and the writings of the great exponents of religious freedom—Jefferson, Madison, John Adams, Benjamin Franklin—are totally wanting in justification for a claim by dissidents of exceptional immunity from civic measures of general applicability, measures not in fact disguised assaults upon such dissident views. The great leaders of the American Revolution were determined to remove political support from every religious establishment. They put on an equality the different religious sects—Episcopalians, Presbyterians, Catholics, Baptists, Methodists, Quakers, Huguenots—which, as dissenters, had been under the heel of the various orthodoxies that prevailed in different colonies. So far as the state was concerned, there was to be neither orthodoxy nor heterodoxy. And so Jefferson and those who followed him wrote guaranties of religious freedom into our constitutions. Religious minorities as well as religious majorities were to be equal in the eyes of the political state. But Jefferson and the others also knew that minorities may disrupt society. It never would have occurred to them to write into the Constitution the subordination of the general civil authority of the state to sectarian scruples.

The constitutional protection of religious freedom terminated disabilities, it did not create new privileges. It gave religious equality, not civil immunity. Its essence is freedom from conformity to religious dogma, not freedom from conformity to law because of religious dogma.

Religious loyalties may be exercised without hindrance from the state, not the state may not exercise that which except by leave of religious loyalties is within the domain of temporal power. Otherwise each individual could set up his own censor against obedience to laws conscientiously deemed for the public good by those whose business it is to make laws.

The prohibition against any religious establishment by the government placed denominations on an equal footing—it assured freedom from support by the government to any mode of worship and the freedom of individuals to support any mode of worship. Any person may therefore believe or disbelieve what he pleases. He may practice what he will in his own house of worship or publicly within the limits of public order. But the lawmaking authority is not circumscribed by the variety of religious beliefs, otherwise the constitutional guaranty would be not a protection of the free exercise of religion but a denial of the exercise of legislation.

The essence of the religious freedom guaranteed by our Constitution is therefore this: no religion shall either receive the state's support or incur its hostility. Religion is outside the sphere of political government. This does not mean that all matters on which religious organizations or beliefs may pronounce are outside the sphere of government. Were this so, instead of the separation of church and state, there would be the subordination of the state on any matter deemed within the sovereignty of the religious conscience. Much that is the concern of temporal authority affects the spiritual interests of men. But it is not enough to strike down a non-discriminatory law that it may hurt or offend some dissident view. It would be too easy to cite numerous prohibitions and injunctions to which laws run counter if the variant interpretations of the Bible were made the tests of obedience to law. The validity of secular laws cannot be measured by their conformity to religious doctrines. It is only in a theocratic state that ecclesiastical doctrines measure legal right or wrong.

An act compelling profession of allegiance to a religion, no matter how subtly or tenuously promoted, is bad. But an act promoting good citizenship and national allegiance is within the domain of governmental authority and is therefore to be judged by the same considerations of power and of constitutionality as those involved in the many claims of immunity from civil obedience because of religious scruples.

That claims are pressed on behalf of sincere religious convictions does not of itself establish their constitutional validity. Nor does waving the banner of religious freedom relieve us from examining into the power we are asked to deny the states. Otherwise the doctrine of separation of church and state, so cardinal in the history of this nation and for the liberty of our people, would mean not the disestablishment of a state church but the establishment of all churches and of all religious groups.

The subjection of dissidents to the general requirement of saluting the flag, as a measure conducive to the training of children in good citizenship, is very far from being the first instance of exacting obedience to general laws that have offended deep religious scruples. Compulsory vaccination, see *Jacobson v. Massachusetts,* 197 U. S. 11, food inspection regulations, see *Shapiro v. Lyle,* 30 F.2d 971, the obligation to bear arms, see *Hamilton v. Regents,* 293 U. S. 245, 267, testimonial duties, see *Stansbury v. Marks,* 2 Dall. 213, compulsory medical treatment, see *People v. Vogelgesang,* 221 N. Y. 290, 116 N. E. 977—these are but illustrations of conduct that has often been compelled in the enforcement of legislation of general applicability even though the religious consciences of particular individuals rebelled at the exaction.

Law is concerned with external behavior and not with the inner life of man. It rests in large measure upon compulsion. Socrates lives in history partly because he gave his life for the conviction that duty of obedience to secular law does not presuppose consent to its enactment or belief in its virtue. The consent upon which free government rests is the consent that comes from sharing in the process of making and unmaking laws. The state is not shut out from a domain because the individual conscience may deny the state's claim. The individual conscience may profess what faith it chooses. It may affirm and promote that faith—in the language of the Constitution, it may "exercise" it freely—but it cannot thereby restrict community action through political organs in matters of community concern, so long as the action is not asserted in a discriminatory way either openly or by stealth. One may have the right to practice one's religion and at the same time owe the duty of formal obedience to laws that run counter to one's beliefs. Compelling belief implies denial of opportunity to combat it and to assert dissident views. Such compulsion is one thing. Quite another matter is submission to conformity of action while denying its wisdom or virtue and with ample opportunity for seeking its change or abrogation. . . .

When dealing with religious scruples we are dealing with an almost numberless variety of doctrines and beliefs entertained with equal sincerity by the particular groups for which they satisfy man's needs in his relation to the mysteries of the universe. There are in the United States more than 250 distinctive established religious denominations. In the state of Pennsylvania there are 120 of these, and in West Virginia as many as 65. But if religious scruples afford immunity from civic obedience to laws, they may be invoked by the religious beliefs of any individual even though he holds no membership in any sect or organized denomination. Certainly this Court cannot be called upon to determine what claims of conscience should be recognized and what should be rejected as satisfying the "religion" which the Constitution protects. That would indeed resurrect the very discriminatory treatment of religion which the Constitution sought forever to forbid. And so, when confronted with the task of considering the claims of immunity from obedience to a law dealing with civil affairs because of religious scruples, we cannot conceive religion more narrowly than in the terms in which Judge Augustus N. Hand recently characterized it:

"It is unnecessary to attempt a definition of religion; the content of the term is found in the history of the human race and is incapable of compression into a few words. Religious belief arises from a sense of the inadequacy of reason as a means of relating the individual to his fellowmen and to his universe. . . . (It) may justly be regarded as a response of the individual to an inward mentor, call it conscience or God, that is for many persons at the present time the equivalent of what has always been thought a religious impulse." *United States v. Kauten,* 133 F.2d 703, 708.

Consider the controversial issue of compulsory Bible-reading in public schools. The educational policies of the states are in great conflict over this, and the state courts are divided in their decisions on the issue whether the requirement of Bible-reading offends constitutional provisions dealing with religious freedom. The requirement of Bible-reading has been justified by various state courts as an appropriate means of inculcating ethical precepts and familiarizing pupils with the most lasting expression of great English literature. Is this Court to overthrow such variant state educational policies by denying states the right to entertain such convictions in regard to their school systems because of a belief that the King James version is in fact a sectarian text to which parents of the Catholic and Jewish faiths and of some Protestant persuasions may rightly object to having their children exposed? On the other hand the religious consciences of some parents may rebel at the absence of any Bible-reading in the schools. See *State of Washington ex rel. Clithero v. Showalter,* 284 U. S. 573. Or is this Court to enter the old controversy between science and religion by unduly defining the limits within which a state may experiment with its school curricula? The religious consciences of some parents may be offended by subjecting their children to the Biblical account of creation, while another state may offend parents by prohibiting a teaching of biology that contradicts such Biblical account. Compare *Scopes v. State,* 154 Tenn. 105. What of conscientious objections to what is devoutly felt by parents to be the poisoning of impressionable minds of children by chauvinistic teaching of history? This is very far from a fanciful suggestion for in the belief of many thoughtful people nationalism is the seed-bed of war.

There are other issues in the offing which admonish us of the difficulties and complexities that confront states in the duty of administering their local school systems. All citizens are taxed for the support of public schools although this Court has denied the right of a state to compel all children to go to such schools and has recognized the right of parents to send children to privately maintained schools. Parents who are dissatisfied with the public schools thus carry a double educational burden. Children who go to public school enjoy in many states derivative advantages such as free textbooks, free lunch, and free transportation in going to and from school. What of the claims for equality of treatment of those parents who, because of religious scruples, cannot send their children to public schools? What of the claim that if the right to send children to privately maintained schools is partly an exercise of religious conviction, to render effective this right it should be accompanied by a quality of treatment by the state in supplying free textbooks, free lunch, and free transportation to children who go to private schools? What of the claim that such grants are offensive to the cardinal constitutional doctrine of separation of church and state?

These questions assume increasing importance in view of the steady growth of parochial schools both in number and in population. I am not borrowing trouble by adumbrating these issues nor am I parading horrible examples of the consequences of today's decision. I am aware that we must decide the case before us and not some other case. But that does not mean that a case is dissociated from the past and unrelated to the future. We must decide this case with due regard for what went before and no less regard for what may come after. Is it really a fair construction of such a fundamental concept as the right freely to exercise one's religion that a state cannot choose to require all children who attend public school to make the same gesture of allegiance to the symbol of our national life because it may offend the conscience of some children, but that it may compel all children to attend public school to listen to the King James version although it may offend the consciences of their parents? And what of the larger issue of claiming immunity from obedience to a general civil regulation that has a reasonable relation to a public purpose within the general competence of the state? . . .

These questions are not lightly stirred. They touch the most delicate issues and their solution challenges the best wisdom of political and religious statesmen. But it presents awful possibilities to try to encase the solution of these problems within the rigid prohibitions of unconstitutionality.

We are told that a flag salute is a doubtful substitute for adequate understanding of our institutions. The states that require such a school exercise do not have to justify it as the only means for promoting good citizenship in children, but merely as one of diverse means for accomplishing a worthy end. We may deem it a foolish measure, but the point is that this Court is not the organ of government to resolve doubts as to whether it will fulfill its purpose. Only if there be no doubt that any reasonable mind could entertain can we deny to the states the right to resolve doubts their way and not ours.

That which to the majority may seem essential for the welfare of the state may offend the consciences of a minority. But, so long as no inroads are made upon the actual exercise of religion by the minority, to deny the political power of the majority to enact laws concerned with civil matters, simply because they may offend the consciences of a minority, really means that the consciences of a minority are more sacred and more enshrined in the Constitution than the consciences of a majority.

We are told that symbolism is a dramatic but primitive way of communicating ideas. Symbolism is inescapable. Even the most sophisticated live by symbols. But it is not for this Court to make psychological judgments as to the effectiveness of a particular symbol in inculcating concededly indispensable feelings, particularly if the state happens to see fit to utilize the symbol that represents our heritage and our hopes. And surely only flippancy could be responsible for the suggestion that constitutional validity of a requirement to salute our flag implies equal validity of a requirement to salute a dictator. The significance of a symbol lies in what it represents. To reject the swastika does not imply rejection of the Cross. And so it bears repetition to say that it mocks reason and denies our whole history to find in the allowance of a requirement to salute our flag on fitting occasions the seeds of sanction for obeisance to a leader. To deny the power to employ educational symbols is to say that the state's educational system may not stimulate the imagination because this may lead to unwise stimulation. . . .

Of course patriotism cannot be enforced by the flag salute. But neither can the liberal spirit be enforced by judicial invalidation of illiberal legislation. Our constant preoccupation with the constitutionality of legislation rather than with its wisdom tends to preoccupation of the American mind with a false value. The tendency of focusing attention on constitutionality is to make constitutionality synonymous with wisdom, to regard a law as all right if it is constitutional. Such an attitude is a great enemy of liberalism. Particularly in legislation affecting freedom of thought and freedom of speech much which should offend a free-spirited society is constitutional. Reliance for the most precious interests of civilization, therefore, must be found outside of their vindication in courts of law. Only a persistent positive translation of the faith of a free society into the convictions and habits and actions of a community is the ultimate reliance against unabated temptations to fetter the human spirit.

Chapter 3

"Have done with this business of judicially examining other people's faiths"

PERSONAL RELIGIOUS BELIEF is surely the most sensitive and delicate matter specifically dealt with in the Constitution. Nowhere is this more effectively revealed than in Justice Jackson's dissenting opinion in *United States v. Ballard*. The case involved the criminal prosecution for mail fraud of the Ballards, leaders of the "I Am" religious cult. The Ballards claimed supernatural healing powers and the ability to communicate with the Almighty through a divine "Saint Germain."

The Supreme Court held that the ultimate truth of the Ballards' beliefs was not at issue, but their honesty and good faith in claiming such beliefs was. Thus, if they honestly believed in their supernatural powers and the other aspects of their dogma they could not be guilty of mail fraud even though those beliefs were incredible to others. In so holding, the Court was obviously creating a strong bulwark of religious freedom.

But this did not go far enough for Justice Jackson. He insisted that, under the rule of the majority of the Court, the good faith of the Ballards would inescapably be settled by the credibility of their beliefs in the eyes of the jury. It followed, in his logic, that the Ballards would stand or fall, then, on the ultimate truth of their beliefs. And freedom of religion would be gone. But let Justice Jackson say it in his own words, in one of the most moving and incisive opinions ever to emanate from the Supreme Court.

UNITED STATES v. BALLARD
Supreme Court of the United States, 1944, 322 U. S. 78

JACKSON, J., *dissenting*:

  I should say that the defendants have done just that for which they are indicted. If I might agree to their conviction without creating a precedent, I cheerfully would do so. I can see in their teachings nothing but humbug, untainted by any trace of truth. But that does not dispose of the constitutional question whether misrepresentation of religious experience or belief is prosecutable; it rather emphasizes the danger of such prosecutions.

  The Ballard family claimed miraculous communication with the spirit world and supernatural power to heal the sick. They were brought to trial for mail fraud on an indictment which charged that their representations were false and that they "well knew" they were false. The trial judge, obviously troubled, ruled that the court could not try whether the statements were untrue, but could inquire whether the defendants knew them to be untrue; and if so, they could be convicted.

  I find it difficult to reconcile this conclusion with our traditional religious freedoms.

  In the first place, as a matter of either practice or philosophy I do not see how we can separate an issue as to what is believed from considerations as to what is believable. The most convincing proof that one believes his statements is to show that they have been true in his experience. Likewise, that one knowingly falsified is best proved by showing that what he said happened never did happen. How can the Government prove these persons knew something to be false which it cannot prove to be false? If we try religious sincerity severed from religious verity, we isolate the dispute from the very considerations which in common experience provide its most reliable answer.

  In the second place, any inquiry into intellectual honesty in religion raises profound psychological problems. William James, who wrote on these matters as a scientist, reminds us that it is not theology and ceremonies which keep religion going. Its vitality is in the religious experiences of many people. "If you ask what these experiences are, they are conversations with the unseen, voices and visions, responses to prayer, changes of heart, deliverances from fear, inflowings of help, assurances of support, whenever certain persons set their own internal attitude in certain appropriate ways." If religious liberty includes, as it must, the right to communicate such experiences to others, it seems to me an impossible task for juries to separate fancied ones from real ones, dreams from happenings, and hallucinations from true clairvoyance. Such experiences, like some tones and colors, have existence for one, but none at all for another. They cannot be verified to the minds of those whose field of consciousness does not include religious insight. When one comes to trial which turns on any aspect of religious belief or representation, unbelievers among his judges are likely not to understand and are almost certain not to believe him.

And then I do not know what degree of skepticism or disbelief in a religious representation amounts to actionable fraud. James points out that "Faith means belief in something concerning which doubt is theoretically possible." Belief in what one may demonstrate to the senses is not faith. All schools of religious thought make enormous assumptions, generally on the basis of revelations authenticated by some sign of miracle. The appeal in such matters is to a very different plane of credulity than is invoked by representations of secular fact in commerce. Some who profess belief in the Bible read literally what others read as allegory or metaphor, as they read Aesop's fables. Religious symbolism is even used by some with the same mental reservations one has in teaching of Santa Claus or Uncle Sam or Easter bunnies or dispassionate judges. It is hard in matters so mystical to say how literally one is bound to believe the doctrine he teaches and even more difficult to say how far it is reliance upon a teacher's literal belief which induces followers to give him money.

There appear to be persons—let us hope not many—who find refreshment and courage in the teachings of the "I Am" cult. If the members of the sect get comfort from the celestial guidance of their "Saint Germain," however doubtful it seems to me, it is hard to say that they do not get what they pay for. Scores of sects flourish in this country by teaching what to me are queer notions. It is plain that there is wide variety in American religious taste. The Ballards are not alone in catering to it with a pretty dubious product.

The chief wrong which false prophets do to their following is not financial. The collections aggregate a tempting total, but individual payments are not ruinous. I doubt if the vigilance of the law is equal to making money stick by over-credulous people. But the real harm is on the mental and spiritual plane. There are those who hunger and thirst after higher values which they feel wanting in their humdrum lives. They live in mental confusion or moral anarchy and seek vaguely for truth and beauty and moral support. When they are deluded and then disillusioned, cynicism and confusion follow. The wrong of these things, as I see it, is not in the money the victims part with half so much as in the mental and spiritual poison they get. But that is precisely the thing the Constitution put beyond the reach of the prosecutor, for the price of freedom of religion or of speech or of the press is that we must put up with, and even pay for, a good deal of rubbish.

Prosecutions of this character easily could degenerate into religious persecution. I do not doubt that religious leaders may be convicted of fraud for making false representations on matters other than faith or experience, as for example if one represents that funds are being used to construct a church when in fact they are being used for personal purposes. But that is not this case, which reaches into wholly dangerous ground. When does less than full belief in a professed credo become actionable fraud if one is soliciting gifts or legacies? Such inquiries may discomfort orthodox as well as unconventional religious teachers, for even the most regular of them are sometimes accused of taking their orthodoxy with a grain of salt.

I would dismiss the indictment and have done with this business of judicially examining other people's faiths.

Chapter 4

"And I should think I would then have thought"

A BRIEF INTERRUPTION in the exploration of religious freedom under the Constitution is warranted at this point to consider another opinion by Justice Jackson, since he has been the present center of our attention. Here he extricates himself from an exceedingly embarrassing position with a whimsical and slyly humorous opinion which is nothing less than a delight.

The case involved a citizen of Denmark who came to this country to see the New York World's Fair and was prevented from returning to his homeland by the outbreak of World War II. Since he found himself unable to leave this country, he obtained employment to support himself even though this was in violation of his visitor's permit. He claimed exemption from the draft on the ground that he was a citizen of a friendly nation. Later, he met an American woman and married her. This led to his decision at the conclusion of the war to remain in the United States. However, the government started proceedings to deport him on the ground that he had violated his visitor's permit by obtaining employment. He countered this move by asking for a permit to remain in the United States permanently since he was now married to a United States citizen. The Immigration Act would clearly have allowed him to remain under this circumstance except for another provision that "resident aliens" who claimed exemption from the draft lost their eligibility to become citizens and could be deported. As presented to the Supreme Court, then, the question was whether this Danish citizen was a "resident alien" of the United States at the time he claimed draft exemption.

The Court held that Kristensen, the Danish citizen, was not subject to deportation because he was not a "resident alien" at the time he claimed draft exemption. The phrase "resident alien" in the Immigration Act was interpreted to refer only to aliens actually making their residence in the United States, not to visitors or those, like Kristensen, who had come to the United States as visitors and had been unable to leave because of the war.

Justice Jackson concurred. But he was faced with the fact that while he had been Attorney General he had rendered a contrary opinion to the Secretary of War—he had asserted that those in Kristensen's position were to be treated as "resident aliens." So Justice Jackson had to explain away his own prior decision, rendered as Attorney General. This is how he did it.

McGRATH v. KRISTENSEN

Supreme Court of the United States, 1950, 340 U. S. 162

JACKSON, J., *concurring*:

I concur in the judgment and opinion of the Court. But since it is contrary to an opinion which, as Attorney General, I rendered in 1940, I owe some word of explanation. I am entitled to say of that opinion what any discriminating reader must think of it—that it was as foggy as the statute the Attorney General was asked to interpret. It left the difficult borderline questions posed by the Secretary of War unanswered, covering its lack of precision with generalities which, however, gave off overtones of assurance that the Act applied to nearly every alien from a neutral country caught in the United States under almost any circumstances which required him to stay overnight.

The opinion did not at all consider aspects of our diplomatic history, which I now think, and should think I would then have thought, ought to be considered in applying any conscription Act to aliens.

In times gone by, many United States citizens by naturalization have returned to visit their native lands. There they frequently were held for military duty by governments which refused to recognize a general right of expatriation. The United States consistently has asserted the right of its citizens to be free from seizure for military duty by reason of temporary and lawful presence in foreign lands. Immunities we have asserted for our own citizens we should not deny to those of other friendly nations. Nor should we construe our legislation to penalize or prejudice such aliens for asserting a right we have consistently asserted as a matter of national policy in dealing with other nations. Of course, if an alien is not a mere sojourner but acquires residence here in any permanent sense, he submits himself to our law and assumes the obligations of a resident toward this country.

The language of the Selective Service Act can be interpreted consistently with this history of our international contentions. I think the decision of the Court today does so. Failure of the Attorney General's opinion to consider the matter in this light is difficult to explain in view of the fact that he personally had urged this history upon this Court in arguing *Perkins v. Elg,* 307 U. S. 325. Its details may be found in the briefs and their cited sources. It would be charitable to assume that neither the nominal addressee nor the nominal author of the opinion read it. That, I do not doubt, explains Mr. Stimson's acceptance of an answer so inadequate to his questions. But no such confession and avoidance can excuse the then Attorney General.

Precedent, however, is not lacking for ways by which a judge may recede from a prior opinion that has proven untenable and perhaps misled others. See Chief Justice Taney, *License Cases,* 5 How. 504, recanting views he had pressed upon the Court as Attorney General of Maryland in *Brown v. State of Maryland,* 12 Wheat. 419. Baron Bramwell extricated himself from a somewhat similar embarrassment by saying, "The matter does not appear to me now as it appears to have appeared to me then." *Andrews v. Styrap,* 26 L.T.R. (N.S.) 704, 706. And Mr. Justice Story, accounting for his contradiction of his own former opinion, quite properly put the matter: "My own error, however, can furnish no ground for its being adopted by this Court . . . ."

United States v. Gooding, 12 Wheat. 460, 478. Perhaps Dr. Johnson really went to the heart of the matter when he explained a blunder in his dictionary—"Ignorance, sir, ignorance." But an escape less self-depreciating was taken by Lord Westbury, who, it is said, rebuffed a barrister's reliance upon an earlier opinion of his Lordship: "I can only say that I am amazed that a man of my intelligence should have been guilty of giving such an opinion." If there are other ways of gracefully and good-naturedly surrendering former views to a better considered position, I invoke them all.

Chapter 5

"This is not just a little case over bus fares"

CONSTITUTIONAL RELIGIOUS FREEDOM has two facets. The first, freedom of religious belief and experience, has already been considered.

But the First Amendment also abjures governmental laws respecting an "establishment of religion." In common parlance, this is the "separation of church and state." It means that the government cannot aid a particular religion or all religions, nor can it discourage any or all religions. The government can give police and fire protection to a church, but it cannot grant money for the construction of the building or in aid of the church program. These obvious distinctions are relatively easy to perceive.

But in the last few years the Supreme Court has been beleaguered by hard cases. One of these is the Everson case, which involved the constitutionality of a state's paying the bus fares of children going to parochial schools. A hard case and a close result. The Court divided five to four in upholding state power to supply transportation to parochial school students against the claim that such a program aided an "establishment of religion." Justice Black wrote the opinion for the majority of the Court.

Justice Hugo L. Black, a Democrat from Alabama, was the first Supreme Court appointment of President Franklin Roosevelt. He was born and reared in Alabama and took his law degree at the state uni-

357

versity. After his admission to the Bar, he engaged in private practice in Birmingham except for eighteen months as a police judge and two years as a prosecuting attorney. In 1927 he was elected to the United States Senate and served there until his elevation to the Court ten years later. Black is a judge of great force and independence, whose opinions successfully blend clarity with a lawyer's precision. He need bow only to Jackson as a literary stylist among the members of the modern Court.

The customary serenity of a judicial career upon the highest Court of the land has been marred in the case of Justice Black by two unseemly episodes. The first of these occurred immediately after Black had been named to the Court. An enterprising newspaper reporter dug up the fact that in the early 1920's Justice Black had been a member of the Ku Klux Klan for a brief period. At the time of this revelation Black was abroad on vacation before assuming his judicial duties. He returned to the country and made a nationwide radio address in which he admitted the membership, asserted its casualness, and made a firm statement upon racial and religious tolerance. It is to Black's honor and credit that he has been as zealous as any member of the Court, and more zealous than most, in protecting the liberties of racial and religious minority groups. In his judging, the taint of his Ku Klux Klan membership has been completely obliterated.

The other episode occurred in 1946, at the time Chief Justice Vinson was named to the Court. A number of newspapers contemporaneously reported rumors of a behind-the-scenes "feud" upon the Court. The rumors were true; Justice Jackson brought them out into the open. From Nuremberg, Germany, where he was serving as chief prosecutor in the War Crimes Trials, Justice Jackson sent an open letter to the congressional Judiciary Committee stating that the reason for the dissension was the failure of Justice Black to disqualify himself from sitting in judgment upon a case which his former law partner had argued before the Court. This attack upon Black was totally unjustified. The other attorney had been Black's law partner for a scant two years exactly nineteen years earlier. It has always been accepted in the Court that justices could hear and decide cases argued by former law partners, close friends, and associates. As we have noted previously in this volume, Justices Field and Curtis often heard cases argued by their brothers, where the chance of bias would obviously be far greater than in the case of a law partner of years ago. In recent years Justices Frankfurter, Douglas, and Rutledge have heard cases argued by former associates on law faculties—close personal friends. Justice Roberts decided cases involving corporations in which he had been a director up to the time he was appointed to the Court. Recent justices, other than Black, who heard cases argued by former law associates and partners include Chief Justice Stone, Justices Holmes, Brandeis, Cardozo, and Butler.

Throughout the great excitement in the newspapers over the Jackson blast, Justice Black played the statesmanlike role of aloofness. He never dignified the charges by replying to them although a devastating retort was at his fingertips simply through the recital of the above facts. Unquestionably in this ugly affair Justice Jackson came off second best. His outburst is now attributed to "war nerves" coupled with possible disappointment, as rumor would have it, in not being named Chief Justice. The disqualification of a Supreme Court justice from sitting on a case remains a personal prerogative of the justice concerned, as it always has been.

A scholarly and comprehensive opinion on behalf of the dissenters in the Everson case was written by Justice Wiley B. Rutledge. The death in 1949 of Justice Rutledge, at the age of fifty-five, cut short a judicial career which was giving promise of carrying him to an exalted niche among all the Supreme Court justices of history. President Roosevelt appointed Rutledge, a Democrat from Iowa, in 1943. A native of Kentucky, he did his undergraduate work at the University of Wisconsin and received his law degree from the University of Colorado Law School. After two years of law practice in Boulder, Colorado, he returned to the university as a law professor. Two years later he joined the faculty of the Washington University (St. Louis) Law School. He spent nine years there, the last four as dean. In 1935 he became dean of the University of Iowa Law School, where he remained until President Roosevelt appointed him to the Court of Appeals of the District of Columbia in 1939. His promotion to the Supreme Court came four years later.

Rutledge was a man of humility and warmth. He was a thorough and competent legal scholar of the highest ability, but he had difficulty expressing himself with clarity and succinctness. The prolixity of his opinions sometimes gives the feeling that he was compelled to express every tentacle of his thought upon the subject. But, as in his dissent in the Everson case, the determination and fervor of the man often rose up in demonstration of his deep conviction, and therefore in spite of the lack of polished style, some of his opinions are truly monumental. They photographically reveal the inner workings of the mind of a great judge struggling to decide the hard cases.

Are state-paid bus fares of parochial school children a proper safety measure or are they a state aid to religious training and, hence, unconstitutional? The opposing opinions are presented. But in your judging it is well to note the words of Justice Rutledge that "this is not just a little case over bus fares." Its significance grows as it is recalled that one of the most sorely contested issues implicit in federal aid to education is whether financial aid can be given to parochial schools for textbooks, supplies, free lunches, and maintenance. The Court builds its legal structures upon precedent. This case is precedent when those future cases arise. Will it control or will it be distinguished away?

In most of the cases involving individual freedom discussed in Part Six, the holding is in denial of the freedom asserted. It is well to note that these are the hard and close cases—and they are included for this very reason. In some quarters it is felt that the Supreme Court has gone too far in the last few years in restricting freedom in these hard cases. On the other hand, it should be recognized that the Court has already established broad and effective protections of the freedoms of speech and religion. At most, the cases here reported are only peripheral inroads upon individual liberties; in their most crucial aspects the freedoms involved have already been made secure.

EVERSON v. BOARD OF EDUCATION OF EWING TP.

Supreme Court of the United States, 1947, 330 U. S. 1

BLACK, J.:

The "establishment of religion" clause of the First Amendment means at least this: Neither a state nor the Federal Government can set up a church. Neither can pass laws which aid one religion, aid all religions, or prefer one religion over another. Neither can force nor influence a person to go to or to remain away from church against his will or force him to profess a belief or disbelief in any religion. No person can be punished for entertaining or professing religious beliefs or disbeliefs, for church attendance or non-attendance. No tax in any amount, large or small, can be levied to support any religious activities or institutions, whatever they may be called, or whatever form they may adopt to teach or practice religion. Neither a state nor the Federal Government can, openly or secretly, participate in the affairs of any religious organizations or groups and vice versa. In the words of Jefferson, the clause against establishment of religion by law was intended to erect "a wall of separation between Church and State."

We must consider the New Jersey statute in accordance with the foregoing limitations imposed by the First Amendment. But we must not strike that state statute down if it is within the state's constitutional power even though it approaches the verge of that power. New Jersey cannot consistently with the "establishment of religion" clause of the First Amendment contribute tax-raised funds to the support of an insitution which teaches the tenets and faith of any church. On the other hand, other language of the amendment commands that New Jersey cannot hamper its citizens in the free exercise of their own religion. Consequently, it cannot exclude individual Catholics, Lutherans, Mohammedans, Baptists, Jews, Methodists, Non-believers, Presbyterians, or the members of any faith, *because of their faith, or lack of it,* from receiving the benefits of public welfare legislation. While we do not mean to intimate that a state could not provide transportation only to children attending public schools, we must be careful, in protecting the citizens of New Jersey against state-established churches, to be sure that we do not inadvertently prohibit New Jersey from extending its general state law benefits to all its citizens without regard to their religious belief.

Measured by these standards, we cannot say that the First Amendment prohibits New Jersey from spending tax-raised funds to pay the bus fares of parochial school pupils as a part of a general program under which it pays the fares of pupils attending public and other schools. It is undoubtedly true that children are helped to get to church schools. There is even a possibility that some of the children might not be sent to the church schools if the parents were compelled to pay their children's bus fares out of their own pockets when transportation to a public school would have been paid for by the state. The same possibility exists where the state requires a local transit company to provide reduced fares to school children including those attending parochial schools, or where a municipally owned transportation system undertakes to carry all school children free of charge. Moreover, state-paid policemen, detailed to protect children going to and from church schools from the very real hazards of traffic, would serve much the same purpose and accomplish much the same result as state provisions intended to guarantee free transportation of a kind which the state deems to be best for the school children's welfare. And parents might refuse to risk their children to the serious danger of traffic accidents going to and from parochial schools, the approaches to which were not protected by policemen. Similarly, parents might be reluctant to permit their children to attend schools which the state had cut off from such general government services as ordinary police and fire protection, connections for sewage disposal, public highways and sidewalks. Of course, cutting off church schools from these services, so separate and so indisputedly marked off from the religious function, would make it far more difficult for the schools to operate. But such is obviously not the purpose of the First Amendment. That Amendment requires the state to be a neutral in its relations with groups of religious believers and non-believers; it does not require the state to be their adversary. State power is no more to be used so as to handicap religions, than it is to favor them.

This Court has said that parents may, in the discharge of their duty under state compulsory education laws, send their children to a religious rather than a public school if the school meets the secular educational requirements which the state has power to impose. See *Pierce v. Society of Sisters,* 268 U.S. 510. It appears that these parochial schools meet New Jersey's requirements. The State contributes no money to the schools. It does not support them. Its legislation, as applied, does no more than provide a general program to help parents get their children, regardless of their religion, safely and expeditiously to and from accredited schools.

The First Amendment has erected a wall between church and state. That wall must be kept high and impregnable. We could not approve the slightest breach. New Jersey has not breached it here.

RUTLEDGE, J., *dissenting*:

"Congress shall make no law respecting an establishment of religion, or prohibiting the free exercise thereof. . . ." U. S. Const. Am. Art. I.

. . . .

"Well aware that Almighty God hath created the mind free; . . . that to compel a man to furnish contributions of money for the propagation of opinions which he disbelieves, is sinful and tyrannical; . . .

"We the General Assembly, do enact, That no man shall be compelled to frequent or support any religious worship, place, or ministry whatsoever, nor shall be enforced, restrained, molested, or burthened in his body or goods, nor shall otherwise suffer on account of his religious opinions or belief. . . ."

I cannot believe that the great author of those words, or the men who made them law, could have joined in this decision. Neither so high nor so impregnable today as yesterday is the wall raised between church and state by Virginia's great statute of religious freedom and the First Amendment, now made applicable to all the states by the Fourteenth. . . .

This case forces us to determine squarely for the first time what was "an establishment of religion" in the First Amendment's conception; and by that measure to decide whether New Jersey's action violates its command. . . .

No provision of the Constitution is more closely tied to or given content by its generating history than the religious clause of the First Amendment. It is at once the refined product and the terse summation of that history. The history includes not only Madison's authorship and the proceedings before the First Congress, but also the long and intensive struggle for religious freedom in America, more especially in Virginia, of which the Amendment was the direct culmination. In the documents of the times, particularly of Madison, who was leader in the Virginia struggle before he became the Amendment's sponsor, but also in the writings of Jefferson and others and in the issues which engendered them is to be found irrefutable confirmation of the Amendment's sweeping content.

For Madison, as also for Jefferson, religious freedom was the crux of the struggle for freedom in general. Madison was co-author with George Mason of the religious clause in Virginia's great Declaration of Rights of 1776. He is credited with changing it from a mere statement of principle of tolerance to the first official legislative pronouncement that freedom of conscience and religion are inherent rights of the individual. He sought also to have the Declaration expressly condemn the existing Virginia establishment. But the forces supporting it were then too strong.

Accordingly Madison yielded on this phase but not for long. At once he resumed the fight, continuing it before succeeding legislative sessions. As a member of the General Assembly in 1779 he threw his full weight behind Jefferson's historic Bill for Establishing Religious Freedom. That bill was a prime phase of Jefferson's broad program of democratic reform undertaken on his return from the Continental Congress in 1776 and submitted for the General Assembly's consideration in 1779 as his proposed revised Virginia code. With Jefferson's departure for Europe in 1784, Madison became the Bill's prime sponsor. Enactment failed in successive legislatures from its introduction in June, 1779, until its adoption in January, 1786. But during all this time the fight for religious freedom moved forward in Virginia on various fronts with growing intensity. Madison led throughout, against Patrick Henry's powerful opposing leadership until Henry was elected governor in November, 1784.

The climax came in the legislative struggle of 1784–1785 over the Assessment Bill. This was nothing more nor less than a taxing measure for the support of religion, designed to revive the payment of tithes suspended since 1777. So long as it singled out a particular sect for preference it incurred the active and general hostility of dissentient groups. It was broadened to include them, with the result that some subsided temporarily in their opposition. As altered, the bill gave to each taxpayer the privilege of designating which church should receive his share of the tax. In default of designation the legislature applied it to pious uses. But what is of the utmost significance here, "in its final form the bill left the taxpayer the option of giving his tax to education."

Madison was unyielding at all times, opposing with all his vigor the general and nondiscriminatory as he had the earlier particular and discriminatory assessments proposed. The modified Assessment Bill passed second reading in December, 1784, and was all but enacted. Madison and his followers, however, maneuvered deferment of final consideration until November, 1785. And before the Assembly reconvened in the fall he issued his historic Memorial and Remonstrance.

This is Madison's complete, though not his only, interpretation of religious liberty. It is a broadside attack upon all forms of "establishment" of religion, both general and particular, nondiscriminatory or selective. Reflecting not only the many legislative conflicts over the Assessment Bill and the Bill for Establishing Religious Freedom but also, . . . the struggles for religious incorporations and the continued maintenance of the glebes, the Remonstrance is at once the most concise and the most accurate statement of the views of the First Amendment's author concerning what is "an establishment of religion." Because it behooves us in the dimming distance of time not to lose sight of what he and his co-workers had in mind when, by a single sweeping stroke of the pen, they forbade an establishment of religion and secured its free exercise, the text of the Remonstrance is appended at the end of this opinion for its wider current reference, together with a copy of the bill against which it was directed. [The texts of the Remonstrance and the bill are omitted here, but they can be read in the original report, 330 U.S., p. 63.]

The Remonstrance, stirring up a storm of popular protest, killed the Assessment Bill. It collapsed in committee shortly before Christmas, 1785. With this, the way was cleared at last for enactment of Jefferson's Bill for Establishing Religious Freedom. Madison promptly drove it through in January of 1786, seven years from the time it was first introduced. This dual victory substantially ended the fight over establishments, settling the issue against them.

The next year Madison became a member of the Constitutional Convention. Its work done, he fought valiantly to secure the ratification of its great product in Virginia as elsewhere, and nowhere else more effectively. Madison was certain in his own mind that under the Constitution "there is not a shadow of right in the general government to intermeddle with religion" and that "this subject is, for the honor of America, perfectly free and unshackled. The Government has no jurisdiction over it. . . ." Nevertheless he pledged that he would work for a

Bill of Rights, including a specific guaranty of religious freedom, and Virginia, with other states, ratified the Constitution on this assurance.

Ratification thus accomplished, Madison was sent to the First Congress. There he went at once about performing his pledge to establish freedom for the nation as he had done in Virginia. Within a little more than three years from his legislative victory at home he had proposed and secured the submission and ratification of the First Amendment as the first article of our Bill of Rights.

All the great instruments of the Virginia struggle for religious liberty thus became warp and woof of our constitutional tradition, not simply by the course of history, but by the common unifying force of Madison's life, thought and sponsorship. He epitomized the whole of that tradition in the Amendment's compact, but nonetheless comprehensive, phrasing.

As the Remonstrance discloses throughout, Madison opposed every form and degree of official relation between religion and civil authority. For him religion was a wholly private matter beyond the scope of civil power either to restrain or to support. Denial or abridgment of religious freedom was a violation of rights both of conscience and of natural equality. State aid was no less obnoxious or destructive to freedom and to religion itself than other forms of state interference. "Establishment" and "free exercise" were correlative and coextensive ideas, representing only different facets of the single great and fundamental freedom. The Remonstrance, following the Virginia statute's example, referred to the history of religious conflicts and the effects of all sorts of establishments, current and historical, to suppress religion's free exercise. With Jefferson, Madison believed that to tolerate any fragment of establishment would be by so much to perpetuate restraint upon that freedom. Hence he sought to tear out the institution not partially but root and branch, and to bar its return forever.

In no phase was he more unrelentingly absolute than in opposing state support or aid by taxation. Not even "three pence" contribution was thus to be exacted from any citizen for such a purpose. Tithes had been the life blood of establishment before and after other compulsions disappeared. Madison and his co-workers made no exceptions or abridgments to the complete separation they created. Their objection was not to small tithes. It was to any tithes whatsoever. "If it were lawful to impose a small tax for religion the admission would pave the way for oppressive levies." Not the amount but "the principle of assessment was wrong." And the principle was as much to prevent "the interference of law in religion" as to restrain religious intervention in political matters. In this field the authors of our freedom would not tolerate "the first experiment on our liberties" or "wait till usurped power had strengthened itself by exercise, and entangled the question in precedents." Nor shall we.

In view of this history no further proof is needed that the Amendment forbids any appropriation, large or small, from public funds to aid or support any and all religious exercises. But if more were called for, the debates in the First Congress and this Court's consistent expressions, whenever it has touched on the matter directly, supply it. . . .

Does New Jersey's action furnish support for religion by use of the taxing power? Certainly it does, if the test remains undiluted as Jefferson and Madison made it, that money taken by taxation from one is not to be used or given to support another's religious training or belief, or indeed one's own. Today as then the furnishing of "contributions of money for the propagation of opinions which he disbelieves" is the forbidden exaction; and the prohibition is absolute for whatever measure brings that consequence and whatever amount may be sought or given to that end. . . .

New Jersey's action . . . exactly fits the type of exaction and kind of evil at which Madison and Jefferson struck. Under the test they framed it cannot be said that the cost of transportation is no part of the cost of education or of the religious instruction given. That it is a substantial and a necessary element is shown most plainly by the continuing and increasing demand for the state to assume it. Nor is there pretence that it relates only to the secular instruction given in religious schools or that any attempt is or could be made toward allocating proportional shares as between the secular and the religious instruction. It is precisely because the instruction is religious and relates to a particular faith, whether one or another, that parents send their children to religious schools. . . . And the very purpose of the state's contribution is to defray the cost of conveying the pupil to the place where he will receive not simply secular, but also and primarily religious, teaching and guidance. . . .

An appropriation from the public treasury to pay the cost of transportation to Sunday school, to weekday special classes at the church or parish house, or to the meetings of various young people's religious societies, such as the Y.M.C.A., the Y.W.C.A., the Y.M.H.A., the Epworth League, could not withstand the constitutional attack. This would be true, whether or not secular activities were mixed with the religious. If such an appropriation could not stand, then it is hard to see how one becomes valid for the same thing upon the more extended scale of daily instruction. Surely constitutionality does not turn on where or how often the mixed teaching occurs.

Finally, transportation, where it is needed, is as essential to education as any other element. Its cost is as much a part of the total expense, except at times in amount, as the cost of textbooks, of school lunches, of athletic equipment, of writing and other materials; indeed of all other items composing the total burden. Now as always the core of the educational process is the teacher-pupil relationship. Without this the richest equipment and facilities would go for naught. But the proverbial Mark Hopkins conception no longer suffices for the country's requirements. Without buildings, without equipment, without library, textbooks and other materials, and without transportation to bring teacher and pupil together in such an effective teaching environment, there can be not even the skeleton of what our times require. Hardly can it be maintained that transportation is the least essential of these items, or that it does not in fact aid, encourage, sustain and support, just as they do, the very process which is its purpose to accomplish. No less essential is it, or the payment of its cost, than the very teaching in the classroom or payment of the teacher's sustenance. Many types of equipment, now considered essential, better could be done without.

For me, therefore, the feat is impossible to select so indispensable an item from the composite of total costs, and characterize it as not aiding, contributing to, promoting or sustaining the propagation of beliefs which it is the very end of all to bring about. Unless this can be maintained, and the Court does not maintain it, the aid thus given is outlawed. Payment of transportation is no more, nor is it any the less essential to education, whether religious or secular, than payment for tuitions, for teachers' salaries, for buildings, equipment and necessary materials. Nor is it any the less directly related, in a school giving religious instruction, to the primary religious objective all those essential items of cost are intended to achieve. No rational line can be drawn between payment for such larger, but not more necessary, items and payment for transportation. The only line that can be so drawn is one between more dollars and less. Certainly in this realm such a line can be no valid constitutional measure. . . .

The reasons underlying the Amendment's policy have not vanished with time or diminished in force. Now as when it was adopted the price of religious freedom is double. It is that the church and religion shall live both within and upon that freedom. There cannot be freedom of religion, safeguarded by the state, and intervention by the church or its agencies in the state's domain or dependency on its largesse. The great condition of religious liberty is that it be maintained free from sustenance, as also from other interferences, by the state. For when it comes to rest upon that secular foundation it vanishes with the resting. Public money devoted to payment of religious costs, educational or other, brings the quest for more. It brings too the struggle of sect against sect for the larger share or for any. Here one by numbers alone will benefit most, there another. That is precisely the history of societies which have had an established religion and dissident groups. It is the very thing Jefferson and Madison experienced and sought to guard against, whether in its blunt or in its more screened forms. The end of such strife cannot be other than to destroy the cherished liberty. The dominating group will achieve the dominant benefit; or all will embroil the state in their dissensions.

Exactly such conflicts have centered of late around providing transportation to religious schools from public funds. The issue and the dissension work typically, in Madison's phrase, to "destroy that moderation and harmony which the forbearance of our laws to intermeddle with Religion, has produced amongst its several sects." This occurs, as he well knew, over measures at the very threshold of departure from the principle.

In these conflicts wherever success has been obtained it has been upon the contention that by providing the transportation the general cause of education, the general welfare, and the welfare of the individual will be forwarded; hence that the matter lies within the realm of public function, for legislative determination. State courts have divided upon the issue, some taking the view that only the individual, others that the institution receives the benefit. A few have recognized that this dichotomy is false, that both in fact are aided.

The majority here does not accept in terms any of those views. But neither does it deny that the individual or the school, or indeed both, are benefited directly and substantially. To do so would cut the ground from under the public function—social legislation thesis. On the contrary, the opinion concedes that the children are aided by being helped to get to the religious schooling. By converse necessary implication as well as by the absence of express denial, it must be taken to concede also that the school is helped to reach the child with its religious teaching. The religious enterprise is common to both, as it is the interest in having transportation for its religious purposes provided.

Notwithstanding the recognition that this two-way aid is given and the absence of any denial that religious teaching is thus furthered, the Court concludes that the aid so given is not "support" of religion. It is rather only support of education as such, without reference to its religious content, and thus becomes public welfare legislation. To this elision of the religious element from the case is added gloss in two respects, one that the aid extended partakes of the nature of a safety measure, the other that failure to provide it would make the state unneutral in religious matters, discriminating against or hampering such children concerning public benefits all others receive. . . .

The one gloss is contradicted by the facts of record and the other is of whole cloth with the "public function" argument's excision of the religious factor. But most important is that this approach, if valid, supplies a ready method for nullifying the Amendment's guaranty, not only for this case and others involving small grants in aid for religious education, but equally for larger ones. The only thing needed will be for the Court again to transplant the "public welfare—public function" view from its proper nonreligious due process bearing to First Amendment application, holding that religious education is not "supported" though it may be aided by the appropriation, and that the cause of education generally is furthered by helping the pupil to secure that type of training.

This is not therefore just a little case over bus fares. In paraphrase of Madison, distant as it may be in its present form from a complete establishment of religion, it differs from it only in degree; and is the first step in that direction. Today as in his time "the same authority which can force a citizen to contribute three pence only . . . for the support of any one [religious] establishment, may force him" to pay more; or "to conform to any other establishment in all cases whatsoever." And now, as then, "either . . . we must say, that the will of the Legislature is the only measure of their authority; and that in the plentitude of this authority, they may sweep away all our fundamental rights; or, that they are bound to leave this particular right untouched and sacred."

The realm of religious training and belief remains, as the Amendment made it, the kingdom of the individual man and his God. It should be kept inviolately private, not "entangled . . . in precedents" or confounded with what legislatures legitimately may take over into the public domain.

No one conscious of religious values can be unsympathetic toward the burden which our constitutional separation puts on parents who desire religious instruction mixed with secular for their children. They pay taxes for other's children's education, at the same time the added cost of instruction for their own. Nor can one happily see benefits denied to children which others receive, because in conscience they or their parents for them desire a different kind of training others do not demand.

But if those feelings should prevail, there would be an end to our historic constitutional policy and command. No more unjust or discriminatory in fact is it to deny attendants at religious schools the cost of their transportation than it is to deny them tuitions, substance for their teachers, or any other educational expense which others receive at public cost. Hardship in fact there is which none can blink. But, for assuring to those who undergo it the greater, the most comprehensive freedom, it is one written by design and firm intent into our basic law.

Of course discrimination in the legal sense does not exist. The child attending the religious school has the same right as any other to attend the public school. But he foregoes exercising it because the same guaranty which assures this freedom forbids the public school or any agency of the state to give or aid him in securing the religious instruction he seeks.

Were he to accept the common school, he would be the first to protest the teaching there of any creed or faith not his own. And it is precisely for the reason that their atmosphere is wholly secular that children are not sent to public schools under the *Pierce* doctrine. But that is a constitutional necessity, because we have staked the very existence of our country on the faith that complete separation between the state and religion is best for the state and best for religion. . . .

Short treatment will dispose of what remains. Whatever might be said of some other application of New Jersey's statute, the one made here has no semblance of bearing as a safety measure or, indeed, for securing expeditious conveyance. The transportation supplied is by public conveyance, subject to all the hazards and delays of the highway and the streets incurred by the public generally in going about its multifarious business.

Nor is the case comparable to one of furnishing fire or police protection, or access to public highways. These things are matters of common right, part of the general need for safety. Certainly the fire department must not stand idly by while the church burns. Nor is this reason why the state should pay the expense of transportation or other items of the cost of religious education. . . .

Two great drives are constantly in motion to abridge, in the name of education, the complete division of religion and civil authority which our forefathers made. One is to introduce religious education and observances into the public schools. The other, to obtain public funds for the aid and support of various private religious schools. In my opinion both avenues were closed by the Constitution. Neither should be opened by this Court. The matter is not one of quantity, to be measured by the amount of money expended. Now as in Madison's day it is one of principle, to keep separate the separate spheres as the First Amendment drew them; to prevent the first experiment upon our liberties; and to keep the question from becoming entangled in corrosive precedents. We should not be less strict to keep strong and untarnished the one side of the shield of religious freedom than we have been of the other.

Chapter 6

"We are a religious people"

IN THE LAST FEW YEARS, many states or their political subdivisions have instituted "released time" programs of sectarian religious instruction for public school children. Obviously, these programs raise an acute question of separation of church and state. One such plan, that of the city of Champaign, Illinois, was struck down by the Supreme Court in 1948, in *People of the State of Illinois ex rel. McCollum v. Board of Education,* 333 U. S. 203. The Champaign system consisted of holding sectarian classes at a given hour during the school day in the school building. The teachers of these religious classes were not paid by public funds. Each student was given the option of attending such a class in religious training or remaining in a class which was part of the regular secular curriculum of the school. The Court found two invalidating elements in the program, the use of public school property for the holding of the sectarian classes, and the compulsion in forcing the child to remain in school whether or not he desired the religious training. Justice Black wrote the opinion of the Court and only Justice Reed dissented.

In 1952 a "released time" program was again before the Court, this time the plan employed in the New York City schools. Here students were excused from school to leave the school premises and go elsewhere for sectarian religious instruction. Those who did not take this training were required to remain in school at secular tasks. Roll was taken at the various religious classes and reported back to the school to detect truancy. This time, in *Zorach v. Clauson,* the program was upheld as not in contravention of the separation of church and state. Justice Douglas wrote the opinion for the majority of six. Justices Black, Jackson, and Frankfurter dissented. Unquestionably, this decision represents a significant narrowing of the scope of the McCollum case. Whether this was justified is for you to decide, by reading the majority opinion of Justice Douglas and the dissenting opinions of Justices Black and Jackson.

We have already become acquainted with Black and Jackson. Now meet Justice William O. Douglas. A Connecticut Democrat, he was appointed to the Court by President Roosevelt in 1939. At the age of forty-one, he was, except for Justice William Johnson, who was appointed in 1804 at the age of thirty-three, the youngest man so far called to the Court. He did his undergraduate work at Whitman College and took his law degree at Columbia Law School. After three years of practicing law in New York City and teaching at Columbia Law School, in 1928 he became a full-time member of the Yale Law School faculty. In 1934 he went to Washington to direct an important study of stockholders' protective committees, under the supervision of the Securities and Exchange Commission, and he became, in 1936, a commissioner of the SEC, and later its chairman. Many persons outside the legal profession have come to know Justice Douglas through his penetrating books recording his extensive travels in Asia in the last few years; a recent book, *Of Men and Mountains,* is an appreciation of nature and also an insight into his personal philosophy.

Justice Douglas is the most versatile man now on the Court, equally at home in an obscure and technical corporation law or taxation problem or in a case of simpler facts raising grave questions of human liberty. He and Justice Black come closer to forming a "team," in the sense that Justices Holmes and Brandeis were a team, than any two men on the Court. Their alignment on opposite sides in the Zorach case is the exception rather than the rule. In style and manner of opinion writing, too, Douglas and Black are brothers. Douglas, like Black, writes with appealing literary craftsmanship, but style is never allowed to stand in the way of clarity and incisive analysis. However, Douglas has been more mercurial and unpredictable than Black, especially in the later years. A marked characteristic of his judging is the calling of each case as he sees it, with small stress upon a broader cohesive and consistent pattern in the law. To him, justice is not necessarily a regular and evenly balanced structure—or, perhaps, not even a structure at all, but the rocks, hills, trees, shrubs, flowers and grasses that together blend into a landscape of nature.

ZORACH v. CLAUSON
Supreme Court of the United States, 1952, 343 U. S. 306

DOUGLAS, J.:

New York City has a program which permits its public schools to release students during the school day so that they may leave the school buildings and school grounds and go to religious centers for religious instruction or devotional exercises. A student is released on written request of his parents. Those not released stay in the classrooms. The churches make weekly reports to the schools, sending a list of children who have been released from public school but who have not reported for religious instruction.

This "released time" program involves neither religious instruction in public school classrooms nor the expenditure of public funds. All costs, including the application blanks, are paid by the religious organizations. The case is therefore unlike *McCollum v. Board of Education,* 333 U. S. 203, which involved a "released time" program from Illinois. In that case the classrooms were turned over to religious instructors. We accordingly held that the program violated the First Amendment which (by reason of the Fourteenth Amendment) prohibits the states from establishing religion or prohibiting its free exercise. . . .

Our problem reduces itself to whether New York by this system has either prohibited the "free exercise" of religion or has made a law "respecting an establishment of religion" within the meaning of the First Amendment.

It takes obtuse reasoning to inject any issue of the "free exercise" of religion into the present case. No one is forced to go to the religious classroom and no religious exercise or instruction is brought to the classrooms of the public schools. A student need not take religious instruction. He is left to his own desires as to the manner or time of his religious devotions, if any.

There is a suggestion that the system involves the use of coercion to get public school students into religious classrooms. There is no evidence in the record before us that supports that conclusion. The present record indeed tells us that the school authorities are neutral in this regard and do no more than release students whose parents so request. If in fact coercion were used, if it were established that any one or more teachers were using their office to persuade or force students to take the religious instruction, a wholly different case would be presented. Hence we put aside that claim of coercion both as respects the "free exercise" of religion and "an establishment of religion" within the meaning of the First Amendment.

Moreover, apart from that claim of coercion, we do not see how New York by this type of "released time" program has made a law respecting an establishment of religion within the meaning of the First Amendment. There is much talk of the separation of Church and State in the history of the Bill of Rights and in the decisions clustering around the First Amendment. There cannot be the slightest doubt that the First Amendment reflects the philosophy that Church and State should be separated. And so far as interference with the "free exercise" of religion and an "establishment" of religion are concerned, the separation must be complete and unequivocal. The First Amendment within the scope of its coverage permits no exception; the prohibition is absolute. The First Amendment, however, does not say that in every and all respects there shall be a separation of Church and State. Rather, it studiously defines the manner, the specific ways, in which there shall be no concert or union or dependency one on the other. That is the common sense of the matter. Otherwise the state and religion would be aliens to each other—hostile, suspicious, and even unfriendly. Churches could not be required to pay even property taxes. Municipalities would not be permitted to render police or fire protection to religious groups. Policemen who helped parishioners into their places of worship would violate the Constitution. Prayers in our legislative halls; the appeals to the Almighty in the messages of the Chief Executive; the proclamation making Thanksgiving Day a holiday; "so help me God" in our courtroom oaths—these and all other references to the Almighty that run through our laws, our public rituals, our ceremonies would be flouting the First Amendment. A fastidious atheist or agnostic could even object to the supplication with which the Court opens each session: "God save the United States and this Honorable Court."

We would have to press the concept of separation of Church and State to these extremes to condemn the present law on constitutional grounds. The nullification of this law would have wide and profound effects. A Catholic student applies to his teacher for permission to leave the school during hours on a Holy Day of Obligation to attend a mass. A Jewish student asks his teacher for permission to be excused for Yom Kippur. A Protestant wants the afternoon off for a family baptismal ceremony. In each case the teacher requires parental consent in writing. In each case the teacher, in order to make sure the student is not a truant, goes further and requires a report from the priest, the rabbi, or the minister. The teacher in other words cooperates in a religious program to the extent of making it possible for her students to participate in it. Whether she does it occasionally for a few students, regularly for one, or pursuant to a systematized program designed to further the religious needs of all the students does not alter the character of the act.

We are a religious people whose institutions presuppose a Supreme Being. We guarantee the freedom to worship as one chooses. We make room for as wide a variety of beliefs and creeds as the spiritual needs of man deem necessary. We sponsor an attitude on the part of government that shows no partiality to any one group and that lets each flourish according to the zeal of its adherents and the appeal of its dogma. When the state encourages religious instruction or cooperates with religious authorities by adjusting the schedule of public events to sectarian needs, it follows the best of our traditions. For it then respects the religious nature of our people and accommodates the public service to their spiritual needs. To hold that it may not would be to find in the Constitution a requirement that the government show a callous indifference to religious groups. That would be preferring those who believe in no religion over those who do believe. Government may not finance religious groups nor undertake religious instruction nor blend secular and sectarian education nor use secular institutions to force one or some religion on any person. But we find no constitutional requirement which makes it necessary for government to be hostile to religion and to throw its weight against efforts to widen the effective scope of religious influence. The government must be neutral when it comes to competition between sects. It may not thrust any sect on any person. It may not make a religious observance compulsory. It may not coerce anyone to attend church, to observe a religious holiday, or to take religious instruction. But it can close its doors or suspend its operations as to those who want to repair to their religious sanctuary for worship or instruction. No more than that is undertaken here. . . .

In the *McCollum* case the classrooms were used for religious instruction and the force of the public school was used to promote that instruction. Here, as we have said, the public schools do no more than accommodate their schedules to a program of outside religious instruction. We follow the *McCollum* case. But we cannot expand it to cover the present released time program unless separation of Church and State means that public institutions can make no adjustments of their schedules to accommodate the religious needs of the people. We cannot read into the Bill of Rights such a philosophy of hostility to religion.

BLACK, J., *dissenting*:

Illinois ex rel. McCollum v. Board of Education, 333 U. S. 203, held invalid as an "establishment of religion" an Illinois system under which school children, compelled by law to go to public schools, were freed from some hours of required school work on condition that they attend special religious classes held in the school buildings. Although the classes were taught by sectarian teachers neither employed nor paid by the state, the state did use its power to further the program by releasing some of the children from regular class work, insisting that those released attend the religious classes, and requiring that those who remained behind do some kind of academic work while the others received their religious training. We said this about the Illinois system:

"Pupils compelled by law to go to school for secular education are released in part from their legal duty upon the condition that they attend the religious classes. This is beyond all question a utilization of the tax-established and tax-supported public school system to aid religious groups to spread their faiths. And it falls squarely under the ban of the First Amendment . . . ." *McCollum v. Board of Education,* supra, 333 U. S. at pages 209–210.

I see no significant difference between the invalid Illinois system and that of New York here sustained. Except for the use of the school buildings in Illinois, there is no difference between the systems which I consider even worthy of mention. In the New York program, as in that of Illinois, the school authorities release some of the children on the condition that they attend the religious classes, get reports on whether they attend, and hold the other children in the school building until the religious hour is over. As we attempted to make categorically clear, the *McCollum* decision would have been the same if the religious classes had not been held in the school buildings. We said:

"Here *not only* are the state's tax-supported public school buildings used for the dissemination of religious doctrines. The State *also* affords sectarian groups an invaluable aid in that it helps to provide pupils for their religious classes through use of the state's compulsory public school machinery. *This* is not separation of Church and State." (Emphasis supplied.) *McCollum v. Board of Education, supra,* 333 U. S. at page 212.

McCollum thus held that Illinois could not constitutionally manipulate the compelled classroom hours of its compulsory school machinery so as to channel children into sectarian classes. Yet that is exactly what the Court holds New York can do. . . .

Difficulty of decision in the hypothetical situations mentioned by the Court, but not now before us, should not confuse the issues in this case. Here the sole question is whether New York can use its compulsory education laws to help religious sects get attendants presumably too unenthusiastic to go unless moved to do so by the pressure of this state machinery. That this is the plan, purpose, design and consequence of the New York program cannot be denied. The state thus makes religious sects beneficiaries of its power to compel children to attend secular schools. Any use of such coercive power by the state to help or hinder some religious sects or to prefer all religious sects over nonbelievers or vice versa is just what I think the First Amendment forbids. In considering whether a state has entered this forbidden field the question is not whether it has entered too far but whether it has entered at all. New

York is manipulating its compulsory education laws to help religious sects get pupils. This is not separation but combination of Church and State.

The Court's validation of the New York system rests in part on its statement that Americans are "a religious people whose institutions presuppose a Supreme Being." This was at least as true when the First Amendment was adopted; and it was just as true when eight Justices of this Court invalidated the released time system in *McCollum* on the premise that a state can no more "aid all religions" than it can aid one. It was precisely because Eighteenth Century Americans were a religious people divided into many fighting sects that we were given the constitutional mandate to keep Church and State completely separate. Colonial history had already shown that, here as elsewhere zealous sectarians entrusted with governmental power to further their causes would sometimes torture, maim and kill those they branded "heretics," "atheists" or "agnostics." The First Amendment was therefore to insure that no one powerful sect or combination of sects could use political or governmental power to punish dissenters whom they could not convert to their faith. Now as then, it is only by wholly isolating the state from the religious sphere and compelling it to be completely neutral, that the freedom of each and every denomination and of all nonbelievers can be maintained. It is this neutrality the Court abandons today when it treats New York's coercive system as a program which *merely* "encourages religious instruction or cooperates with religious authorities." The abandonment is all the more dangerous to liberty because of the Court's legal exaltation of the orthodox and its derogation of unbelievers.

Under our system of religious freedom, people have gone to their religious sanctuaries not because they feared the law but because they loved their God. The choice of all has been as free as the choice of those who answered the call to worship moved only by the music of the old Sunday morning church bells. The spiritual mind of man has thus been free to believe, disbelieve, or doubt, without repression, great or small, by the heavy hand of government. Statutes authorizing such repression have been stricken. Before today, our judicial opinions have refrained from drawing invidious distinctions between those who believe in no religion and those who do believe. The First Amendment has lost much if the religious follower and the atheist are no longer to be judicially regarded as entitled to equal justice under law.

State help to religion injects political and party prejudices into a holy field. It too often substitutes force for prayer, hate for love, and persecution for persuasion. Government should not be allowed, under cover of the soft euphemism of "co-operation," to steal into the sacred area of religious choice.

JACKSON, J., *dissenting*:

This released time program is founded upon a use of the State's power of coercion, which, for me, determines its unconstitutionality. Stripped to its essentials, the plan has two stages, first, that the State compel each student to yield a large part of his time for public secular education and, second, that some of it be "released" to him on condition that he devote it to sectarian religious purposes.

No one suggests that the Constitution would permit the State directly to require this "released" time to be spent "under the control of a duly constituted religious body." This program accomplishes that forbidden result by indirection. If public education were taking so much of the pupil's time as to injure the public or the students' welfare by encroaching upon their religious opportunity, simply shortening everyone's school day would facilitate voluntary and optional attendance at Church classes. But that suggestion is rejected upon the ground that if they are made free many students will not go to the Church. Hence, they must be deprived of freedom for this period, with Church attendance put to them as one of the two permissible ways of using it.

The greater effectiveness of this system over voluntary attendance after school hours is due to the truant officer who, if the youngster fails to go to the Church school, dogs him back to the public schoolroom. Here schooling is more or less suspended during the "released time" so the nonreligious attendants will not forge ahead of the churchgoing absentees. But it serves as a temporary jail for a pupil who will not go to Church. It takes more subtlety of mind than I possess to deny that this is governmental constraint in support of religion. It is as unconstitutional, in my view, when exerted by indirection as when exercised forthrightly.

As one whose children, as a matter of free choice, have been sent to privately supported Church schools, I may challenge the Court's suggestion that opposition to this plan can only be antireligious, atheistic, or agnostic. My evangelistic brethren confuse an objection to compulsion with an objection to religion. It is possible to hold a faith with enough confidence to believe that what should be rendered to God does not need to be decided and collected by Caesar.

The day that this country ceases to be free for irreligion it will cease to be free for religion—except for the sect that can win political power. The same epithetical jurisprudence, used by the Court today to beat down those who oppose pressuring children into some religion can devise as good epithets tomorrow against those who object to pressuring them into a favored religion. And after all if we concede to the State power and wisdom to single out "duly constituted religious" bodies as exclusive alternatives for compulsory secular instruction, it would be logical to also uphold the power and wisdom to choose the true faith among those "duly constituted." We start down a rough road when we begin to mix compulsory public education with compulsory godliness.

A number of Justices just short of a majority of the majority that promulgates today's passionate dialectics joined in answering them in *Illinois ex rel. McCollum v. Board of Education,* 333 U. S. 203. The distinction attempted between that case and this is trivial, almost to the point of cynicism, magnifying its nonessential details and disparaging compulsion which was the underlying reason for invalidity. A reading of the Court's opinion in that case along with its opinion in this case will show such difference of overtones and undertones as to make clear that the *McCollum* case has passed like a storm in a teacup. The wall which the Court was professing to erect between Church and State has become even more warped and twisted than I expected. Today's judgment will be more interesting to students of psychology and of the judicial processes than to students of constitutional law.

Chapter 7

*"We cannot bind the government to
wait until the catalyst is added"*

EVALUATING CONSTITUTIONAL ISSUES by reading the majority and dissenting opinions in the same case is not a game. Rather, it is an exercise in statecraft which stimulates consideration and evaluation of the all-important tenets of our American life. A forceful current example arises in the awesome challenge to the doctrine of free speech posed by Communism. To some, the toleration in our midst of Communists and others who would subvert our cherished freedoms is an act of courageous faith in political liberty. To others this toleration is foolhardy. With the passage of the Smith Act in 1940, Congress went on record as believing that the toleration of Communists had gone too far. The provisions of this law made it a crime to teach or advocate the overthrow of the government by force, or to create or join any organization teaching revolutionary doctrine.

In 1948 the leaders of the Communist Party in the United States were indicted for violation of the Smith Act. There was no charge that they were engaging in sabotage or other open revolutionary conduct. The indictment was limited to the teaching of revolution and the forming of an organization, the Communist Party, which taught revolution.

The trial of these indicted Communist leaders, before Federal Judge

Harold R. Medina, covered a period of nine months. This was the trial which provided mountains of newspaper copy because of the constant bickering between Judge Medina and the battery of lawyers defending the Communists. Fascinating verbatim excerpts from these interchanges between the judge and the lawyers can be found in the Appendix to the report of the case of *Sacher v. United States,* 343 U. S. 1, at pages 42–89, and in the Appendix to the report of the same case in the lower federal court, 182 F. 2d 416, at pages 430–453. At the conclusion of the trial of the Communist leaders, Judge Medina held their lawyers in contempt of court for their conduct during the trial. The Sacher case is the appeal of those lawyers from the contempt convictions. Judge Medina's action was upheld by the Supreme Court in the Sacher case, but not without dissent.

The Communist Party leaders were convicted of violation of the Smith Act. The case goes under the name of *Dennis v. United States.* In the appeal to the Supreme Court it was conceded that the Communist leaders had violated the Act—had taught and advocated the overthrow of the government and had formed an organization, the Communist Party, so to teach and advocate. The sole question before the Court was whether the Smith Act was unconstitutional because such teaching and advocacy fell in the area of privileged free speech.

In the Dennis case the Supreme Court upheld the constitutionality of the Smith Act and affirmed the conviction of the Communist leaders. Justices Black and Douglas dissented. Of the six majority justices (one justice did not hear the case), Jackson and Frankfurter wrote their own concurring opinions. The other four of the majority joined in an opinion by Chief Justice Vinson, which, as the only group opinion among the majority justices, is the one presented here, together with Justice Douglas' dissent. Both opinions, of necessity, are substantially shortened; the full report of the Dennis case occupies ninety-eight pages. Both the Vinson and Douglas opinions rely upon the Holmes "clear and present danger" test in defining the scope of free speech. Vinson sees a clear and present danger, and Douglas does not. Further comment upon the opinions is superfluous; they both sharply etch the respective positions.

The twelfth Chief Justice, Fred M. Vinson, a Democrat from Kentucky, was named by President Truman in 1946. His college work, both undergraduate and law, was taken at Centre College. He practiced law in Kentucky until in 1923 he became a member of the U. S. House of Representatives, where he served seven terms, missing only the 1929–31 term. President Roosevelt named him an associate justice of the

U. S. Court of Appeals of the District of Columbia in 1937. After five years, he resigned this judgeship to become the director of Economic Stabilization during World War II. Successive positions of high responsibility followed. He was Federal Loan administrator, director of War Mobilization and Reconversion, and finally, 1945–46, the Secretary of the Treasury in President Truman's cabinet. While in this cabinet post, he was appointed the Chief Justice of the United States. And in this capacity he served for seven years, until his sudden death in 1953 at the age of sixty-three.

"Quiet craftsmanship" is probably the best phrase to describe Chief Justice Vinson's work on the Court. His opinions follow the same general pattern as those of his predecessor, Chief Justice Stone. They are opinions for lawyers, quietly leading one through the intricate paths of past precedent. But Vinson was not the giant of legal scholarship that Stone was. His particular place in history will probably be that of a thoroughly competent and adequate Chief Justice, but one not truly outstanding.

Justice Holmes said in his dissenting opinion in the Gitlow case, "If in the long run the beliefs expressed in proletarian dictatorship are destined to be accepted by the dominant forces of the community, the only meaning of free speech is that they should be given their chance and have their way." With this statement as a guide we should probably conclude that Holmes and probably Brandeis, if alive today, would have aligned themselves with Black and Douglas in dissenting in the Dennis case. But Holmes and Brandeis were sometimes wrong. Further, they did not live amid today's world-Communist threat. No—evaluation of the Dennis case is not a game. It is a most serious endeavor. The correct balance must be found between successful resistance to the Communist menace and the preservation of our liberties, those freedoms that make resistance to Communism worth while.

DENNIS v. UNITED STATES
Supreme Court of the United States, 1951, 341 U. S. 494.

Vinson, C. J.:

Petitioners were indicted in July, 1948, for violation of the conspiracy provisions of the Smith Act, 54 Stat. 671, 18 U. S. C. (1946 ed) § 11, during the period of April, 1945, to July, 1948....

Sections 2 and 3 of the Smith Act, 54 Stat. 671, 18 U. S. C. (1946 ed) §§ 10, 11 (see present 18 U. S. C. § 2385), provide as follows:

"Sec. 2.

"(a) It shall be unlawful for any person—

"(1) to knowingly or willfully advocate, abet, advise, or teach the duty, necessity, desirability, or propriety of overthrowing or destroying any government in the United States by force or violence, or by the assassination of any officer of any such government;

"(2) with intent to cause the overthrow or destruction of any government in the United States, to print, publish, edit, issue, circulate, sell, distribute, or publicly display any written or printed matter advocating, advising, or teaching the duty, necessity, desirability, or propriety of overthrowing or destroying any government in the United States by force or violence;

"(3) to organize or help to organize any society, group, or assembly of persons who teach, advocate, or encourage the overthrow or destruction of any government in the United States by force or violence; or to be or become a member of, or affiliate with, any such society, group, or assembly of persons, knowing the purposes thereof.

"(b) For the purposes of this section, the term 'government in the United States' means the Government of the United States, the government of any State, Territory, or possession of the United States, the government of the District of Columbia, or the government of any political subdivision of any of them.

"Sec. 3. It shall be unlawful for any person to attempt to commit, or to conspire to commit, any of the acts prohibited by the provisions of this title."

The indictment charged the petitioners with willfully and knowingly conspiring (1) to organize as the Communist Party of the United States of America a society, group and assembly of persons who teach and advocate the overthrow and destruction of the Government of the United States by force and violence, and (2) knowingly and wilfully to advocate and teach the duty and necessity of overthrowing and destroying the Government of the United States by force and violence. The indictment further alleged that § 2 of the Smith Act proscribes these acts and that any conspiracy to take such action is a violation of § 3 of the Act....

The obvious purpose of the statute is to protect existing Government, not from change by peaceable, lawful and constitutional means, but from change by violence, revolution and terrorism. That it is within the *power* of Congress to protect the Government of the United States from armed rebellion is a proposition which requires little discussion. Whatever theoretical merit there may be to the argument that there is a "right" to rebellion against dictatorial governments is without force where the existing structure of the government provides for peaceful and orderly change. We reject any principle of governmental helplessness in the face of preparation for revolution, which principle, carried to its logical conclusion, must lead to anarchy. No one could conceive that it is not within the power of Congress to prohibit acts intended to overthrow the Government by force and violence. The question with which we are concerned here is not whether Congress has such *power*, but whether the *means* which it has employed conflict with the First and Fifth Amendments to the Constitution.

One of the bases for the contention that the means which Congress has employed are invalid takes the form of an attack on the face of the statute on the grounds that by its terms it prohibits academic discussion of the merits of Marxism-Leninism, that it stifles ideas and is contrary to all concepts of a free speech and a free press....

The very language of the Smith Act negates the interpretation which petitioners would have us impose on that Act. It is directed at advocacy, not discussion. Thus, the trial judge properly charged the jury that they could not convict if they found that petitioner did "no more than pursue peaceful studies and discussions or teaching and advocacy in the realm of ideas." He further charged that it was not unlawful "to conduct in an American college and university a course explaining the philosophical theories set forth in the books which have been placed in evidence." Such a charge is in strict accord with the statutory language, and illustrates the meaning to be placed on those words. Congress did not intend to eradicate the free discussion of political theories, to destroy the traditional rights of Americans to discuss and evaluate ideas without fear of governmental sanction. Rather Congress was concerned with the very kind of activity in which the evidence showed these petitioners engaged.

But although the statute is not directed at the hypothetical cases which petitioners have conjured, its application in this case has resulted in convictions for the teaching and advocacy of the overthrow of the Government by force and violence, which, even though coupled with the intent to accomplish that overthrow, contains an element of speech. For this reason, we must pay special heed to the demands of the First Amendment marking out the boundaries of speech. . . .

Overthrow of the Government by force and violence is certainly a substantial enough interest for the Government to limit speech. Indeed, this is the ultimate value of any society, for if a society cannot protect its very structure from armed internal attack, it must follow that no subordinate value can be protected. If, then, this interest may be protected, the literal problem which is presented is what has been meant by the use of the phrase "clear and present danger" of the utterances bringing about the evil within the power of Congress to punish.

Obviously, the words cannot mean that before the Government may act, it must wait until the *putsch* is about to be executed, the plans have been laid and the signal is awaited. If Government is aware that a group aiming at its overthrow is attempting to indoctrinate its members and to commit them to a course whereby they will strike when the leaders feel the circumstances permit, action by the Government is required. The argument that there is no need for Government to concern itself, for Government is strong, it possesses ample powers to put down a rebellion, it may defeat the revolution with ease needs no answer. For that is not the question. Certainly an attempt to overthrow the Government by force, even though doomed from the outset because of inadequate numbers or power of the revolutionists, is a sufficient evil for Congress to prevent. The damage which such attempts create both physically and politically to a nation makes it impossible to measure the validity in terms of the probability of success, or the immediacy of a successful attempt. In the instant case the trial judge charged the jury that they could not convict unless they found that petitioners intended to overthrow the Government "as speedily as circumstances would permit." This does not mean, and could not properly mean, that they would not strike until there was certainty of success. What was meant was that the revolutionists would strike when they thought the time was ripe. We must therefore reject the contention that success or probability of success is the criterion....

Chief Judge Learned Hand, writing for the majority below, interpreted the phrase as follows: "In each case [courts] must ask whether the gravity of the 'evil,' discounted by its improbability, justifies such invasion of free speech as is necessary to avoid the danger." 183 F. 2d at 212. We adopt this statement of the rule. As articulated by Chief Judge Hand, it is as succinct and inclusive as any other we might devise at this time. It takes into consideration those factors which we deem relevant, and relates their significances. More we cannot expect from words.

Likewise, we are in accord with the court below, which affirmed the trial court's findings that the requisite danger existed. The mere fact that from the period 1945 to 1948 petitioners' activities did not result in an attempt to overthrow the Government by force and violence is of course no answer to the fact that there was a group that was ready to make the attempt. The formation by petitioners of such a highly organized conspiracy, with rigidly disciplined members subject to call when the leaders, these petitioners, felt that the time had come for action, coupled with the inflammable nature of world conditions, similar uprising in other countries, and the touch-and-go nature of our relations with countries with whom petitioners were in the very least ideologically attuned, convince us that their convictions were justified on this score. And this analysis disposes of the contention that a conspiracy to advocate, as distinguished from the advocacy itself, cannot be constitutionally restrained, because it comprises only the preparation. It is the existence of the conspiracy which creates the danger. If the ingredients of the reaction are present, we cannot bind the Government to wait until the catalyst is added....

DOUGLAS, J., *dissenting*:

If this were a case where those who claimed protection under the First Amendment were teaching the techniques of sabotage, the assassination of the President, the filching of documents from public files, the planting of bombs, the art of street warfare, and the like, I would have no doubts. The freedom to speak is not absolute; the teaching of methods of terror and other seditious conduct should be beyond the pale along with obscenity and immorality. This case was argued as if those were the facts. The argument imported much seditious conduct into the record. That is easy and it has popular appeal, for the activities of Communists in plotting and scheming against the free world are common knowledge. But the fact is that no such evidence was introduced at the trial. There is a statute which makes a seditious conspiracy unlawful. Petitioners, however, were not charged with a "conspiracy to overthrow" the Government. They were charged with a conspiracy to form a party and groups and assemblies of people who teach and advocate the overthrow of our Government by force or violence and with a conspiracy to advocate and teach its overthrow by force and violence. It may well be that indoctrination in the techniques of terror to destroy the Government would be indictable under either statute. But the teaching which is condemned here is of a different character.

So far as the present record is concerned, what petitioners did was to organize people to teach and themselves teach the Marxist-Leninist doctrine contained chiefly in four books: Foundations of Leninism by Stalin (1924); The Communist Manifesto by Marx and Engels (1848); State and Revolution by Lenin (1917); History of the Communist Party of the Soviet Union (B.) (1939).

Those books are to Soviet Communism what Mein Kampf was to Nazism. If they are understood, the ugliness of Communism is revealed, its deceit and cunning are exposed, the nature of its activities becomes apparent, and the chances of its success less likely. That is not, of course, the reason why petitioners chose these books for their classrooms. They are fervent Communists to whom these volumes are gospel. They preached the creed with the hope that some day it would be acted upon.

The opinion of the Court does not outlaw these texts nor condemn them to the fire, as the Communists do literature offensive to their creed. But if the books themselves are not outlawed, if they can lawfully remain on library shelves, by what reasoning does their use in a classroom become a crime? It would not be a crime under the Act to introduce these books to a class, though that would be teaching what the creed of violent overthrow of the Government is. The Act, as construed, requires the element of intent—that those who teach the creed believe in it. The crime then depends not on what is taught but on who the teacher is. That is to make freedom of speech turn not on *what is said,* but on the *intent* with which it is said. Once we start down that road we enter territory dangerous to the liberties of every citizen.

There was a time in England when the concept of constructive treason flourished. Men were punished not for raising a hand against the king but for thinking murderous thoughts about him. The framers of the Constitution were alive to that abuse and took steps to see that the practice would not flourish here. Treason was defined to require overt acts—the evolution of a plot against the country into an actual project. The present case is not one of treason. But the analogy is close when the illegality is made to turn on intent, not on the nature of the act. We then start probing men's minds for motive and purpose; they become entangled in the law not for what they did but for *what they thought;* they get convicted not for what they said but for the purpose with which they said it. . . .

Free speech has occupied an exalted position because of the high service it has given our society. Its protection is essential to the very existence of a democracy. The airing of ideas releases pressures which otherwise might become destructive. When ideas compete in the market for acceptance, full and free discussion exposes the false and they gain few adherents. Full and free discussion even of ideas we hate encourages the testing of our own prejudices and preconceptions. Full and free discussion keeps a society from becoming stagnant and unprepared for the stresses and strains that work to tear all civilizations apart.

Full and free discussion has indeed been the first article of our faith. We have founded our political system on it. It has been the safeguard of every religious, political, philosophical, economic, and racial group amongst us. We have counted on it to keep us from embracing what is cheap and false; we have trusted the common sense of our people to choose the doctrine true to our genius and to reject the rest. This has been the one single outstanding tenet that has made our institutions the symbol of freedom and equality. We have deemed it more costly to liberty to suppress a despised minority than to let them vent their spleen. We have above all else feared the political censor. We have wanted a land where our people can be exposed to all the diverse creeds and cultures of the world.

There comes a time when even speech loses its constitutional immunity. Speech innocuous one year may at another time fan such destructive flames that it must be halted in the interests of the safety of the Republic. That is the meaning of the clear and present danger test. When conditions are so critical that there will be no time to avoid the evil that the speech threatens, it is time to call a halt. Otherwise, free speech which is the strength of the Nation will be the cause of its destruction.

Yet free speech is the rule, not the exception. The restraint to be constitutional must be based on more than fear, on more than passionate opposition against the speech, on more than a revolted dislike for its contents. There must be some immediate injury to society that is likely if speech is allowed....

The nature of Communism as a force on the world scene would, of course, be relevant to the issue of clear and present danger of petitioners' advocacy within the United States. But the primary consideration is the strength and tactical position of petitioners and their converts in this country. On that there is no evidence in the record. If we are to take judicial notice of the threat of Communists within the nation, it should not be difficult to conclude that as a *political party* they are of little consequence. Communists in this country have never made a respectable or serious showing in any election. I would doubt that there is a village, let alone a city or county or state, which the Communists could carry. Communism in the world scene is no bogey-man; but Communism as a political faction or party in this country plainly is. Communism has been so thoroughly exposed in this country that it has been crippled as a political force. Free speech has destroyed it as an effective political party. It is inconceivable that those who went up and down this country preaching the doctrine of revolution which petitioners espouse would have any success. In days of trouble and confusion, when bread lines were long, when the unemployed walked the streets, when people were starving, the advocates of a short-cut by revolution might have a chance to gain adherents. But today there are no such conditions. The country is not in despair; the people know Soviet Communism; the doctrine of Soviet revolution is exposed in all of its ugliness and the American people want none of it.

How it can be said that there is a clear and present danger that this advocacy will succeed is, therefore, a mystery. Some nations less resilient than the United States, where illiteracy is high and where democratic traditions are only budding, might have to take drastic steps and jail these men for merely speaking their creed. But in America they are miserable merchants of unwanted ideas; their wares remain unsold. The fact that their ideas are abhorrent does not make them powerful.

The political impotence of the Communists in this country does not, of course, dispose of the problem. Their numbers; their positions in industry and government; the extent to which they have in fact infiltrated the police, the armed services, transportation, stevedoring, power plants, munitions works, and other critical places—these facts all bear on the likelihood that their advocacy of the Soviet theory of revolution will endanger the Republic. But the record is silent on these facts. If we are to proceed on the basis of judicial notice, it is impossible for me to say that the Communists in this country are so potent or so strategically deployed that they must be suppressed for their speech. I could not so hold unless I were willing to conclude that the activities in recent years of committees of Congress, of the Attorney General, of labor unions, of the state legislatures, and of Loyalty Boards were so futile as to leave the country on the edge of grave peril. To believe that petitioners and their following are placed in such critical positions as to endanger the Nation is to believe the incredible. It is safe to say that the followers of the creed of Soviet Communism are known to the F. B. I.; that in case of war with Russia they will be picked up overnight as were all prospective saboteurs at the commencement of World War II; that the invisible army of petitioners is the best known, the most beset, and the least thriving of any fifth column in history. Only those held by fear and panic could think otherwise.

This is my view if we are to act on the basis of judicial notice. But the mere statement of the opposing views indicates how important it is that we know the facts before we act. Neither prejudice nor hate nor senseless fear should be the basis of this solemn act. Free speech—the glory of our system of government—should not be sacrificed on anything less than plain and objective proof of danger that the evil advocated is imminent. On this record no one can say that petitioners and their converts are in such a strategic position as to have even the slightest chance of achieving their aims.

The First Amendment provides that "Congress shall make no law . . . abridging the freedom of speech." The Constitution provides no exception. This does not mean, however, that the Nation need hold its hand until it is in such weakened condition that there is no time to protect itself from incitement to revolution. Seditious conduct can always be punished. But the command of the First Amendment is so clear that we should not allow Congress to call a halt to free speech except in the extreme case of peril from the speech itself. The First Amendment makes confidence in the common sense of our people and in their maturity of judgment the great postulate of our democracy. Its philosophy is that violence is rarely, if ever, stopped by denying civil liberties to those advocating resort to force. The First Amendment reflects the philosophy of Jefferson "that it is time enough for the rightful purposes of civil government, for its officers to interfere when principles break out into overt acts against peace and good order." The political censor has no place in our public debates. Unless and until extreme and necessitous circumstances are shown our aim should be to keep speech unfettered and to allow the processes of law to be invoked only when the provocateurs among us move from speech to action.

Vishinsky wrote in 1938 in The Law of the Soviet State, "In our state, naturally, there is and can be no place for freedom of speech, press, and so on for the foes of socialism."

Our concern should be that we accept no such standard for the United States. Our faith should be that our people will never give support to these advocates of revolution, so long as we remain loyal to the purposes for which our Nation was founded.

Chapter 8

"The imminence of great disorder"

THOSE WHO KNOW London's Hyde Park and New York's Union Square realize that one of the cogs in the free speech mechanism is the right of anyone to climb upon his soap box in some public place and harangue all those who will listen. The Supreme Court has regularly struck down laws which give a licensing power to some public official whereby the holding of public meetings can be limited to selected groups and public speeches to selected persons. Any laws designed to give discretion to government officials to decide who shall be heard in public are an anathema to the Court.

But the lack of state power to control speech by licensing does not make street-corner oratory or public meetings absolutely privileged. Obviously, in any public speech there can come a point where the words are so inciting to violence or riot that they must be stopped. Short of this point, however, there must be an area of police protection to an unpopular speaker whose words may be provoking his disagreeing listeners to physical attempts to silence him.

These issues are neatly posed by the majority opinion of Chief Justice Vinson and the dissent of Justice Black in *Feiner v. New York*. Again— you be the judge.

FEINER v. NEW YORK
Supreme Court of the United States, 1951, 340 U. S. 315

VINSON, C. J.:
    Petitioner was convicted of the offense of disorderly conduct, a misdemeanor under the New York penal laws, in the Court of Special Sessions of the City of Syracuse and was sentenced to thirty days in the county penitentiary....

On the evening of March 8, 1949, petitioner Irving Feiner was addressing an open-air meeting at the corner of South McBride and Harrison Streets in the City of Syracuse. At approximately 6:30 p.m., the police received a telephone complaint concerning the meeting, and two officers were detailed to investigate. One of these officers went to the scene immediately, the other arriving some twelve minutes later. They found a crowd of about seventy-five or eighty people, both Negro and white, filling the sidewalk and spreading out into the street. Petitioner, standing on a large wooden box on the sidewalk, was addressing the crowd through a loud-speaker system attached to an automobile. Although the purpose of his speech was to urge his listeners to attend a meeting to be held that night in the Syracuse Hotel, in its course he was making derogatory remarks concerning President Truman, the American Legion, the Mayor of Syracuse, and other local political officials.

The police officers made no effort to interfere with petitioner's speech, but were first concerned with the effect of the crowd on both pedestrian and vehicular traffic. They observed the situation from the opposite side of the street, noting that some pedestrians were forced to walk in the street to avoid the crowd. Since traffic was passing at the time, the officers attempted to get the people listening to petitioner back on the sidewalk. The crowd was restless and there was some pushing, shoving and milling around. One of the officers telephoned the police station from a nearby store, and then both policemen crossed the street and mingled with the crowd without any intention of arresting the speaker.

At this time, petitioner was speaking in a "loud, high-pitched voice."

He gave the impression that he was endeavoring to arouse the Negro people against the whites, urging that they rise up in arms and fight for equal rights. The statements before such a mixed audience "stirred up a little excitement." Some of the onlookers made remarks to the police about their inability to handle the crowd and at least one threatened violence if the police did not act. There were others who appeared to be favoring petitioner's arguments. Because of the feeling that existed in the crowd both for and against the speaker, the officers finally "stepped in to prevent it from resulting in a fight." One of the officers approached the petitioner, not for the purpose of arresting him, but to get him to break up the crowd. He asked petitioner to get down off the box, but the latter refused to accede to his request and continued talking. The officer waited for a minute and then demanded that he cease talking. Although the officer had thus twice requested petitioner to stop over the course of several minutes, petitioner not only ignored him but continued talking. During all this time, the crowd was pressing closer around petitioner and the officer. Finally, the officer told petitioner he was under arrest and ordered him to get down from the box, reaching up to grab him. Petitioner stepped down, announcing over the microphone that "the law has arrived, and I suppose they will take over now." In all, the officer had asked petitioner to get down off the box three times over a space of four or five minutes. Petitioner had been speaking for over a half hour. . . .

The courts below recognized petitioner's right to hold a street meeting at this locality, to make use of loud-speaking equipment in giving his speech, and to make derogatory remarks concerning public officials and the American Legion. They found that the officers in making the arrest were motivated solely by a proper concern for the preservation of order and protection of the general welfare, and that there was no evidence which could lend color to a claim that the acts of the police were a cover for suppression of petitioner's views and opinions. Petitioner was thus neither arrested nor convicted for the making or the content of his speech. Rather, it was the reaction which it actually engendered.

The language of *Cantwell v. State of Connecticut,* 1940, 310 U. S. 296, is appropriate here. "The offense known as breach of the peace embraces a great variety of conduct destroying or menacing public order and tranquility. It includes not only violent acts but acts and words likely to produce violence in others. No one would have the hardihood to suggest that the principle of freedom of speech sanctions incitement to riot or that religious liberty connotes the privilege to exhort others to physical attack upon those belonging to another sect. When clear and present danger of riot, disorder, interference with traffic upon the public streets, or other immediate threat to public safety, peace, or order, appears, the power of the State to prevent or punish is obvious." 310 U. S. at page 308. The findings of the New York courts as to the condition of the crowd and the refusal of petitioner to obey the police requests, supported as they are by the record of this case, are persuasive that the conviction of petitioner for violation of public peace, order and authority does not exceed the bounds of proper state police action. This Court respects, as it must, the interest of the community in maintaining peace and order on its streets. We cannot say that the preservation of that interest here encroaches on the constitutional rights of this petitioner.

We are well aware that the ordinary murmurings and objections of a hostile audience cannot be allowed to silence a speaker, and are also mindful of the possible danger of giving overzealous police officials complete discretion to break up otherwise lawful public meetings. "A state may not unduly suppress free communication of views, religious or other, under the guise of conserving desirable conditions." *Cantwell v. State of Connecticut,* supra, 310 U. S. at page 308. But we are not faced here with such a situation. It is one thing to say that the police cannot be used as an instrument for the suppression of unpopular views, and another to say that, when as here the speaker passes the bounds of argument or persuasion and undertakes incitement to riot, they are powerless to prevent a breach of the peace. Nor in this case can we condemn the considered judgment of three New York courts approving the means which the police, faced with a crisis, used in the exercise of their power and duty to preserve peace and order. The findings of the state courts as to the existing situation and the imminence of greater disorder coupled with petitioner's deliberate defiance of the police officers convince us that we should not reverse this conviction in the name of free speech.

BLACK, J., *dissenting*:

The record before us convinces me that petitioner, a young college student, has been sentenced to the penitentiary for the unpopular views he expressed on matters of public interest while lawfully making a street-corner speech in Syracuse, New York. ...

The end result of the affirmance here is to approve a simple and readily available technique by which cities and states can with impunity subject all speeches, political or otherwise, on streets or elsewhere, to the supervision and censorship of the local police. I will have no part or parcel in this holding which I view as a long step toward totalitarian authority. ...

The Court's opinion apparently rests on this reasoning: The policeman, under the circumstances detailed, could reasonably conclude that serious fighting or even riot was imminent; therefore he could stop petitioner's speech to prevent a breach of peace; accordingly, it was "disorderly conduct" for petitioner to continue speaking in disobedience of the officer's request. As to the existence of a dangerous situation on the street corner, it seems far-fetched to suggest that the "facts" show any imminent threat of riot or uncontrollable disorder. It is neither unusual nor unexpected that some people at public street meetings mutter, mill about, push, shove, or disagree, even violently, with the speaker. Indeed, it is rare where controversial topics are discussed that an outdoor crowd does not do some or all of these things. Nor does one isolated threat to assault the speaker forebode disorder. Especially should the danger be discounted where, as here, the person threatening was a man whose wife and two small children accompanied him and who, so far as the record shows, was never close enough to petitioner to carry out the threat.

Moreover, assuming that the "facts" did indicate a critical situation, I reject the implication of the Court's opinion that the police had no obligation to protect petitioner's constitutional right to talk. The police of course have power to prevent breaches of the peace. But if, in the name of preserving order, they ever can interfere with a lawful public speaker, they first must make all reasonable efforts to protect him. Here the policemen did not even pretend to try to protect petitioner. According to the officers' testimony, the crowd was restless but there is no showing of any attempt to quiet it; pedestrians were forced to walk into the street, but there was no effort to clear a path on the sidewalk; one person threatened to assault petitioner but the officer did nothing to discourage this when even a word might have sufficed. Their duty was to protect petitioner's right to talk, even to the extent of arresting the man who threatened to interfere. Instead, they shirked that duty and acted only to suppress the right to speak. . . .

In my judgment, today's holding means that as a practical matter, minority speakers can be silenced in any city. Hereafter, despite the First and Fourteenth Amendments, the policeman's club can take heavy toll of a current administration's public critics. Criticism of public officials will be too dangerous for all but the most courageous. . . .

In this case I would reverse the conviction, thereby adhering to the great principles of the First and Fourteenth Amendments as announced for this Court in 1940 by Mr. Justice Roberts:

"In the realm of religious faith, and in that of political belief, sharp differences arise. In both fields the tenets of one man may seem the rankest error to his neighbor. To persuade others to his own point of view, the pleader, as we know, at times, resorts to exaggeration, to vilification of men who have been, or are, prominent in church or state, and even to false statement. But the people of this nation have ordained in the light of history, that, in spite of the probability of excesses and abuses, these liberties are, in the long view, essential to enlightened opinion and right conduct on the part of the citizens of a democracy." *Cantwell v. State of Connecticut,* 310 U. S. 296, 310.

I regret my inability to persuade the Court not to retreat from this principle.

Chapter 9

" 'Another such victory and I am undone' "

JUSTICE JACKSON implied in his opinion in the Ballard case that a belief in dispassionate judging must include the kind of mental reservation which usually accompanies belief in Santa Claus, Uncle Sam, and the Easter bunny. Undoubtedly he is right—we shall never see the completely dispassionate judge. And undoubtedly we are the better for it. Nevertheless, for the sake of the preservation of significant rights and the protection of orderly governmental processes, a worthy judge must from time to time reach decisions in opposition to his own deeply held sympathies. One such instance was revealed in Justice Frankfurter's dissenting opinion in the Barnette case, previously considered. Another instance is Justice Black's dissenting opinion in *Beauharnais v. Illinois*. Beauharnais was convicted of violating an Illinois statute prohibiting any publication which portrayed "depravity, criminality, unchastity, or lack of virtue of a class of citizens of any race, color, creed or religion" and thereby exposed such group to "contempt, derision, or obloquy." Beauharnais published a petition in Chicago attacking the Negro race and asking for local segregation laws. That he was in violation of the statute was clear; the question was whether the statute was constitutional.

The Supreme Court held the statute valid on the ground that it was a law prohibiting "libel"—a group libel law. The opinion for the majority of the Court, written by Justice Frankfurter, is omitted here because it is a technical discussion of libel and slander laws. Suffice it to say that the opinion is based upon a most curious and apparently illogical twist. Frankfurter says that since this is a libel law it follows that no free speech question is involved, the statute need not even be tested by the constitutional free speech protections. Justice Black, in dissent, ill conceals his astonishment at this reasoning, as he argues that the constitutional test must come first, and only if the law passes the test can we decide what kind of law, libel or otherwise, it is.

Those who know the work of Justice Black on the Court realize that he must have had nothing but the lowest contempt for the activities of Beauharnais. No member of the present Court has been more zealous in upholding the liberties of racial and religious minorities against governmental encroachment. His sympathies surely lay strongly with the maligned racial group in this case. But when it came to prohibiting a citizen from employing strong and even scurrilous abuse as part of his advocacy of political change, Justice Black firmly and even vehemently said, "No!" Whether or not you find yourself in accord with this opinion, it deserves thoughtful consideration as a trenchant assertion that freedom of speech requires tolerance of the intolerant.

BEAUHARNAIS v. ILLINOIS

Supreme Court of the United States, 1952, 343 U. S. 250

BLACK, J., *dissenting*:

This case is here because Illinois inflicted criminal punishment on Beauharnais for causing the distribution of leaflets in the city of Chicago. The conviction rests on the leaflet's contents, not on the time, manner or place of distribution. Beauharnais is head of an organization that opposes amalgamation and favors segregation of white and colored people. After discussion, an assembly of his group decided to petition the mayor and council of Chicago to pass laws for segregation. Volunteer members of the group agreed to stand on street corners, solicit signers to petitions addressed to the city authorities, and distribute leaflets giving information about the group, its beliefs and its plans. In carrying out this program a solicitor handed out a leaflet which was the basis of this prosecution. . . .

That Beauharnais and his group were making a genuine effort to petition their elected representatives is not disputed. Even as far back as 1689, the Bill of Rights exacted of William and Mary said: "It is the Right of the Subjects to petition the King, and all Commitments and Prosecutions for such petitioning are illegal." And 178 years ago the Declaration of Rights of the Continental Congress proclaimed to the monarch of that day that his American subjects had "a right peaceably to assemble, consider of their grievances, and petition the King; and that all prosecutions, prohibitory proclamations, and commitments for the same, are illegal." After independence was won, Americans stated as the first unequivocal command of their Bill of Rights: "Congress shall make no law . . . abridging the freedom of speech, or of the press; or the right of the people peaceably to assemble, and to petition the Government for a redress of grievances." Without distortion, this First Amendment could not possibly be read so as to hold that Congress has power to punish Beauharnais and others for petitioning Congress as they have here sought to petition the Chicago authorities. And we have held in a number of prior cases that the Fourteenth Amendment makes the specific prohibitions of the First Amendment equally applicable to the states.

In view of these prior holdings, how does the Court justify its holding today that states can punish people for exercising the vital freedoms intended to be safeguarded from suppression by the First Amendment? The prior holdings are not referred to; the Court simply acts on the bland assumption that the First Amendment is wholly irrelevant. It is not even accorded the respect of a passing mention. This follows logically, I suppose, from recent constitutional doctrine which appears to measure state laws solely by this Court's notions of civilized "canons of decency," reasonableness, etc. Under this "reasonableness" test, state laws abridging First Amendment freedoms are sustained if found to have a "rational basis." . . . Today's case degrades First Amendment freedoms to the "rational basis" level. It is now a certainty that the new "due process" coverall offers far less protection to liberty than would adherence to our former cases compelling states to abide by the unequivocal First Amendment command that its defined freedoms shall not be abridged.

The Court's holding here and the constitutional doctrine behind it leave the rights of assembly, petition, speech and press almost completely at the mercy of state legislative, executive, and judicial agencies. I say "almost" because state curtailment of these freedoms may still be invalidated if a majority of this Court conclude that a particular infringement is "without reason," or is "a wilful and purposeless restriction unrelated to the peace and well being of the State." But lest this encouragement should give too much hope as to how and when this Court might protect these basic freedoms from state invasion, we are cautioned that state legislatures must be left free to "experiment" and to make "legislative" judgments. We are told that mistakes may be made during the legislative process of curbing public opinion. In such event the Court fortunately does not leave those mistakenly curbed, or any of us for that matter, unadvised. Consolation can be sought and must be found in the philosophical reflection that state legislative error in stifling speech and press "is the price to be paid for the trial-and-error inherent in legislative efforts to deal with obstinate social issues." My own belief is that no legislature is charged with the duty or vested with the power to decide what public issues Americans can discuss. In a free country that is the individual's choice, not the state's. State experimentation in curbing freedom of expression is startling and frightening doctrine in a country dedicated to self-government by its people. I reject the holding that either state or nation can punish people for having their say in matters of public concern. . . .

The Court condones this expansive state censorship by painstakingly analogizing it to the law of criminal libel. As a result of this refined analysis, the Illinois statute emerges labeled "a group libel law." This label may make the Court's holding more palatable for those who sustain it, but the sugar-coating does not make the censorship less deadly. However tagged, the Illinois law is not that criminal libel which has been "defined, limited and constitutionally recognized time out of mind." For as "constitutionally recognized" that crime has provided for punishment of false, malicious, scurrilous charges against individuals, not against huge groups. This limited scope of the law of criminal libel is of no small importance. It has confined state punishment of speech and expression to the narrowest of areas involving nothing more than purely private feuds. Every expansion of the law of criminal libel so as to punish discussions of matters of public concern means a corresponding invasion of the area dedicated to free expression by the First Amendment. ...

Unless I misread history the majority is giving libel a more expansive scope and more respectable status than it was ever accorded even in the Star Chamber. For here it is held to be punishable to give publicity to any picture, moving picture, play, drama or sketch, or any printed matter which a judge may find unduly offensive to any race, color, creed or religion. In other words, in arguing for or against the enactment of laws that may differently affect huge groups, it is now very dangerous indeed to say something critical of one of the groups. And any "person, firm or corporation" can be tried for this crime. "Person, firm or corporation" certainly includes a book publisher, newspaper, radio or television station, candidate or even a preacher.

It is easy enough to say that none of this latter group have been proceeded against under the Illinois Act. And they have not—yet. But emotions bubble and tempers flare in racial and religious controversies, the kind here involved. It would not be easy for any court, in good conscience, to narrow this Act so as to exclude from it any of those I have mentioned. ...

This Act sets up a system of state censorship which is at war with the kind of free government envisioned by those who forced adoption of our Bill of Rights. The motives behind the state law may have been to do good. But the same can be said about most laws making opinions punishable as crimes. History indicates that urges to do good have led to the burning of books and even to the burning of "witches."

No rationalization on a purely legal level can conceal the fact that state laws like this one present a constant overhanging threat to freedom of speech, press and religion. Today Beauharnais is punished for publicly expressing strong views in favor of segregation. Ironically enough, Beauharnais, convicted of crime in Chicago, would probably be given a hero's reception in many other localities, if not in some parts of Chicago itself. Moreover, the same kind of state law that makes Beauharnais a criminal for advocating segregation in Illinois can be utilized to send people to jail in other states for advocating equality and nonsegregation.

What Beauharnais said in his leaflet is mild compared with usual arguments on both sides of racial controversies.

We are told that freedom of petition and discussion are in no danger "while this Court sits." This case raises considerable doubt. Since those who peacefully petition for changes in the law are not to be protected "while this Court sits," who is? I do not agree that the Constitution leaves freedom of petition, assembly, speech, press or worship at the mercy of a case-by-case, day-by-day majority of this Court. I had supposed that our people could rely for their freedom on the Constitution's commands, rather than on the grace of this Court on an individual case basis. To say that a legislative body can, with this Court's approval, make it a crime to petition for and publicly discuss proposed legislation seems as farfetched to me as it would be to say that a valid law could be enacted to punish a candidate for President for telling the people his views. I think the First Amendment, with the Fourteenth, "absolutely" forbids such laws without any "ifs" or "buts" or "whereases." Whatever the danger, if any, in such public discussions, it is a danger the Founders deemed outweighed by the danger incident to the stifling of thought and speech. The Court does not act on this view of the Founders. It calculates what it deems to be the danger of public discussion, holds the scales are tipped on the side of state suppression, and upholds state censorship. This method of decision offers little protection to First Amendment liberties "while this Court sits."

If there be minority groups who hail this holding as their victory, they might consider the possible relevancy of this ancient remark:

"Another such victory and I am undone."

Chapter 10

"Such wheat overhangs the market"

CONSTITUTIONAL LIBERTIES of individuals has been the main theme of the modern Supreme Court because the decisions of the spring of 1937 largely eliminated questions concerning the scope of federal regulatory power. Today's broad sweep of congressional power under the commerce clause, as it is now defined by the Court, is the inevitable outgrowth of *National Labor Relations Board v. Jones and Laughlin Steel Corp*. Once it was decided in this case that producing businesses in general were within federal control because of their effect upon interstate commerce, production, no matter how small, was to fall within the federal ambit. Thus the case of *Wickard v. Filburn*.

The Filburn case involved the constitutionality of the second Agricultural Adjustment Act, the first having been declared unconstitutional in *United States v. Butler*. This time Congress based the Act upon the federal power over commerce rather than upon the taxing and spending power, as had been the foundation of the earlier invalid act. After the Jones and Laughlin case, the power of Congress under the commerce clause to organize the interstate market in farm products would have appeared obvious. So Congress undertook to do so through the plan of setting an over-all national quota for selected agricultural products and apportioning this quota among the producers of the commodities. Farmers were paid benefits for restricting their production in accordance with the quotas. Overproduction ended and prices rose.

407

But Filburn's was the extreme case. He was producing wheat for his own use upon his own farm and was not selling it on the market. He produced in excess of quota. The question posed in his case was whether the federal power over commerce could reach so far as to control agricultural production by a small farmer who was producing only for his own use. The Supreme Court upheld the congressional power even in this extremity.

Justice Jackson wrote the opinion. He conceded that Filburn's production *alone* would obviously have no measurable effect upon the interstate wheat market. But the *cumulative* effect of *all* small domestic production, like Filburn's, could and probably would have a most significant impact upon the program of regulation. Note particularly how Jackson relied heavily upon the factual pattern of wheat production to establish the cumulative burden upon interstate commerce which could result from a multitude of small deviations from quotas. In sum, if Congress has the power generally to organize the interstate wheat market, it must have all the power necessary to do so. To hold otherwise, said Justice Jackson, would be to deny this power in fact by making it impossible to use effectively.

The decision was unanimous. Even Justice Roberts, still on the Court, concurred. Yet he was the "swing man" of the Court of the "Nine Old Men," the justice who had denied any federal power at all to control production until his shift, in the spring of 1937, that led to the decision in the Jones and Laughlin case. Now, he willingly went beyond that case because of the inevitable progression of broad congressional power it presaged. To all the members of the Court, we had become one national economic unit as a natural product of the modern growth of commerce. Thus we see clearly why the modern Court is little concerned with questions involving federal power to engage in general economic regulation. Local economic needs have become, by and large, national economic needs. And federal economic control can no longer be successfully challenged by claiming that the power is not delegated to the national government but resides in the states. So says the Supreme Court.

WICKARD v. FILBURN
Supreme Court of the United States, 1942, 317 U. S. 111

JACKSON, J.:

The appellee for many years past has owned and operated a small farm in Montgomery County, Ohio, maintaining a herd of dairy cattle, selling milk, raising poultry, and selling poultry and eggs. It has been his practice to raise a small acreage of winter wheat, sown in the Fall and harvested in the following July; to sell a portion of the crop; to feed part to poultry and livestock on the farm, some of which is sold; to use some in making flour for home consumption; and to keep the rest for the following seeding. The intended disposition of the crop here involved has not been expressly stated.

In July of 1940, pursuant to the Agricultural Adjustment Act of 1938, as then amended, there were established for the appellee's 1941 crop a wheat acreage allotment of 11.1 acres and a normal yield of 20.1 bushels of wheat an acre. He was given notice of such allotment in July of 1940, before the Fall planting of his 1941 crop of wheat, and again in July of 1941, before it was harvested. He sowed, however, 23 acres, and harvested from his 11.9 acres of excess acreage 239 bushels, which under the terms of the Act as amended on May 26, 1941, constituted farm marketing excess, subject to a penalty of 49 cents a bushel, or $117.11 in all. The appellee has not paid the penalty and he has not postponed or avoided it by storing the excess under regulations of the Secretary of Agriculture, or by delivering it up to the Secretary. The Committee, therefore, refused him a marketing card, which was, under the terms of Regulations promulgated by the Secretary, necessary to protect a buyer from liability to the penalty and upon its protecting lien.

The general scheme of the Agriculture Adjustment Act of 1938 as related to wheat is to control the volume moving in interstate and foreign commerce in order to avoid surpluses and shortages and the consequent abnormally low or high wheat prices and obstructions to commerce. Within prescribed limits and by prescribed standards the Secretary of Agriculture is directed to ascertain and proclaim each year a national acreage allotment for the next crop of wheat, which is then apportioned to the states and their counties, and is eventually broken up into allotments for individual farms. Loans and payments to wheat farmers are authorized in stated circumstances.

The Act further provides that whenever it appears that the total supply of wheat as of the beginning of any marketing year, beginning July 1, will exceed a normal year's domestic consumption and export by more than 35 per cent, the Secretary shall so proclaim not later than May 15 prior to the beginning of such marketing year; and that during the marketing year a compulsory national marketing quota shall be in effect with respect to the marketing of wheat. Between the issuance of the proclamation and June 10, the Secretary must, however, conduct a referendum of farmers who will be subject to the quota to determine whether they favor or oppose it; and if more than one-third of the farmers voting in the referendum do oppose, the Secretary must prior to the effective date of the quota by proclamation suspend its operation....

Pursuant to the Act, the referendum of wheat growers was held on May 31, 1941. According to the required published statement of the Secretary of Agriculture, 81 per cent of those voting favored the marketing quota, with 19 per cent opposed....

It is urged that under the Commerce Clause of the Constitution, Article 1, § 8, clause 3, Congress does not possess the power it has in this instance sought to exercise. The question would merit little consideration . . . except for the fact that this Act extends federal regulation to production not intended in any part for commerce but wholly for consumption on the farm. The Act includes a definition of "market" and its derivatives so that as related to wheat in addition to its conventional meaning it also means to dispose of "by feeding (in any form) to poultry or livestock which, or the products of which, are sold, bartered, or exchanged, or to be so disposed of." Hence, marketing quotas not only embrace all that may be sold without penalty but also what may be consumed on the premises. Wheat produced on excess acreage is designated as "available for marketing" as so defined and the penalty is imposed thereon. Penalties do not depend upon whether any part of the wheat either within or without the quota is sold or intended to be sold. The sum of this is that the Federal Government fixes a quota including all that the farmer may harvest for sale or for his own farm needs, and declares that wheat produced on excess acreage may neither be disposed of nor used except upon payment of the penalty or except it is stored as required by the Act or delivered to the Secretary of Agriculture.

Appellee says that this is a regulation of production and consumption of wheat. Such activities are, he urges, beyond the reach of Congressional power under the Commerce Clause, since they are local in character, and their effects upon interstate commerce are at most "indirect." In answer the Government argues that the statute regulates neither production nor consumption, but only marketing; and, in the alternative, that if the Act does go beyond the regulation of marketing it is sustainable as a "necessary and proper" implementation of the power of Congress over interstate commerce.

The Government's concern lest the Act be held to be a regulation of production or consumption, rather than of marketing, is attributable to a few dicta and decisions of this Court which might be understood to lay it down that activities such as "production," "manufacturing," and "mining" are strictly "local" and, except in special circumstances which are not present here, cannot be regulated under the commerce power because their effects upon interstate commerce are, as matter of law, only "indirect." Even today, when this power has been held to have great latitude, there is no decision of the Court that such activities may be regulated where no part of the product is intended for interstate commerce or intermingled with the subjects thereof. . . .

In the *Shreveport Rate Cases (Houston, E. & W. T. R. Co. v. United States)*, 234 U. S. 342, the Court held that railroad rates of an admittedly intrastate character and fixed by authority of the state might, nevertheless, be revised by the Federal Government because of the economic effects which they had upon interstate commerce. The opinion of Mr. Justice Hughes found federal intervention constitutionally authorized because of "matters having such a close and substantial relation to interstate traffic that the control is essential or appropriate to the security of that traffic, to the efficiency of the interstate service, and to the maintenance of conditions under which interstate commerce may be conducted upon fair terms and without molestation or hindrance."

The Court's recognition of the relevance of the economic effects in the application of the Commerce Clause exemplified by this statement has made the mechanical application of legal formulas no longer feasible. Once an economic measure of the reach of the power granted to Congress in the Commerce Clause is accepted, questions of federal power cannot be decided simply by finding the activity in question to be "production" nor can consideration of its economic effects be foreclosed by calling them "indirect." The present Chief Justice [Stone] has said in summary of the present state of the law: "The commerce power is not confined in its exercise to the regulation of commerce among the states. It extends to those activities intrastate which so affect interstate commerce, or the exertion of the power of Congress over it, as to make regulation of them appropriate means to the attainment of a legitimate end, the effective execution of the granted power to regulate interstate commerce. . . . The power of Congress over interstate commerce is plenary and complete in itself, may be exercised to its utmost extent, and acknowledges no limitations other than are prescribed in the Constitution. . . . It follows that no form of state activity can constitutionally thwart the regulatory power granted by the commerce clause to Congress. Hence the reach of that power extends to those intrastate activities which in a substantial way interfere with or obstruct the exercise of the granted power." *United States v. Wrightwood Dairy Co.,* 315 U. S. 110, 119.

Whether the subject of the regulation in question was "production," "consumption," or "marketing" is, therefore, not material for purposes of deciding the question of federal power before us. . . . Even if appellee's activity be local and though it may not be regarded as commerce, it may still, whatever its nature, be reached by Congress if it exerts a substantial economic effect on interstate commerce and this irrespective of whether such effect is what might at some earlier time have been defined as "direct" or "indirect."

The parties have stipulated a summary of the economics of the wheat industry. Commerce among the states in wheat is large and important. Although wheat is raised in every state but one, production in most states is not equal to consumption. Sixteen states on average have had a surplus of wheat above their own requirements for feed, seed, and food. Thirty-two states and the District of Columbia, where production has been below consumption, have looked to these surplus-producing states for their supply as well as for wheat for export and carryover.

The wheat industry has been a problem industry for some years. Largely as a result of increased foreign production and import restrictions, annual exports of wheat and flour from the United States during the ten-year period ending in 1940 averaged less than 10 per cent of total production, while during the 1920's they averaged more than 25 per cent. The decline in the export trade has left a large surplus in production which in connection with an abnormally large supply of wheat and other grains in recent years caused congestion in a number of markets; tied up railroad cars; and caused elevators in some instances to turn away grains, and railroads to institute embargoes to prevent further congestion.

Many countries, both importing and exporting, have sought to modify the impact of the world market conditions on their own economy. Importing countries have taken measures to stimulate production and self-sufficiency. The four large exporting countries of Argentina, Australia, Canada, and the United States have all undertaken various programs for the relief of growers. Such measures have been designed in part at least to protect the domestic price received by producers. Such plans have generally evolved towards control by the central government.

In the absence of regulation the price of wheat in the United States would be much affected by world conditions. During 1941 producers who cooperated with the Agricultural Adjustment program received an average price on the farm of about $1.16 a bushel as compared with the world market price of 40 cents a bushel.

Differences in farming conditions, however, make these benefits mean different things to different wheat growers. There are several large areas of specialization in wheat, and the concentration on this crop reaches 27 per cent of the crop land, and the average harvest runs as high as 155 acres. Except for some use of wheat as stock feed and for seed, the practice is to sell the crop for cash. Wheat from such areas constitutes the bulk of the interstate commerce therein.

On the other hand, in some New England states less than one per cent of the crop land is devoted to wheat, and the average harvest is less than five acres per farm. In 1940 the average percentage of the total wheat production that was sold in each state, as measured by value, ranged from 29 per cent thereof in Wisconsin to 90 per cent in Washington. Except in regions of large-scale production, wheat is usually grown in rotation with other crops; for a nurse crop for grass seeding; and as a cover crop to prevent soil erosion and leaching. Some is sold, some kept for seed, and a percentage of the total production much larger than in areas of specialization is consumed on the farm and grown for such purpose. Such farmers, while growing some wheat, may even find the balance of their interest on the consumer's side.

The effect of consumption of home-grown wheat on interstate commerce is due to the fact that it constitutes the most variable factor in the disappearance of the wheat crop. Consumption on the farm where grown appears to vary in an amount greater than 20 per cent of average production. The total amount of wheat consumed as food varies but relatively little, and use as seed is relatively constant.

The maintenance by government regulation of a price for wheat undoubtedly can be accomplished as effectively by sustaining or increasing the demand as by limiting the supply. The effect of the statute before us is to restrict the amount which may be produced for market and the extent as well to which one may forestall resort to the market by producing to meet his own needs. That appellee's own contribution to the demand for wheat may be trivial by itself is not enough to remove him from the scope of federal regulation where, as here, his contribution, taken together with that of many others similarly situated, is far from trivial.

It is well established by decisions of this Court that the power to regulate commerce includes the power to regulate the prices at which commodities in that commerce are dealt in and practices affecting such prices. One of the primary purposes of the Act in question was to increase the market price of wheat and to that end to limit the volume thereof that could affect the market. It can hardly be denied that a factor of such volume and variability as home-consumed wheat would have a substantial influence on price and market conditions. This may arise because being in marketable condition such wheat overhangs the market and if induced by rising prices tends to flow into the market and check price increases. But if we assume that it is never marketed, it supplies a need of the man who grew it which would otherwise be reflected by purchases in the open market. Home-grown wheat in this sense competes with wheat in commerce. The stimulation of commerce is a use of the regulatory function quite as definitely as prohibitions or restrictions thereon. This record leaves us in no doubt that Congress may properly have considered that wheat consumed on the farm where grown, if wholly outside the scheme of regulation, would have a substantial effect in defeating and obstructing its purpose to stimulate trade therein at increased prices.

It is said, however, that this Act, forcing some farmers into the market to buy what they could provide for themselves, is an unfair promotion of the markets and prices of specializing wheat growers. It is of the essence of regulation that it lays a restraining hand on the self-interest of the regulated and that advantages from the regulation commonly fall to others. The conflicts of economic interest between the regulated and those who advantage by it are wisely left under our system to resolution by the Congress under its more flexible and responsible legislative process. Such conflicts rarely lend themselves to judicial determination. And with the wisdom, workability, or fairness, of the plan of regulation we have nothing to do. . . .

Chapter 11

"Separate educational facilities are inherently unequal"

IT WAS WILLIAM MARBURY'S ATTEMPT to obtain the relatively obscure position of justice of the peace in the District of Columbia that led to the case of *Marbury v. Madison,* which established the momentous American principle of court review of the constitutionality of legislative and executive acts. It was the plight of Lambdin Milligan, a previously unnoted citizen of Indiana, in being held by military authorities, that led to the great case of *Ex parte Milligan,* which assures American citizens of freedom from control by the military. So also, in 1954, it was an eleven-year-old Negro schoolgirl named Linda Brown, living in Topeka, Kansas, who gives her name to a case which will stamp American history with an indelible impact of social, economic, and political change. This, of course, is the case outlawing racial segregation in the public schools of the United States. There is no better proof of the vital role which the Supreme Court plays in securing the freedoms of each individual American than reflection upon the names of Supreme Court decisions. The names of previously unnoticed "little people" are the names of many of the greatest constitutional cases. Note well the name of *Brown v. Board of Education of Topeka.* The obscure individual protecting her own little world scores again before the highest court of the land.

The life of Linda Brown is now forever interwoven with the life of the thirteenth Chief Justice of the United States, Earl Warren, of California. Rarely does it come to any Supreme Court justice to write in his first year an opinion which is so memorable that his name will forever be more closely associated with that case than any other. Yet such is the likely event with Chief Justice Warren and the Public School Segregation Case. Although many years of productive and significant work are ahead for the new Chief Justice, it may well be that never again in his tenure will there be a case destined to have the fame of the case of Linda Brown.

His first two years on the Bench seem to have set the pattern for Earl Warren's tenure as the thirteenth Chief Justice. His opinions of these years are most noteworthy for shining clarity. The Chief Justice writes so that none may doubt and all may understand. To the administrative side of the duties of the Chief Justice, Warren is eminently suited. Almost all of his professional life has been in public service. Upon his graduation from the University of California Law School, he practiced law only a short time before beginning his public career. After periods of service as assistant county attorney and assistant district attorney, he became the district attorney of Oakland, then attorney general of California, and then governor. There can hardly be a whisper of doubt, even at this early stage, that the appointment by President Eisenhower of this native son of California to the highest judicial office of the land was in the finest tradition of the Supreme Court.

There is no need to detail the history of the problem of racial segregation in the public schools. The opinion of the Court succinctly accomplishes this. Worthy of particular mention, however, was the unique procedure of announcing the principle in formal opinion but postponing for further consideration the determination of the means to carry out the principle so announced. Thus, one hundred and sixty-five years after the adoption of the Constitution a new constitutional technique was created. And who can say that this is not the best means of accomplishing the readjustment of delicate human relationships which the Court has decreed? The predicate has been laid and responsibility for implementation assumed.

BROWN v. BOARD OF EDUCATION OF TOPEKA

Supreme Court of the United States, 1954, 1955, 347 U. S. 483, 349 U. S. 294

WARREN, C. J.

These cases come to us from the States of Kansas, South Carolina, Virginia, and Delaware. They are premised on different facts and different local conditions, but a common legal question justifies their consideration together in this consolidated opinion.

In each of the cases, minors of the Negro race, through their legal representatives, seek the aid of the courts in obtaining admission to the public schools of their community on a nonsegregated basis. In each instance, they have been denied admission to schools attended by white children under laws requiring or permitting segregation according to race. This segregation was alleged to deprive the plaintiffs of the equal protection of the laws under the Fourteenth Amendment. In each of the cases other than the Delaware case, a three-judge federal district court denied relief to the plaintiffs on the so-called "separate but equal" doctrine announced by this Court in *Plessy v. Ferguson,* 163 U. S. 537. Under that doctrine, equality of treatment is accorded when the races are provided substantially equal facilities, even though these facilities be separate. In the Delaware case, the Supreme Court of Delaware adhered to that doctrine, but ordered that the plaintiffs be admitted to the white schools because of their superiority to the Negro schools.

The plaintiffs contend that segregated public schools are not "equal" and cannot be made "equal," and that hence they are deprived of the equal protection of the laws. . . . Argument was heard in the 1952 Term, and reargument was heard this Term on certain questions propounded by the Court.

Reargument was largely devoted to the circumstances surrounding the adoption of the Fourteenth Amendment in 1868. It covered exhaustively consideration of the Amendment in Congress, ratification by the States, then existing practices in racial segregation, and the views of proponents and opponents of the Amendment. This discussion and our own investigation convince us that, although these sources cast some light, it is not enough to resolve the problem with which we are faced. At best, they are inconclusive. The most avid proponents of the post-War Amendments undoubtedly intended them to remove all legal distinctions among "all persons born or naturalized in the United States." Their opponents, just as certainly, were antagonistic to both the letter and the spirit of the Amendments and wished them to have the most limited effect. What others in Congress and the state legislatures had in mind cannot be determined with any degree of certainty.

An additional reason for the inconclusive nature of the Amendment's history, with respect to segregated schools, is the status of public education at that time. In the south, the movement toward free common schools, supported by general taxation, had not yet taken hold. Education of white children was largely in the hands of private groups. Education of Negroes was almost nonexistent, and practically all of the race were illiterate. In fact, any education of Negroes was forbidden by law in some states. Today, in contrast, many Negroes have achieved outstanding success in the arts and sciences as well as in the business and professional world. It is true that public school education at the time of the Amendment had advanced further in the North, but the effect of the Amendment on Northern States was generally ignored in the congressional debates. Even in the North, the conditions of public education did not approximate those existing today. The curriculum was usually rudimentary; ungraded schools were common in rural areas; the school term was but three months a year in many states; and compulsory school attendance was virtually unknown. As a consequence, it is not surprising that there should be so little in the history of the Fourteenth Amendment relating to its intended effect on public education.

In the first cases in this Court construing the Fourteenth Amendment, decided shortly after its adoption, the Court interpreted it as proscribing all state-imposed discriminations against the Negro race. The doctrine of "separate but equal" did not make its appearance in this Court until 1896 in the case of *Plessy v. Ferguson,* supra, involving not education but transportation. American courts have since labored with the doctrine for over half a century. In this Court, there have been six cases involving the "separate but equal" doctrine in the field of public education. In *Cumming v. Board of Education of Richmond County,* 175 U. S. 528, and *Gong Lum v. Rice,* 275 U. S. 78, the validity of the doctrine itself was not challenged. In more recent cases, all on the graduate school level, inequality was found in that specific benefits enjoyed by white students were denied to Negro students of the same educational qualifications. *State of Missouri ex rel. Gaines v. Canada,* 305 U. S. 337, *Sipuel v. Board of Regents of University of Oklahoma,* 332 U. S. 631, *Sweatt v. Painter,* 339 U. S. 629, *McLaurin v. Oklahoma State Regents,* 339 U. S. 637. In none of these cases was it necessary to re-examine the doctrine to grant relief to the Negro plaintiff. And in *Sweatt v. Painter,* the Court expressly reserved decision on the question whether *Plessy v. Ferguson* should be held inapplicable to public education.

In the instant cases, that question is directly presented. Here, unlike *Sweatt v. Painter,* there are findings below that the Negro and white schools involved have been equalized, or are being equalized, with respect to buildings, curricula, qualifications and salaries of teachers, and other "tangible" factors. Our decision, therefore, cannot turn on merely a comparison of these tangible factors in the Negro and white schools involved in each of the cases. We must look instead to the effect of segregation itself on public education.

In approaching this problem, we cannot turn the clock back to 1868 when the Amendment was adopted, or even to 1896 when *Plessy v. Ferguson* was written. We must consider public education in the light of its full development and its present place in American life throughout the Nation. Only in this way can it be determined if segregation in public schools deprives these plaintiffs of the equal protection of the laws.

Today, education is perhaps the most important function of state and local governments. Compulsory school attendance laws and the great expenditures for education both demonstrate our recognition of the importance of education to our democratic society. It is required in the performance of our most basic public responsibilities, even service in the armed forces. It is the very foundation of good citizenship. Today it is a principal instrument in awakening the child to cultural values, in preparing him for later professional training, and in helping him to adjust normally to his environment. In these days, it is doubtful that any child may reasonably be expected to succeed in life if he is denied the opportunity of an education. Such an opportunity, where the state has undertaken to provide it, is a right which must be made available to all on equal terms.

We come then to the question presented: Does segregation of children in public schools solely on the basis of race, even though the physical facilities and other "tangible" factors may be equal, deprive the children of the minority group of equal educational opportunities? We believe that it does.

In *Sweatt v. Painter,* in finding that a segregated law school for Negroes could not provide them equal educational opportunities, this Court relied in large part on "those qualities which are incapable of objective measurement but which make for greatness in a law school." In *McLaurin v. Oklahoma State Regents,* the Court, in requiring that a Negro admitted to a white graduate school be treated like all other students, again resorted to intangible considerations: ". . . his ability to study, to engage in discussions and exchange views with other students, and, in general, to learn his profession." Such considerations apply with added force to children in grade and high schools. To separate them from others of similar age and qualifications solely because of their race generates a feeling of inferiority as to their status in the community that may affect their hearts and minds in a way unlikely ever to be undone. The effect of this separation on their educational opportunities was well stated by a finding in the Kansas case by a court which nevertheless felt compelled to rule against the Negro plaintiffs:

"Segregation of white and colored children in public schools has a detrimental effect upon the colored children. The impact is greater when it has the sanction of the law; for the policy of separating the races is usually interpreted as denoting the inferiority of the negro group. A sense of inferiority affects the motivation of a child to learn. Segregation with the sanction of law, therefore, has a tendency to [retard] the educational and mental development of negro children and to deprive them of some of the benefits they would receive in a racial[ly] integrated school system." Whatever may have been the extent of psychological knowledge at the time of *Plessy v. Ferguson,* this finding is amply supported by modern authority. Any language in *Plessy v. Ferguson* contrary to this finding is rejected.

We conclude that in the field of public education the doctrine of "separate but equal" has no place. Separate educational facilities are inherently unequal. Therefore, we hold that the plaintiffs and others similarly situated for whom the actions have been brought are, by reason of the segregation complained of, deprived of the equal protection of the laws guaranteed by the Fourteenth Amendment. . . .

Because these are class actions, because of the wide applicability of this decision, and because of the great variety of local conditions, the formulation of decrees in these cases presents problems of considerable complexity. On reargument, the consideration of appropriate relief was necessarily subordinated to the primary question—the constitutionality of segregation in public education. We have now announced that such segregation is a denial of the equal protection of the laws. In order that we may have the full assistance of the parties in formulating decrees, the cases will be restored to the docket, and the parties are requested to present further argument on Questions 4 and 5 previously propounded by the Court for the reargument this Term. The Attorney General of the United States is again invited to participate. The Attorneys General of the states requiring or permitting segregation in public education will also be permitted to appear as *amici curiae* upon request to do so. . . .

It is so ordered.

On May 31, 1955, the Supreme Court implemented this ruling in a further unanimous decision and opinion. The accomplishment is for the future, as the nation is contemplative and moves toward initial steps. And the world watches and waits.

WARREN, C. J.:

These cases were decided on May 17, 1954. The opinions of that date, declaring the fundamental principle that racial discrimination in public education is unconstitutional, are incorporated herein by reference. All provisions of federal, state, or local law requiring or permitting such discrimination must yield to this principle. There remains for consideration the manner in which relief is to be accorded. . . .

Full implementation of these constitutional principles may require solution of varied local school problems. School authorities have the primary responsibility for elucidating, assessing, and solving these problems; courts will have to consider whether the action of school authorities constitutes good faith implementation of the governing constitutional principles. Because of their proximity to local conditions and the possible need for further hearings, the courts which originally heard these cases can best perform this judicial appraisal. Accordingly, we believe it appropriate to remand the cases to those courts.

In fashioning and effectuating the decrees, the courts will be guided by equitable principles. Traditionally, equity has been characterized by a practical flexibility in shaping its remedies and by a facility for adjusting and reconciling public and private needs. These cases call for the exercise of these traditional attributes of equity power. At stake is the personal interest of the plaintiffs in admission to public schools as soon as practicable on a nondiscriminatory basis. To effectuate this interest may call for elimination of a variety of obstacles in making the transition to school systems operated in accordance with the constitutional principles set forth in our May 17, 1954, decision. Courts of equity may properly take into account the public interest in the elimination of such obstacles in a systematic and effective manner. But it should go without saying that the vitality of these constitutional principles cannot be allowed to yield simply because of disagreement with them.

While giving weight to these public and private considerations, the courts will require that the defendants make a prompt and reasonable start toward full compliance with our May 17, 1954, ruling. Once such a start has been made, the courts may find that additional time is necessary to carry out the ruling in an effective manner. The burden rests upon the defendants to establish that such time is necessary in the public interest and is consistent with good faith compliance at the earliest practicable date. To that end, the courts may consider problems related to administration, arising from the physical condition of the school plant, the school transportation system, personnel, revision of school districts and attendance areas into compact units to achieve a system of determining admission to the public schools on a nonracial basis, and revision of local laws and regulations which may be necessary in solving the foregoing problems. They will also consider the adequacy of any plans the defendants may propose to meet these problems and to effectuate a transition to a racially nondiscriminatory school system. During this period of transition, the courts will retain jurisdiction of these cases.

The judgments below, . . . are accordingly reversed and the cases are remanded to the District Courts to take such proceedings and enter such orders and decrees consistent with the opinion as are necessary and proper to admit to public schools on a racially nondiscriminatory basis with all deliberate speed the parties to these cases. . . .

Epilogue

NEW CASES will come before the Supreme Court, and new faces will be seen on its Bench, but the tradition of continuity, which we lack in the other branches of the government, will undoubtedly still surround the Court. The political winds shift abruptly and often in the Congress and in the Administration. Not so in the Court. And this tradition of the Court has engendered reverence, somewhat akin to the reverence toward the monarchy in Great Britain. Our Supreme Court is a symbol of orderly constitutional government.

But the Court is also far more than just a symbol. Government by law purely for the sake of order is tyranny; government by law so that the lowest and the highest among us are equally protected and equally controlled is the road to freedom. Here is the curious paradox. The Supreme Court is the undemocratic organ of our government, in the sense that the justices are appointive and that they serve for life. If there was to be order for its own sake—tyranny—in our system, we would expect its manifestation first in the Court. Yet we have seen that the importance of the Court as a protector of human liberty is past measuring. Our Court is an integral part of the tradition of freedom.

Because of its power to pass upon the constitutionality of legislation, the Supreme Court of the United States is the most powerful judicial body in the world. This power compels awesome responsibility. The carrying out of this responsibility has been the subject of our investigation in this book. And that the Supreme Court has acquitted itself in this trust with exceeding honor, there can be no shadow of doubt. The strength, well-being, prosperity, and eminence of the United States is absolute attestation. The nation, and indeed the world, listens when the Supreme Court speaks.

APPENDIXES

Appendix I

The Constitution of the United States

WE THE PEOPLE of the United States, in Order to form a more perfect Union, establish Justice, insure domestic Tranquility, provide for the common defence, promote the general Welfare, and secure the Blessings of Liberty to ourselves and our Posterity, do ordain and establish this CONSTITUTION for the United States of America.

ARTICLE. I.

SECTION. 1. All legislative Powers herein granted shall be vested in a Congress of the United States, which shall consist of a Senate and House of Representatives.

SECTION. 2. The House of Representatives shall be composed of members chosen every second Year by the People of the several States, and the Electors in each State shall have the Qualifications requisite for Electors of the most numerous Branch of the State Legislature.

No Person shall be a Representative who shall not have attained the Age of twenty five Years, and been seven Years a Citizen of the United States, and who shall not, when elected, be an Inhabitant of that State in which he shall be chosen.

Representatives and direct Taxes shall be apportioned among the several States which may be included within this Union, according to their respective Numbers, which shall be determined by adding to the

APPENDIX I

whole Number of free Persons, including those bound to Service for a Term of Years, and excluding Indians not taxed, three fifths of all other Persons. The actual Enumeration shall be made within three Years after the first Meeting of the Congress of the United States, and within every subsequent Term of ten Years, in such Manner as they shall by law direct. The Number of Representatives shall not exceed one for every thirty Thousand, but each State shall have at Least one Representative; and until such enumeration shall be made, the State of New Hampshire shall be entitled to chuse three, Massachusetts eight, Rhode-Island and Providence Plantations one, Connecticut five, New-York six, New Jersey four, Pennsylvania eight, Delaware one, Maryland six, Virginia ten, North Carolina five, South Carolina five, and Georgia three.

When vacancies happen in the Representation from any State, the Executive Authority thereof shall issue Writs of Election to fill such Vacancies.

The House of Representatives shall chuse their Speaker and other Officers; and shall have the sole Power of Impeachment.

Section. 3. The Senate of the United States shall be composed of two Senators from each State, chosen by the Legislature thereof, for six Years; and each Senator shall have one Vote.

Immediately after they shall be assembled in Consequence of the first Election, they shall be divided as equally as may be into three Classes. The Seats of the Senators of the first Class shall be vacated at the Expiration of the second Year, of the second Class at the Expiration of the fourth Year, and of the third Class at the Expiration of the sixth Year, so that one third may be chosen every second Year; and if Vacancies happen by Resignation, or otherwise, during the Recess of the Legislature of any State, the Executive thereof may make temporary Appointments until the next Meeting of the Legislature, which shall then fill such Vacancies.

No Person shall be a Senator who shall not have attained to the Age of thirty Years, and been nine Years a Citizen of the United States, and who shall not, when elected, be an Inhabitant of that State for which he shall be chosen.

The Vice President of the United States shall be President of the Senate, but shall have no Vote, unless they be equally divided.

The Senate shall chuse their other Officers, and also a President pro tempore, in the Absence of the Vice President, or when he shall exercise the Office of President of the United States.

The Senate shall have the sole Power to try all Impeachments. When sitting for that Purpose, they shall be on Oath or Affirmation. When the President of the United States is tried, the Chief Justice shall preside: And no Person shall be convicted without the Concurrence of two thirds of the Members present.

Judgment in Cases of Impeachment shall not extend further than to removal from Office, and disqualification to hold and enjoy any Office of honor, Trust or Profit under the United States: but the Party convicted shall nevertheless be liable and subject to Indictment, Trial, Judgment and Punishment, according to Law.

SECTION. 4. The Times, Places and Manner of holding Elections for Senators and Representatives, shall be prescribed in each State by the Legislature thereof; but the Congress may at any time by Law make or alter such Regulations, except as to the Places of chusing Senators.

The Congress shall assemble at least once in every Year, and such Meeting shall be on the first Monday in December, unless they shall by Law appoint a different Day.

SECTION. 5. Each House shall be the Judge of the Elections, Returns and Qualifications of its own Members, and a Majority of each shall constitute a Quorum to do Business; but a smaller Number may adjourn from day to day, and may be authorized to compel the attendance of absent Members, in such Manner, and under such Penalties as each House may provide.

Each House may determine the Rules of its Proceedings, punish its Members for Disorderly Behaviour, and, with the Concurrence of two thirds, expel a Member.

Each House shall keep a Journal of its Proceedings, and from time to time publish the same, excepting such Parts as may in their Judgment require Secrecy; and the Yeas and Nays of the Members of either House on any question shall, at the Desire of one fifth of those Present, be entered on the Journal.

Neither House, during the Session of Congress, shall, without the Consent of the other, adjourn for more than three days, nor to any other Place than that in which the two Houses shall be sitting.

SECTION. 6. The Senators and Representatives shall receive a Compensation for their Services, to be ascertained by Law, and paid out of the Treasury of the United States. They shall in all Cases, except Treason, Felony and Breach of the Peace, be privileged from Arrest during their Attendance at the Session of their respective Houses, and in going to and returning from the same; and for any Speech or Debate in either House, they shall not be questioned in any other Place.

APPENDIX I

No Senator or Representative shall, during the Time for which he was elected, be appointed to any civil Office under the Authority of the United States, which shall have been created, or the Emoluments whereof shall have been encreased during such time; and no Person holding any Office under the United States, shall be a member of either House during his Continuance in Office.

SECTION. 7. All Bills for raising Revenue shall originate in the House of Representatives; but the Senate may propose or concur with Amendments as on other Bills.

Every Bill which shall have passed the House of Representatives and the Senate, shall, before it becomes a Law, be presented to the President of the United States; If he approve he shall sign it, but if not he shall return it, with his Objections to that House in which it shall have originated, who shall enter the Objections at large on their Journal, and proceed to reconsider it. If after such Reconsideration two thirds of that House shall agree to pass the Bill, it shall be sent, together with the Objections, to the other House, by which it shall likewise be reconsidered, and if approved by two thirds of that House, it shall become a Law. But in all such Cases the Votes of both Houses shall be determined by Yeas and Nays, and the Names of the Persons voting for and against the Bill shall be entered on the Journal of each House respectively. If any Bill shall not be returned by the President within ten Days (Sundays excepted) after it shall have been presented to him, the same shall be a Law, in like Manner as if he had signed it, unless the Congress by their Adjournment prevent its Return, in which Case it shall not be a Law.

Every Order, Resolution, or Vote to which the Concurrence of the Senate and House of Representatives may be necessary (except on a question of Adjournment) shall be presented to the President of the United States; and before the same shall take Effect, shall be approved by him, or being disapproved by him, shall be repassed by two thirds of the Senate and House of Representatives, according to the Rules and Limitations prescribed in the Case of a Bill.

SECTION. 8. The Congress shall have Power To lay and collect Taxes, Duties, Imposts and Excises, to pay the Debts and provide for the common Defence and general Welfare of the United States; but all Duties, Imposts and Excises shall be uniform throughout the United States;

To borrow Money on the credit of the United States;

To regulate Commerce with foreign Nations, and among the several States, and with the Indian Tribes;

To establish an uniform Rule of Naturalization, and uniform Laws on the subject of Bankruptcies throughout the United States;

To coin Money, regulate the Value thereof; and of foreign Coin, and fix the Standard of Weights and Measures;

To provide for the Punishment of counterfeiting the Securities and current Coin of the United States;

To establish Post Offices and post Roads;

To promote the Progress of Science and useful Arts, by securing for limited Times to Authors and Inventors the exclusive Right to their respective Writings and Discoveries;

To constitute Tribunals inferior to the supreme Court;

To define and punish Piracies and Felonies committed on the high Seas, and Offences against the Law of Nations;

To declare War, grant Letters of Marque and Reprisal, and make Rules concerning Captures on Land and Water;

To raise and support Armies, but no Appropriation of Money to that Use shall be for a longer Term than two Years;

To provide and maintain a Navy;

To make Rules for the Government and Regulation of the land and naval Forces;

To provide for calling forth the Militia to execute the Laws of the Union, suppress Insurrections and repel Invasions;

To provide for organizing, arming, and disciplining, the Militia, and for governing such Part of them as may be employed in the Service of the United States, reserving to the States respectively, the Appointment of the Officers, and the Authority of training the Militia according to the discipline prescribed by Congress;

To exercise exclusive Legislation in all Cases whatsoever, over such District (not exceeding ten Miles square) as may, by Cession of particular States, and the Acceptance of Congress, become the Seat of the Government of the United States, and to exercise like Authority over all Places purchased by the Consent of the Legislature of the State in which the same shall be, for the Erection of Forts, Magazines, Arsenals, dock-Yards, and other needful Buildings;—And

To make all Laws which shall be necessary and proper for carrying into Execution the foregoing Powers, and all other Powers vested by this Constitution in the Government of the United States, or in any Department or Officer thereof.

SECTION. 9. The Migration or Importation of such Persons as any of the States now existing shall think proper to admit, shall not be pro-

APPENDIX I

hibited by the Congress prior to Year one thousand eight hundred and eight, but a Tax or duty may be imposed on such Importation, not exceeding ten dollars for each Person.

The Privilege of the Writ of Habeas Corpus shall not be suspended, unless when in Cases of Rebellion or Invasion the public Safety may require it.

No Bill of Attainder or ex post facto Law shall be passed.

No Capitation, or other direct, Tax shall be laid, unless in Proportion to the Census or Enumeration herein before directed to be taken.

No Tax or Duty shall be laid on Articles exported from any State.

No Preference shall be given by any Regulation of Commerce or Revenue to the Ports of one State over those of another: nor shall Vessels bound to, or from, one State, be obliged to enter, clear, or pay Duties in another.

No Money shall be drawn from the Treasury, but in Consequence of Appropriations made by Law; and a regular Statement and Account of the Receipts and Expenditures of all public Money shall be published from time to time.

No Title of Nobility shall be granted by the United States: And no Person holding any Office of Profit or Trust under them, shall, without the Consent of the Congress, accept of any present, Emolument, Office, or Title, of any kind whatever, from any King, Prince, or foreign State.

SECTION. 10. No State shall enter into any Treaty, Alliance, or Confederation; grant Letters of Marque and Reprisal; coin Money; emit Bills of Credit; make any Thing but gold and silver Coin a Tender in Payment of Debts; pass any Bill of Attainder, ex post facto Law, or Law impairing the Obligation of Contracts, or grant any Title of Nobility.

No State shall, without the Consent of the Congress, lay any Imposts or Duties on Imports or Exports, except what may be absolutely necessary for executing its inspection Laws: and the net Produce of all Duties and Imposts, laid by any State on Imports or Exports, shall be for the Use of the Treasury of the United States; and all such Laws shall be subject to the Revision and Control of the Congress.

No State shall, without the Consent of Congress, lay any Duty of Tonnage, keep Troops, or Ships of War in time of Peace, enter into any Agreement or Compact with another State, or with a foreign Power, or engage in War, unless actually invaded, or in such imminent Danger as will not admit of delay.

THE CONSTITUTION OF THE UNITED STATES
ARTICLE. II.

SECTION. 1. The executive Power shall be vested in a President of the United States of America. He shall hold his Office during the Term of four Years, and, together with the Vice President, chosen for the same Term, be elected, as follows

Each State shall appoint, in such Manner as the Legislature thereof may direct, a Number of Electors, equal to the whole Number of Senators and Representatives to which the State may be entitled in the Congress: but no Senator or Representative, or Person holding an Office of Trust or Profit under the United States, shall be appointed an Elector.

The Electors shall meet in their respective States, and vote by Ballot for two Persons, of whom one at least shall not be an Inhabitant of the same State with themselves. And they shall make a List of all the Persons voted for, and of the Number of Votes for each; which List they shall sign and certify, and transmit sealed to the Seat of the Government of the United States, directed to the President of the Senate. The President of the Senate shall, in the Presence of the Senate and House of Representatives, open all the Certificates, and the Votes shall then be counted. The Person having the greatest Number of Votes shall be the President, if such Number be a Majority of the whole Number of Electors appointed; and if there be more than one who have such Majority, and have an equal Number of Votes, then the House of Representatives shall immediately chuse by Ballot one of them for President; and if no Person have a Majority, then from the five highest on the List the said House shall in like Manner chuse the President. But in chusing the President, the Votes shall be taken by States, the Representation from each State having one Vote; A quorum for this Purpose shall consist of a Member or Members from two thirds of the States, and a Majority of all the States shall be necessary to a Choice. In every Case, after the Choice of the President, the Person having the greatest Number of Votes of the Electors shall be the Vice President. But if there should remain two or more who have equal Votes, the Senate shall chuse from them by Ballot the Vice President.

The Congress may determine the Time of chusing the Electors, and the Day on which they shall give their Votes; which Day shall be the same throughout the United States.

No Person except a natural born Citizen, or a Citizen of the United States, at the time of the Adoption of this Constitution, shall be eligible to the Office of President; neither shall any Person be eligible to that

APPENDIX I

Office who shall not have attained to the Age of thirty five Years, and been fourteen Years a Resident within the United States.

In Case of the Removal of the President from Office, or of his Death, Resignation, or Inability to discharge the Powers and Duties of the said Office, the Same shall devolve on the Vice President, and the Congress may by Law provide for the Case of Removal, Death, Resignation, or Inability, both of the President and Vice President, declaring what Officer shall then act as President, and such Officer shall act accordingly, until the Disability be removed, or a President shall be elected.

The President shall, at stated Times, receive for his Services, a Compensation, which shall neither be encreased nor diminished during the Period for which he shall have been elected, and he shall not receive within that Period any other Emolument from the United States, or any of them.

Before he enter on the Execution of his Office, he shall take the following Oath or Affirmation:—"I do solemnly swear (or affirm) that I will faithfully execute the Office of President of the United States, and will to the best of my Ability, preserve, protect and defend the Constitution of the United States."

SECTION. 2. The President shall be Commander in Chief of the Army and Navy of the United States, and of the Militia of the several States, when called into the actual Service of the United States; he may require the Opinion, in writing, of the principal Officer in each of the executive Departments, upon any Subject relating to the Duties of their respective Offices, and he shall have Power to grant Reprieves and Pardons for Offences against the United States, except in Cases of Impeachment.

He shall have Power, by and with the Advice and Consent of the Senate, to make Treaties, provided two thirds of the Senators present concur; and he shall nominate, and by and with the Advice and Consent of the Senate, shall appoint Ambassadors, other public Ministers and Consuls, Judges of the supreme Court, and all other Officers of the United States, whose Appointments are not herein otherwise provided for, and which shall be established by Law: but the Congress may by Law vest the Appointment of such inferior Officers, as they think proper, in the President alone, in the Courts of Law, or in the Heads of Departments.

The President shall have Power to fill up all Vacancies that may happen during the Recess of the Senate, by granting Commissions which shall expire at the End of their next Session.

SECTION. 3. He shall from time to time give to the Congress Information of the State of the Union, and recommend to their Consideration such Measures as he shall judge necessary and expedient; he may on extraordinary Occasions, convene both Houses, or either of them, and in Case of Disagreement between them, with Respect to the Time of Adjournment, he may adjourn them to such Time as he shall think proper; he shall receive Ambassadors and other public Ministers; he shall take Care that the Laws be faithfully executed, and shall Commission all the Officers of the United States.

SECTION. 4. The President, Vice President and all civil Officers of the United States, shall be removed from Office on Impeachment for, and Conviction of, Treason, Bribery, or other high Crimes and Misdemeanors.

ARTICLE. III.

SECTION. 1. The judicial Power of the United States, shall be vested in one supreme Court, and in such inferior Courts as the Congress may from time to time ordain and establish. The Judges, both of the supreme and inferior Courts, shall hold their Offices during good Behaviour, and shall, at stated Times, receive for their Services, a Compensation, which shall not be diminished during their Continuance in Office.

SECTION. 2. The judicial Power shall extend to all Cases, in Law and Equity, arising under this Constitution, the Laws of the United States, and Treaties made, or which shall be made, under their Authority;—to all Cases affecting Ambassadors, other public Ministers and Consuls;—to all Cases of admiralty and maritime jurisdiction;—to Controversies to which the United States shall be a Party;—to Controversies between two or more States;—between a State and Citizens of another State;— between Citizens of different States,—between Citizens of the same State claiming Lands under Grants of different States, and between a State, or the Citizens thereof, and foreign States, Citizens or Subjects.

In all Cases affecting Ambassadors, other public Ministers and Consuls, and those in which a State shall be Party, the supreme Court shall have original Jurisdiction. In all the other Cases before mentioned, the supreme Court shall have appellate Jurisdiction, both as to Law and Fact, with such Exceptions, and under such Regulations as the Congress shall make.

The Trial of all Crimes, except in Cases of Impeachment, shall be by Jury; and such Trial shall be held in the State where the said Crimes shall have been committed; but when not committed within any State, the Trial shall be at such Place or Places as the Congress may by Law have directed.

SECTION. 3. Treason against the United States, shall consist only in levying War against them, or in adhering to their Enemies, giving them Aid and Comfort. No Person shall be convicted of Treason unless on the Testimony of two Witnesses to the same overt Act, or on Confession in open Court.

The Congress shall have Power to declare the Punishment of Treason, but no Attainder of Treason shall work Corruption of Blood, or Forfeiture except during the Life of the Person attainted.

ARTICLE. IV.

SECTION. 1. Full Faith and Credit shall be given in each State to the public Acts, Records, and judicial Proceedings of every other State. And the Congress may by general Laws prescribe the Manner in which such Acts, Records and Proceedings shall be proved, and the Effect thereof.

SECTION. 2. The Citizens of each State shall be entitled to all Privileges and Immunities of Citizens in the several States.

A Person charged in any State with Treason, Felony, or other Crime, who shall flee from Justice, and be found in another State, shall on Demand of the executive Authority of the State from which he fled, be delivered up, to be removed to the State having Jurisdiction of the Crime.

No Person held to Service or Labour in one State, under the Laws thereof, escaping into another, shall, in Consequence of any Law or Regulation therein, be discharged from such Service or Labour, but shall be delivered up on Claim of the Party to whom such Service or Labour may be due.

SECTION. 3. New States may be admitted by the Congress into this Union; but no new State shall be formed or erected within the Jurisdiction of any other State; nor any State be formed by the Junction of two or more States, or Parts of States, without the Consent of the Legislatures of the States concerned as well as of the Congress.

The Congress shall have Power to dispose of and make all needful Rules and Regulations respecting the Territory or other Property belonging to the United States; and nothing in this Constitution shall be so construed as to Prejudice any Claims of the United States or of any particular State.

SECTION. 4. The United States shall guarantee to every State in this Union a Republican Form of Government, and shall protect each of them against Invasion; and on Application of the Legislature, or of the Executive (when the Legislature cannot be convened) against domestic Violence.

ARTICLE. V.

The Congress, whenever two thirds of both Houses shall deem it necessary, shall propose Amendments to this Constitution, or, on the Application of the Legislatures of two thirds of the several States, shall call a Convention for proposing Amendments, which, in either Case, shall be valid to all Intents and Purposes, as Part of this Constitution, when ratified by the Legislatures of three fourths of the several States, or by Conventions in three fourths thereof, as the one or the other Mode of Ratification may be proposed by the Congress; Provided that no Amendment which may be made prior to the Year One thousand eight hundred and eight shall in any Manner affect the first and fourth Clauses in the Ninth Section of the first Article; and that no State, without its Consent, shall be deprived of its equal Suffrage in the Senate.

ARTICLE. VI.

All Debts contracted and Engagements entered into, before the Adoption of this Constitution, shall be as valid against the United States under this Constitution, as under the Confederation.

This Constitution, and the Laws of the United States which shall be made in Pursuance thereof; and all Treaties made, or which shall be made, under the Authority of the United States, shall be the supreme Law of the Land; and the Judges in every State shall be bound thereby, any Thing in the Constitution or Laws of any State to the Contrary notwithstanding.

The Senators and Representatives before mentioned, and the Members of the several State Legislatures, and all executive and judicial Officers, both of the United States and of the several States, shall be bound by Oath or Affirmation, to support this Constitution; but no religious Test shall ever be required as a Qualification to any Office or public Trust under the United States.

APPENDIX I

ARTICLE. VII.

The Ratification of the Conventions of nine States, shall be sufficient for the Establishment of this Constitution between the States so ratifying the Same.

ARTICLES in addition to and Amendment of the Constitution of the United States of America, proposed by Congress, and ratified by the Legislatures of the several States, pursuant to the fifth Article of the original Constitution.

[The first ten articles declared in force Dec. 15, 1791]

ARTICLE I.

Congress shall make no law respecting an establishment of religion, or prohibiting the free exercise thereof; or abridging the freedom of speech, or of the press; or the right of the people peaceably to assemble, and to petition the Government for a redress of grievances.

ARTICLE II.

A well regulated Militia, being necessary to the security of a free State, the right of the people to keep and bear Arms, shall not be infringed.

ARTICLE III.

No Soldier shall, in time of peace be quartered in any house, without the consent of the Owner, nor in time of war, but in a manner to be prescribed by law.

ARTICLE IV.

The right of the people to be secure in their persons, houses, papers, and effects, against unreasonable searches and seizures, shall not be violated, and no Warrants shall issue, but upon probable cause, supported by Oath or Affirmation, and particularly describing the place to be searched, and the persons or things to be seized.

ARTICLE V.

No person shall be held to answer for a capital, or otherwise infamous crime, unless on a presentment or indictment of a Grand Jury, except in cases arising in the land or naval forces, or in the Militia, when in actual service in time of War or public danger; nor shall any person be subject for the same offence to be twice put in jeopardy of life or limb; nor shall be compelled in any criminal case to be a witness against himself, nor be deprived of life, liberty, or property, without due process of law; nor shall private property be taken for public use, without just compensation.

ARTICLE VI.

In all criminal prosecutions the accused shall enjoy the right to a speedy and public trial, by an impartial jury of the State and district wherein the crime shall have been committed, which district shall have been previously ascertained by law, and to be informed of the nature and cause of the accusation; to be confronted with the witnesses against him; to have compulsory process for obtaining witnesses in his favor, and to have the Assistance of Counsel for his defence.

ARTICLE VII.

In suits at common law, where the value in controversy shall exceed twenty dollars, the right of trial by jury shall be preserved, and no fact tried by a jury shall be otherwise re-examined in any Court of the United States, than according to the rules of the common law.

ARTICLE VIII.

Excessive bail shall not be required, nor excessive fines imposed, nor cruel and unusual punishments inflicted.

ARTICLE IX.

The enumeration in the Constitution, of certain rights, shall not be construed to deny or disparage others retained by the people.

ARTICLE X.

The powers not delegated to the United States by the Constitution, nor prohibited by it to the States, are reserved to the States respectively, or to the people.

APPENDIX I

ARTICLE XI.
[Ratified Jan. 8, 1798]

The Judicial power of the United States shall not be construed to extend to any suit in law or equity, commenced or prosecuted against one of the United States by Citizens of another State, or by Citizens or Subjects of any Foreign State.

ARTICLE XII.
[Ratified Sept. 25, 1804]

The Electors shall meet in their respective states, and vote by ballot for President and Vice-President, one of whom, at least, shall not be an inhabitant of the same state with themselves; they shall name in their ballots the person voted for as President, and in distinct ballots the person voted for as Vice-President, and they shall make distinct lists of all persons voted for as President, and of all persons voted for as Vice-President, and of the number of votes for each, which lists they shall sign and certify, and transmit sealed to the seat of the government of the United States, directed to the President of the Senate;— The President of the Senate shall, in the presence of the Senate and House of Representatives, open all the certificates and the votes shall then be counted;— The person having the greatest number of votes for President, shall be the President, if such number be a majority of the whole number of Electors appointed; and if no person have such majority, then from the persons having the highest numbers not exceeding three on the list of those voted for as President, the House of Representatives shall choose immediately, by ballot, the President. But in choosing the President, the votes shall be taken by states, the representation from each state having one vote; a quorum for this purpose shall consist of a member or members from two-thirds of the states, and a majority of all the states shall be necessary to a choice. And if the House of Representatives shall not choose a President whenever the right of choice shall devolve upon them, before the fourth day of March next following, then the Vice-President shall act as President, as in the case of the death or other constitutional disability of the President.—The person having the greatest number of votes as Vice-President, shall be the Vice-President, if such number be a majority of the whole number of Electors appointed, and if no person have a majority, then from the two highest numbers on the list, the Senate shall choose the Vice-President; a quorum for the purpose shall consist of two-thirds of the whole number of Senators, and a majority of the whole number shall be necessary to a choice. But no person constitutionally ineligible to the office of President shall be eligible to that of Vice-President of the United States.

ARTICLE XIII.
[Ratified Dec. 18, 1865]

SECTION 1. Neither slavery nor involuntary servitude, except as a punishment for crime whereof the party shall have been duly convicted, shall exist within the United States, or any place subject to their jurisdiction.

SECTION 2. Congress shall have power to enforce this article by appropriate legislation.

ARTICLE XIV.
[Ratified July 28, 1868]

SECTION 1. All persons born or naturalized in the United States, and subject to the jurisdiction thereof, are citizens of the United States and of the State wherein they reside. No State shall make or enforce any law which shall abridge the privileges or immunities of citizens of the United States; nor shall any State deprive any person of life, liberty, or property, without due process of law; nor deny to any person within its jurisdiction the equal protection of the laws.

SECTION 2. Representatives shall be apportioned among the several States according to their respective numbers, counting the whole number of persons in each State, excluding Indians not taxed. But when the right to vote at any election for the choice of electors for President and Vice President of the United States, Representatives in Congress, the Executive and Judicial officers of a State, or the members of the Legislature thereof, is denied to any of the male inhabitants of such State, being twenty-one years of age, and citizens of the United States, or in any way abridged, except for participation in rebellion, or other crime, the basis of representation therein shall be reduced in the proportion which the number of such male citizens shall bear to the whole number of male citizens twenty-one years of age in such State.

SECTION 3. No person shall be a Senator or Representative in Congress, or elector of President and Vice President, or hold any office, civil or military, under the United States, or under any State, who, having previously taken an oath, as a member of Congress, or as an officer of the United States, or as a member of any State legislature, or as an executive or judicial officer of any State, to support the Constitution of the United States, shall have engaged in insurrection or rebellion against the same, or given aid or comfort to the enemies thereof. But Congress may by a vote of two-thirds of each House remove such disability.

SECTION 4. The validity of the public debt of the United States, authorized by law, including debts incurred for payment of pensions and bounties for services in suppressing insurrection or rebellion, shall not be questioned. But neither the United States nor any State shall assume or pay any debt or obligation incurred in aid of insurrection or rebellion against the United States, or any claim for the loss or emancipation of any slave; but all such debts, obligations and claims shall be held illegal and void.

SECTION 5. The Congress shall have power to enforce, by appropriate legislation, the provisions of this article.

ARTICLE XV.
[Ratified March 30, 1870]

SECTION 1. The right of citizens of the United States to vote shall not be denied or abridged by the United States or by any State on account of race, color, or previous condition of servitude.

SECTION 2. The Congress shall have power to enforce this article by appropriate legislation.

ARTICLE XVI.
[Ratified Feb. 25, 1913]

The Congress shall have power to lay and collect taxes on incomes, from whatever source derived, without apportionment among the several States, and without regard to any census or enumeration.

ARTICLE XVII.
[Ratified May 31, 1913]

The Senate of the United States shall be composed of two Senators from each State, elected by the people thereof, for six years; and each Senator shall have one vote. The electors in each State shall have the qualifications requisite for electors of the most numerous branch of the State legislatures.

When vacancies happen in the representation of any State in the

Senate, the executive authority of such State shall issue writs of election to fill such vacancies: *Provided,* That the legislature of any State may empower the executive thereof to make temporary appointments until the people fill the vacancies by election as the legislature may direct.

This amendment shall not be so construed as to affect the election or term of any Senator chosen before it becomes valid as part of the Constitution.

ARTICLE XVIII.
[Ratified Jan. 29, 1919; repealed by 21st Amendment]

SECTION 1. After one year from the ratification of this article the manufacture, sale, or transportation of intoxicating liquors within, the importation thereof into, or the exportation thereof from the United States and all territory subject to the jurisdiction thereof for beverage purposes is hereby prohibited.

SECTION 2. The Congress and the several States shall have concurrent power to enforce this article by appropriate legislation.

SECTION 3. This article shall be inoperative unless it shall have been ratified as an amendment to the Constitution by the legislatures of the several States, as provided in the Constitution, within seven years from the date of the submission hereof to the States by the Congress.

ARTICLE XIX.
[Ratified Aug. 26, 1920]

The right of citizens of the United States to vote shall not be denied or abridged by the United States or by any State on account of sex.

Congress shall have power to enforce this article by appropriate legislation.

ARTICLE XX.
[Ratified Feb. 6, 1933]

SECTION 1. The terms of the President and Vice President shall end at noon on the 20th day of January, and the terms of Senators and Representatives at noon on the 3d day of January, of the years in which such terms would have ended if this article had not been ratified; and the terms of their successors shall then begin.

SECTION 2. The Congress shall assemble at least once in every year, and such meeting shall begin at noon on the 3d day of January, unless they shall by law appoint a different day.

APPENDIX I

Section 3. If, at the time fixed for the beginning of the term of the President, the President elect shall have died, the Vice President elect shall become President. If a President shall not have been chosen before the time fixed for the beginning of his term, or if the President elect shall have failed to qualify, then the Vice President elect shall act as President until a President shall have qualified; and the Congress may by law provide for the case wherein neither a President elect nor a Vice President elect shall have qualified, declaring who shall then act as President, or the manner in which one who is to act shall be selected, and such person shall act accordingly until a President or Vice President shall have qualified.

Section 4. The Congress may by law provide for the case of the death of any of the persons from whom the House of Representatives may choose a President whenever the right of choice shall have devolved upon them, and for the case of the death of any of the persons from whom the Senate may choose a Vice President whenever the right of choice shall have devolved upon them.

Section 5. Sections 1 and 2 shall take effect on the 15th day of October following the ratification of this article.

Section 6. This article shall be inoperative unless it shall have been ratified as an amendment to the Constitution by the legislatures of three-fourths of the several States within seven years from the date of its submission.

ARTICLE XXI.
[Ratified Dec. 5, 1933]

Section 1. The eighteenth article of amendment to the Constitution of the United States is hereby repealed.

Section 2. The transportation or importation into any State, Territory, or possession of the United States for delivery or use therein of intoxicating liquors, in violation of the laws thereof, is hereby prohibited.

Section 3. This article shall be inoperative unless it shall have been ratified as an amendment to the Constitution by conventions in the several States, as provided in the Constitution, within seven years from the date of the submission hereof to the States by the Congress.

ARTICLE XXII.
[Ratified Feb. 26, 1951]

Section 1. No person shall be elected to the office of the President more than twice, and no person who has held the office of President, or acted as President, for more than two years of a term to which some other person was elected President shall be elected to the office of President more than once. But this Article shall not apply to any person holding the office of President when this Article was proposed by the Congress, and shall not prevent any person who may be holding the office of President, or acting as President, during the term within which this Article becomes operative from holding the office of President or acting as President during the remainder of such term.

SECTION 2. This article shall be inoperative unless it shall have been ratified as an amendment to the Constitution by the legislatures of three-fourths of the several States within seven years from the date of its submission to the States by the Congress.

Appendix II

The Justices of the United States Supreme Court

Following the name of each justice there appears the state of his residence, the years of birth and death (in parentheses) and the years of Court service (in brackets). The names of the Chief Justices are printed in italics.

Appointments of President Washington
   Jay, John, N.Y. (1745–1829) [1789–1795]
   Rutledge, John, S.C. (1739–1800) [1789–1791]
   Cushing, William, Mass. (1732–1810) [1789–1810]
   Wilson, James, Pa. (1742–1798) [1789–1798]
   Blair, John, Va. (1732–1800) [1789–1796]
   Iredell, James, N.C. (1751–1799) [1790–1799]
   Johnson, Thomas, Md. (1732–1819) [1791–1793]
   Paterson, William, N.J. (1745–1806) [1793–1806]
   Chase, Samuel, Md. (1741–1811) [1796–1811]
   Ellsworth, Oliver, Conn. (1745–1807) [1796–1800]
Appointments of President John Adams
   Washington, Bushrod, Va. (1762–1829) [1798–1829]
   Moore, Alfred, N.C. (1755–1810) [1799–1804]
   Marshall, John, Va. (1755–1835) [1801–1835]
Appointments of President Jefferson
   Johnson, William, S.C. (1771–1834) [1804–1834]
   Livingston, Brockholst, N.Y. (1757–1823) [1806–1823]
   Todd, Thomas, Ky. (1765–1826) [1807–1826]

APPENDIX II

Appointments of President Madison
  Duval, Gabriel, Md. (1752–1844) [1811–1835]
  Story, Joseph, Mass. (1779–1845) [1811–1845]

Appointment of President Monroe
  Thompson, Smith, N.Y. (1768–1843) [1823–1843]

Appointment of President John Quincy Adams
  Trimble, Robert, Ky. (1777–1828) [1826–1828]

Appointments of President Jackson
  McLean, John, Ohio (1785–1861) [1829–1861]
  Baldwin, Henry, Pa. (1780–1844) [1830–1844]
  Wayne, James M., Ga. (1790–1867) [1835–1867]
  Taney, Roger B., Md. (1777–1864) [1836–1864]
  Barbour, Philip P., Va. (1783–1841) [1836–1841]

Appointments of President Van Buren
  Catron, John, Tenn. (1786–1865) [1837–1865]
  McKinley, John, Ala. (1780–1852) [1837–1852]
  Daniel, Peter V., Va., (1784–1860) [1841–1860]

Appointment of President Tyler
  Nelson, Samuel, N.Y. (1792–1873) [1845–1872]

Appointments of President Polk
  Woodbury, Levi, N.H. (1789–1851) [1845–1851]
  Grier, Robert C., Pa. (1794–1870) [1846–1870]

Appointment of President Fillmore
  Curtis, Benjamin R., Mass. (1809–1874) [1851–1857]

Appointment of President Pierce
  Campbell, John A., Ala. (1811–1889) [1853–1861]

Appointment of President Buchanan
  Clifford, Nathan, Me. (1803–1881) [1858–1881]

Appointments of President Lincoln
  Swayne, Noah H., Ohio (1804–1884) [1862–1881]
  Miller, Samuel F., Iowa (1816–1890) [1862–1890]
  Davis, David, Ill. (1815–1886) [1862–1877]
  Field, Stephen J., Cal. (1816–1899) [1863–1897]
  Chase, Salmon P., Ohio (1808–1873) [1864–1873]

Appointments of President Grant
  Strong, William, Pa. (1808–1895) [1870–1880]
  Bradley, Joseph P., N.J. (1813–1892) [1870–1892]

THE JUSTICES OF THE UNITED STATES SUPREME COURT

Appointments of President Grant *(continued)*
  Hunt, Ward, N.Y. (1810–1886) [1872–1882]
  Waite, Morrison R., Ohio (1816–1888) [1874–1888]
Appointments of President Hayes
  Harlan, John Marshall, Ky. (1833–1911) [1877–1911]
  Woods, William B., Ga. (1824–1887) [1880–1887]
Appointment of President Garfield
  Matthews, Stanley, Ohio (1824–1889) [1881–1889]
Appointments of President Arthur
  Gray, Horace, Mass. (1828–1902) [1881–1902]
  Blatchford, Samuel, N.Y. (1820–1893) [1882–1893]
Appointments of President Cleveland (first term)
  Lamar, Lucius Q. C., Miss. (1825–1893) [1888–1893]
  Fuller, Melville W., Ill. (1833–1910) [1888–1910]
Appointments of President Harrison
  Brewer, David J., Kan. (1837–1910) [1889–1910]
  Brown, Henry B., Mich. (1836–1913) [1890–1906]
  Shiras, George, Pa. (1832–1924) [1892–1903]
  Jackson, Howell E., Tenn. (1832–1895) [1893–1895]
Appointments of President Cleveland (second term)
  White, Edward D., La. (1845–1921) [1894–1910], promoted to Chief Justice in 1910
  Peckham, Rufus W., N.Y. (1838–1909) [1895–1909]
Appointment of President McKinley
  McKenna, Joseph, Cal. (1843–1926) [1898–1925]
Appointments of President Theodore Roosevelt
  Holmes, Oliver Wendell, Mass. (1841–1935) [1902–1932]
  Day, William R., Ohio (1849–1923) [1903–1922]
  Moody, William H., Mass. (1853–1917) [1906–1910]
Appointments of President Taft
  Lurton, Horace H., Tenn. (1844–1914) [1910–1914]
  Hughes, Charles Evans, N.Y. (1862–1948) [1910–1916]
  White, Edward D., La. (1845–1921) [1910–1921]
  Van Devanter, Willis, Wyo. (1859–1941) [1911–1937]
  Lamar, Joseph R., Ga. (1857–1916) [1911–1916]
  Pitney, Mahlon, N.J. (1858–1924) [1912–1922]
Appointments of President Wilson
  McReynolds, James C., Tenn. (1862–1946) [1914–1941]

451

APPENDIX II

Appointments of President Wilson (*continued*)
    Brandeis, Louis D., Mass. (1856–1941) [1916–1939]
    Clarke, John H., Ohio (1857–1945) [1916–1922]

Appointments of President Harding
    Taft, William Howard, Conn. (1857–1930) [1921–1930]
    Sutherland, George, Utah (1862–1942) [1922–1938]
    Butler, Pierce, Minn. (1866–1939) [1922–1939]
    Sanford, Edward T., Tenn. (1865–1930) [1923–1930]

Appointment of President Coolidge
    Stone, Harlan F., N.Y. (1872–1946) [1925–1941], promoted to Chief Justice in 1941

Appointments of President Hoover
    Hughes, Charles Evans, N.Y. (1862–1948) [1930–1941]
    Roberts, Owen J., Pa. (1875–1955) [1930–1945]
    Cardozo, Benjamin N., N.Y. (1870–1938) [1932–1938]

Appointments of President Franklin D. Roosevelt
    Black, Hugo L., Ala. (1886——) [1937——]
    Reed, Stanley F., Ky. (1884——) [1938——]
    Frankfurter, Felix, Mass. (1882——) [1939——]
    Douglas, William O., Conn. (1898——) [1939——]
    Murphy, Frank, Mich. (1890–1949) [1940–1949]
    Byrnes, James F., S.C. (1879——) [1941–1942]
    Stone, Harlan F., N.Y. (1872–1946) [1941–1946]
    Jackson, Robert H., N.Y. (1892–1954) [1941–1954]
    Rutledge, Wiley B., Iowa (1894–1949) [1943–1949]

Appointments of President Truman
    Burton, Harold H., Ohio (1888——) [1945——]
    Vinson, Fred M., Ky. (1890–1953) [1946–1953]
    Clark, Tom C., Tex. (1899——) [1949——]
    Minton, Sherman, Ind. (1890——) [1949——]

Apointments of President Eisenhower
    Warren, Earl, Cal. (1891——) [1953——]
    Harlan, John Marshall, N.Y. (1899——) [1955——]

INDEX

Index

Ableman v. Booth: 80–81
 opinion of Chief Justice Taney quoted, 81–88
Abrams v. United States: 210
 dissenting opinion of Justice Holmes quoted, 211–12
Acts of Congress: *see* Congress
Adams, Charles Francis: 216
Adams, John: 3–4
Agricultural Adjustment Act, first: held unconstitutional, 283–85; dissent quoted, 286–91
 second, upheld, 407–15
Alien and Sedition Acts of 1798: 3–4
American Steel Foundries v. Tri-City Central Trades Council: 255–56
 opinion of Chief Justice Taft quoted, 256–61
Anarchy case, New York: 213–15
Antitrust legislation: 185
Appeal, right of: ix
Assembly, freedom of: and public meetings inciting to riot, 395–400

Ballard case: *see United States v. Ballard*
Bank of the United States: 29; *see also* Second Bank of the United States
Barnette case: *see West Virginia Board of Education v. Barnette*
Bearing of arms obligation: applied to citizenship case, 244–46
Beauharnais v. Illinois: 401–402
 dissenting opinion of Justice Black quoted, 402–406
Beck, James M.: *The Constitution of the United States,* viii
Bill of attainder: loyalty oath requirement as, 106–12
Bill of Rights: read into Fourteenth Amendment, 309–10
 Fifth Amendment rights, 310–15
 First Amendment rights, 213–14
 Sixth Amendment rights, 310, 316–18
Bituminous Coal Conservation Act: held unconstitutional, 283, 294–96
Black, Hugo L.: 357–59
 opinions quoted: Beauharnais case, dissenting, 402–406; Everson case, 360–62; Feiner case, dissenting, 399–400; *Zorach v. Clauson,* dissenting, 378–81

455

INDEX

Blockade, Union, of southern ports: *Prize Cases* dealing with, 89–96
Booth case: *see Ableman v. Booth*
Borah, William E.: 217
Bradley, Joseph P.: 115–16
  opinions quoted: Bradwell case, concurring, 124–26; *Civil Rights Cases,* 156–60; *Legal Tender Cases,* 116–22
Bradwell v. Illinois: 124–26
Brandeis, Louis D.: 217–18
  appointment to Court opposed, 216–17
  opinions quoted: Coronado case, dissenting, 231–33; *Olmstead v. United States,* dissenting, 225–29; Whitney case, concurring, 219–23
Brewer, David: 106
Brown, Henry B.: 191–92
  opinion in *Holden v. Hardy* quoted, 192–98
Brown v. Board of Education of Topeka: 416–17
  opinion of Chief Justice Warren quoted, 418–24
Burnet v. Coronado Oil & Gas Co.: 231
  dissenting opinion of Justice Brandeis quoted, 231–33
Burr, Aaron: tried for treason, 11–12
Business, control of: 132, 185–86
  New Deal legislation, held unconstitutional, 283–91, 294–96; upheld by Court, 293, 295, 296–303
  by states, during depression, 266–73, 275–82
  ticket-scalping case, 241–43
  see also Interstate commerce; Labor legislation; Labor unions
Butler case: *see United States v. Butler*

California Criminal Syndicalism Law: 218
Cardozo, Benjamin Nathan: 304–305
  books by, on legal philosophy, 305 n.
  opinions quoted: *Helvering v. Davis,* 305–308; Palko case, 311–15; Snyder case, 316–18

Carter v. Carter Coal Company: 283, 294
  opinion of Justice Sutherland quoted, 295–96
Certiorari, petitions for: ix
Chase, Salmon P.: 128–29
  opinion in *Texas v. White* quoted, 129–30
Chase, Samuel: impeachment of, 11
Church and state: *see* Religion, freedom of
Citizenship case: 244–46
Civil Rights Cases: 154–55
  opinion of Justice Bradley quoted, 156–60
  dissenting opinion of Justice Harlan quoted, 160–65
  see also Due process clause; Public school segregation case; Religion, freedom of; Trial procedures
Civil War: amendments, 131–33
  constitutional status of southern states during, 127–30
  Prize Cases, 89–96
  see also Cummings v. Missouri; Milligan, Ex parte
Clay, Henry: 66
Commerce: *see* Business, control of; Interstate commerce
Commercial cases: in federal courts, 144
Communism: cases dealing with, 213–15, 218–23, 383–94
Communist party: trial of leaders, 383–94
Condemnation of property: *see* Eminent domain
Confederacy: constitutional status of states in, 127–30
Confiscation of property without just compensation: and Dred Scott case, 67, 72–79
  and permissible governmental regulation, 236–37
  Prize Cases, 89–92, 94–96; *United States v. Lee,* 139–43; *see also* Eminent domain
Congress: acts of, and Supreme Court, 5–10
  and civil rights legislation, 154–60

456

INDEX

and declaration of war, in *Prize Cases,* 89–90, 92–94
"implied" powers of, 30–45
Connecticut: appeal by, of criminal case verdict, 310–15
Constitutionality of statutes: Supreme Court power to decide, 5–10
Constitution of United States: 429–47
broad construction of, according to Marshall, 30–31, 52–53; quoted, 33–45, 54–59; necessity for, stated by Brown, 193–95
Contract, freedom of: Court doctrine of, 185–86, 191, 199–200
limited, 275–82, 293
Contracts: validity of "lobbying," 145–49
mortgages as, 266–73
Cooley v. Board of Wardens of Port of Philadelphia: 67–68
Copyright case: 247–48
Coronado case: *see Burnet v. Coronado Oil & Gas Co.*
Criminal trials: *see* Trial procedures
Cummings v. Missouri: 105–106
opinion of Justice Field quoted, 107–13
Currency, devaluation of: *see Legal Tender Cases*
Curtis, Benjamin R.: 67–68
dissenting opinion in Dred Scott case quoted, 75–79
Curtis, George Ticknor: 68
Custis-Lee estate (Arlington): case involving, 139–43

Davidson v. New Orleans: 151
opinion of Justice Miller quoted, 151–53
Davis, David: 98
opinion in Milligan case quoted, 99–104
Democratic party: split over Dred Scott decision, 68
Democratic-Republicans: 3–4, 12–14, 29–31
Dennis v. United States: 384
opinion of Chief Justice Vinson quoted, 386–89

dissenting opinion of Justice Douglas quoted, 390–94
Depression legislation and Court decisions: 265–66
federal authority denied, 283–91
state authority upheld, 266–73, 275–82
Devalued currency: as legal tender, 114–23
Double jeopardy: scope of prohibition against, 310–15
Douglas, William O.: 274–75
opinions quoted: Dennis case, dissenting, 390–94; *Zorach v. Clauson,* 375–78
Dred Scott v. Sandford: 65–68
opinion of Chief Justice Taney quoted, 68–75
dissenting opinion of Justice Curtis quoted, 75–79
Due process clause: of Fifth and Fourteenth Amendments, 132–33, 191–93, 195–96
applied to freedom of contract, 186
applied to ticket scalping, 241–43
protection of Bill of Rights read into Fourteenth Amendment, 309–10; Fifth Amendment rights, 310–15; First Amendment rights, 213–14; Sixth Amendment rights, 310, 316–18
Duval, Gabriel: 12

Ellsworth, Oliver: 5
Eminent domain, government power of: 236–37
Gettysburg case, 166–70
Holmes on, 238–40
see also Confiscation of property
Everson v. Board of Education of Ewing Tp.: 357, 360
opinion of Justice Black quoted, 360–62
dissenting opinion of Justice Rutledge quoted, 363–72
Expenditures: *see* Spending
Ex post facto law: loyalty oath requirement as, 106–13

Farm produce quotas: upheld, 407–15

457

INDEX

Federal authority: to create bank, 30–45
  over individual freedoms, 131–33; see also Confiscation of property; Due process clause; Eminent domain
  over interstate commerce, 51–53, 67–68; held not to extend to early New Deal legislation, 283–84, 294–96; Marshall quoted on, 54–61; modern interpretation of scope, 293, 295, 296–303; second Agricultural Adjustment Act upheld, 407–15
  to spend money "for general welfare," 284–91, 293, 304–308
  supremacy of, over states, 13–28, 80–88, 174, 179–84, 321–22
Federal Bureau of Investigation: and wire-tapping, 224
Federal statutes: see Congress, acts of
Feiner v. New York: 395
  opinion of Chief Justice Vinson quoted, 396–98
  dissenting opinion of Justice Black quoted, 399–400
Field, Cyrus: 106
Field, David Dudley: 106
Field, Stephen J.: 106
  in Neagle case, 174–84
  opinions quoted: Cummings case, 107–13; *Legal Tender Cases,* dissenting, 122–23
Fifth Amendment: see Confiscation of property; Due process clause; Eminent domain
Filburn case: see *Wickard v. Filburn*
First Amendment: see Bill of Rights; Religion, freedom of; Speech, freedom of
Flag salute, compulsory: held constitutional, 322–23; dissent to, 323–28
  held unconstitutional, 329–30, 332–39; dissent to, 330–31, 339–48
Fourteenth Amendment: 131–32
  broad construction of, 132–33, 137–38, 150–53
  enforcement by Supreme Court, 150–51
  narrow construction of, 132–37

  and racial discrimination: *Civil Rights Cases,* 154–65; public school segregation case, 416–24
  women's rights under, as decided in Bradwell case, 124–26
  see also Due process clause
Fox, Austen W.: 216
Frankfurter, Felix: 329–31
  dissenting opinion in Barnette case quoted, 339–48
"Freedom of contract": see Contract
Fugitive slave law: found unconstitutional in Wisconsin, 80–81
Fuller, Melville W.: 187
Fulton, Robert: 51–53

Garland, Ex parte: 106
General welfare: see Spending "for general welfare"
Gettysburg National Park case: 166–70
Gibbons v. Ogden: 51–53
  opinion of Chief Justice Marshall quoted, 54–61
Gitlow v. New York: 213–14
  dissenting opinion of Justice Holmes quoted, 214–15
Gobitis case: see *Minersville District v. Gobitis*
Grange movement: 185
Grant, U. S.: accused of "packing" Supreme Court, 115–16
Grier, Robert C.: 89–90
  opinion in *Prize Cases* quoted, 90–96

Habeas corpus, writ of: suspension of, during war, 97–104
Hamilton, Alexander: 3, 29
Harlan, John Marshall: 155–56
  dissenting opinion in *Civil Rights Cases* quoted, 160–65
Harvard Law Review: cited, 207
Harvard Law School: Holmes' lectures at, 206
Helvering v. Davis: 304
  opinion of Justice Cardozo quoted, 305–308

458

INDEX

Hepburn v. Griswold: 114–15
Herbert v. Shanley Co.: 247
   opinion of Justice Holmes quoted, 248
Holden v. Hardy: 191–92
   opinion of Justice Brown quoted, 191–98
Holmes, Oliver Wendell: 205–207
   "clear and present danger" test of, 210–11, 213–14
   legal philosophy of, 207–10
   opinions quoted: Abrams case, dissenting, 211–12; Gitlow case, dissenting, 214–15; Herbert case, 247–48; Lochner case, dissenting, 200–202; Pennsylvania Coal Company case, 237–40; Schwimmer case, dissenting, 244–46; *Tyson & Brother v. Banton,* dissenting, 241–43
Home Building & Loan Association v. Blaisdell: 266–67
   opinion of Chief Justice Hughes quoted, 268–73
Hopkinson, Joseph: 30
Hughes, Charles Evans: 267–68
   opinions quoted: Jones and Laughlin case, 295–303; Mortgage Moratorium case, 268–73
   quoted on Constitution, viii

"I Am" religious cult case: 349–52
Illinois: and religious instruction in public schools, 373
Immigration Act: "resident aliens" under, 353–56
Impeachment: of Associate Justice Samuel Chase, 11
   of President Johnson, 99, 128
   John Marshall threatened with, 11, 12
Implied powers of Congress: *see* Broad construction of Constitution
Income tax, federal: 185
   held unconstitutional, 186–87; dissenting opinion quoted, 187–90
Individual freedoms: 265
   under Fifth Amendment: *see* Confiscation of property; Due process clause; Eminent domain
   under First Amendment: *see* Religion, freedom of; Speech, freedom of
   under Fourteenth Amendment, 131–33; extended by Bill of Rights, 213–14, 309–18; *see also* Fourteenth Amendment
   under Sixth Amendment: *see* Trial procedures
   and state counterdepression measures, 265–73
Industrial Revolution: 185
Interstate commerce, federal control of: and *Cooley v. Board of Wardens of Port of Philadelphia,* 67–68; as defined in *Gibbons v. Ogden,* 51–61; as defined in New Deal legislation cases, 283–84, 293–303
   and second Agricultural Adjustment Act, 407–15
   stockyards and slaughtering as, 249–54
Interstate Commerce Commission: creation of, 185

Jackson, Andrew: 32, 53, 65–66
Jackson, Robert H.: 329–31, 358–59
   opinions quoted: Ballard case, dissenting, 349–52; Barnette case, 332–39; Filburn case, 408–15; Kristensen case, concurring, 354–56; *Zorach v. Clauson,* dissenting, 381–82
Jefferson, Thomas: 3–6, 11–12
   states' rights concept of, 32
Jehovah's Witnesses: case involving, 322–28
Johnson, Andrew: 98–99, 128
Johnson, William: 14
   concurring opinions quoted: *Gibbons v. Ogden,* 53; *Martin v. Hunter's Lessee,* 26–28
Jones, Walter: 30
Jones and Laughlin Steel case: 295
   opinion of Chief Justice Hughes quoted, 296–303

459

INDEX

Judicial supremacy over legislative bodies: principle of, 5–10
Judiciary Act of 1789: 5
  declared unconstitutional, 5–10
Jurisdiction of Supreme Court: in appealed case, ix
  in Dred Scott case, 66–67
  and Judiciary Act of 1789, 5–6
Justices of Supreme Court: *see* Supreme Court

Kent, James: 52
Kentucky Resolutions: 4
Knox v. Lee: 115

Labor legislation: 185
  maximum hour legislation, 191–202
  minimum wage legislation, 293
  National Labor Relations Act: held constitutional, 294–95, 296–303
Labor unions: strikes and picketing by, 255–61
La Follette, Robert M.: 217
Laissez-faire economic philosophy of Court: 185–87, 191, 199–200
Law: Holmes' philosophy of, 207–209
Lee estate: case involving, 139–43
Legal Tender Cases: 114–16
  concurring opinion of Justice Bradley quoted, 116–22
  dissenting opinion of Justice Field quoted, 122–23
Legislation: judicial review of, established, 5–10
Libel law: Illinois statute held to be, 401–406
Lincoln, Abraham: 128
  and blockade of southern ports, 89–94
  suspension of writ of *habeas corpus* by, 97–104
Livingston, Robert: 51–53
"Lobbying" contract: validity of, 145–49
Lochner v. New York: 199–200
  dissenting opinion of Justice Holmes quoted, 200–202

Lodge, Henry Cabot: 216
Lowell, A. L.: 216
Loyalty oaths: law requiring, found unconstitutional, 105–13

McCollum case: 373
McCulloch v. Maryland: 29–31
  opinion of Chief Justice Marshall quoted, 32–50
McGrath v. Kristensen: 353–54
  concurring opinion of Justice Jackson quoted, 354–56
Madison, James: 3–4, 30
Mail fraud: "I Am" leaders tried for, 349–52
Marbury v. Madison: 4–6
  opinion of Chief Justice Marshall quoted, 6–10
Marshall, John: 4–6, 11–13, 29–32, 51–53
  and conflict with Jeffersonians, 11–13
  and constitutionality of acts of Congress, 4–6; opinion in *Marbury v. Madison* quoted, 6–10
  and federal control over interstate commerce, 51–53; opinion in *Gibbons v. Ogden* quoted, 54–61
  and state attempt to tax United States Bank, 30–32; opinion in *McCulloch v. Maryland* quoted, 32–50
  in trial of Aaron Burr for treason, 12
Martin, Luther: 11, 30
Martin v. Hunter's Lessee: 13–14
  opinion of Justice Story quoted, 14–25
  concurring opinion of Justice Johnson quoted, 26–28
Maryland: and Second United States Bank, 30–50
Maximum hour legislation: *see* Labor legislation
Medina, Harold R.: 383–84
Military jurisdiction over civilians: 97–104
Miller, Samuel F.: 139, 144
  opinions quoted: *Davidson v. New*

INDEX

Orleans, 151–53; Neagle case, 174–84; *Slaughterhouse Cases,* 133–37; *United States v. Lee,* 140–43

Milligan, Ex parte: 97–99
  opinion of Justice Davis quoted, 99–104

Minersville District v. Gobitis: 322–23
  dissenting opinion of Justice Stone quoted, 323–29
  decision overruled, 339

Minimum wage and maximum hour legislation: *see* Labor legislation

Minnesota Mortgage Moratorium case: 266–73

Missouri: loyalty oaths in, after Civil War, 105–13

Missouri Compromise: 32
  and Dred Scott case, 66–67, 69–79

Monopoly: government action against and Court protection of, 185–86
  slaughterhouse, in Louisiana, 132–38
  steamboat, New York State, 51–53

Mortgage Moratorium case, 266–73

Music: and copyright statute, 247–48

National Industrial Recovery Act: held unconstitutional, 283

National Labor Relations Act: held constitutional, 294, 295, 296–303

Neagle, In re: 173–74
  opinion of Justice Miller quoted, 174–84

Nebbia v. New York: 275
  opinion of Justice Roberts quoted, 276–82

"Necessary and proper" clause of Constitution: Marshall interpretation of, 31, 38–44

New Deal legislation: held unconstitutional, 283–91, 294–96
  held constitutional, 293–95, 296–308

New Jersey: and New York steamboat monopoly, 51–53

New York: maximum hours statute of, 199–200

and religious instruction for public school children, 373–82
steamboat monopoly, 51–53
"Nine Old Men," Court of: 292–95

Ogden, Aaron: *see Gibbons v. Ogden*

Old age pension legislation: held constitutional, 304–308

Olmstead v. United States: 224–25
  dissenting opinion of Justice Brandeis quoted, 225–29

Overthrow of government: cases concerned with, 213–15, 218–23, 383–94

Pacifism: and citizenship, 244–46

Packers and Stockyards Act of 1921: 250–54

Palko v. Connecticut: 309–10
  opinion of Justice Cardozo quoted, 311–15

Paper money: *see* Legal Tender Cases

Parker v. Davis: 115

Parochial schools: and state-paid bus transportation, 357, 360–72

Pearl Harbor report: 274

Peckham, Rufus W.: 166–67
  decision of, in *Lochner v. New York,* 199
  opinion in Gettysburg case quoted, 167–70

Pennsylvania Coal Company v. Mahon: 237–38
  opinion of Justice Holmes quoted, 238–40

People of State of Illinois ex rel. McCollum v. Board of Education: 373

Petition, freedom of: and abusive language, 401–406

Picketing by strikers: *see* Labor unions

Pinkney, William: 30

Police power: regulations and restrictions as exercise of, 185–86; *see also* Business, control of

Police protection: for public speaker, 395–400

461

INDEX

Pollock v. Farmers' Loan and Trust Co.: 186–87
  dissenting opinion of Justice White quoted, 187–90
Populist movement: 185
President, war powers of: as defined in *Prize Cases,* 89–94
  suspension of writ of *habeas corpus* by, 97–104
Price fixing: held constitutional, 275–82
Prize Cases: 89–90
  opinion of Justice Grier quoted, 90–96
Progressive Party: 200
Property rights: *see* Confiscation; Due process clause; Eminent domain
Publication, abusive: and libel, 401–406
Public school segregation case: 416–17
  opinions of Chief Justice Warren quoted, 418–24
Public utilities: state authority over, 132, 275, 279–80

Racial discrimination: by private citizens, 154–60
  segregated public schools held unconstitutional, 416–24
Railroads: government control of, 185
Reconstruction: constitutional status of southern states during, 127–30
Religion, freedom of: 322
  and compulsory flag salute, 322–48
  and alleged mail fraud by "I Am" cult, 350–52
  and separation of church and state, 359; "released time" program, 373–82; state-paid bus transportation to parochial schools, 357, 360–72
Res judicata, theory of: 230
Roberts, Owen J.: 266, 274–75, 292, 294, 408
  opinions quoted: Nebbia case, 276–82; *Smith v. Allwright,* dissenting, 231, 234–35
Roosevelt, Franklin D.: 283, 285, 292–93

Roosevelt, Theodore: 200
Root, Elihu: 216
Rutledge, Wiley B.: 359
  dissenting opinion in Everson case quoted, 363–72

Sacher v. United States: 384
Schechter Poultry Corp. v. United States: 283
Schenck v. United States: 210
Schools, parochial: state-paid bus transportation to, 357, 360–72
  "released time" programs at school, 373; away from school, 373–82
  segregation held unconstitutional, 416–24
Schwimmer case: *see United States v. Schwimmer*
Search and seizure: and wire-tapping, 224–29
Secession: constitutional status of states during, 127–30
Second Bank of United States: 30–50, 65–66
Sharon, Frederick W.: 173–76
Sharon, William: 173
Sherman Antitrust Act: 185
Sixteenth Amendment: 187
Sixth Amendment: *see* Bill of Rights; Trial procedures
Slaughterhouse Cases, Louisiana: 131–32
  opinion of Justice Miller quoted, 133–37
  dissenting opinion of Justice Swayne quoted, 137–38
  see also Stockyards and slaughtering
Slavery: Dred Scott decision on, 66–79
  and Missouri Compromise, 32
  role of, in post–Civil War constitutional amendments, 133–36
Smith Act, 383–84
  upheld, 384–89; dissenting opinion quoted, 390–94
Smith v. Allwright: dissenting opinion of Justice Roberts quoted, 234–35

462

Snyder v. Massachusetts: 310
   opinion of Justice Cardozo quoted, 316–18
Social Security legislation: held constitutional, 304–308
Speech, freedom of: Brandeis on, 218–23
   and Holmes' "clear and present danger" test, 210–15, 218
   and abusive pamphlets, 401–406
   and public meetings inciting to riot, 395–400
   and Smith Act, 383–89; dissenting opinion quoted, 390–94
Spending "for general welfare": 284–91, 293, 304–308
Stafford v. Wallace: 250
   opinion of Chief Justice Taft quoted, 251–54
Stare decisis: doctrine of, 230–31
   Brandeis on, 231–33
   nonapplication, in *Legal Tender Cases,* 114–16
   Roberts on, 234–35
State action: required by Fourteenth Amendment, 154–60
State and federal authority: areas of, 266
   and federal supremacy, 13–28, 80–88, 174, 179–84, 321–22
   over individual freedoms, 131–33; see also Fourteenth Amendment
   to postpone foreclosure of mortgages, 266–73
   over interstate commerce, 51–61
   over prices, 275–82
   over public utilities, 132
   to tax federal institutions, 30–31, 45–50
State banks: 29–30
State boundaries: federal power over interstate commerce in, 52–59
State laws: and federal courts in commercial cases, 144
States: constitutional indestructibility of, 127–30
Steamboat monopoly, New York: 51–53
Stockyards and slaughtering: federal control of, 249–54

Stone, Harlan Fiske: 284–85
   dissenting opinions quoted: Butler case, 286–91; Gobitis case, 323–28
Story, Joseph: 12–14
   opinion in *Martin v. Hunter's Lessee* quoted, 14–25
Strikes: see Labor unions
Strong, William: 115
   opinion in *Ex parte Virginia* quoted, 150
Supremacy clause of Constitution: 321–22
Supreme Court: argument before, ix–x
   current types of cases, 321–22
   decisions, announcement of, viii–ix, x; making of, x
   disqualification of Justice from sitting on case, 358–59
   hearings, procedure of, ix–x
   Justices and Chief Justices, list of, 449–52
   number of Justices, viii; Franklin D. Roosevelt's effort to increase, 292–93
   opinions, writing of, x
   terms of Justices, viii
Sutherland, George: 294
   opinion in Carter case quoted, 295–96
Swayne, Noah H.: 144–45
   opinions quoted: *Slaughterhouse Cases,* dissenting, 137–38; *Trist v. Child,* 145–49

Taft, William Howard: 216, 250–51, 255
   opinions quoted: *American Steel Foundries v. Tri-City Central Trades Council,* 256–61; *Stafford v. Wallace,* 251–54
Taney, Roger Brooke: 65–67, 81
   as Attorney General, 32
   opinions quoted: *Ableman v. Booth,* 80–82; Dred Scott case, 68–75
Taxation: direct and indirect, constitutional provision for, 186
   of income, held unconstitutional, 186–87; dissenting opinion quoted, 187–90

463

INDEX

Taxation *(continued)*
  by states, of federal institution, 31, 45–60
Territories: power of Congress to regulate, 67, 69–72
Terry, David S.: 173–84
Terry, Sarah Althea: 173–81
Test oaths: *see* Loyalty oaths
Texas v. White: 127–28
  opinion of Chief Justice Chase quoted, 129–30
Treason: constitutional mandate on conviction for, 12
Trial procedures: appeal by state of criminal case verdict held constitutional, 310–15
  jury "view" held not part of trial, 310, 316–18
Trist v. Child: 145
  opinion of Justice Swayne quoted, 145–49
Tyson & Brother v. Banton: 241
  dissenting opinion of Justice Holmes quoted, 242–43

Unconstitutionality of statutes: *see* Constitutionality
Unemployment compensation legislation: held constitutional, 304
Unions: *see* Labor unions
United States: constitutional indestructibility of, 127–30
United States Bank: *see* Bank of United States; Second Bank of United States
United States v. Ballard: 349
  dissenting opinion of Justice Jackson quoted, 350–52
United States v. Butler: 283–85
  dissenting opinion of Justice Stone quoted, 286–91
United States v. Gettysburg Railway: 166–67
  opinion of Justice Peckham quoted, 167–70
United States v. Schwimmer: 244
  dissenting opinion of Justice Holmes quoted, 244–46

Utah: maximum hours statute of, 191–98

Vinson, Fred M.: 384–85
  opinions quoted: Dennis case, 386–89; Feiner case, 396–98
Virginia: resolutions of, against Alien and Sedition Acts, 4
Virginia, Ex parte: quoted, 150
Virginia Supreme Court: in defiance of United States Supreme Court, 13

Wage and hour laws: *see* Labor legislation
War: and insurrection, in *Prize Cases,* 89–96
  powers of President in, as defined in *Prize Cases,* 89–90, 92–94
  suspension of writ of *habeas corpus* in, 97–104
Warren, Earl: 416–17
  opinions in public school segregation case quoted, 418–24
Webster, Daniel: 66
  in *Gibbons v. Ogden,* 52
  in *McCulloch v. Maryland,* 30, 31
West Virginia Board of Education v. Barnette: 329–30
  opinion of Justice Jackson quoted, 332–39
  dissenting opinion of Justice Frankfurter quoted, 339–48
White, Edward D.: 187
  dissenting opinion in federal income tax case quoted, 187–90
Whitney v. California: 218
  concurring opinion of Justice Brandeis quoted, 219–23
Wickard v. Filburn: 407–408
  opinion of Justice Jackson quoted, 409–15
Wilkinson, General James: and Aaron Burr, 12
Wire-tapping: Court decision on, 224–29
Wirt, William: 30

Wisconsin Supreme Court: in defiance of United States Supreme Court, 80–81

Women's rights: denial of, in Bradwell case, 124–26

Zorach v. Clauson: 373–74
opinion of Justice Douglas quoted, 375–78
dissenting opinions quoted: Justice Black, 378–81; Justice Jackson, 381–82